DAY HIKING
Central
Cascades

Previous page: Saddle Rock hovers high above the city of Wenatchee.

A Townsend's warbler taking an early autumn break in a larch tree

Spectacular autumn crimson slopes along Poet Ridge between Irving Pass and Poe Mountain

Golden larch trees surrounding Larch Lake

Glacier Peak dominates the view north from the Alpine Lookout.

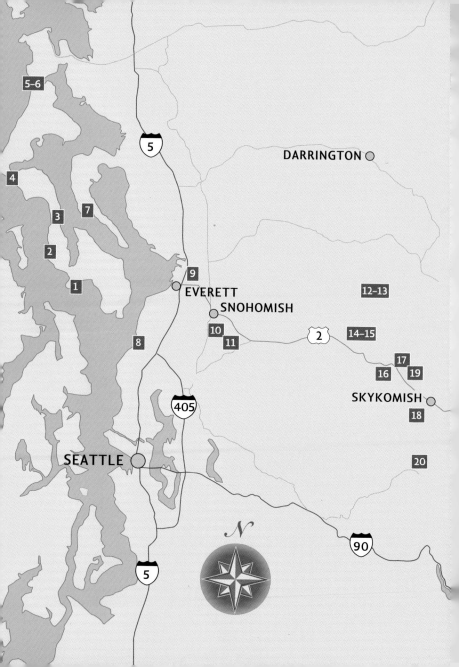

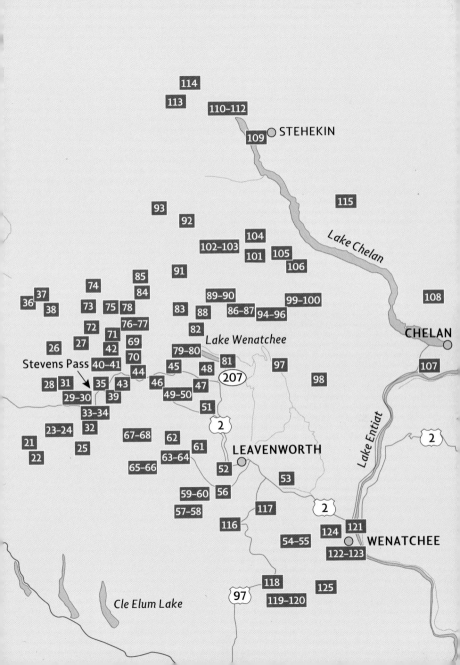

Looking down glacially carved Phelps Creek valley and Spider Meadow

Columbia lewisia, a lovely wildflower found on the east side of the Cascade crest

A great blue heron patiently waits while hunting in a slough at Spencer Island.

Deep blue Lake Chelan seen from the summit of Crow Hill

DAY HIKING

Central
Cascades

stevens pass/alpine lakes/lake wenatchee

Craig Romano
photography by
Alan L. Bauer

THE MOUNTAINEERS BOOKS

THE MOUNTAINEERS BOOKS
*is the nonprofit publishing arm of The Mountaineers, an
organization founded in 1906 and dedicated to the exploration,
preservation, and enjoyment of outdoor and wilderness areas.*

1001 SW Klickitat Way, Suite 201, Seattle, WA 98134

© 2009 by Craig Romano and Alan Bauer

First edition: First printing 2009, second printing 2010, third printing 2012, fourth printing 2014,
fifth printing 2016

Manufactured in the United States of America

Copy Editor: Julie Van Pelt
Cover and Book Design: The Mountaineers Books
Layout: Mayumi Thompson
Cartographer: Moore Creative Design
All photographs by Alan Bauer unless otherwise noted.

Cover photograph: *Glacier Peak from the Garland Peak hike*
Frontispiece: *Autumn colors and Labyrinth Mountain reflected in Minotaur Lake*

The majority of the maps shown in this book were produced using
National Geographic's TOPO! software. For more information, go to
www.nationalgeographic.com/topo.

Library of Congress Cataloging-in-Publication Data
Romano, Craig.
 Day hiking. Central Cascades / by Craig Romano, photographs by Alan
Bauer.
    p. cm.
 ISBN-13: 978-1-59485-094-3
 ISBN-10: 1-59485-094-1
 1. Hiking—Washington (State)—Guidebooks. 2. Hiking—Cascade Range—Guidebooks. 3.
Washington (State)—Guidebooks. 4. Cascade Range—Guidebooks. I. Bauer, Alan. II. Title. III.
Title: Central Cascades.
 GV199.42.W2R635 2009
 796.5109797'5—dc22

                    2008047485

ISBN (paperback): 978-1-59485-094-3
ISBN (ebook): 978-1-59485-319-7

Table of Contents

Lake Chelan

Peshastin Creek and Blewett Pass

Wenatchee

LEGEND

Symbol	Meaning	Symbol	Meaning
5	Interstate Highway	) (	Pass
2	U.S. Highway	~	River/Stream
SR 20	State Highway	~	Falls
—	Secondary Road	▬	Lake
=======	Unpaved Road	Å	Lookout
== 24 ==	Forest Road	■	Ranger Station
----------	Hiking Route	ᵮ	Picnic Area
··········	Other Trail	)(	Bridge
—·—·—	Wilderness Boundary	‖	Footbridge
1	Hike Number	■	Building
❶	Trailhead	Ɱ	View
▲	Campground or Campsite	✿	Wildflowers
▲	Summit	●—○	Gate

Hikes at a Glance

HIKE	DISTANCE (ROUND-TRIP)	DIFFICULTY	HIKEABLE ALL YEAR	KID-FRIENDLY
ISLANDS AND PUGET SOUND				
1. Double Bluff	4 miles	1	x	x
2. South Whidbey State Park	2.7 miles	2	x	x
3. Greenbank Farm	3 miles	1	x	x
4. Ebey's Landing	5.6 miles	2	x	x
5. Goose Rock	2.5 miles	2	x	x
6. Hoypus Point	3.2 miles	2	x	x
7. Camano Island State Park	2.5 miles	2	x	x
8. Lunds Gulch	2.5 miles	1	x	x
9. Spencer Island	2.6 miles	1	x	x
10. Bob Heirman Wildlife Preserve	3 miles	1	x	x
11. Lord Hill	2.2/3.5/5.2 miles	1/2/3	x	x
SKYKOMISH RIVER VALLEY				
12. Greider Lakes	8.6 miles	3		
13. Boulder Lake	13.8 miles	4		
14. Wallace Falls	5.5 miles	3	x	x
15. Wallace Lake	8.2 miles	3	x	x
16. Bridal Veil Falls/Lake Serene	4.4/7.2 miles	2/3		x
17. Heybrook Lookout	2.6 miles	2	x	x
18. Lake Elizabeth	0.7 mile	1		x
19. Barclay Lake	4.4 miles	1		x
20. Lakes Dorothy, Bear and Deer	3.5/11.5 miles	1/3		x
21. Evans Lake	1 mile	1		x
22. West Fork Foss Lakes	13 miles	5		
23. Mount Sawyer and Tonga Ridge	6 miles	2		x
24. Fisher Lake	10 miles	3		
25. Deception Creek	11 miles	3		
26. Evergreen Mountain Lookout	3 miles	3		x
27. Fortune Ponds	13 miles	4		
28. Johnson Ridge	9 miles	4		
29. Iron Goat Loop	5.7 miles	2		x
30. Iron Goat Trail to Wellington	12 miles	3		x
31. Kelley Creek	7 miles	4		
32. Surprise and Glacier Lakes	11 miles	4		x

DOG-FRIENDLY	HISTORICAL	WILDERNESS	OLD-GROWTH	SOLITUDE	WILD-FLOWERS	ALPINE VIEWS	CAR CAMP NEARBY	BACK-PACKING
X								
X			X				X	
X	X							
	X				X		X	
	X		X				X	
X			X	X			X	
X							X	
X	X							
	X							
	X							
X								
X								X
X			X	X				X
							X	
X				X			X	
						X		
X	X						X	
X			X	X				
X			X					
X		X	X					X
X		X	X					
		X	X			X		X
X		X	X		X	X		
X		X	X	X	X	X		X
X		X	X	X				X
	X	X	X		X	X		
X		X	X	X				X
		X				X	X	
	X							
	X							
X		X	X	X				
X		X	X					X

HIKE	DISTANCE (ROUND-TRIP)	DIFFICULTY	HIKEABLE ALL YEAR	KID-FRIENDLY
33. Hope and Mig Lakes	4.6 miles	3		x
34. Trap Lake	11 miles	4		
35. Skyline Lake	2.5 miles	3		
36. Blanca Lake	8.4 miles	4		
37. Quartz Creek	8.4 miles	2		x
38. Benchmark Mountain	14.4 miles	5		
NASON CREEK AND WENATCHEE RIVER VALLEYS				
39. Josephine Lake	10 miles	3		
40. Lake Valhalla	12 miles	3		x
41. Mount McCausland	7 miles	3		
42. Lake Janus/Grizzly Peak	7.2/16.8 miles	2/5		x
43. Lanham Lake	3.2 miles	3		x
44. Rock Mountain via Rock Lake	11/9.5 miles	5/5		
45. Merritt Lake/Lost Lake	6/9 miles	3/4		x
46. Whitepine Creek	5 miles	2		x
47. Lake Ethel	10 miles	4		
48. Alpine Lookout	10 miles	3		
49. Larch Lake	12 miles	4		
50. Lake Julius and Loch Eileen	7 miles	3		x
51. Chiwaukum Creek	12 miles	3		
52. Tumwater Pipeline Trail	2.4 miles	1		x
53. Peshastin Pinnacles	1.5 miles	2		x
54. Mission Ridge	14 miles	4		
55. Devils Gulch	9 miles	2		
56. Snow Lakes	13 miles	5		
57. Colchuck Lake	8.4 miles	4		
58. Lake Stuart	10 miles	3		x
59. Eightmile Lake	6.6 miles	2		x
60. Lake Caroline	11.5 miles	4		
61. Icicle Ridge via Fourth of July Creek	12 miles	5		
62. Lake Edna	12.5 miles	5		
63. Icicle Gorge	4 miles	1		x
64. Icicle Gorge View Trail	2.25 miles	2		x
65. Trout Lake	11.5 miles	3		
66. Bootjack Mountain	8 miles	5		
67. Upper Icicle Creek	10 miles	2		x
68. French Ridge	14 miles	5		

DOG-FRIENDLY	HISTORICAL	WILDERNESS	OLD-GROWTH	SOLITUDE	WILD-FLOWERS	ALPINE VIEWS	CAR CAMP NEARBY	BACK-PACKING
X		X	X		X			
X		X	X		X	X		X
					X	X		
		X	X		X	X		X
X		X	X	X				
X		X	X		X	X		
X		X	X		X			X
X	X	X	X					X
X		X	X			X		
X		X	X		X	X		X
X			X					
					X	X		
X								X
X		X	X	X				X
X		X	X	X		X		X
	X				X	X		
X		X	X	X	X	X		X
X		X	X					X
X		X	X	X	X		X	X
X	X							
					X			
			X	X	X	X		
X			X	X	X			X
		X			X	X	X	X
		X	X			X	X	X
		X	X				X	X
		X					X	
		X			X	X	X	X
	X		X		X	X	X	
		X	X		X	X	X	X
	X						X	
				X			X	
X		X	X				X	X
		X	X	X	X	X	X	
X		X	X				X	X
		X	X	X	X	X	X	

HIKE	DISTANCE (ROUND-TRIP)	DIFFICULTY	HIKEABLE ALL YEAR	KID-FRIENDLY
LAKE WENATCHEE				
69. Minotaur Lake	3.5 miles	4		
70. Rock Mountain via Snowy Creek	9.8 miles	4		
71. Heather Lake	6.6 miles	3		x
72. Pear Lake	12 miles	4		
73. Cady Ridge	13 miles	4		
74. Meander Meadow	12.5 miles	3		
75. Poe Mountain	6 miles	4		
76. Little Wenatchee Gorge	3 miles	2		x
77. Soda Springs Big Trees	0.5 mile	1		x
78. Poe Mountain via Irving Pass	6 miles	3		
79. Hidden Lake	1.2 miles	2		x
80. Lake Wenatchee South Shore Trail	2.4 miles	1		x
81. Lake Wenatchee State Park	2.5 miles	1		x
82. Dirtyface Lookout Site	9 miles	4		
83. Twin Lakes	8 miles	3		x
84. Mount David	14 miles	5		
85. Indian Creek	8 miles	3		x
86. Basalt Peak	8.4 miles	4		
87. Garland Peak	10.4 miles	5		
88. Schaefer Lake	10 miles	4		
89. Rock Creek	14 miles	3		
90. Estes Butte	8.5 miles	4		
91. Little Giant Pass	10 miles	5		
92. Carne Mountain	8 miles	4		
93. Spider Meadow and Phelps Basin	13 miles	3		x
ENTIAT MOUNTAINS				
94. Blue Creek Meadow	11.6 miles	3		x
95. Whistling Pig Meadow	11.4 miles	3		x
96. Cougar Mountain	10 miles	3		
97. Miners Ridge	4 miles	3		
98. Lower Mad River Valley	6.5 miles	3		
99. Silver Falls	1.8 miles	2		x
100. Silver Falls Interpretive Trail	1.2 miles	1		x
101. Duncan Hill	13.6 miles	4		
102. Myrtle Lake	8 miles	2		x
103. Larch Lakes	15.5 miles	5		
104. Fern Lake	15 miles	5		

DOG-FRIENDLY	HISTORICAL	WILDERNESS	OLD-GROWTH	SOLITUDE	WILD-FLOWERS	ALPINE VIEWS	CAR CAMP NEARBY	BACK-PACKING
		X			X	X		
X			X		X	X		
X		X	X			X		X
X		X	X		X	X		X
		X	X		X	X		X
X		X			X	X		X
	X	X			X	X		
X				X			X	
X			X	X			X	
X	X				X	X		
X			X				X	
							X	
							X	
				X	X	X	X	
X	X	X	X				X	
	X	X			X	X	X	
X		X	X	X			X	X
X					X	X	X	
				X	X	X	X	
X		X	X		X	X	X	X
X		X	X	X	X		X	X
					X	X	X	
		X		X	X	X	X	
				X	X	X	X	
X		X			X	X	X	X
X	X				X			X
X	X			X	X			X
X				X	X	X		
				X	X	X		
X				X	X		X	
							X	
			X			X		
X				X	X	X	X	
X		X					X	X
X		X		X	X	X	X	X
X				X		X	X	X

HIKE	DISTANCE (ROUND-TRIP)	DIFFICULTY	HIKEABLE ALL YEAR	KID-FRIENDLY
105. Pugh Ridge	12.4 miles	5		
106. Crow Hill	4 miles	2		x
LAKE CHELAN				
107. Chelan Butte	4.2 miles	3		
108. Echo Ridge	2.25 miles	2		x
109. Chelan Lakeshore Trail	10 miles	3		x
110. Rainbow Loop	4.4 miles	3		x
111. Buckner Orchard	2.8 miles	1		x
112. Stehekin River Trail	7 miles	2		x
113. Agnes Gorge	5.5 miles	2		x
114. Howard Lake	3.3 miles	2		x
115. North Navarre Peak	5 miles	3		
PESHASTIN CREEK AND BLEWETT PASS				
116. Ingalls Creek	11 miles	3		x
117. Camas Meadows	2 miles	2		x
118. Swauk Forest Discovery Trail	2.8 miles	2		x
119. Naneum Meadow	7 miles	3		
120. Mount Lillian	6.5 miles	3		
WENATCHEE				
121. Horan Natural Area	2.5 miles	1	x	x
122. Sage Hills	5.5 miles	2		x
123. Saddle Rock	3 miles	3		
124. Twin Peaks	7 miles	3		
125. Clara and Marion Lakes	3.2 miles	2		x

DOG-FRIENDLY	HISTORICAL	WILDERNESS	OLD-GROWTH	SOLITUDE	WILD-FLOWERS	ALPINE VIEWS	CAR CAMP NEARBY	BACK-PACKING
X				X	X	X	X	
X				X	X	X		
	X				X	X		
X					X	X		
	X				X		X	X
					X	X	X	
	X						X	
X			X	X	X		X	X
	X			X			X	
X	X			X			X	
				X	X	X		
X		X	X	X	X			X
				X	X	X		
X					X		X	
X	X			X	X	X		
X					X	X		
							X	
					X		X	
					X		X	
X				X	X	X	X	
X			X		X			

Acknowledgments

In addition to my trusty pickup truck and several (now well-worn) pairs of hiking shoes, writing this book could not have been possible without the help and support of the following people.

First, a big *grazie* to all of the great people at The Mountaineers Books, especially publisher Helen Cerullo, editor-in-chief Kate Rogers, and project manager Mary Metz. To Mary, especially, for keeping me from melting down in the face of deadlines.

I want to acknowledge my editor, Julie Van Pelt. Once again, it has been great working with you. Your professionalism and attention to detail have greatly contributed to making this book a finer volume. I look forward to working with you on yet another guidebook. You have suffered much from my bad puns and illusive alliteration and yet still want to work with me. *Grazie mille!*

I also want to acknowledge guidebook pioneers Ira Spring and Harvey Manning for their inspiration and invaluable knowledge. It is an honor to walk in their boot prints. And to my photographer, Alan Bauer—not just for providing the wonderful images for this book, but for some great companionship on the trail as well.

Thank you to Andy Dappen for providing me with background on the exciting trails around Wenatchee. Thanks, too, to Don and Chris Hanson at Scottish Lakes High Camp for shuttling and accommodating me.

Thanks to my mother-in-law, Virginia Scott, for letting me use the time-share in Leavenworth while researching. Thanks to my brother, Doug Romano, for accompanying me on some of the more challenging and interesting routes in this book. And thanks to my cat, Giuseppe, for putting a smile on my face when I was stressed out working on the manuscript.

And lastly, but most importantly, I want to thank my dear wife, Heather, for believing in me and supporting me while I worked hard on yet another book. Thanks for hiking with me, too, to so many of the special places in this book. And *mille, mille grazie* for all of the back massages after all my long nights in front of the keyboard.

Preface

It was the mountains that lured me to Washington State in the summer of 1989, and the mountains that have kept me firmly planted here ever since. And while there's no shortage of excellent hiking destinations here in the Evergreen State, I find myself spending inordinate amounts of time in the Central Cascades. Part of the reason is pure convenience. They're close to my home. But most of the reason is because of these mountains' wild, yet accessible demeanor; their endless array of sparkling alpine lakes, unbroken tracts of primeval forest, and sprawling high-country meadows awash in dazzling wildflowers. Especially that latter reason! The Henry M. Jackson Wilderness, which encompasses over 100,000 acres along the Central Cascades crest, ranks supreme for its alpine meadows. It's one of my absolute favorite places on the planet. And that's saying quite a bit, considering that it keeps company with such gems as Mount Rainier, Patagonia, the Apennines, the Pyrenees, Quebec's Chic-Choc Mountains, the White Mountains of New Hampshire, and just about all of British Columbia!

The Central Cascades is where I spent a good part of my first couple of years exploring after making Washington my home. "Leave no trail unhiked" was my unofficial motto. And I darn near did so, returning time and again to this amazing and diverse area. Working on this book was heaven-sent, giving me a strong incentive to revisit many old favorites. I have hiked every hike in this book, many of them several times and almost all of them recently. It is my pleasure to share this region with you.

And like so many natural areas that I have a strong affinity for, the Central Cascades are no different. It was here in June of 1996 that I first introduced the wonderful world of hiking and the Central Cascades to a young woman I met while studying at the University of Washington. That woman became my wife. The hike? Surprise Lake. A nice surprise indeed! And I'm sure that you, too, will find many a pleasant surprise while exploring the trails of this region.

And with that, it's time to repeat my battle cry from previous books in the Day Hiking series. As our world continues to urbanize, its denizens grow more sedentary, materialistic, and disconnected from the natural world. Life for many on this course has lost its real meaning. Nature may need us to protect it from becoming another hallowed urban center, but we need nature to protect us from the encroaching world of meaningless consumption and pursuits. So, shun the mall, turn off the TV, skip the casino, and hit the trail. I've lined up 125 magnificent hikes to help you celebrate nature, life, the incredible landscapes of the Central Cascades, and you. Yes, you! Go take a hike! Celebrate life, and return from the natural world a better and more content person.

Henry David Thoreau proclaimed, "In wildness is the preservation of the world." And I would like to add, "In wildness is the salvation of our souls, the meaning of life, and the preservation of our humanness."

If I'm preaching to the choir, then help me to introduce new disciples to the sacred world of nature. For while we sometimes relish our solitude on the trail, we need more like-minded souls to help us keep what little wildlands remain. Help nature by introducing family members, coworkers, your neighbors, children, and politicians to our wonderful trails. I'm convinced that a society that hikes is not only good for our wild and natural places (people will be willing to protect them), but is also good for us (helping us to live healthy and connective lives).

Enjoy this book. I've enjoyed writing it. I'm convinced that we can change our world for the better, one hike at a time. I hope to see you on the trail. Happy hiking!

Introduction

Why day hike? It's great exercise for one thing. And God knows we Americans don't get enough of that. But day hiking offers more than just physical exercise—we can get that running around the block or sweating to hip-hop at the local fitness club. Day hiking also offers exercise for our souls, a chance to get out of the city and reflect on what's truly important—like the natural world and our role in it. Day hiking is a great excuse to leave the TV, computer, video games, BlackBerry, and all those other electronic devices that were supposed to make our lives simpler—but instead have cluttered them—behind. As America grows ever more urban, and as we Americans grow ever more disconnected from nature, day hiking may well be one of our last portals to a simpler yet more fulfilling life.

When was the last time you were stuck in traffic on a mountaintop? Forced to give a presentation at an alpine lake? Had to pay bills in a meadow of wildflowers? Felt inadequate watching a field full of elk? Felt unloved in a world full of natural beauty? So seek rejuvenation and give day hiking a try if you haven't before. And if you're already well-versed on the trail, then introduce your fellow humans to this wonderful pastime.

Why day hiking as opposed to backpacking? Day hiking is more egalitarian. It can be done by just about anyone at almost any time. Backpacking involves more skill and planning, and is often more restrictive (for example, it can be more regulated). Now, don't get me wrong. I love to backpack too. But the scope of this book is what you can do in a day—often on a whim, and sometimes with the sole intent of making a quick getaway for sanity's sake. Of course many of the hikes in this book can easily be turned into overnighters, and I encourage you to so if you're so inclined and the area permits it.

Now, to help you get out on the trails and out exploring, start turning the pages of this book, one of seven volumes (and counting) in The Mountaineers Books Day Hiking series. This series sets out to find the best routes that can be enjoyed as day hikes in each of the regions covered. Of course, depending on where you live, some destinations may be too far for you to travel to, hike, and travel back in a day. In that case, look at these trips as daily excursions you can make from that weeklong cabin rental or three-day car-camping weekend.

The book you are now holding focuses on hiking routes found throughout the Central Cascades and Whidbey Island—basically, all the good day hikes from Deception Pass to Stevens Pass, Lake Wenatchee to Lake Chelan, Everett to Wenatchee along US 2, and all of the great river valleys like the North Fork Skykomish and Icicle that radiate from that highway. You'll find short walks close to population centers and all-day treks deep into wilderness areas, including in Washington's newest, the Wild Sky. Beaches, islands, riversides, lakefronts, old-growth forests, alpine meadows, mountaintops, and fire lookouts—they're all in here. Hikes in national parks, national forests, wilderness areas, state, and county parks. Hikes perfect for children, friendly to dogs, accessible year-round, popular and remote. You'll find them in this book. New trails, historic trails,

There may be no gold at this rainbow's end, but it's a priceless sight nonetheless.

and revitalized trails. Where to find wildlife, where to escape crowds, and where to get the best bang for your boot. It's all included in this packed-with-adventure volume.

The Central Cascades region is home to incredible biological diversity. With some of the largest tracts of wilderness in the Pacific Northwest, wildlife flourishes here. Martens and marmots, bobcat and cougar, bear, deer, elk, and even moose. The Central Cascades are easily accessible to millions of people. It's possible to leave downtown Seattle in the morning and be deep in the wilderness by noon.

The Central Cascades consists of dramatic mountains, from the snowy volcano Glacier Peak (the fourth-highest summit in the state) to the sun-baked basalt- and sandstone-flanked Mission Ridge. The region contains great biological and geological diversity, from pockets of rainforest on western slopes to pockets of desert steppe on eastern slopes. The Central Cascades also contain one of the highest concentrations of alpine lakes in the Pacific Northwest, some of the finest and largest tracts of old-growth forest in the Pacific Northwest, and some of the loveliest and largest alpine meadows within the entire Cascade Range.

The area is rich in human history too. First Nations, European explorers, French-Canadian voyageurs, African, Asian, and European American pioneers and homesteaders have all traveled through these mountains and along the region's waterways. Stevens Pass, the heart of the Central Cascades, is and has been for centuries one of the busiest transportation corridors in the Northwest. Humans of all walks have hunted, mined, fished, and harvested the region's great natural resources. In many cases, their marks still scar the land. In many other cases, the land has recovered. Traces of past dreams and schemes can be found throughout this region.

And what better way for you to explore this heartland of the Washington Cascades than by taking a hike through it? Hundreds of miles of trails traverse the Central Cascades, ensuring no shortage of day hiking options.

USING THIS BOOK

These Day Hiking guidebooks strike a fine balance. They were developed to be easy to use while still providing enough detail to help you explore a region. As a result, *Day Hiking: Central Cascades* includes all the information you need to find and enjoy the hikes, but leaves enough room for you to make your own discoveries as you venture into areas new to you. And yes, I have hiked every mile of trail described in this book (many of the routes several times), so you can follow my directions and advice with confidence. Conditions do change, however—more on that in a little bit.

What the Ratings Mean

Every trail described in this book features a detailed "trails facts" section. Not all of the details are facts, however.

Each hike starts with two subjective ratings: each has a rating of 1 to 5 stars for its overall appeal, and each route's difficulty is rated on a scale of 1 to 5. This is subjective, based on my impressions of each route, but the ratings do follow a formula of sorts. The overall rating is based on scenic beauty, natural wonder, and other unique qualities, such as solitude potential and wildlife-viewing opportunities. Here are the guidelines I followed:

* ***** Unmatched hiking adventure, great scenic beauty, and wonderful trail experience
* **** Excellent experience, sure to please all
* *** A great hike, with one or more fabulous features to enjoy
* ** May lack the "killer view" features, but offers lots of little moments to enjoy
* * Worth doing as a refreshing wild-country walk, especially if you're in the neighborhood

The difficulty rating is based on trail length, the steepness of the trail, and how difficult it is to hike. Generally, trails that are rated more difficult (4 or 5) are longer and steeper than average. But it's not a simple equation. A short, steep trail over talus slopes may be rated 5, while a long, smooth trail with little elevation gain may be rated 2. Here's what the difficulty ratings mean:

* 5 Extremely difficult: Excessive elevation gain and/or more than 6 miles one-way, and/or bushwhacking required
* 4 Difficult: Some steep sections, possibly rough trail or poorly maintained trail
* 3 Moderate: A good workout, but no real problems
* 2 Moderately easy: Relatively flat or short route with good trail
* 1 Easy: A relaxing stroll in the woods

To help explain these difficulty ratings, you'll also find the round-trip mileage, total elevation gain, and high point for each hike. The distances are not always exact mileages—trails weren't measured with calibrated instruments—but the mileages are generally those used by cartographers and land managers (who have measured many of the trails). The elevation gains report the cumulative difference between the high and low point on the route—in other words, the total amount you will go up on a hike. It's worth noting that not all high points are at the end of the trail—a route may run over a high ridge before dropping to a lake basin, for instance.

Many trails can be enjoyed from the time they lose their winter snowpack right up until they are buried in fresh snow the following fall. But snowpacks vary from year to year, so a trail that is open in May one year may be snow-covered until mid-July the next. The recommended season for each trail is an estimate; before you venture out it's worth contacting the land manager to get current conditions.

This guidebook also lists the maps you'll want to have on your hike as well as what agency or organization to contact to get current trail and road conditions. Hikes typically reference Green Trails maps, which are based on the standard 7.5-minute USGS topographical maps. Green Trails maps are available at most outdoor retailers in the state, as well as at many National Park Service and U.S. Forest Service visitor centers.

Important notes, if any, follow. These consist of information pertinent to your planning, such as road closures, trail restrictions, or whether a parking pass is required.

GPS coordinates for each trailhead are also provided—use this both to get to the trail and to help you get back to your car if you get caught out in a storm or wander off-trail.

Finally, icons at the start of each hike description give you a quick overview of the trail's highlights. Kid-friendly hikes are generally easier, pose few if any obstacles, and often consist of natural features that should intrigue and engage youngsters. A dog-friendly hike is one on which dogs are not only allowed, but is a trip that usually will be easy on the paws and that has adequate shade and water. A beachcombing hike is one that is either on or to a beach. Do leave all living organisms for the health of our coastal ecosystems and for others to enjoy, though. Hikes with especially abundant seasonal wildflowers are also spotlighted. Historical hikes highlight the region's human story in mining relics, fire lookouts, and early settlements. Endangered Trails are threatened due to lack of maintenance, motorized encroachment, or other actions detrimental to their exis-

tence. Saved Trails, on the other hand, are reasons to rejoice—these hikes have been revived and restored, often by passionate hikers just like you.

Kid-friendly

Dog-friendly

Beachcombing

Wildflowers

Historical

Endangered Trail

Saved Trail

The route descriptions themselves provide detailed descriptions of the hike and some of the things you might find along the way, including geographic features, scenic views, flora and fauna potential, and more. Thorough driving directions get you to the trailhead, and in most cases options for extending your trip give additional suggestions for exploring.

Of course, you'll need some information long before you ever leave home. So, as you plan your trips, consider the following issues.

PERMITS, REGULATIONS, FEES

As our public lands have become increasingly popular, and as funding from both state and national levels has continued to decline, regulations and permits have become necessary components in managing our natural heritage. It's important that you know, understand, and abide by them. To help keep our wilderness areas wild and our trails safe and well-maintained, land managers—especially the National Park Service and U.S. Forest Service—have implemented a sometimes complex set of rules and regulations governing the use of these lands.

Generally, any developed trailhead in Washington's national forests (Oregon, too) falls under the Region 6 Forest Pass Program. Simply stated, in order to park legally at these designated national forest trailheads, you must display a Northwest Forest Pass in your windshield. These sell for $5 per day or $30 for an annual pass good throughout Region 6.

In Washington's national parks, popular access points in Olympic and Mount Rainier require a national park entrance fee, currently $15 for a one-week pass, $30 for an annual pass, or $50 for an annual pass good in all national parks in the country. There are no trailhead fees in the North Cascades National Park Complex. Your best bet if you hike a lot in both national parks and forests is to buy an America the Beautiful Pass for $80 (http://store.usgs.gov/pass). This pass grants you and three other adults in your vehicle (children under sixteen are admitted free) access to all federal recreation sites that charge a day-use fee. These include national parks, national forests, national wildlife refuges, and Bureau of Land Management areas, not only here in Washington but throughout the country. Washington State Parks, Department of Natural Resource properties, and Washington Department of Fish and Wildlife properties require a Discover Pass; currently $10 for a day or $30 for an annual pass and available online (www.discoverpass.wa.gov), at some parks, and from most sporting goods outlets.

It can be confusing to keep track of who charges what, which is why the America the Beautiful Pass makes sense (see "Whose Land Is This?" below). Even if you don't hike much, all park and forest pass monies go directly to the agencies managing our lands. It is money well spent. You can purchase passes at national park and forest visitors centers, as well as from many area outdoor retailers. They are good for one year from the day of purchase.

Signposts offer help as to which way to go.

WHOSE LAND IS THIS?

Almost all of the hikes in this book are on public land. That is, they belong to you and me and the rest of the citizenry. What's confusing, however, is just who exactly is in charge of this public trust. Over a half dozen different governing agencies manage lands described in this guide.

Most of the hikes in this book are managed by the U.S. Forest Service. A division of the U.S. Department of Agriculture, the Forest Service strives to "sustain the health, diversity, and productivity of the nation's forests and grasslands to meet the needs of present and future generations." The agency purports to do this under the notion of "multiple use." However, supplying timber products, managing wildlife habitat, and developing motorized and nonmotorized recreation options have a tendency to conflict with each other. Some of these uses may not exactly sustain the health of the forest either. Several areas within national forests, however, have been afforded stringent protections as federal wilderness areas, barring development, roads, and motorized recreation (see "Untrammeled Central Cascades" in the Skykomish River Valley section).

The National Park Service, a division of the U.S. Department of the Interior, manages more than 60,000 acres of land in the Central Cascades as the Lake Chelan National Recreation Area, part of the North Cascades National Park Complex. The Ebey's Landing National Historical Reserve on Whidbey Island is also managed by the Park Service, but most of its land is state and privately owned (see "Ebey's Landing" in the Islands and Puget Sound section). The Park Service's primary objective is quite different from the Forest Service. They aim "to conserve the scenery and natural and historic objects and the wildlife therein and to provide for the enjoyment of the same in such a manner and by such means as will leave them unimpaired for the enjoyment of future generations." In other words, the primary focus of the Park Service is preservation.

Other public lands you'll encounter in this book are Washington's state parks, managed primarily for recreation and preservation. Washington Department of Natural Resources lands are managed primarily for timber harvesting, with pockets of natural area preserves. Washington Department of Fish and Wildlife lands are managed primarily for hunting and fishing. And county parks are often like state parks, but on a regional level.

It's important that you know who manages the land you'll be hiking on, for each agency has its own fees and rules (like for dogs: generally no in national parks, yes in national forests, and yes but on-leash in state parks—with notable exceptions). Confusing? Yes. But it's our land and we should understand how it is managed for us. And remember that we also have a say in how our lands are managed and can let the agencies know whether we like what they are doing or not.

WEATHER

Mountain weather in general is famously unpredictable, and in the Central Cascades with its multitude of microclimates, you'll be completely baffled (or intrigued) trying to figure it out. Weather patterns west and east of the Cascade crest are two different stories. The western slopes are characterized by a marine climate, influenced by prevailing winds off of the Pacific. Rainfall is heavy from November to April, with higher altitudes receiving much of the precipitation as snow. Summers are generally temperate, with extended periods of no or low rainfall. Mid-July through early October is generally a delightful time to hike the region.

East of the Cascade crest, weather patterns reflect a continental climate, with cold winters (snowfall heavy in high elevations) and hot, dry summers. As storm clouds move eastward and are pushed up over the moun-tains, they cool and release their moisture. Peaks closer to Puget Sound wring the most moisture, Mount Baker being one the best wringers of them all. The big volcano, second to Rainier as the most glaciated Cascade peak, holds the distinction of being one of the snowiest places on earth. During the winter of 1998–99, 1140 inches (95 ft) of snow fell on Mount Baker, setting a world record for annual snowfall. Trails on and near the mountain that summer never melted out.

Whidbey Island enjoys temperate weather and low rainfall year-round (snowfall is rare), thanks to being in the Olympic Mountains rain shadow. On any given day it can be sunny at Ebey's Landing on Whidbey, pouring rain at Lake Dorothy in the Skykomish River valley, snowing on Benchmark Mountain up the North Fork Skykomish, sunny on Alpine Lookout near Lake Wenatchee, and down-right hot on Mount Lillian near Blewett Pass.

Lightning lights up an evening sky.

Plan your hike according to your weather preference. But no matter where you hike in the Central Cascades, always pack raingear. Being caught in a sudden rain and wind storm without adequate clothing can lead to hypothermia (loss of body temperature), which is deadly if not immediately treated. Most hikers who die of exposure (hypothermia) do so not in winter, but during the milder months when a sudden change of temperature accompanied by winds and rain sneaks up on them. Always carry extra clothing layers, including rain and wind protection.

While snow blankets the high country primarily from November through May, it can occur any time of year. Be prepared. Lightning is rare along the west slope, but quite common during the summer months east of the Cascade crest. If you hear thunder, waste no time getting off of summits and away from water. Take shelter, but not under big trees or rock ledges. If caught in an electrical storm, crouch down, making minimal contact with the ground, and wait for the boomer to pass. Remove metal-framed packs and ditch the trekking poles! For more detailed information and fascinating reading on this subject, refer to Jeff Renner's excellent book, *Lightning Strikes: Staying Safe Under Stormy Skies* (The Mountaineers Books, 2002).

Other weather hazards you should be aware of are the results of past episodes of rain and snow. River and creek crossings can be extremely dangerous to traverse after periods of heavy rain or snowmelt. Always use caution and sound judgment when fording.

Also be aware of snowfields left over from the previous winter's snowpack. Depending on the severity of the past winter, and the weather conditions of the spring and early summer, some trails may not melt out until well into summer or not at all. In addition to treacherous footing and difficulties in routefinding, lingering snowfields can be prone to avalanches or slides. Use caution crossing them.

ROAD AND TRAIL CONDITIONS

In general, trails change little year to year. But change can and does occur, sometimes very quickly. A heavy storm can cause a river to jump its channel, washing out sections of trail or an access road in moments. The record rainfall in November 2006 caused significant flooding, wreaking substantial damage on trails and access roads in the Central and North Cascades, as well as in Mount Rainier National Park. Many of these trails and roads remain closed as financially strapped land managers (specifically the Forest Service) grapple with insufficient resources to restore them. Windstorms can blow down trees across trails by the hundreds, making the paths unhikable. And snow can bury trails well into summer. Avalanches, landslides, and forest fires can also bring serious damage and obliteration to our trails.

With this in mind, each hike included in this book lists the land manager's contact information so you can phone the agency prior to your trip and ensure that your chosen road and trail are open and safe to travel.

On the topic of trail conditions, it is vital that we thank the countless volunteers who donate tens of thousands of hours to trail maintenance each year. The Washington Trails Association (WTA) alone coordinates upward of eighty thousand hours of volunteer trail maintenance each year.

As enormous as the volunteer efforts have

Opposite: A mountain bike comes in handy for negotiating road washouts.

become, there is always a need for more. Our trail system faces ever-increasing threats, including (but not limited to) ever-shrinking trail funding, inappropriate trail uses, and conflicting land management policies and practices. Decades ago the biggest threat to our trails was the overharvesting of timber and the wanton building of logging roads. Ironically, as timber harvesting has all but ceased on much of our federal forests, one of the biggest threats to our trails now is access. Many roads once used for hauling timber (and for getting to trailheads) are no longer being maintained. Many of these roads are slumping and growing over and are becoming downright dangerous to drive. Many, too, are washing out, severing access to trails. While this author supports the decommissioning of many of the trunk roads that go "nowhere" as both economically and environmentally prudent, I am deeply disturbed by the number of main roads that are falling into disrepair. Once a road has been closed for several years, the trails radiating from it often receive no maintenance, which often leads them to become unhikable.

On the other end of the threat scale is the increased motorized use of many of our trails (particularly on the east slope). Despite still being open to hikers and equestrians, motorized trails tend to discourage these users because dirt biking—with its noise, speed, and impact on the natural environment—is not compatible with quiet, muscle-powered modes of backcountry travel. Motorcycles have a heavy impact on trails. Even when users obey rules and regulations—and most do—wheels tear up tread far more than boots do. This is especially true in the high country, where fragile pumice soils and lush meadows can easily be shredded. Further, the noise that many of the machines emit is simply

incompatible with Leave No Trace backcountry principles.

While I have shared trails with responsible motorcyclists, hiking on a speedway is simply not a wilderness experience. And while I support the right of motorized recreation users to have access to public lands, many of the trails currently open to them (and in particular the southern Entiat Mountains) should not be. In this book I clearly state which trails are open to motorcycles and what you can do to perhaps return them to a motor-free state (federal wilderness protection being the strongest safeguard against the incursion of wheels). Many of these trails qualify as Endangered Trails and are so noted. When it comes to public policy, the squeaky wheel gets the grease. Hikers better start motoring their mouths to their public officials about what they want from their lands, or take a back seat to ORV users, who are organized and vocal. The Saved Trails marked in this book show you that individual efforts do make a difference.

WILDERNESS ETHICS

As wonderful as volunteer trail maintenance programs are, they aren't the only way to help save our trails. Indeed, these on-the-ground efforts provide quality trails today, but to ensure the long-term survival of our trails—and more specifically, the wildlands they cross—then we must embrace and practice a sound wilderness ethic.

A strong, positive wilderness ethic includes making sure you leave the wilderness as good (or even better) than you found it. But sound wilderness ethics go deeper than simply picking up after ourselves (and others) when we go for a hike. Wilderness ethics must carry over into our daily lives. We need to ensure that our elected officials and public-land managers recognize and respond to our wilderness needs and desires. Get involved with groups and organizations that safeguard, watchdog, and advocate for land protection. And get on the phone and keyboard and let land managers and public officials know how important protecting lands and trails is to you.

TRAIL GIANTS

I grew up in rural New Hampshire and was introduced to hiking and respect for our wildlands at a young age. I grew to admire the men and women responsible for saving and protecting many of our trails and wilderness areas as I became more aware of the often tumultuous history behind the preservation efforts.

When I moved to Washington in 1989 I immediately gained a respect for Harvey Manning and Ira Spring. Through their pioneering 100 Hikes guidebooks, I was introduced to and fell in love with the Washington backcountry. I bought the whole series and voraciously devoured them on the trail and on the sofa. I joined the Mountaineers Club, the WTA, Conservation Northwest, and other local trail and conservation organizations so that I could help a little to protect these places and carry on this legacy for future generations.

While I never met Ira Spring, I was honored to work on his last book after he passed away (*Best Wildflower Hikes in Washington*, The Mountaineers Books, 2004). I believe 100 percent in what he termed "green bonding." We must, in Ira's words, "get people onto trails. They need to bond with the wilderness." This is essential in building public support for trails and trail funding. When hikers get complacent, trails suffer.

And while I often chuckled at Harvey Manning's tirades and diatribes as he lam-basted public officials' short-sighted and misguided land practices, I almost always tacitly agreed with him. Sometimes I thought Harvey was a bit combative, a tad too polarizing, perhaps even risked turning off potential allies. On the other hand, sometimes you have to raise a little hell to get results.

As you get out and hike the trails you find described here, consider that many of these trails would have long ago ceased to exist without the phenomenal efforts of people like Ira Spring, Harvey Manning, Louise Marshall, Robert Wood, Fred Darvill, and Greg Ball, not to mention the scores of unnamed hikers who joined them in their push for wildland protection, trail funding, and strong environmental stewardship programs.

When you get home, take a page from their playbook and write a letter to your congressperson or state representative asking for better trail and public lands funding. Call your local Forest Service office to say you've enjoyed the trails in their jurisdiction and that you want these routes to remain wild and accessible for use by you and your children. Let them know your disapproval of converting wilderness trails into motorized trails.

If you're not already a member, consider joining an organization devoted to wilderness, backcountry trails, or other wild-country issues. Organizations like the Mountaineers Club, Washington Trails Association, Volunteers for Outdoor Washington, Washington's National Park Fund, Conservation Northwest, and countless others leverage individual contributions and efforts to help ensure the future of our trails and the wonderful wilderness legacy we've inherited. Buy a specialty license plate for Washington's national parks or state parks and let everybody on the way to the trailhead see what you value and are willing to work for.

TRAIL ETIQUETTE

We need to not only be sensitive to the environment surrounding our trails, but to other trail users as well. Many of the trails in this book are open to an array of trail users. Some are hiker-only, but others allow equestrians and mountain bikers too (a few are open to motorbikes).

When you encounter other trail users, whether they are hikers, climbers, runners, bicyclists, or horse riders, the only hard-and-fast rule is to follow common sense and exercise simple courtesy. It's hard to overstate just how vital these two things—common sense and courtesy—are to maintaining an enjoyable, safe, and friendly situation when different types of trail users meet.

A small northern Pacific rattlesnake slowly makes its way across a bed of pine needles.

With this Golden Rule of Trail Etiquette firmly in mind, here are other things you can do during trail encounters to make everyone's trip more enjoyable:

- **Right-of-way.** When meeting other hikers, the group traveling uphill has the right-of-way. There are two reasons for this. First, on steep ascents, hikers may be watching the trail and might not notice the approach of descending hikers until they are face-to-face. More importantly, it is easier for descending hikers to break their stride and step off the trail than it is for those who have gotten into a good, climbing rhythm. But by all means, if you are the uphill trekker and you wish to grant passage to oncoming hikers, go right ahead with this act of trail kindness.
- **Moving off-trail.** When meeting other user groups (like bicyclists and horseback riders), the hiker should move off the trail. This is because hikers are more mobile and flexible than other users, making it easier for them to step off the trail.
- **Encountering horses.** When meeting horseback riders, the hiker should step off the downhill side of the trail unless the terrain makes this difficult or dangerous. In that case, move to the uphill side of the trail, but crouch down a bit so you do not tower over the horses' heads. Also, make yourself visible so as not to spook the big beasties, and talk in a normal voice to the riders. This calms the horses. If hiking with a dog, keep your buddy under control.
- **Stay on trails,** and practice minimum impact. Don't cut switchbacks, take shortcuts, or make new trails. If your destination is off-trail, stick to snow and rock when possible so as not to damage fragile alpine meadows. Spread out when traveling off-trail; don't hike in line if in a group, as this

greatly increases the chance of compacting thin soils and crushing delicate plant environments.

- **Obey the rules** specific to the trail you are visiting. Many trails are closed to certain types of use, including hiking with dogs (e.g., in parts of the Alpine Lakes Wilderness) or riding horses.
- **Hiking with dogs.** Hikers who take dogs on the trails should have their dog on a leash or under very strict voice command at all times. And if leashes are required (such as in all state parks) then this *does* apply to you. Too many dog owners flagrantly disregard this regulation, setting themselves up for tickets, hostile words from fellow hikers, and the possibility of losing the right to bring Fido out on that trail in the future. One of the most contentious issues in hiking circles is whether dogs should be allowed on trails. Far too many hikers (this author included, who happens to love dogs) have had very negative trail encounters with dogs (actually, with the dog owners). Remember that many hikers are not fond of dogs on the trail. Respect their right to not be approached by your loveable Lab. A well-behaved leashed dog, however, can certainly help warm up these hikers to your buddy.
- **Avoid disturbing wildlife,** especially in winter and in calving areas. Observe from a distance, resist the urge to move closer to wildlife (use your telephoto lens). This not only keeps you safer, but it prevents the animal from having to exert itself unnecessarily fleeing from you.
- **Take only photographs.** Leave all natural things, features, and historic artifacts as you found them for others to enjoy.
- **Never roll rocks off trails or cliffs.** You risk endangering lives below you.

Photographing wildlife requires a little luck and a lot of patience.

These are just a few of the things you can do to maintain a safe and harmonious trail environment. And while not every situation is addressed by these rules, you can avoid problems by always remembering that common sense and courtesy are in order.

Remember too, that anything you pack in must be packed out, even biodegradable items like apple cores and pistachio shells. "Leave only footprints, take only pictures," is a worthy slogan to live by when visiting the wilderness.

Another important Leave No Trace principle focuses on the business of taking care of business. The first rule of backcountry bathroom etiquette says that if an outhouse exists, use it. While you may be tempted not to (they really aren't that bad—we're not talking city public restrooms here), remember that they help keep backcountry water supplies free from contamination and the surrounding countryside from turning into a minefield of human waste decorated with toilet-paper flowers. Composting privies can actually improve the environment. I once spent a summer as a backcountry ranger, and one of my duties was composting the duty. Once the "stew" was sterile, we spread it on damaged alpine meadows, helping to restore the turf.

When privies aren't provided, however, the key factor to consider is location. Choose a site at least 200 feet from water, campsites, and the trail. Dig a cat hole. Once you're done, bury your waste with organic duff, sticks, rocks, and a "Microbes at Work" sign (just kidding about the last one).

Water

As a general rule you should treat all backcountry water sources. There is quite a bit of debate on how widespread nasties like *Giardia* (a waterborne parasite) are in water sources. New evidence suggests that the threat is greatly overblown. However, it's still better to assume that all water is contaminated. You don't want to risk it. I have contracted giardiasis on several occasions (in places as diverse as Paraguay and Vermont) and it's no treat—especially for the people around you.

Treating water can be as simple as boiling it, chemically purifying it (adding tiny iodine tablets), or pumping it through a water filter and purifier. (Note: Pump units labeled as filters generally remove everything but viruses, which are too small to be filtered out. Pumps labeled as purifiers use a chemical element, usually iodine, to render viruses inactive after filtering all the other bugs out).

Cleanup

When washing your hands, rinse off as much dust and dirt as you can in just plain water first. If you still feel the need for a soapy wash, collect a pot of water from a lake or stream and move at least 100 feet away. Apply a tiny bit of biodegradable soap to your hands, dribble on a little water, and lather up. Use a bandanna or towel to wipe away most of the soap, and then rinse with the water in the pot.

Hunting

Hikers should be aware that many of our public lands are opened to hunting. Season dates vary, but big-game hunting generally begins in early August and ends in late November.

While hiking in areas frequented by hunters, it is best to make yourself visible by donning an orange cap and vest. If hiking with a dog, your buddy should wear an orange vest too.

The majority of hunters are responsible, decent folks (and are conservationists who also support our public lands), so you should have little concern when encountering them in the backcountry. Still, if being around outdoors people who schlep rifles is unnerving to you, then stick to hiking in national and state parks, where hunting is prohibited.

WILDLIFE
The Bear Essentials

The Central Cascades is one of the best places in Washington for observing bears. While an extremely small population of grizzlies struggle to survive in the greater North Cascades ecosystem, the bear you're most likely to see is the ubiquitous black bear. Your encounter will most likely involve just catching a glimpse of his bear behind. But occasionally the bruin may actually want to get a look at *you*. In very rare cases (and I repeat, rare), a bear may act aggressively. To avoid an un-*bear*-able encounter, also heed the following advice, compliments of fellow guidebook writer and man of many bear encounters, Dan Nelson:

- **Respect a bear's need for personal space.** If you see a bear in the distance, make a wide detour around it, or if that's not possible (i.e., if the trail leads close to the bear), leave the area.
- **Remain calm.** If you encounter a bear at close range, remain calm. Do not run, as this may trigger a predator-prey reaction from the bear.
- **Talk in a low, calm manner** to the bear to help identify yourself as a human.
- **Appear large** by holding your arms out from your body, or if wearing a jacket, hold open the front so you seem as big as possible.
- **Don't stare directly at the bear.** The bear may interpret this as a direct threat or challenge. Watch the animal without making direct eye-to-eye contact.
- **Slowly move upwind** of the bear if you can do so without crowding the bear. The bear's strongest sense is its sense of smell, and if it can sniff you and identify you as human, it may retreat.
- **Know how to interpret bear actions.** A nervous bear will often rumble in its chest, clack its teeth, and "pop" its jaw. It may paw the ground and swing its head violently from side to side. If the bear does this, watch it closely (without staring directly at it). Continue speaking calmly and in a low voice.
- **A bear may bluff-charge**—run at you, but stop well before reaching you—to try and intimidate you. Resist the urge to run from this charge, as that may turn the bluff into a real charge, and you will *not* be able to outrun the bear. (Black bears can run at speeds up to 35 miles per hour through log-strewn forests.)
- If you surprise a bear and it does charge from close range, **lie down and play dead.** A surprised bear will leave you once the perceived threat is neutralized. However, if the bear wasn't attacking because it was surprised—if it charges from a long distance, or **if it has had a chance to identify you and still attacks—you should fight back.** A bear in this situation is behaving in a predatory manner (as opposed to the defensive attack of a surprised bear) and is looking at you as food. Kick, stab, punch at the bear. If it knows you will fight back, it may leave you and search for easier prey.

Look for wildlife signs, such as bear claw marks on aspens.

- **Carry a 12-ounce (or larger) can of pepper spray bear deterrent.** The spray—a high concentration of oils from hot peppers—should fire out at least 20 or 30 feet in a broad mist. Don't use the spray unless a bear is actually charging and is in range of the spray.
- **Avoid an encounter in the first place.** This is your best defense. Read the land for bear sign: fresh tree scrapings, scat, footprints, and overturned topsoil. If it looks like Yogi and company have been around, start talking if hiking in a group, or start singing if you're solo. Keep dogs leashed and under control. The intent is to not startle the bear if he's in the area.

This Is Cougar Country

Very few hikers ever see cougars in the wild. I've been tracked by them, but in all of my hiking throughout North and South America I have yet to see one of these elusive kitties. Shy and solitary, there are about 2500 to 3000 of them roaming the state of Washington. The Central Cascades support a healthy population of *Felix concolor*.

While cougar encounters are rare in the Central Cascades, they do occur. To make sure the encounter is a positive one (at least for you), you need to understand these wild cats. Cougars are curious (after all, they're cats). They will follow hikers simply to see what kind of beasts we are, but they rarely (almost never) attack adult humans.

If you do encounter a cougar, remember that they rely on prey that can't, or won't, fight back. Fellow guidebook writer Dan Nelson, a WSU Cougar, also grew up in cougar country (the Blue Mountains of southeast Washington). He offers the following advice should you run into one of these cats:

- **Do not run!** Running may trigger a cougar's attack instinct.
- **Stand up and face the cat.** Virtually every recorded cougar attack on humans has been a predator-prey attack. If you appear to the cougar as another aggressive predator rather than as prey, the cat will back down.
- **Try to appear large.** Wave your arms or a jacket over your head.
- **Pick up children and small dogs.**
- **Maintain eye contact** with the animal. The cougar will interpret this as a show of dominance on your part.
- **Back away slowly** if you can safely do so.
- **Do not turn your back** or take your eyes off the cougar. Remain standing.
- **Throw things,** provided you don't have to bend down to pick them up. If you have a water bottle on your belt, chuck it at the cat. Wave your trekking pole, and if the cat gets close enough, whack it *hard* with your trekking pole.
- **Shout loudly.**
- **Fight back** aggressively.

And you can minimize the already slim chances of having a negative cougar encounter by heeding the following:

- **Do not hike or run alone** (runners look like fleeing prey to a predator).
- **Keep children within sight** and close at all times.
- **Avoid dead animals.**
- **Keep dogs leashed and under control.** A cougar may attack a loose, solitary dog, but a leashed dog next to you makes two foes for the cougar to deal with—and cougars are too smart to take on two aggressive animals at once.
- **Be alert** to the surroundings.
- **Carry a walking stick** or trekking poles.

NERVOUS TICKS AND RATTLED NERVES

Compared with other parts of the world I have hiked in, natural nuisances in the Central Cascades are few (if you don't count the mosquitoes!). Two that you should be concerned with, and only minimally at that, are snakes that rattle and arachnids that hitch a ride.

Rattlesnakes. On the wet west side of the Cascades, there's no need for concern—rattlers are absent. On the east side of the crest, and in particular in low-elevation, dry canyon areas, northern Pacific rattlesnakes may be found.

A viper that is as intent on avoiding you as you are him, rattlesnakes generally keep to themselves. But if you get too close, they'll set off an alarm by rattling their tails. Walk away, allowing the snake to retreat. Never ever try to catch, provoke, or pursue one.

Rattlesnake bites in Washington are extremely rare, deaths by rattlesnake bites even more so. If bit, remain calm. Wash the bite. Immobilize the limb. Apply a wet wrap. Seek medical attention immediately.

Ticks. These pests are a nuisance that you should be far more concerned with. Other than the fact that most people (this author included) find these hard-shelled arachnids disgusting (and fascinating too, I admit), it's their role as a disease vector that raises alarm.

Ticks are parasites that live off of the blood of their host. Hikers make great hosts, and ticks will cling to them if given the opportunity. Generally active in the spring (and mainly on the lower slopes of the eastern side of the Cascade crest), ticks inhabit shrubs and tall grasses. When these plants are brushed up against, the tick is given the opportunity to hitch a ride.

During tick season, wear long sleeves and tuck pant legs into socks. Be sure to check yourself (while singing Brad Paisley songs), particularly waist and sock lines, after hiking in tick country.

And if one of the little buggers has fastened himself to you, get your tweezers. Gently squeeze its head until it lets go (try not to break its head off, or the tick body may become lodged and infected). Wash and disinfect the bite area. Most ticks in the Northwest do not carry Lyme disease. Still, it's best to monitor the bite. If a rash develops, immediately seek medical help.

A wood tick rests on a wildflower, waiting to catch a ride on a new host.

GEAR

No hiker should venture far up a trail without being properly equipped. Starting with the feet, a good pair of boots can make all the difference between a wonderful hike and a blistering affair. Keep your feet happy and you'll be happy.

But you can't talk boots without talking socks. Only one rule here: wear whatever is most comfortable, unless it's cotton. I prefer a synthetic liner under a wool sock. Cotton is a wonderful fabric, but not the best to hike in. When it gets wet, it stays wet and lacks any insulation value. In fact, wet cotton sucks away body heat, leaving you susceptible to hypothermia. Still, I encounter hundreds of hikers who prefer jeans and cotton T-shirts—my preference for campground wear, but not for the trails.

While the list of what you pack will vary from what another hiker on the same trail is carrying, there are a few items everyone should have in their packs. Every hiker who ventures into the woods should be prepared to spend the night out, with emergency food and shelter on hand. Mountain storms can whip up in a hurry, catching fair-weather hikers by surprise. What was an easy-to-follow trail during a calm, clear day can disappear into a confusing world of fog and rain—or snow. Therefore, every member of the party should pack the Ten Essentials, as well as a few other items that aren't necessarily essential, but that would be good to have in an emergency.

The Ten Essentials

1. **Navigation (map and compass).** Carry a topographic map of the area you plan to be in and knowledge of how to read it. Likewise a compass—again, make sure you know how to use it.

2. **Sun protection (sunglasses and sunscreen).** Even on wet days I always carry sunscreen and sunglasses; you never know when the clouds will lift. At higher elevations your exposure to UV rays is much more intense than at sea level. You can easily burn on snow and near water. Protect yourself.

3. **Insulation (extra clothing).** It may be 70 degrees at the trailhead, but at the summit it could be 45 and windy. Also, storms can and do blow in rapidly. In the high country it can snow any time of the year. Be sure to carry raingear, wind gear, and extra layers. If you get injured or lost, you won't be moving around generating heat, so you'll need to be able to bundle up.

4. **Illumination (flashlight/headlamp).** If caught after dark, you'll need a headlamp or flashlight to be able to follow the trail. If forced to spend the night, you'll need it to set up emergency camp, gather wood, and so on. Carry extra batteries and bulb too.

5. **First-aid supplies.** At the very least your kit should include bandages, gauze, scissors, tape, tweezers, pain relievers, antiseptics, and perhaps a small manual. It is also recommended that you take a first-aid training course through a program such as MOFA (Mountaineering Oriented First Aid).

6. **Fire (firestarter and matches).** If forced to spend the night, you can build an emergency campfire to provide warmth. Be sure you keep your matches dry. I use sealable plastic bags. A candle can come in handy too.

7. **Repair kit and tools (including a knife).** A knife is helpful, a multitool is better. You never know when you might need a small pair of pliers or scissors, both of which are commonly found

on compact multitools. A basic repair kit should include nylon cord, a small roll of duct tape, some 1-inch webbing and extra webbing buckles (to fix broken pack straps), and a small tube of superglue. A handful of safety pins can do wonders too.

8. **Nutrition (extra food).** Always pack more food than what you need for your hike. If you are forced to spend the night, you'll be prepared. Better to have and not need than the other way around. I also pack a couple of energy bars for emergency pick-me-ups.

9. **Hydration (extra water).** I carry two full water bottles all the time, unless I'm hiking entirely along a water source. You'll need to carry iodine tablets or a filter too, so as not to catch any waterborne nasties like *Giardia.*

10. **Emergency shelter.** This can be as simple as a garbage bag, or something more efficient like a reflective space blanket. My poncho doubles as an emergency tarp.

TRAILHEAD CONCERNS

Sadly, the topic of trailhead and trail crime must be addressed. As urban areas continuously encroach upon our green spaces, societal ills follow along. While violent crime is extremely rare (practically absent on most of our public lands, thankfully), it is a grim reminder that we are never truly free from the worst elements of society.

Common sense and vigilance are in order. This is true for all hikers, but particularly so for solo hikers. (Solo hiking sparks much debate over whether it is prudent or not. I hike solo 90 percent of the time, reaping rewards of deep reflection, self-determination, amazing wildlife observations, and a complete wilderness experience. You must decide for yourself.) Be aware of your surroundings at all times. Leave your itinerary with someone back home. If something doesn't feel right, it probably isn't. Take action by leaving the place or situation immediately. But remember, most hikers are friendly, decent people. Some may be a little introverted, but that's no cause for worry.

By far your biggest concern should be with trailhead theft. Car break-ins, sadly, are a far-too-common occurrence at some of our trailheads. Do not, absolutely under no circumstances, leave anything of value in your vehicle while out hiking. Take your wallet, cell phone, and listening devices with you—or better yet, don't bring them along in the first place. Don't leave anything in your car that may appear valuable. A duffle bag on the back seat may contain dirty T-shirts, but a thief may think there's a laptop in it. Save yourself the hassle of returning to a busted window by not giving criminals a reason to clout your car.

If you arrive at a trailhead and someone looks suspicious, don't discount your intuition. Take notes on the person and his or her vehicle. Record the license plate and report the behavior to the authorities. Do not confront the person. Leave and go to another trail.

While most car break-ins are crimes of opportunity by drug addicts looking for loot to support their fix, organized bands intent on stealing IDs have also been known to target parked cars at trailheads. While some trailheads are regularly targeted, and others rarely if at all, there's no sure way of preventing this from happening to you other than being dropped off at the trailhead or taking the bus (rarely an option, either way). But you can make your car less of a target by not leaving anything of value in it. And contact your government officials and demand that law enforcement be a priority in our national forests. We taxpayers have a right to recreate safely in our public lands.

ENJOY THE TRAILS

Most importantly, though, be safe and enjoy the trails in this book. They exist for our enjoyment and for the enjoyment of future generations of hikers. We can use them and protect them at the same time if we are careful with our actions, as well as forthright with our demands on Congress and state legislators to continue to further the protection of our state's wildlands.

Throughout the last century, wilderness lovers helped secure protection for many of the lands we enjoy today. President Theodore Roosevelt was visionary in establishing the national forest system and in greatly expanding our public lands (to over 40 million acres). President Franklin Roosevelt was ingenious in bringing infrastructure to our public lands and also in expanding our parks and preserves. President Obama, will you be a leader in protecting our public lands?

Republicans, Democrats, city dwellers, country folks, Americans of all walks of life have helped establish and protect our open spaces and wilderness areas. As we cruise into the twenty-first century, we must see to it that those protections continue and that the last bits of wildlands are preserved for the enjoyment of future generations.

If you enjoy these trails, get involved! Trails may wind through trees, but they don't grow on them. Your involvement can be as simple as picking up trash, attending a work party, joining a trail advocacy group, educating fellow citizens, or writing to your congressional and state representatives. All of these seemingly small acts can make a big difference. Introduce children to our trails. We need to continue a legacy of good trail stewards. At the end of this book you'll find a list of organizations working on behalf of our trails and wildlands in Washington. Consider getting involved with a few of them.

Happy hiking!

A NOTE ABOUT SAFETY

Safety is an important concern in all outdoor activities. No guidebook can alert you to every hazard or anticipate the limitations of every reader. Therefore, the descriptions of roads, trails, routes, and natural features in this book are not representations that a particular place or excursion will be safe for your party. When you follow any of the routes described in this book, you assume responsibility for your own safety. Under normal conditions, such excursions require the usual attention to traffic, road and trail conditions, weather, terrain, the capabilities of your party, and other factors. Because many of the lands in this book are subject to development and/or change of ownership, conditions may have changed since this book was written that make your use of some of these routes unwise. Always check for current conditions, obey posted private property signs, and avoid confrontations with property owners or managers. Keeping informed on current conditions and exercising common sense are the keys to a safe, enjoyable outing.

—The Mountaineers Books

Opposite: Looking west from Goose Rock toward Deception Island and Rosario Strait

islands and puget sound

Whidbey and Camano Islands

With rural landscapes, fine beaches, and an agreeable climate thanks to the Olympic Mountains rain shadow, Whidbey and Camano islands offer excellent year-round hiking. Most of the hikes are short, but all-day romps can be found at Ebey's Landing, where you'll also find some of the best beach walking in all of Puget Sound.

1 Double Bluff

RATING/ DIFFICULTY	ROUND-TRIP	ELEV GAIN/ HIGH POINT	SEASON
★★★★/1	4 miles	None/ Sea level	Year-round

Map: USGS Hansville; **Contact:** Island County Parks, (360) 240-5532, www.islandcounty.net /gsa/parks/ParkLocations.htm; **Note:** Dogs must be leashed accessing off-leash area; **GPS:** N 47 58.908, W 122 30.846

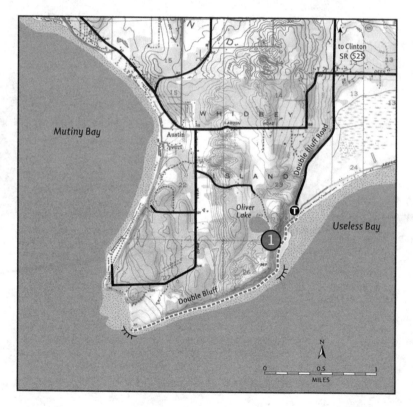

One of the finest beach hikes in Washington, Double Bluff offers a rare mix of wide sandy shores, stunning Puget Sound scenery, and easy accessibility. A favorite spot among Whidbey Islanders and their dogs, Double Bluff is also perfect for antsy children and anxious city folk needing a good dose of beach walking.

GETTING THERE
Take the Washington State Ferry from Mukilteo to Clinton on Whidbey Island. Continue north on State Route 525 for 8.5 miles, turning left onto Double Bluff Road (just before milepost 17). Proceed for 2 miles to road end at Double Bluff Park and the trailhead (elev. sea level). Parking is tight, but more space is available on the road. Privy available.

ON THE TRAIL
While the beaches of Double Bluff can usually be hiked in all tides, low tide is preferable because of the extensive tidal flats. The walking is good here, on hard-packed sand—a far cry from the cobbled coastline prevalent throughout the Sound. The 2-mile strand of beach spread before you is public property administered by Island County Parks, Washington State Parks, and the Washington Department of Natural Resources. The towering bluffs and other surrounding uplands, however, are private property, so please respect owners by not trespassing. Besides, why would you bother, with such a top-notch beach at your feet?

Head west along the sandy shoreline that cups Useless Bay. The shallow inlet may not have been much value to ancient mariners, but pelagic and shorebirds (no albatrosses!) find it plenty useful. After

Rocky shoreline beneath Double Bluff

about a half mile, approach the first of the towering Double Bluffs. Among the highest coastal bluffs on Puget Sound, they exceed 300 feet in height.

As impressive a geologic landmark as the bluffs are, your attention will be drawn seaward. Stare south to Mount Rainier and the Seattle skyline shimmering on the salty horizon. Watch vessels ply Admiralty Inlet. Look east to Mounts Baker, White Chuck, Pilchuck, and Three Fingers. Continue marching westward and watch a diorama of Olympic peaks unfold before you.

At 1.75 miles the beach grows rockier, the bluff revealing a conglomerate composition. Carry on for another 0.25 mile to round Double Bluff and call it quits. Find a nice rock to perch on. Mutiny Bay lies just to the north, but there's no need to jump ship just yet. Relax and stay for a while, absorbing the splendid coastal scenery.

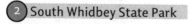

2 South Whidbey State Park

RATING/ DIFFICULTY	LOOP	ELEV GAIN/ HIGH POINT	SEASON
★★/2	2.7 miles	200 feet/ 400 feet	Year-round

Map: USGS Freeland; **Contact:** South Whidbey State Park, (360) 331-4559, www.parks.wa.gov; **Notes:** Dogs must be leashed; Discover Pass required; **GPS:** N 48 03.370, W 122 35.445

The beach is grand and the campground most inviting, but South Whidbey's best attribute is its forest: it's over 250 years old, sporting massive cedars and Douglas-firs. One of the finest tracts of old growth remaining on the Puget Sound shoreline, it was nearly logged in the 1970s. Today a trail bearing the name of the husband and wife responsible for mobilizing the public to protect it weaves through the impressive grove.

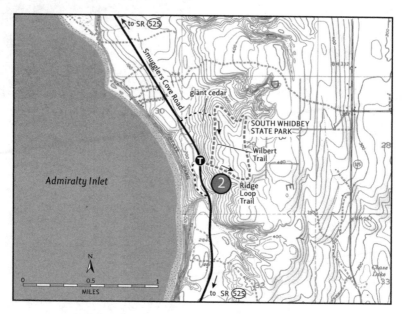

A U.S. Coast Guard ship on Admiralty Inlet seen from the Forest Discovery Trail

GETTING THERE

Take the Washington State Ferry from Mukilteo to Clinton on Whidbey Island. Continue north on State Route 525 for 9.4 miles, turning left onto Bush Point Road. After 2.2 miles the road becomes Smugglers Cove Road. Continue for another 2.7 miles to South Whidbey State Park. Turn left into the day-use parking area (elev. 250 ft). Privy and water available.

ON THE TRAIL

Locate the forest trailhead on the east side of Smugglers Cove Road, and immediately come to a junction at a big Sitka spruce. The trail left, the Wilbert Trail, is your return route. Head right on the Ridge Loop Trail. Climbing gradually, pass big firs and a "holy hemlock." The way winds east under a lush canopy and through thickets of kinnikinnick (bearberry) and big boughs of ferns.

After traversing an alder grove at 0.5 mile, the trail swings west, following an old Washington Department of Natural Resources road. With elevation gain now complete, enjoy

easy walking. Intersect another old road and continue straight. At 1.3 miles leave old road for trail, beginning a short descent into a dark draw of massive fir and spruce. Listen for wrens, chickarees, and the occasional owl.

After crossing a wet flat, intersect the Wilbert Trail at 1.8 miles. But before returning left, strut right for a short distance to the "Giant Cedar," a lone behemoth five centuries old. Read the plaque about the couple whose "tree hugging" led to the preservation of this cedar and 255 acres of surrounding forest.

Now return right to the Wilbert Trail, passing the Ridge Loop junction and continuing through beautiful groves of ancient cedar and spruce. After a small climb, come to what possibly may be the biggest tree on Whidbey Island. Continue a short distance to return to the trailhead.

EXTENDING YOUR TRIP

There's a lot more to explore at this wonderful 347-acre state park. Check out the 1-mile Forest Discovery Loop Trail, or head down the

0.5-mile Beach Trail to where nearly a mile of public shoreline awaits your footprints. The Ryan Trail, named for Al and Maurine Ryan, is in the works at the park. The trail is a fitting tribute to these conservationists who were instrumental in protecting several Whidbey gems (Keystone Spit among them).

3 Greenbank Farm

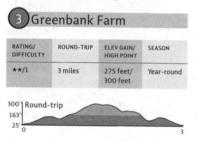

RATING/ DIFFICULTY	ROUND-TRIP	ELEV GAIN/ HIGH POINT	SEASON
★★/1	3 miles	275 feet/ 300 feet	Year-round

Map: USGS Freeland; **Contact:** Greenbank Farm, (360) 678-7700, http://greenbank farm .com; **Note:** Some trails open to equestrians; **GPS:** N 48 06.453, W 122 34.507

A historic farm once destined to become a 700-home self-contained community is now, thanks to local residents and the Trust for Public Land, a living history farm, cultural community center, and scenic and recreational gem. Numerous trails traverse the fielded and forested sprawling farm that straddles the narrowest point on Whidbey Island. From Greenbank's rolling pastures, heartily feast on inspiring maritime and mountain views.

Greenbank Farm

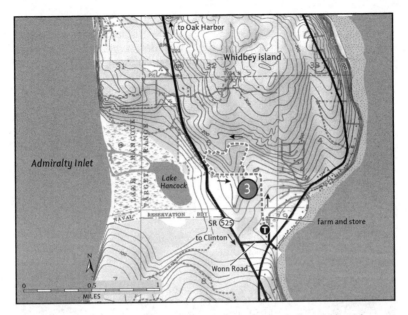

GETTING THERE

Take the Washington State Ferry from Mukilteo to Clinton on Whidbey Island. Continue north on State Route 525 for 14 miles to the small community of Greenbank. Pass Coupe's Greenbank Store and turn right onto Wonn Road. (From the north, the turnoff is 5 miles south of the SR 20/SR 525 junction.) Proceed for 0.2 mile, turning left into a large parking area for Greenbank Farm. The trail begins by the alpaca enclosure (elev. 25 ft).

ON THE TRAIL

From dairying to the largest loganberry farm in the United States, Greenbank has had a productive and flavorful history on Washington's largest island. But in the 1990s wine producer Chateau Ste. Michelle wanted to turn this scenic and serene piece of our agricultural heritage into a sprawling suburban housing tract. *Mon dieu!* What were they thinking?!

Lucky for us who believe farmland is better off unpaved, local citizens convinced the vintner to negotiate with the Trust for Public Land instead, which had far nobler intentions for the 522-acre tract of rural beauty. The Trust in turn sold the land to Island County, the Port of Coupeville, and the Nature Conservancy to be preserved and managed as a living history farm for all to enjoy.

And dog owners in particular enjoy Greenbank Farm. If well-behaved and nonaggressive, Rover and company are allowed to roam the premises (away from the farm buildings) unfettered from their leashes. If you're not fond of man and woman's best friend, you may want to opt for a different destination. Weekends are particularly busy here at Greenbank with those of the four-legged persuasion.

Children will be fond of Greenbank as well. This hike begins beside a small pen of alpacas. After admiring these fine sweater providers, take to the fields. Several trails traverse them and they all make for fine ambling. The center one, however, follows along a ridge crest granting the best viewing. Gallivant for a half mile across the grassy ridge, grazing on views east across Saratoga Passage to Camano Island, Three Fingers, and Mount Pilchuck, and west across Admiralty Inlet to the craggy eastern front of the Olympic Mountains.

Come to field's edge along a row of blackberries and alder and find a signed fence post marking the beginning of the forest trails. Continue into a forest of hemlock and fir. On good tread the trail winds through thickets of waxy leaf salal, bearberry, and rhododendron.

After about 0.4 mile, come to a junction.

Head right for a pleasant loop through quiet forest. After about a mile arrive at another junction. The trail right leads to an alternative trailhead on SR 525. Head left, and after a 0.25 mile or so come to a familiar junction. Bear right and retrace earlier steps back to your vehicle.

EXTENDING YOUR TRIP

Take time to scope out Greenbank Farm's other trails. Be sure to check out the stately century-old buildings on the premises as well. There's a good chance that a farmers market or other event will be going on.

④ Ebey's Landing

RATING/ DIFFICULTY	LOOP	ELEV GAIN/ HIGH POINT	SEASON
★★★★★/2	5.6 miles	260 feet/ 260 feet	Year-round

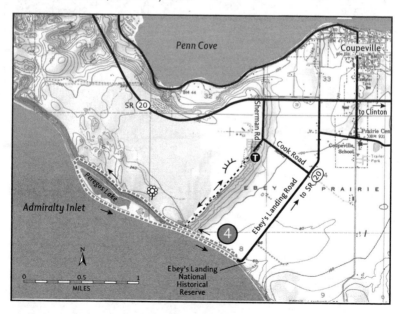

A hiker admires Peregos Lake from high above a bluff at Ebey's Landing.

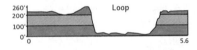

Map: USGS Coupeville; **Contact:** Ebey's Landing National Historical Reserve, (360) 678-6084, www.nps.gov/ebla; **Note:** Dogs must be leashed; **GPS:** N 48 12.297, W 122 42.360

👪 ✂ ⚙ 🏠 *Stroll across rolling emerald fields, climb coastal bluffs towering above crashing surf, and wander along a driftwood-strewn beach, gazing across busy coastal waters to a backdrop of snowcapped Olympic Mountains. And there's more! Prairie flowers, bald eagles, shorebirds, and historic relics. One of the finest coastal hikes in the Northwest, Ebey's Landing is one of Washington's most naturally diverse as well as historically significant places.*

GETTING THERE

Take the Washington State Ferry from Mukilteo to Clinton on Whidbey Island. Continue north on State Route 525 for 19 miles to the junction with SR 20. Bear right onto SR 20 and continue for 5.5 miles to the town of Coupeville. At the traffic light, continue north on SR 20 for 0.8 mile, turning left onto Sherman Road. (From the north, the turnoff is 9 miles from Oak Harbor.) Proceed for 0.3 mile and turn right onto Cemetery Road. After another 0.3 mile reach the Prairie Overlook and trailhead (elev. 200 ft).

ON THE TRAIL

Rife with history as well as natural beauty, Ebey's Landing was named for Colonel Isaac Neff Ebey, who in the 1850s became one of the first non-Native settlers on Whidbey Island. The blockhouse he erected to defend his land claim from Native attacks still stands, looking above prairies that have been in continual agricultural use for over 150 years. Prominent in territorial affairs, Ebey was slain in 1857 by a band of Haidas seeking revenge for the killing of one of their own chieftains by settlers. The blockhouse, prairies, and much of the surrounding lands are now protected within a special unit of the National Park Service (see "Ebey's Land-Inc." in this section).

Starting from the Prairie Overlook, head west on a combination of trail and gravel road. Pass a restored 1850s homestead that now serves as a visitor center. Continue toward the sea across emerald lawns reminiscent of Ireland. At 1 mile reach a junction (elev. 150 ft). This is a lollipop loop. You'll be returning left. Head right climbing golden coastal bluffs lined with contorted firs and speckled with blossoms in the spring. Reaching heights of 270 feet, these are among the highest coastal bluffs in Washington.

Gaze out to the snowcapped Olympics, the Strait of Juan de Fuca, Vancouver Island, and the San Juan Islands. Watch ferries and ocean vessels ply busy Admiralty Inlet. Look for majestic bald eagles perched in ghostly snags and notice the prickly-pear cactus growing on the sun-kissed slopes. Stare straight down at Peregos Lake, a lagoon bursting with shorebirds and formed by a narrow spit littered with giant drift logs.

Walk along the bluff crest for a good mile, coming to a junction with a short spur trail heading to an excellent viewpoint. Back on the main trail, steeply descend, coming to the trail's end at a wide beach of hard-packed sand and polished stones. Turn left and walk south along the beach, rounding the spit and reaching the Ebey's Landing Wayside at 4.25 miles.

Pick up the trail once again, climbing stairs back up the coastal bluff and reaching a familiar junction at 4.6 miles. Your vehicle can be retrieved one mile to the east. Head back or linger longer.

EBEY'S LAND-INC.

When President Carter signed into law the bill establishing Ebey's Landing National Historical Reserve in 1978, he did more than just create a new unit of the National Park Service (NPS)—he created a new type of park. Ebey's Landing differs from other park units in that most of the lands within it remain in private ownership, and it's managed through partnerships and overseen by a trust consisting of representatives from the NPS, state, county, and local governments as well as residents from the area. While the NPS does own several parcels within the reserve, as does Washington State Parks and the Nature Conservancy, the majority of the land remains privately owned. On many of these lands the NPS purchases development rights, assuring their historic and scenic integrity. And many of these parcels, 5500 acres of the reserve's 17,400 acres, are still being used for agriculture, as they have been since pioneers settled them over 150 years ago.

Similar to many European national parks, this model should be expanded here in America to other areas of historic, cultural, and natural significance where buying property outright (and taking it out of historic use and off the tax rolls) makes little sense. Other areas in Washington worth exploring for this type of reserve are the Snoqualmie and lower Columbia River valleys. In New England, Congress has established several National Historic Corridors, similar in concept and also worth looking into.

EXTENDING YOUR TRIP

Hike the beach north 2.2 miles to Fort Ebey State Park or south 2.5 miles to Fort Casey State Park. More bluff-running trails can be found at Fort Ebey as well as excellent family-friendly camping. Near Fort Casey, the state-protected Keystone Spit makes for nice coastal wandering too.

5 Goose Rock

RATING/ DIFFICULTY	LOOP	ELEV GAIN/ HIGH POINT	SEASON
★★★/2	2.5 miles	550 feet/ 480 feet	Year-round

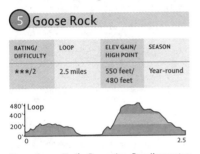

Map: Green Trails Deception Pass/Anacortes Community Forest Lands No. 41S; **Contact:** Deception Pass State Park, (360) 675-2417, www.parks.wa.gov; **Notes:** Dogs must be leashed; Discover Pass required; **GPS:** N 48 24.203, W 122 38.848

One of the highest points on Whidbey, Goose Rock offers the closest thing to "mountain climbing" on the island. Though not exactly a lofty summit, Goose Rock gives spectacular and far-reaching views. From open grassy slopes and mossy rocky ledges, bask in sunshine while catching a gander of a gaggle of surrounding peaks and islands.

GETTING THERE

From Burlington (exit 230 on I-5) head west on State Route 20 for about 12 miles to a major junction with SR 20 Spur. Turn left, continuing on SR 20 and coming to the Deception Pass Bridge in 6 miles. One mile beyond, at a traffic light, turn right into Deception Pass State Park. Proceed past the park entrance station and in 0.4 mile turn right at a junction (signed for North Beach). Continue another 0.7 mile to a large parking area and the trailhead (elev. 50 ft). Privy and water available.

ON THE TRAIL

With over three million annual visitors, Deception Pass is Washington's most popular state park. It was created during the Great

Madrona trees grace the Goose Rock Loop.

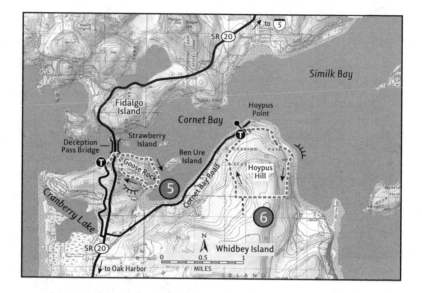

Depression, but great elation is what you'll feel after taking to this park's trails. Over 40 miles of them traverse the 4000-plus-acre park. Many trails were developed in the 1930s by the Civilian Conservation Corps (CCC). Park staff and volunteers continue maintenance of these well-trodden paths while retaining their original charm.

Start by hiking 0.2 mile through old-growth forest, climbing about 100 feet to the Deception Pass Bridge. Built in 1935 as a Public Works Administration (PWA) project, the attractive 976-foot steel cantilever bridge along with its sister, 511-foot steel-arched Canoe Pass Bridge, are two of the most photographed structures in the state. Marvel at them and then down below at the turbulent waters funneling though Deception Pass. Admire, too, the view out to Deception Island and the rugged headlands comprising the pass.

Hike under the bridge and come to a junc-

tion. The trail right, the Northwest Goose Rock Summit Trail is your return route. Head left down the Goose Rock Perimeter Trail, taking in more views of the pass as well as of Strawberry and Ben Ure islands. The latter was named for a notorious human trafficker.

At 0.5 mile ignore a side trail right. At 1 mile, along water's edge, ignore a side trail left and begin to climb. Ascend about 150 feet up a grassy ledge above sparkling Cornet Bay. Check out all of the handsome madronas (arbutus if you're Canadian) clinging to the sunny hillside. Then lose all that elevation, dropping back to sea level and a well-signed trail junction.

Take the trail right, the one marked Goose Rock Summit Trail—the one that immediately begins climbing steeply. Twisting and turning and gaining over 400 feet in 0.4 mile, reach Goose Rock's open summit. An unsigned but obvious side trail veers left

0.1 mile to a series of open ledges, granting excellent viewing. Look north to Mount Erie, west to the Strait of Juan de Fuca, the Olympic Mountains, and the San Juan Islands, and south to Rainier rising above a rolling Whidbey countryside. Watch fighters take off from the nearby naval air base.

Once through gazing, return to the main trail and turn left. Ignore a side trail right and another one heading left shortly afterward. Then descend quickly, coming to a familiar junction at the Deception Pass Bridge. The trailhead is 0.2 mile to the left. You know the way from here.

EXTENDING YOUR TRIP
Miles of trails nearby offer all kinds of options for extending your hike or planning a return trip. Hike down to North Beach to an attractive CCC shelter and breathtaking views of the Deception Pass Bridge. Hike 0.7 mile to West Beach for excellent beach strolling and combing. Cranberry Lake offers nice walking as well, and don't forget about the park trails across the pass on Fidalgo Island. Consider spending the night here camping, but don't forget to make a reservation.

6 Hoypus Point

RATING/ DIFFICULTY	LOOP	ELEV GAIN/ HIGH POINT	SEASON
★★/2	3.2 miles	360 feet/ 380 feet	Year-round

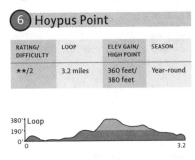

Mount Baker as seen from Hoypus Point

Map: Green Trails Deception Pass/Anacortes Community Forest Lands No. 41S; **Contact:** Deception Pass State Park, (360) 675-2417, www.parks.wa.gov; **Notes:** Dogs must be leashed. Discover Pass required. Access road is occasionally gated at Cornet Bay Marina, in which case, walk road 0.3 mile to south Hoypus Point trailhead; **GPS:** N 48 24.553, W 122 36.697

Seek solitude from the Deception Pass masses at this quiet corner of the sprawling park. Amble amid ancient conifers through a tract of Whidbey Island that has withstood the pressures of the modern world. Admire towering firs that witnessed Captain George Vancouver's 1789 sailing where he mistakenly took the island for a peninsula. Realizing his error, Vancouver bestowed the name Deception upon the strait that he mistook for a river.

GETTING THERE

From Burlington (exit 230 on I-5) head west on State Route 20 for about 12 miles to a major junction with SR 20 Spur. Turn left, continuing on SR 20 and coming to the Deception Pass Bridge in 6 miles. One mile beyond, at a traffic light, turn left onto Cornet Bay Road. In 1.4 miles, come to Cornet Marina (privy available and alternative parking). Continue for another 0.7 mile to the road end at a picnic area and the trailhead (elev. 25 ft).

ON THE TRAIL

Before heading off to Hoypus Hill, consider a short side trip to Hoypus Point. Follow a gated old road a level 0.25 mile to a splendid view of Similk Bay, Skagit Island, Mount Erie, and Mount Baker. When tides are low, explore the area's excellent sandy beaches. For the Hoypus Hill loop, take the old road-trail just to the

right of the Hoypus Point access road-trail.

Immediately enter thick timber. Alders, ferns, and hemlock line the way. Soon, big old-growth Douglas-firs appear. Ancient cedars will follow. These trees are among the largest and oldest on the island, and surely they would have been logged if Washington State Parks hadn't acquired this tract from the Washington Department of Natural Resources back in 1992. In what is now managed as a Natural Forest Area, these trees will continue to defy the ages and amaze their admirers.

After a short climb reach a junction with the CCC Crossing Trail, your return route. Continue straight on the East Hoypus Point Trail, a pleasant way through towering trees. After about a half mile, the way climbs. In 1 mile it brushes up against the backyards of a few residences as it follows the park boundary. Catch glimpses of Ala Spit and Hope Island out in Skagit Bay.

At 1.4 miles the way makes a sharp turn right, now following the Fireside Trail. After a short, steep climb the trail crosses a 380-foot saddle on Hoypus Hill. It then steeply drops on a sometimes muddy and slick track. Pass the Forest Grove Trail that shoots off left, and arrive at a junction with the West Hoypus Point Trail shortly afterward.

Turn right on a level grade through lush bottomlands. Pass the ruins of an old truck before coming to a trail junction. The trail left leads back to Cornet Bay Road. It passes a massive Douglas-fir and makes for a nice side trip. Continue right. In 0.2 mile reach the CCC Crossing Trail. Head right once more and in 0.4 mile reach a familiar junction. Head left 0.2 mile back to the trailhead.

If you're still wondering what a Hoypus is, you're not alone. Named by famed explorer Charles Wilkes in 1841, he left no explanation as to what it means. Come to your own conclusion.

EXTENDING YOUR TRIP

Hoypus Hill sports several other trails to the south of this loop. Most are multiuse—open to horses and mountain bikes—but make good walking nevertheless, especially during the quiet winter months.

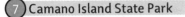

7 Camano Island State Park

RATING/ DIFFICULTY	LOOP	ELEV GAIN/ HIGH POINT	SEASON
★★/2	2.5 miles	300 feet/ 300 feet	Year-round

Map: USGS Juniper Beach; **Contact:** Camano Island State Park, (360) 387-3031, www.parks. wa.gov; **Note:** Dogs must be leashed; Discover Pass required; **GPS:** N 48 07.318, W 122 29.461

Stroll manicured trails weaving through blotchy-barked madronas and stately firs along coastal bluffs, with stunning views of lofty peaks that hover over sparkling waters. Camano Island State Park offers dramatic glimpses of a less developed Puget Sound—one where shorelines aren't marred by wall-to-wall houses and one that Captain George Vancouver would perhaps still recognize.

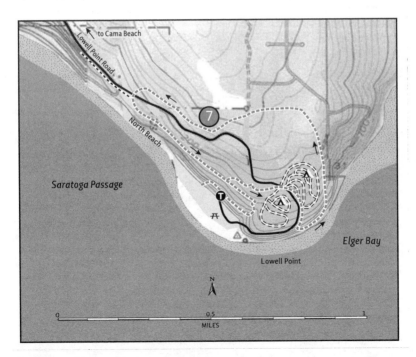

GETTING THERE

From exit 212 on I-5, travel west on State Route 532 for 5.5 miles to the town of Stanwood. Continue west on SR 532 for 4.5 miles to the junction of NE Camano and N Camano drives. Bear left onto NE Camano Drive and proceed for 3 miles, bearing left again onto SE Camano Drive. In 3.4 miles bear right onto S Elger Bay Road and continue for 1.9 miles, turning right onto Mountain View Road. In 1.7 miles turn left onto Lowell Point Road and follow this road 0.7 mile to Camano Island State Park. Proceed for 0.2 mile, turning left and following the park road (passing the camping area) for 1.1 mile to its end at a large day-use parking area (elev. sea level). Privy and water available.

ON THE TRAIL

Begin on the Marsh Trail, which runs parallel to the large parking area and takes you to the main trailhead, located a short distance back on the access road. Along the way be sure to look for eagles perched on tall firs. At the main trailhead, study the posted map of the park's trail system. Your objective is to follow the Loop Trail, but feel free to divert onto interesting side trails at any time. The park is small, just under 140 acres, so don't worry about venturing too far off course.

Head up an attractive ravine shaded by mature maples and cloaked with waxy salal and boughs of ferns. Immediately come to a junction. Turn left. With the aid of steps, steeply but briefly climb out of the ravine. Come to another junction. You'll be returning on the left, so head right. Bear right at yet another junction and continue climbing, coming to the group camp area after about 0.2 mile. Go right, through the cabin camp area, and then pick up trail once more. Pass the amphitheater, weave through the campground, cross the main park road, and

Inviting beach and towering bluffs at Camano Island State Park

then parallel it south for a short distance, eventually heading back into the woods.

Now get ready to enjoy spectacular Puget Sound scenery. The trail turns left, hugging the rim of a 150-foot bluff rising above Elger Bay. Stop at numerous viewpoints to marvel straight down at Saratoga Passage's gleaming waters. Scope out familiar summits on the eastern horizon: Pilchuck, Baring, which others?

Continue along the bluff, soaking up scenery and sea breezes. The trail eventually turns landward, coming to another junction. Head right in thick forest along the park periphery. Reach a 300-foot high point before beginning a slow descent, dipping in and out of small ravines along the way. Pass some giant old-growth Doug-firs before coming to another junction. The trail left returns to the campground. Head right instead, dropping steeply.

Cross the park road, pass Roy's Trail on your left (an alternative return) and the Cama Beach Connector Trail on your right, and then follow the Loop Trail left along more high bluffs, back to the trailhead. Pause frequently to take in captivating views across the Sound of jagged Olympic Mountain peaks rising above Whidbey Island's chalky bluffs and emerald forests.

EXTENDING YOUR TRIP

Stay a night or two in the park's bluff-perched campground. When tides are low, descend from the bluffs and walk 1 mile of cobblestone beach. For a good leg stretcher follow the Cama Beach Connector Trail 1 mile to Washington's newest state park, Cama Beach. Once an early twentieth-century beachside cabin retreat, this 400-plus-acre property was acquired by the state in the 1990s. The cabins have been restored to their early charm, offering cozy lodging. A mile of public beach set beneath steep bluffs cloaked in maple and madrona invites exploring, and the park contains several miles of good trails.

Puget Lowlands

Rapidly urbanizing and suburbanizing, much of the central Puget Lowlands won't be of interest to hikers and lovers of the natural world. The area's shoreline and foothills are rapidly being covered in housing, strip malls, and pavement. And there's no end in sight to the frenzied development that is transforming this region into another south King County. Sigh. Most hikers will be content racing up US 2 to greener hills and pastures. But if you look hard within this urban sprawl, you'll discover a few pockets of green worthy of wandering. Greenbelts, parks, and preserves were protected through the foresight and dedication of residents and conservationists not resigned to seeing the entire area morph into suburbia. Visit these gems and rejoice over their creation. Then return energized by nature's healing powers and mobilize to protect the remaining wild tracts.

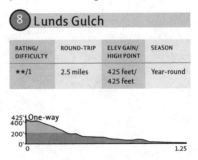

8 Lunds Gulch

RATING/ DIFFICULTY	ROUND-TRIP	ELEV GAIN/ HIGH POINT	SEASON
★★/1	2.5 miles	425 feet/ 425 feet	Year-round

Map: USGS Edmonds East; **Contact:** Snohomish County Parks, (425) 388-6600, http://www1.co.snohomish.wa.us/departments/parks; **Note:** Dogs must be leashed; **GPS:** N 47 51.350, W 122 19.051

Hike through a deep green ravine sliced by a salmon-spawning stream in Lynnwood of all places. But there's more; finish at a quiet Puget Sound beach with sweeping views of Whidbey Island and the Olympic Mountains. Lunds Gulch forms a green swath in heavily suburbanized south Snohomish County. Protected within the 105-acre Meadowdale County Park, Lunds Gulch is not only a refuge to area wildlife, but also to area residents.

GETTING THERE

From Everett, head 10 miles south on I-5 to exit 183. Follow 164th Street SW west for 1.5 miles, bearing left onto 44th Avenue W to a traffic light. Turn right onto 168th Street SW and continue west, passing State Route 99. After a shy half mile, turn right onto 52nd Avenue W. In another half mile, turn left on 160th Street SW (signed for Meadowdale County Park). In 0.25 mile, turn right on 56th Avenue W. In another 0.25 mile, turn left onto 156th Street SW and follow it a short distance to the park entrance.

ON THE TRAIL

The hike through Lunds Gulch begins in a small opening on a forested bluff. The wide and well-built trail immediately enters a mature forest of Douglas-fir and wastes no time dropping 400 feet into the emerald ravine. Big boughs of ferns line the way. So do hefty cedar and hemlock stumps, testaments to the giants that once flourished here before pioneering loggers "discovered" them.

Not all of the big trees were harvested, though. A few giant firs and cottonwoods

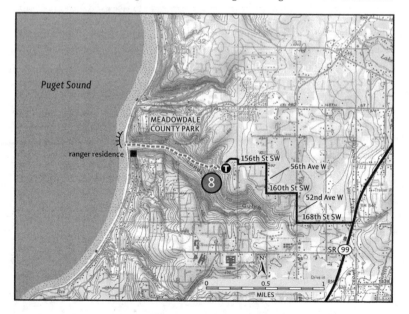

Hikers stroll down the forested trail at Lunds Gulch.

still stand tall within the lush gulch. John Lund first homesteaded this rugged tract of paradise back in 1878, and it's nicely reverting back to its wilder days. The trail follows the small creek also named after Lund. Bubbling and babbling, it makes its short journey to the Sound. Come each fall, a handful of salmon make their way up the creek to spawn.

In 1 mile the trail comes to a junction. The path left leads to the ranger's residence and to picnic tables scattered about on a manicured lawn. Much of this area once sported a country club complete with an Olympic-sized swimming pool and bath houses. In 1968 the county parks department acquired this property and began transforming it into a top-notch natural and recreational gem.

Continue hiking straight along the creek and through forest, eventually coming to a railroad underpass. Make tracks under the tracks to reach the beach. Rest on a driftwood log, comb the shore, and enjoy a splendid view of Whidbey Island and the Olympic Mountains. Sunsets are supreme here, but don't forget to allot yourself some daylight for the return to your vehicle.

9 Spencer Island

RATING/ DIFFICULTY	ROUND-TRIP	ELEV GAIN/ HIGH POINT	SEASON
★★/1	2.6 miles	None/ 10 feet	Year-round

Map: USGS Everett; **Contact:** Snohomish County Parks, (425) 388-6600, http://www1 .co.snohomish.wa.us/departments/parks; **Notes:** Dogs prohibited. Fish and Wildlife manages the northern half of the island, which is

An old hay rake farm implement on Spencer Island

open seasonally to hunting, http://wdfw.wa.gov;
GPS: N 47 59.571, W 122 10.379

👪 🏠 *Just minutes from downtown Everett, Spencer Island sits in the heart of the Snohomish River estuary, a wildlife-rich ecosystem where salt- and freshwater mix. Surrounded by snaking sloughs, this 400-acre island offers a slew of scenic delights, from glistening mudflats to glimpses of snowcapped peaks. And bird-watching opportunities here rank among the best in western Washington.*

GETTING THERE
From Everett, take exit 195 off of I-5, turning left onto E Grand Avenue. In 0.5 mile bear right onto E Marine View Drive, following it for 1 mile to State Route 529. Continue north on SR 529, crossing the Snohomish River onto Smith Island. After 0.5 mile turn right onto 35th Avenue NE (signed for Langus Riverfront Park), and proceed south for 0.5 mile, turning left onto Smith Island Road. (From Marysville, follow SR 529 south for 1 mile, turning right onto 36th Place NE. Continue for 1 mile, passing under SR 529 and coming to a junction with 35th Avenue NE and Smith Island Road.) Follow Smith Island Road south. At 1 mile bear right at a Y intersection. In another mile pass under I-5, where the road takes a sharp left and becomes 4th Street SE. Continue for 0.3 mile, passing a water treatment plant, to a parking lot on your right. Park here. The hike begins on the road.

ON THE TRAIL
Starting by the water treatment plant, hold your breath and walk 0.4 mile down gravel 4th Street SE, coming to the trailhead proper at

the old Jackknife Bridge. A paved trail leads right 2 miles to the City of Everett's Langus Riverfront Park. Continue straight onto the historic bridge. The bridge spanned nearby Ebey Slough from 1914 to 1980. In 1993 it was moved here to Union Slough, providing pedestrian access to Spencer Island. It is one of the last remaining bascule bridges (counterweight drawbridges) in the country.

Upon stepping foot on the island, come to a junction. The trail left follows a levee north to open-to-hunting (check seasons) Fish and Wildlife land. It terminates in 1 mile at a breach. Directly ahead is a short trail (often flooded in winter and spring), leading to a boardwalk providing excellent wildlife viewing. An old barn once stood here. A favorite subject for visiting photographers, it was toppled by a 2006 windstorm.

For the Spencer Island Loop, follow the levee trail south. In 0.2 mile come to a junction with the Cross Island Levee Trail, your return. Continue right, soon arriving at a bridge, one of several spanning breaches in the levee. These breaches were intentionally made by land managers to allow much of the island to revert back to a tide-influenced wetland. Scan the reeds, cattails, and sedges for myriad waterfowl and songbirds. Enjoy, too, the view east across the saturated flats to Mount Pilchuck and Three Fingers. Note the profusion of homes marching up the hills toward them. The constant buzz of traffic in the air also reminds you just how close the "civilized world" is to this wildlife refuge.

Continue hiking on the levee trail toward the southern tip of the island. Alders line the way, with an occasional birch or spruce adding a little arboreal diversity. The way then

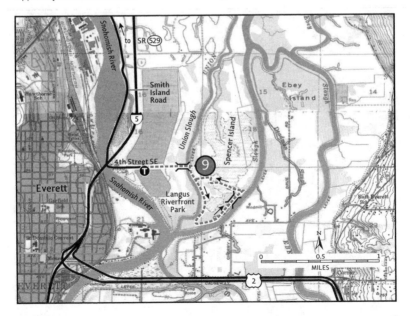

turns north, following alongside Steamboat Slough. Cross another breach bridge and come to a junction. The trail north dead-ends at an unbridged breach. Head left instead on the Cross Levee Trail, traversing wetlands teeming with life. Watch for hawks, herons, harriers, widgeons, and ruddy and wood ducks. Look, too, for bald eagles, river otters, coyotes, and deer.

In 0.5 mile the Cross Levee Trail leads back to the main trail. Turn right to return to the Jackknife Bridge.

EXTENDING YOUR TRIP

The 2.2-mile paved Smith Island Trail to the Langus Riverfront Park makes a great addition to this hike. Enjoy excellent viewing of the Snohomish River and its delta environs. On clear days, Mount Rainier can be seen hovering in the distance above the river flats.

10 Bob Heirman Wildlife Preserve

RATING/ DIFFICULTY	ROUND-TRIP	ELEV GAIN/ HIGH POINT	SEASON
★★/1	3 miles	80 feet/ 90 feet	Year-round

Map: USGS Maltby; **Contact:** Snohomish County Parks (425) 388-6600, http://www1.co.snohomish.wa.us/departments/parks; **Note:** Dogs prohibited; **GPS:** N 47 51.608, W 122 05.603

The Bob Heirman Wildlife Preserve protects undeveloped riverfront and important floodplain along the Snohomish River at the Thomas Eddy. Here the powerful river ripples and churns through a pair of tight hairpin turns, occasionally jumping its banks to create new channels and oxbow ponds. Always in flux,

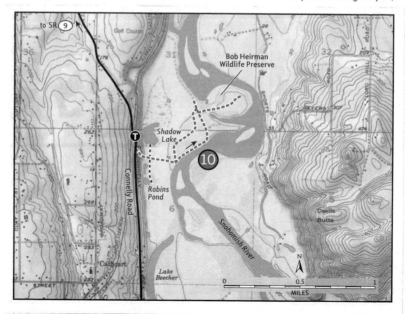

the Snohomish is a dynamic river. Here you can feel its pulse, listen to its rhythm, and embrace its beauty.

GETTING THERE

From the city of Snohomish, travel south on State Route 9 for 3 miles. At the junction with SR 96 (Lowell-Larimer Road), turn left (east) onto Broadway Avenue. In 0.8 mile bear left onto Connelly Road. Travel for another 0.8 mile to the preserve's parking area and trailhead, located on your left (elev. 90 ft).

ON THE TRAIL

Snohomish County Parks manages over 340 acres at the Bob Heirman Wildlife Preserve—open for fishing, bird-watching, and hiking. An old road serving as a central trail leads from the parking area down a short but steep bluff to wildlife-rich flats and wetlands abutting the Snohomish River. At the bottom of the bluff, immediately come to two side trails taking off in opposite directions to cloud-reflecting oxbow ponds teeming with birdlife.

Both Robins Pond and Shadow Lake harbor scores of waterfowl during the winter months. From their alder-lined shorelines, gaze out over placid waters and witness countless ducks, grebes, and swans taking refuge. Then continue on the main trail across marshy meadows to a dike along the Snohomish. The way follows along the dike, heading downstream. Take in good views north of Lord Hill (Hike 11) rising above the river.

At about 0.75 mile from the trailhead, you'll come to a Y intersection. Take the trail to the right across a damp poplar flat to reach a sprawling gravel bed. Explore the shoreline here, admiring glistening gravel and polished stones, or find a spot to cast your line for steelhead. Then retrace your steps to the trail

A cormorant rests on a rock in Shadow Lake at the Bob Heirman Preserve.

junction and continue downriver for another 0.25 mile until a tangle of blackberries prohibits further exploration. For a variation on the return, follow a parallel trail through meadows that were once used to graze livestock.

The preserve has had an industrious past, from gravel mining to farming, and it almost became a housing development. But Bob Heirman and the Snohomish Sportsman Association rallied to protect the area. Thanks Bob—I'm sure the resident wildlife thank you as well.

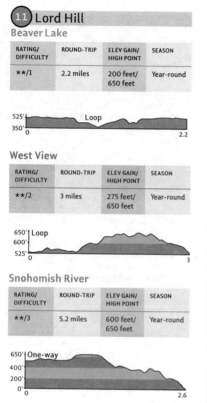

11 Lord Hill

Beaver Lake

RATING/ DIFFICULTY	ROUND-TRIP	ELEV GAIN/ HIGH POINT	SEASON
★★/1	2.2 miles	200 feet/ 650 feet	Year-round

West View

RATING/ DIFFICULTY	ROUND-TRIP	ELEV GAIN/ HIGH POINT	SEASON
★★/2	3 miles	275 feet/ 650 feet	Year-round

Snohomish River

RATING/ DIFFICULTY	ROUND-TRIP	ELEV GAIN/ HIGH POINT	SEASON
★★/3	5.2 miles	600 feet/ 650 feet	Year-round

Map: USGS Maltby; **Contact:** Snohomish County Parks, (425) 388-6600, http://www1.co.snohomish.wa.us/departments/parks; **Note:** Dogs must be leashed; **GPS:** N 47 51.680, W 122 03.526

Pocket wilderness, backyard wilderness, urban wilderness— all are appropriate descriptions of the sprawling forested ridge between the cities of Snohomish and Monroe known as Lord Hill. Over 1400 acres of this emerald upland on the Snohomish River are protected from development within Snohomish County's Lord Hill Regional Park, providing excellent outdoor wanderings close to ever-burgeoning Puget Sound cities.

GETTING THERE

From the city of Snohomish, exit State Route 9 onto 2nd Street. Proceed east for 1 mile. Then turn right onto Lincoln Avenue, which becomes the Old Snohomish–Monroe Highway. After 2.7 miles, turn right (south) onto 127th Avenue SE and proceed for about 1.6 miles to the park entrance and trailhead (elev. 525 ft). Privy available.

ON THE TRAIL

Lord Hill's location alone, situated within easy reach of hundreds of thousands of urban and suburban dwellers, makes it an attractive place. But Lord Hill is a place of natural beauty too, with placid ponds, Snohomish River frontage, scenic lookouts, and lush forests. Its large and varied habitats also support a wide array of wildlife, including bears, cougars, and bobcats.

There are over 11 miles of trail and several miles of old woods roads traversing this park named for Mitchell Lord, who homesteaded here in the 1880s. Several semiloop options exist, from short leg stretchers to all-day explorations. Here are three good suggestions. Feel free to combine them, or better yet, make them into three separate trips.

Beaver Lake: Head down the Main Trail through a cool forest of big trees, coming to a junction in 0.4 mile. Turn left on the Beaver Lake Trail and follow it through a tunnel of alders to the marshy body of water called Beaver Lake. Take a right on the Pipeline Trail, a right on the Pipeline Cutoff Trail, and then another right on the Main Trail to return to the parking lot.

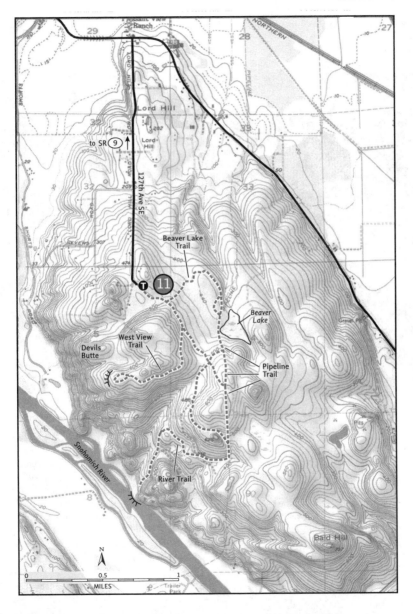

One of the many ponds dotting Lord Hill

West View: Head down the Main Trail through a cool forest of big trees to the junction at 0.4 mile. Turn right, following the Main Trail for 0.3 mile to another junction. Turn right again onto the West View Trail. After 0.8 mile come to a 650-foot knoll with a window view that includes Mount Baker. Take the loop trail around the knoll and back to the West View Trail, retracing your steps back to the parking lot. You can extend this hike by heading up the Devils Butte Trail, which branches off of the West View Trail.

Snohomish River: Head down the Main Trail through a cool forest of big trees, coming to the junction at 0.4 mile. Turn right, continuing on the Main Trail and avoiding all side trails. At 1.6 miles come to a junction with the River Trail. Take it and drop several hundred feet in 1 mile to a quiet and secluded spot on the Snohomish River. Retrace your route, or follow the River Trail Cutoff to the Pipeline Trail to the Beaver Lake Trail back to your vehicle for a more varied 6-mile loop.

Opposite: Mittens waits on the slopes of Mount Sawyer.

skykomish river valley

Sultan Basin

A rugged and remote watershed on the western edge of the Central Cascades, most of the Sultan Basin is lightly visited. Because it houses the Spada Reservoir, the city of Everett's public drinking water supply, access into the basin is regulated. Ironically, while trails in the basin are only open to foot travel (yay!) and backcountry camping is restricted to designated campsites and only open from June 15 to October 15, much of the basin has been intensively (to put it mildly) logged. However, in 1987 the Washington Department of Natural Resources (DNR), which manages much of the basin, did recognize that the area possesses ecological value as well and designated 6700 acres along Greider Ridge a Natural Resources Conservation Area. That is, it's off limits to chain saws. With help from the Student Conservation Association (SCA), the DNR constructed two wonderful trails to a pretty trio of sub-alpine lakes tucked in the ridge. In 2010, bowing to budget restrictions, the DNR could no longer maintain its roads in the basin. Fortunately, the Snohomish County PUD took over road maintenance, but unfortunately reduced access in the process. This has made two formerly easy day hikes in the basin much longer; and with limited trail maintenance much more difficult as well.

Map: Green Trails Index No. 142; **Contact:** Snohomish County Public Utility District, www.snopud.com; **Notes:** Dogs must be leashed. Hikers must register (for free) at the Olney Pass kiosk upon entering Sultan Basin watershed; **GPS:** N 47 58.483, W 121 34.773

A pair of scenic lakes is tucked in an open cirque awash in avalanche greenery and streaming with cascades that tumble down shiny rock ledges. Visit in late spring for the flowers, late summer for the berries, or late autumn for a last hiking hurrah. But no matter the season, keep your senses keen for Ursus americanus, for he's as fond of this valley as you'll soon be.

GETTING THERE

From Everett follow US 2 east to Sultan. At a traffic light east of the town center, just past milepost 23, turn left (north) onto Sultan Basin Road. Follow it for 13.25 miles (the pavement ends at 10.25 miles) to an information kiosk. Stop and sign in, acknowledging that you understand the rules and regulations for visiting Sultan Basin, which is Everett's public water supply. Then continue 500 feet farther to a Y intersection, bearing right onto South Shore Road (formerly FR 61). Reach the trailhead (elev. 1,560 feet) at South Shore Recreation Site in 5.3 miles. Privy available.

ON THE TRAIL

Start by walking on the decommissioned road which has added considerable mileage to this once-short hike. At 1.8 miles, come to the former trailhead. Locate the original

12 Greider Lakes

RATING/ DIFFICULTY	ROUND-TRIP	ELEV GAIN/ HIGH POINT	SEASON
★★★/3	8.6 miles	1370 feet/ 2930 feet	June–Nov

One-way from original trailhead

[elevation profile chart with y-axis values 2930', 2760', 2460', 2160', 1860', 1560' and x-axis 0 to 2.5]

Opposite: Clouds descend upon the Greider Basin.

trail taking off right, skirting the Reflection Ponds, two insect-incubating wetland pools responsible for feeding area frogs, dragonflies, flycatchers, and sparrows. A side trail diverts left to circle the ponds—consider taking it after you reach the Greider Lakes for a slight variation on the return.

The trail quickly heads upward, steeply at first on somewhat rocky and rooty terrain. Traversing slopes that succumbed to fire

many decades ago, you'll see blackened snags punctuate an even-aged canopy of maturing second growth. After climbing 1000 feet on forty switchbacks over a course of 1.5 miles, the grade eases, the tread becomes more agreeable, and old growth fills the backdrop.

At 2 miles, come upon the forested western shoreline of Little Greider Lake (elev. 2900 ft). Look across the placid lake to the herbaceous eastern shoreline, where it's not unusual to witness a critter or two.

Continue hiking past appealing campsites, crossing Greider Creek on sturdy planking and emerging into more open terrain.

Next climb a scant 30 feet or so, passing above a small set of tumbling falls to soon arrive at Big Greider Lake. Quite a contrast from Lower Greider, in addition to being much larger, Big Greider's environs are much more dramatic and rugged. Flanked by slopes of exposed cliffs and avalanche chutes, cascades crash from above into the lake basin. Scoot yourself down on one of

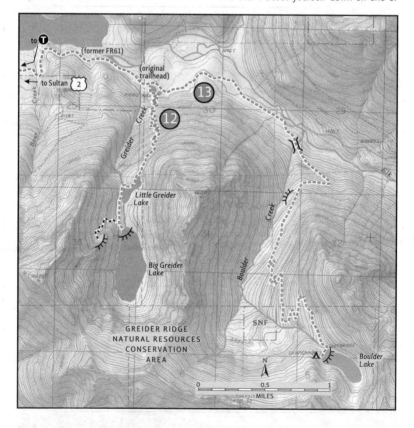

the large smooth logs lining the lake outlet and savor the scene.

EXTENDING YOUR TRIP

A spur trail takes off from Big Greider, climbing 600 feet in 0.5 mile to open meadows above the lake. Much of the way is overgrown, but tenacious hikers will be rewarded with good views.

13 Boulder Lake

RATING/ DIFFICULTY	ROUND-TRIP	ELEV GAIN/ HIGH POINT	SEASON
★★★/4	13.8 miles	2140 feet/ 3700 feet	June–Nov

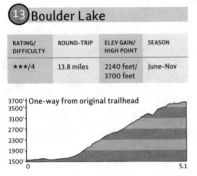

3700'
3500'
3100'
2700'
2300'
1900'
1500'

One-way from original trailhead

0   5.1

Map: Green Trails Index No. 142; **Contact:** Snohomish County Public Utility District, www.snopud.com; **Notes:** Dogs must be leashed. Hikers must register (for free) at the Olney Pass kiosk upon entering Sultan Basin watershed; **GPS:** N 47 58.483, W 121 34.773

Boulder Lake sits in a beautiful basin bounded by big trees and slopes of scree. A delightful destination, the hike to it isn't very pleasant due to a long slog on the decommissioned road and brushy, deteriorating trail. But if not deterred you'll traverse some view-granting open slopes, bubbling bogs, and stands of primeval cedars and hemlocks along the way. Boulder is one of the prettiest backcountry lakes on the western front of the Central Cascades, so it is worth the discomfort of getting there.

GETTING THERE

From Everett follow US 2 east to Sultan. At a traffic light east of the town center, just past milepost 23, turn left (north) onto Sultan Basin Road. Follow it for 13.25 miles (the pavement ends at 10.25 miles) to an information kiosk. Stop and sign in, acknowledging that you understand the rules and regulations for visiting Sultan Basin, which is Everett's public water supply. Then continue 500 feet farther to a Y intersection, bearing right onto South Shore Road (formerly FR 61). Reach the trailhead (elev. 1,560 feet) at South Shore Recreation Site in 5.3 miles. Privy available.

ON THE TRAIL

Start by walking on the decommissioned road which has added considerable mileage to this once short and enjoyable hike. At 1.8 miles, pass the former trailhead to the Greider Lakes. Continue left on the decommissioned road for another 1.3 miles, finally reaching the former trailhead to Boulder Lake. Then, as you walk an old logging road in a dank, dark, scrappy stand of hemlock, you'll likely not immediately see this hike's charm. Stick with it. Cross Boulder Creek on a big wide bridge, steadily climbing on old roadbed lined with alders. Eroded and brushy in spots, the old road makes a wide swing to angle back toward tumbling Boulder Creek. After about 1 mile the grade eases and real trail takes over. Real forest too—and views, as the way traverses the first of several open brushy slopes.

On increasingly pleasant tread, begin switchbacking through an increasingly impressive forest of ancient giants. Some of the finest specimens of cedar, hemlock, and Douglas-fir in all of western Washington can be found here in the Greider Ridge Natural Resources Conservation Area. Straddling the Puget Sound Convergence Zone (an area

A partially frozen Boulder Lake reflects the surrounding ridges.

where prevailing winds split by the Olympic Mountains reconverge, causing updrafts that can lead to convection and abundant rainfall), this is one of the wettest spots in the Central Cascades. The area's 100 to 180 inches of annual rainfall favors fast- and big-growing trees. Witness, too, the excessive runoff and boggy areas along the trail. Good solid cedar puncheon, however, assures dry boots and minimal impact on these important and fragile plant communities.

After brushing up alongside a small creek, the trail switchbacks once again, crosses said creek, and then traverses a gorgeous grassy bog. Boulder Creek soon comes into earshot before the trail swings away, switchbacking once again, albeit gently this time and through yet more magnificent old growth.

At 5.1 miles reach the lake. Yellow cedar, mountain hemlock, and huckleberry grace its shores. Cross the outlet creek on a good bridge to grassy shores ripe for lounging. Stare across shimmering azure waters to rocky pinnacles peaking above boulder fields that slope into the lake. Pretty sight, huh? And a pretty nice place to spend the night too—did you check out those designated campsites?

US 2 West

Some of the most popular hikes in the Central Cascades can be found along US 2 in the Skykomish River valley. With quick and easy access from Seattle and Everett, this should be no surprise. In an area of beautiful alpine lakes, several of which can be reached by short and fairly easy trails, these hikes are prime candidates for introducing children and hiking neophytes to the beauties of the natural world.

14 Wallace Falls

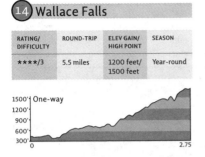

RATING/ DIFFICULTY	ROUND-TRIP	ELEV GAIN/ HIGH POINT	SEASON
★★★★/3	5.5 miles	1200 feet/ 1500 feet	Year-round

Map: Green Trails Index No. 142; **Contact:** Wallace Falls State Park, (360) 793-0420, www .parks.wa.gov; **Notes:** Dogs must be leashed; Discover Pass required; **GPS:** N 47 52.015, W 121 40.683

A series of falls, nine in all, two that are stunning and one—the tallest at 265 feet—that's absolutely spectacular! As Wallace Falls is one of the best known and loved sets of cataracts in the Evergreen State, expect plenty of company on this hike. And while these falls are grand any time of year, visit on a rainy day. Each raindrop that falls from the heavens and makes its way to the Wallace River enhances the intensity and stimulating beauty of this cavalcade of crashing cascades.

GETTING THERE

From Everett follow US 2 for 28 miles east to the hamlet of Gold Bar. Just before milepost 28, turn left onto 1st Street (signed for Wallace Falls State Park). Proceed for 0.4 mile to a four-way stop. Turn right onto May Creek Road and continue for 1.5 miles to Wallace Falls State Park and the trailhead (elev. 300 ft). Privy and water available.

ON THE TRAIL

First, check out the kiosk to read up on the falls, park, and their history. The way begins on a high-voltage line right-of-way. Buzzing along, take in a nice view of Mount Index and Baring Mountain. After 0.25 mile, enter a uniform forest of young hemlocks. The Wallace River becomes audible and its presence felt in the cool breezes funneling down the valley.

At 0.4 mile, come to a junction. Left heads to the falls on an old logging railroad grade. The easy grade attracts runners and mountain bikers. It makes for a nice loop option, adding about a mile and is best done on the return.

Head right on the Woody Trail (named not for the surroundings, but for the late

Cascading North Fork Wallace River

state senator, Frank Woody, who was a great advocate of the state's Youth Corps that helped construct this trail). Follow the trail through dark and dank forest, dropping down to river's edge. A short side trail branches off to a pretty series of small cataracts. But the big tumbles are still ahead. Under colonnades of moss-shrouded trees

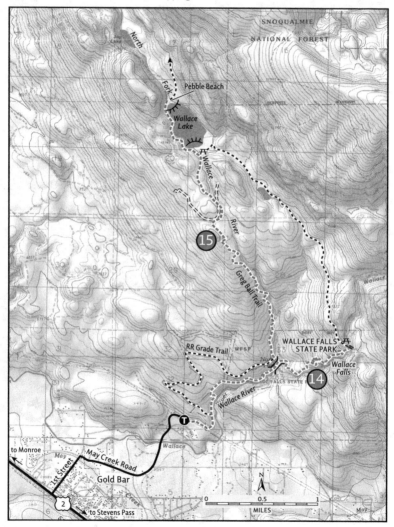

and accompanied by showy boughs of dark green ferns bursting from the ground, continue beside the roiling river. Benches provide spots for contemplation.

Now pulling away from the river, the trail begins to climb. Thanks to the Washington Trails Association, the tread is tough and durable, ready to withstand the thousands of boots that pummel it each season. At a little over a mile, a short side trail veers steeply left to connect with the Railroad Grade Trail. Continue straight, remaining high above the raucous river. At 1.4 miles, come to a junction. Left heads to the Railroad Grade Trail (your return option) and also to Wallace Lake via the Greg Ball Trail (Hike 15).

Proceed straight, dropping to cross the North Fork Wallace River, and then begin a short and steep climb to the Lower Falls viewpoint and picnic shelter. A pretty sight, but what will probably catch your attention is the much bigger falls off in the distance. Continue up the trail. At 2.2 miles reach the viewpoint for the Middle Falls. At 265 feet, this falls is the park's highest, the one you can see from US 2 way down below, and one of the most impressive hydrological shows in the state. From the soggy overlook, stare right into the heart of the tumultuous falls roaring through a narrow chasm.

The Upper Falls are another 0.5 mile beyond. Not quite as impressive, it's still nevertheless worth the 500-foot climb to get there. En route be sure to stop at the ledgy overlook above the Middle Falls for a sweeping view of the Skykomish River valley out to the Olympic Mountains.

EXTENDING YOUR TRIP

Return via the Railroad Grade Trail, or continue beyond the Upper Falls, climbing a couple hundred feet more on a rough trail to an old logging road, which you can follow for 2.6 miles to Wallace Lake (the route is well signed). Then head back to the trailhead via the Greg Ball Trail (Hike 15), arriving at your vehicle after a satisfying 10-mile hike.

15 Wallace Lake

RATING/ DIFFICULTY	ROUND-TRIP	ELEV GAIN/ HIGH POINT	SEASON
★★/3	8.2 miles	1500 feet/ 1800 feet	Year-round

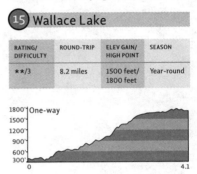

Map: Green Trails Index No. 142; **Contact:** Wallace Falls State Park, (360) 793-0420, www .parks.wa.gov; **Notes:** Dogs must be leashed; Discover Pass required; **GPS:** N 47 52.015, W 121 40.683

A pretty lake—not quite back-country, not quite alpine, but a wonderful hiking destination nevertheless, especially during the dreary months when most real backcountry and alpine lakes are inaccessible. Once reached by a long and unappealing logging road, Wallace Lake is now accessible via the enjoyable Greg Ball Trail, a path built by and honoring one of the greatest trail advocates this state has ever seen.

GETTING THERE

From Everett follow US 2 for 28 miles east to the hamlet of Gold Bar. Just before milepost 28, turn left onto 1st Street (signed for Wallace Falls State Park). Proceed for 0.4 mile to

Wallace Lake

a four-way stop. Turn right onto May Creek Road and continue for 1.5 miles to Wallace Falls State Park and the trailhead (elev. 300 ft). Privy and water available.

ON THE TRAIL

Wallace Lake is by far the best-kept secret in the 4735-acre Wallace Falls State Park, so don't despair if the trailhead parking lot is overflowing with SUVs and sedans. The majority, if not all, of those vehicles belong to hikers intent only on seeing the falls. The lake is all yours!

Start on the main (and busy) trail, traveling under high-tension wires before entering the woods and coming to a junction. Either route will work. Left follows the Railroad Grade Trail 2.2 miles before terminating at the Greg Ball Trail. Right heads 1.1 miles along

the Wallace River before coming to a junction leading 0.2 mile to the Greg Ball Trail. Head right and return on the left-hand trail.

After following along a very scenic stretch of the Wallace River, come to a well-marked junction directing you left for Wallace Lake. After a short, steep climb, emerge onto the Railroad Grade Trail. Turn right, and within a couple hundred feet arrive at the beginning of the Greg Ball Trail (elev. 900 ft). Greg was a former board member and director for the Washington Trails Association (WTA). In 1993 he launched WTA's volunteer trail-maintenance program, which has since grown into the largest state-based program of its kind, contributing over 80,000 hours of volunteer trail work annually. In 2004, at the age of sixty, Greg tragically passed away after battling cancer. He had designed this trail, and it was finished in his memory by WTA volunteers and with support from the Spring Trail Trust.

Paralleling along and above the North Fork Wallace River, the Greg Ball Trail gracefully meanders through mature second growth, climbing gently, all on nice tread. After 0.5 mile the way steepens and the forest grows darker. But an agreeable grade and forest soon returns. At 1.4 miles (3 miles from the trailhead), the river can be seen (use caution) cascading down a narrow chasm.

Now following a level course along the river, the trail continues, terminating at a Washington Department of Natural Resources (DNR) road 3.5 miles from trailhead. Turn right and follow the road for a short 0.1 mile to a junction with an old road taking off left. Follow this near-level forested way for 0.5 mile to arrive at the southern tip of Wallace Lake at its outlet. Though this is a pretty spot in heavy timber with picnic tables and an attractive bridge, the northern end of the lake at Pebble Beach is much better.

Head left, following an old woods road for 0.5 mile to arrive at the beach, a gravel outwash at the base of a small talus slope. Find yourself a nice sun-warmed log and enjoy the view across the placid lake to Mount Index and what's colloquially referred to as Zekes Hill, peeking out in the distance.

EXTENDING YOUR TRIP

You can continue north of Wallace Lake another 0.5 mile to a sliver of a lake, Jay Lake. Better yet, from Wallace's outlet head to Wallace Falls (Hike 14). On a route consisting mostly of DNR roads (some old, some still in use), it's a 2.6-mile trip to the Upper Falls. The way is well-signed. Follow the Woody Trail back to your vehicle, completing a loop of about 10 miles.

16 Bridal Veil Falls and Lake Serene

Bridal Veil Falls

RATING/DIFFICULTY	ROUND-TRIP	ELEV GAIN/HIGH POINT	SEASON
★★★/2	4.4 miles	850 feet/1450 feet	Mar–Dec

Lake Serene

RATING/DIFFICULTY	ROUND-TRIP	ELEV GAIN/HIGH POINT	SEASON
★★★/3	7.2 miles	1920 feet/2520 feet	May–Nov

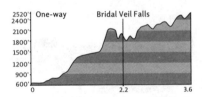

Map: Green Trails Index No. 142; **Contact:** Mount Baker–Snoqualmie National Forest, Skykomish Ranger District, (360) 677-2414, www.fs.fed.us/r6/mbs; **Note:** NW Forest Pass required; **GPS:** N 47 48.546, W 121 34.432

Towering and formidable, Mount Index is perhaps the most awesome and fiercest sight and site along US 2. But softening its stark appearance is Bridal Veil Falls. Emanating from beneath the mountain's austere crags, the tiered and tumbling cataract drapes over granite slabs. To really appreciate this plummeting waterway, however, you'll need to leave your vehicle and hit the trail. And in your journey, discover a secret—there's a beautiful lake perched beneath those rugged spires feeding those falls.

GETTING THERE

From Everett follow US 2 east to the hamlet of Gold Bar. Continue on US 2 for 7 more miles to just before it crosses the Skykomish River (near milepost 35), and turn right onto Mount Index Road. Proceed on this dirt road 0.4 mile, turning right on the spur road signed "Lake Serene Trail 1068." The trailhead and large parking area are 500 feet farther (elev. 600 ft). Privy available.

ON THE TRAIL
Start by following an old road lined with mossy maples and alders. Cross a series of minor tributaries. Pretty in their own right, especially after a storm, these streaming streams are also eroding away chunks of

Bridal Veil Falls crashes down cliffs below Lake Serene.

tread. Next, along a thickly forested slope, the trail gradually ascends. At 1.7 miles, just after leaving the old roadbed, come to a signed junction (elev. 1200 ft). The trail left continues on, heading to "secret" Lake Serene tucked in a deep basin beneath the spires of Mount Index.

For Bridal Veil Falls, head right. The falls is 0.5 mile away. Just follow the roar, using a series of short switchbacks and stairways that steeply climb toward the tumult. Cross several side creeks and expect to get your feet wet. Be sure to pause for a moment or two to look back at the Skykomish Valley spread below. One last grunt, and reach the first of two waterfall viewing platforms.

Except for late summer, when the falls trickle more than pummel, the roar should be pretty deafening at this point. Don your rain parka and set out on a drenched boardwalk to embrace the cascade's full force and beauty. Bridal veil? From this proximity, it's more like a bridal shower. Literally soak up the falls' beauty. When you've had enough, retreat to the trail junction and make a decision. Back to your rig, or up to Lake Serene?

Serene usually wins, so carry on. Continue on the main trail, dropping a little into a damp ravine. Cross Bridal Veil Creek on a well-built bridge, and then begin climbing. On solid tread that occasionally utilizes stone steps and rock cribbing, the trail steeply ascends. A long sweep east—then a long sweep west—the way works under, over, and around cliffs, gaining 1300 feet in about 1.5 miles. Take in fine views of the valley below as well as out to Ragged Ridge and other peaks of the newly minted Wild Sky Wilderness.

And Lake Serene? It lies just a short distance ahead, tucked in a tight basin beneath the ramparts and parapets of fortress Index.

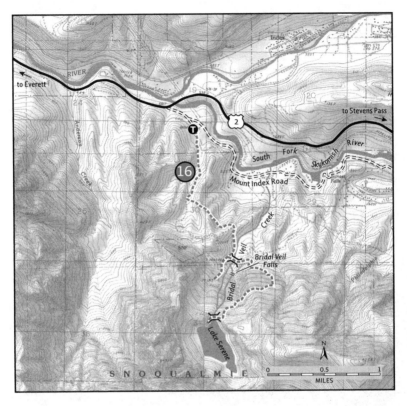

Stare straight up those 3000-vertical-foot stark walls. Hardly serene, it's more like awe-inspiring. But when the basin is calm, those imposing rock faces delicately reflect in the lake's surface. Now, that's serene and quite a sight!

17 Heybrook Lookout

RATING/ DIFFICULTY	ROUND-TRIP	ELEV GAIN/ HIGH POINT	SEASON
★★/2	2.6 miles	850 feet/ 1700 feet	Year-round

Map: Green Trails Index No. 142; **Contact:** Mount Baker–Snoqualmie National Forest, Skykomish Ranger District, (360) 677-2414, www.fs.fed.us/r6/mbs; **Note:** NW Forest Pass required; **GPS:** N 47 48.502, W 121 32.112

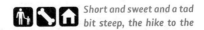

Short and sweet and a tad bit steep, the hike to the

restored Heybrook Lookout makes for a good spring warm-up or late fall frolic, when the surrounding high country is buried deep in snow. From the lookout's lofty balcony, scan the scenic Skykomish Valley, relish the rugged beauty of Ragged Ridge, and stand impressed by Mount Index's imposing facade.

GETTING THERE

From Everett follow US 2 east for 37 miles (approximately 2 miles east of the steel bridge crossing the Skykomish River) to the trailhead (elev. 850 ft), located on the north side of the highway just after entering Mount Baker–Snoqualmie National Forest.

ON THE TRAIL

Quickly leave the busy highway behind and enter a cool, mossy forest of second growth.

After angling east at an easy grade, the way reverses direction and steepens. Via a series of tight switchbacks the trail meanders upward under an emerald canopy. Pass by giant cedar stumps, evidence of past logging. Their blackened scars confirm that even moist forests like this one are subject to fire.

Approach a series of boulders carpeted with moss. Swing east once again and crest the ridge, highway noise now replaced by thrush and wren song. In early season search the forest floor for signs of spring. A blooming trillium qualifies. Continue along the ridge on a gentler incline to eventually bust out of the forest on a ledge just below Heybrook's fire lookout. The views here are good, but they're far better from the top of the 67-foot lookout tower perched on the 1700-foot ridge.

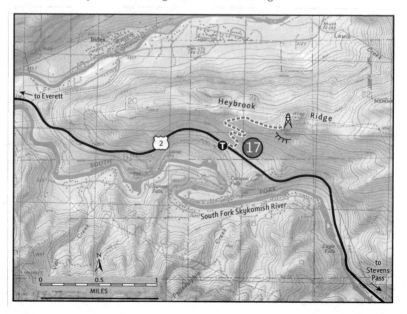

Views across the Skykomish River Valley to Mount Index are highlights of the hike to Heybrook Lookout.

Ascend seven sets of stairs and behold a supreme view of the Skykomish Valley spread below you. First, gaze east toward Stevens Pass and ominous Baring Mountain. Then look west to the forks of the Skykomish—mighty good white water down there. Finally draw your attention south to the massive and awesome rock wall known as Mount Index. Snowfields perpetually cling to its precipitous crags. Bridal Veil Falls careens out of a cleft housing Lake Serene.

The hike out is short so there's no need to return just yet. Hang around awhile and watch the evening sky cast a crimson hue on the impressive and imposing landmark Index. And don't forget to give thanks to the Everett Mountaineers for making all of this viewing possible. It was their idea and hard work that restored the 1964 lookout.

18 Lake Elizabeth

RATING/ DIFFICULTY	ROUND-TRIP	ELEV GAIN/ HIGH POINT	SEASON
★/1	0.7 mile	50 feet/ 2900 feet	Mid-May– mid-Nov

Map: Green Trails Mount Si No. 174; **Contact:** Mount Baker–Snoqualmie National Forest, Skykomish Ranger District, (360) 677-2414, www.fs.fed.us/r6/mbs; **GPS:** N 47 48.072, W 121 31.095

A quiet little lake at the headwaters of Money Creek, Lake Elizabeth makes for an easy family outing. Come in late spring for showy blossoms brightening the forest floor, summer for languid lounging, or fall for berry picking amid pockets of vivid color. And with its short distance, the hike around Elizabeth is ideal for budding explorers.

GETTING THERE

From Everett follow US 2 east for 45 miles. Just before milepost 46 turn right at the sign for "Money Creek Campground" onto the Old Cascade Highway. Proceed for 1.1 mile, turning right onto Miller River Road (Forest Road 6410). Then immediately turn right onto Money Creek Road (FR 6420) and continue 6.8 miles to the easy-to-miss trailhead on your right. The last couple of miles of road are rough.

ON THE TRAIL

The way is pretty straightforward. From the trailhead, drop a few feet to the lake's outlet, Money Creek, and decide your course of circumnavigation. Left or right around the lake? Either way, it's a delightful hike. Aside from constantly having the tranquil

7-acre lake at your side, you'll pass through lovely groves of old cedar, fir, and hemlock, and cross numerous feeder creeks. You'll be granted nice views, too, of the steep, open slopes surrounding Elizabeth.

The only difficulty you may encounter is that this trail, like so many others in the Mount Baker–Snoqualmie National Forest, is slowly deteriorating due to lack of maintenance. The bridge over Money Creek is in need of capital improvements and the trail is brushing-in at many spots. After your hike, let the forest ranger and your representative in Congress know about the trail's condition and why it's a shame to let such a recreational treasure wither away. Better yet, invite them out to see it for themselves—it'll do them some good and hopefully the trail too!

EXTENDING YOUR TRIP

In winter the Money Creek Road makes a good snowshoe or cross-country ski route to

Lake Elizabeth

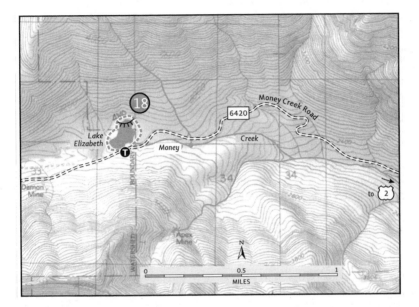

Lake Elizabeth. Before venturing here during the dark, cold months, however, be sure you're properly prepared—in winter this hike is no longer an easy jaunt. And stay away from the open slopes surrounding the lake. They're occasionally prone to avalanches.

19 Barclay Lake

RATING/ DIFFICULTY	ROUND-TRIP	ELEV GAIN/ HIGH POINT	SEASON
★★/1	4.4 miles	225 feet/ 2425 feet	May–mid-Nov

2425' One-way
2200'
0   2.2

Map: Green Trails Monte Cristo No. 143;
Contact: Mount Baker–Snoqualmie National Forest, Skykomish Ranger District, (360) 677-2414, www.fs.fed.us/r6/mbs; **Note:** NW Forest Pass required; **GPS:** N 47 47.504, W 121 27.355

Barclay Lake sits snug between Merchant Peak and Baring Mountain, an awesome pair of imposing peaks. A gentle and easy hike, Barclay is a welcoming portal into the rugged terrain of Washington's newest wilderness, the 106,577-acre Wild Sky. The well-graded and maintained trail gains a little more than 200 feet of elevation in a little more than two miles, making it an ideal trek for children and beginning hikers.

GETTING THERE

From Everett, head 40 miles east on US 2 to the settlement of Baring. Near milepost 41 and across from a convenience store, turn left (north) onto 635th Place NE. Cross railroad tracks and after 0.3 mile come to a junction. Turn left onto Forest Road 6024 and proceed for 4.2 miles to the trailhead (elev. 2200 ft).

ON THE TRAIL

Beginning in an old clear-cut, the trail takes off through a dark tunnel of regenerating forest. Despair over the majestic forest that once blanketed this valley, and say a prayer for the misguided land managers who sanctioned its destruction. Thankfully all was not lost, and mature forest is soon reached. Interspersed with remnant giants and quickly taking on old-growth characteristics, it is a far more attractive and ecologically viable forest than the one you began in. This stand, almost all western hemlocks, is blessed with a high amount of annual precipitation, evidenced by the thick carpets of mosses draping the trees.

Continue up the sliver of a valley, hemmed in by Baring to the south and the craggy, rocky summits of Gunn and Merchant peaks to the north. As rugged and wild as the surroundings may appear, the way to Barclay Lake is as gentle as any trail can be. Soon after crossing Barclay Creek, reach the lake. Stroll alongside it and try to find a quiet spot to sit and enjoy it, for chances are you'll be far from alone here. Barclay has its legions of admirers, from Scouts to artists, from first-time hikers to the very seasoned. Gaze out across the lake and up to the striking northern face of Baring Mountain. An imposing and well-known landmark visible from much of the Skykomish Valley, it is truly stunning when viewed from the lake.

EXTENDING YOUR TRIP

Experienced hikers who don't mind a little sweat and toil can follow an unmarked but

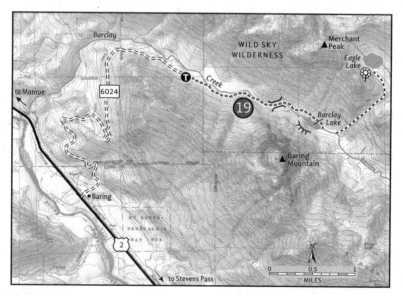

Baring Mountain towers over a frozen Barclay Lake in early winter.

very obvious trail leading north from the far end of the lake into the Wild Sky Wilderness. Follow this rough-and-tumble route for 2 miles, gaining 1500 feet, much of it within the very beginning, to pretty Eagle Lake. En route you'll pass tiny Stone Lake before traversing the aptly named Paradise Meadow. Enjoy the floral show. An old cabin graces Eagle Lake. If you're still feeling ambitious, nearby Townsend Mountain's semi-open slopes invite wandering. But don't be surprised if you're not alone here either—a boot-beaten "backdoor" path along Eagle Creek comes in from FR 6514.

20 Lakes Dorothy, Bear, and Deer

Lake Dorothy

RATING/ DIFFICULTY	ROUND-TRIP	ELEV GAIN/ HIGH POINT	SEASON
★★/1	3.5 miles	800 feet/ 3060 feet	June–mid-Nov

Bear and Deer Lakes

RATING/ DIFFICULTY	ROUND-TRIP	ELEV GAIN/ HIGH POINT	SEASON
★★★/3	11.5 miles	1800 feet/ 3800 feet	July–Oct

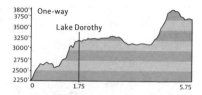

Map: Green Trails Skykomish No. 175; **Contact:** Mount Baker–Snoqualmie National Forest, Skykomish Ranger District, (360) 677-2414, www.fs.fed.us/r6/mbs; **Notes:** NW Forest Pass required. Dogs must be leashed; **GPS:** N 47 36.535, W 121 23.166

One of the largest and easiest to hike to bodies of water within the sprawling 393,360-acre Alpine Lakes Wilderness, Lake Dorothy is not for the solitude seeker. Expect scores of first-time hikers, neophyte backpackers, and fledgling anglers scurrying about the shores of this almost 2-mile-long sparkling lake. If it's a real wilderness experience you seek, and a satisfying day-long hike as well, push farther to the twin lakes of Bear and Deer.

GETTING THERE

From Everett follow US 2 east for 45 miles. Just before milepost 46 turn right at sign for "Money Creek Campground" onto the Old Cascade Highway. Proceed for 1.1 miles, turning right onto Miller River Road (Forest Road 6412). Follow this generally good gravel road for 9.5 miles to its terminus at the trailhead (elev. 2250 ft). Privy available.

ON THE TRAIL

Surrounded by virgin forest centuries old and shiny rocky ledges scoured by ancient ice flows, Lake Dorothy would still be a popular destination if the hike were twice as long. Unfortunately, the short distance that makes this lake an ideal destination for children

Mittens pauses on a rock along the shore of Lake Dorothy.

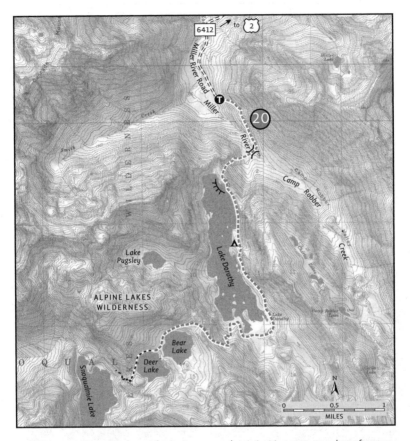

and those not quite yet in shape, also invites visitors unenlightened about Leave No Trace principles and the idea of walking lightly on the land. Do your part to help minimize negative impacts on this special place.

The well-built and well-maintained trail takes off into primeval timber and in little time enters the Alpine Lakes Wilderness. The trail soon comes upon cascading Camp Robber Creek, following it for a bit before crossing it on a sturdy bridge. Here, among polished granite slabs, the creek plunges into a deep pool—an inviting spot on a hot afternoon. The trail then begins to climb more steeply, reaching the long lake's littered-with-logs outlet (elev. 3060 ft) at 1.75 miles. Savor the view south to Big Snow Mountain.

This short and easy hike wasn't always this way. Back in the 1950s the trip to Dorothy required an all-day trek on trail up the East Fork Miller River valley. But by the 1960s the Forest Service (the same agency that converted many of our old-growth forests into "managed" woodlots) converted most of that trail to road. In fact, the bureaucrats were intent on punching the road all the way to the Middle Fork Snoqualmie River, creating a Lake Dorothy Highway. Good grief! Fortunately, the creation of the Alpine Lakes Wilderness in the 1970s permanently put a halt to that scheme, keeping Dorothy and her aquatic neighbors in the backcountry, where they rightfully belong.

If you want to visit those neighbors, carry on. Continue on good albeit at times rocky trail for nearly 2 miles along Dorothy's eastern shoreline. Pass backcountry campsites, lounging ledges, and plenty of scenic spots along the way. At the south end of the lake the trail turns west, crossing a tumbling inlet creek before ascending 750 steep and rocky feet up a forested ridge dividing the Skykomish and Snoqualmie watersheds.

At 4.75 miles from the trailhead, reach a 3800-foot gap in the ridge. Pause for huckleberries and viewing down to island-dotted

Dorothy. Then continue on your way, dropping about 200 feet and reaching Bear Lake (elev. 3610 ft) in about a half mile. Its nearly identical rounded twin, Deer Lake (elev. 3583 ft), is easily reached by walking another half mile of trail. The lakes are ringed with old forest and there's nary another human soul to be found.

EXTENDING YOUR TRIP

One mile beyond Deer and about 400 feet lower in elevation is much larger Snoqualmie Lake. This remote and attractive lake can also be reached by hiking up from the Taylor River valley, but that's an 8.5-mile journey. With its long accesses, Snoqualmie remains mainly within the domain of backpackers.

21 Evans Lake

RATING/ DIFFICULTY	ROUND-TRIP	ELEV GAIN/ HIGH POINT	SEASON
★/1	1 mile	50 feet/ 3700 feet	Mid-June– Oct

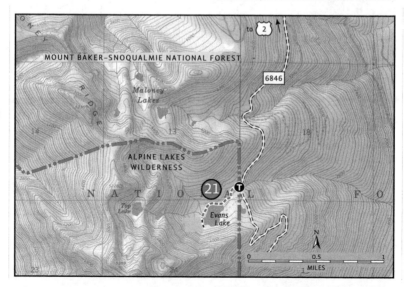

Evans Lake

Map: Green Trails Skykomish No. 175; **Contact:** Mount Baker–Snoqualmie National Forest, Skykomish Ranger District, (360) 677-2414, www.fs.fed.us/r6/mbs; **GPS:** N 47 39.532 W 121 19.379

A long, albeit decent logging road to a short, albeit pleasant trail, the trip to Evans Lake makes for a quick wilderness fix. Come here to snow probe in early season, berry pick in late summer, or reflect in late fall. Except perhaps for a few anglers, it should just be you and the frogs and the dragonflies at this little lake.

GETTING THERE

Drive US 2 east to the small town of Skykomish. Continue east for 1.9 miles (passing the Forest Service ranger station) and turn right onto Foss River Road (Forest Road 68). Continue for 8.1 miles (the pavement ends at 1.1 miles), turning left onto FR 6846. Follow this decent road for 2.7 miles (bear left at 2.2 miles) to the trailhead, located on your right (elev. 3650 ft).

ON THE TRAIL

The wide and well-groomed path immediately enters ancient forest and the Alpine Lakes Wilderness. Back in the logging frenzy of the 1980s and early '90s, the congressionally set wilderness border was all that kept these old trees surrounding Evans Lake from becoming lumber. Following alongside the gently flowing outlet creek, reach the lake within mere minutes. Ringed by grassy shores and old-growth trees, it's a pleasant spot.

The lake is shallow, not good for swimming and only slightly better for fishing. Sit and enjoy the serenity, or continue walking along the small body of water. The formal trail continues a short distance before reverting to a primitive path at the inlet creek. There are other lakes in the vicinity, along Maloney Ridge, but lacking developed trails and requiring considerable climbing, they're not quite as easy to get to as Evans.

22 West Fork Foss Lakes

RATING/ DIFFICULTY	ROUND-TRIP	ELEV GAIN/ HIGH POINT	SEASON
★★★★★/5	13 miles	3700 feet/ 4900 feet	Mid-July– Oct

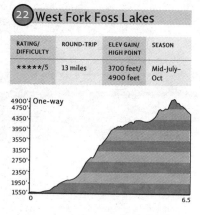

Map: Green Trails Skykomish No. 175; **Contact:** Mount Baker–Snoqualmie National Forest, Skykomish Ranger District, (360) 677-2414, www.fs.fed.us/r6/mbs; **Notes:** NW Forest Pass required. Dogs must be leashed. Trail sustained considerable flood damage in 2006, inquire about status at ranger station; **GPS:** N 47 38.093 W 121 18.214

⭐ *Tucked in tight folds, big basins, and rocky cirques high above the West Fork Foss River are a bevy of big, beautiful alpine lakes—one of the highest concentrations of alpine lakes in the entire Alpine*

Lakes Wilderness, actually. You can spend days here, and many do, but day hiking to several of these aquatic gems isn't out of the question. Just prepare for a tough slog over rough terrain. And prepare for some of the finest alpine scenery this side of Stevens Pass.

GETTING THERE

Drive US 2 east to the small town of Skykomish. Continue east for 1.9 miles (passing the Forest Service ranger station), and turn right onto Foss River Road (Forest Road 68). Continue for 4.7 miles (the pavement ends at 1.1 miles), turning left onto FR 6835. Follow this road for 1.9 miles to its end and the trailhead (elev. 1550 ft).

ON THE TRAIL

How many of the five lakes lying along this trail you choose to visit will depend on your stamina and determination. While this hike isn't the longest in this book, nor does it involve the most elevation gain, it does rank among the toughest. Much of the way is over rock—lots of rock. And much of the climb comes at once in a brushy section fully exposed to the sun. The first mile used to be really rough, but it's gotten a lot better thanks to recent trail work completed by volunteer work crews. If you're up for the challenge, you're in for a real treat. These lakes are among the biggest and most beautiful within the entire 393,360-acre Alpine Lakes Wilderness.

Immediately entering wilderness, the trail begins in a lush mossy river bottomland. In the autumn of 2006 the trail became a river channel when the West Fork Foss flooded. Tread damage was extensive, but the Washington Trails Association assembled several work teams over the summers of 2010 and 2011 and was able to rehabilitate this section of trail.

At about 1.1 miles, come to a sturdy bridge spanning the river. Now continue upvalley, passing some of the largest trees this side of the redwoods. Carefully negotiate through a recent rock-slide area ("the fall of 2006!"), and at 1.5 miles come to Trout Lake (elev. 2000 ft). A shallow lake set amid cliffs and graced with groves of hemlock, it's a popular backpacking destination among anglers and families with children.

Beyond Trout, trail damage is minimal, but the going gets tough. Paralleling a crashing side creek, the trail furiously climbs over rock and brushy slopes out of the deep valley. Following the waterway upward, you'll soon come to a spectacular waterfall. Then, angling right, the trail works its way over the headwall from whence all that water rages. Now in cool forest of yellow cedar and mountain hemlock, carefully cross a side creek on a snow-damaged bridge and continue upward at a saner grade.

At 3.5 miles reach a junction (elev. 3850 ft). The trail right leads 0.2 mile up a steep and brushy route to often overlooked Lake Malachite (elev. 4089 ft), set in a big cirque. Continuing on the main path, reach Copper Lake (elev. 3961 ft) in 0.25 mile, just after crossing its outlet creek above a set of falls.

Call it quits at the grassy outlet, where you can sit and stare across sparkling waters fed by snowmelt cascades, or keep exploring. The trail hugs the lake's rugged eastern shore, revealing fine rocky overlooks among groves of ancient trees. At 5 miles, after passing through heather meadows, reach the next aquatic gem, Little Heart Lake (elev. 4204 ft). Access to this body of water,

Malachite Peak rises to the north of Copper Lake in the Foss Lakes region.

often littered with avalanche debris, is at the campsites near the outlet stream.

To get to Big Heart Lake, the most beautiful yet of the West Fork Foss lakes, keep following the trail, heading about 700 feet up a steep ridge and then dropping 350 feet off of it. Enjoy window views north of Trout Lake in the valley below and Glacier Peak hovering in the horizon beyond. Big Heart Lake at 6.5 miles (elev. 4545 ft) is set against a backdrop

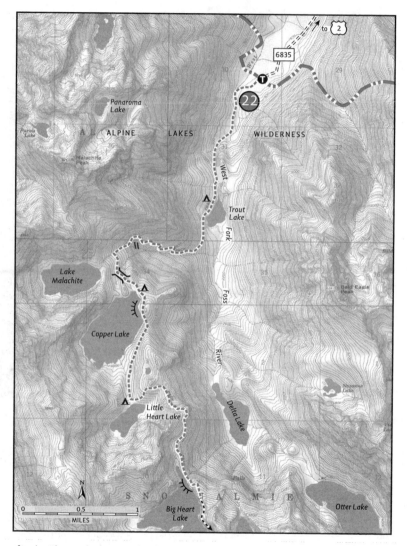

of rocky ridges and snowcapped spires.

The large logjam near its outlet stream cascading into the valley below makes for an ideal spot for sunning, snacking, feet-soaking, and savoring all of this beauty. Rest up. It's a rough journey back, too.

EXTENDING YOUR TRIP

The trail continues another mile, deteriorating into a boot-beaten path on its up-and-over way to gorgeous Angeline Lake. Another half dozen lakes lie beyond, strictly the domain of experienced off-trail travelers with days to explore.

23 Mount Sawyer and Tonga Ridge

RATING/ DIFFICULTY	ROUND-TRIP	ELEV GAIN/ HIGH POINT	SEASON
★★★/2	6 miles	1200 feet/ 5501 feet	July–Oct

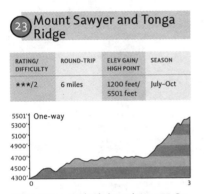

Maps: Green Trails Skykomish No. 175, Stevens Pass No. 176; **Contact:** Mount Baker–Snoqualmie National Forest, Skykomish Ranger District, (360) 677-2414, www.fs.fed.us/r6/mbs; **Note:** NW Forest Pass required; **GPS:** N 47 40.730, W 121 15.887

Amble aimlessly along an easy ridge on the edge of the Alpine Lakes Wilderness. Scrounge for berries or lounge in sun-kissed meadows. Then follow a faint path to a long-ago lookout site still flush in stunning alpine views. Come in summer for dazzling floral displays or in autumn for carpets of crimson unfurled along the way. But no matter the season, come during the week, for Sawyer's admirers are legion.

GETTING THERE

Drive US 2 east to the small town of Skykomish. Continue east for 1.9 miles (passing the Forest Service ranger station), and turn right onto Foss River Road (Forest Road 68). Continue for 3.6 miles (the pavement ends at 1.1 miles), turning left onto FR 6830. Proceed for 6.9 miles to an unsigned junction. Bear right onto FR Spur 310, and after 1.4 miles reach the trailhead at the road's end (elev. 4300 ft).

ON THE TRAIL

The way begins on an old fire break at the edge of an old cut that's quickly being reclaimed by feisty firs and hemlocks. After a short, steep, and rather uninspiring prelude, the score advances to real trail through real

Mittens enjoys summit snow—ignoring the great view of Glacier Peak behind her.

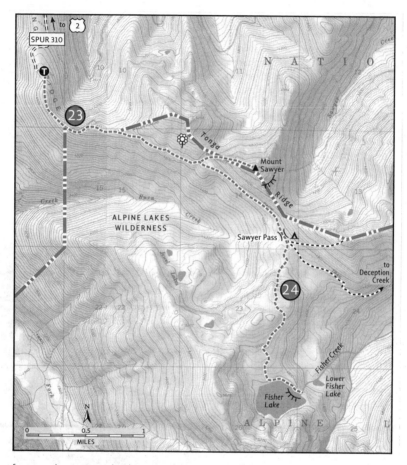

forest and on a near-level course that's a pleasure to hike. At 0.6 mile enter the Alpine Lakes Wilderness. Now watch the forest cover thin—first groves of mountain hemlock, then brushy meadow openings sporting mountain ash and huckleberry.

Skirting the western high point of Tonga Ridge, the trail commences slightly downward. At 2 miles traverse a grassy swale (elev.

4700 ft) that once housed a tarn. Shrubs and grasses and showy wildflowers have claimed the once water-filled depression. Pay attention to your left for an unmarked trail as you continue a short distance, reentering a forested grove.

This is the way to Mount Sawyer, a 5501-foot summit on Tonga Ridge's midsection. Brushy and steep at first, the grade soon eases and the well-defined tread becomes a pleasure to follow. As you make a long traverse across Sawyer's open and brushy southern face (the result of a fire a century ago), rugged mountains to the south come into view.

Rife with blueberry bushes and mountain ash, Sawyer's slopes are atwitter with copious birds. Watch for bears, and try not to let flushed grouse with their thunderous fleeing increase your heart rate.

Steadily ascending, the way makes a few short switchbacks before swinging west along a subalpine fir–draped ridgeline. It's then a short final climb to the old lookout site. Enjoy an awesome view into the heart of the Alpine Lakes Wilderness, where snowy, showy Mounts Daniel and Hinman dominate the scene. Rainier peaks above scores of other summits, grand and small.

EXTENDING YOUR TRIP

Continue along the Tonga Ridge Trail for another mile to Sawyer Pass (elev. 4750 ft), a lovely flat of heather, small pools, and abundant berries in season. Want more? A way trail leads from the pass to the right, to the Fisher Lake Trail (Hike 24), or continue on the main trail, dropping 1500 feet in 2.3 miles to Deception Creek (Hike 25).

24 Fisher Lake

RATING/ DIFFICULTY	ROUND-TRIP	ELEV GAIN/ HIGH POINT	SEASON
★★★/3	10 miles	1350 feet/ 5175 feet	July–Oct

Maps: Green Trails Skykomish No. 175, Stevens Pass No. 176; **Contact:** Mount Baker–Snoqualmie National Forest, Skykomish Ranger District, (360) 677-2414, www.fs.fed .us/r6/mbs; **Note:** NW Forest Pass required; **GPS:** N 47 40.730, W 121 15.887

Rock-rimmed and liberally garnished with huckleberries, Fisher Lake sits snug in a forested bowl high above the deep, dark Deception Creek valley. Because the lake was "discovered" by anxious anglers, the trail to it was never officially built. Expect rough going, but all in the absence of the huddled masses that usually aggregate on nearby Tonga Ridge.

GETTING THERE

Drive US 2 east to the small town of Skykomish. Continue east for 1.9 miles (passing the Forest Service ranger station), and turn right onto Foss River Road (Forest Road 68). Continue for 3.6 miles (the pavement ends at 1.1 miles), turning left onto FR 6830. Proceed for 6.9 miles to an unsigned junction. Bear right onto FR Spur 310, and after 1.4 miles reach the trailhead at the road's end (elev. 4300 ft).

ON THE TRAIL

Start by following the Tonga Ridge Trail (Hike 23) on an easy and delightful romp across subalpine forest and meadow. At 0.6 mile enter the Alpine Lakes Wilderness. At 2.1 miles pass the unmarked trail to Mount Sawyer. Nary gaining elevation, the trail continues, skirting the three prominent summits of Tonga Ridge. In autumn the bountiful berry bushes and clusters of mountain ash set the ridge on fire in shades of crimson.

At just over 3 miles, come to the pool-pocked, heathered flat known as Sawyer

Pass (elev. 4750 ft), where there's an unmarked four-way junction. The path left heads for the open slopes of Tonga Ridge's 5596-foot high point. The trail forward descends 1500 feet in 2.3 miles to reach the Deception Creek Trail (Hike 25). En route it crosses FR 6830, a favorite haunt for winter visitors.

The trail you want to take veers right—with all the side trails to campsites and berry patches, it might be a little difficult deciphering the one that leads to Fisher Lake. Try to stay on the most boot-beaten one. In 0.1 mile stay to the left, and then immediately head right, following a rooty, washed-out path heading south. You'll know you're on the right path if after 0.25 mile you begin a steep rocky climb.

Cresting a 5000-foot ridge the trail continues more gently, traversing rolling parkland brushed with glades of old-growth hemlock and dolloped with reflecting pools. After crossing an open flat, climb again. It's a steep grunt up to a 5150-foot crest, but rejoice, your payoff is nearing. The way now begins a gradual descent, crossing creeklets and beautiful groves of yellow cedars. Several paths divert to hidden tarns and points unknown. Keep to the most boot-beaten way.

At 4.75 miles reach the heavily forested shore of Fisher Lake (elev. 4763 ft). Continue for another 0.25 mile to an opening near the lake's outlet for a good spot for soaking feet, the sun's rays, and the surrounding soothing scenery.

EXTENDING YOUR TRIP

Experienced off-trail travelers may want to venture farther to the even quieter Ptarmigan Lakes. Cross Fisher Creek and follow a very brushy, rough-at-times primitive way path to the two lakes south of Fisher.

A hiker enjoys the serenity of Fisher Lake.

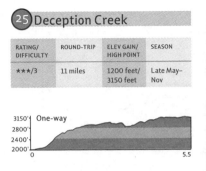

25 Deception Creek

RATING/ DIFFICULTY	ROUND-TRIP	ELEV GAIN/ HIGH POINT	SEASON
★★★/3	11 miles	1200 feet/ 3150 feet	Late May– Nov

Well-built bridge over Deception Creek

Map: Green Trails Stevens Pass No. 176; **Contact:** Mount Baker–Snoqualmie National Forest, Skykomish Ranger District, (360) 677-2414, www.fs.fed.us/r6/mbs; **Note:** NW Forest Pass required; **GPS:** N 47 42.723, W 121 11.618

Venture up a valley cloaked in magnificent old-growth regalia. Deception Creek is one of the finest ancient-forest hikes within the entire Alpine Lakes Wilderness—its treasured trees will have you oohing and aahing the entire way. But there's more to this trail than arboreal admiring. There's the creek itself, a silvery ribbon that slithers over boulders and crashes down rocky sluiceways. Deception Creek is ideal for early season forays, rainy-day sauntering, a midsummer retreat, or whenever you just feel like being alone with nature.

GETTING THERE

Drive US 2 east to the small town of Skykomish. Continue for another 8 miles, turning right onto easy-to-miss Forest Road 6088. The turnoff is 0.25 mile east of the Deception Falls Interpretive Site. Follow FR 6088 for 0.4 mile to its end at the trailhead, located in a powerline swath (elev. 2000 ft).

ON THE TRAIL

A pure delight to hike, this lightly traveled trail has recently received some heavy maintenance thanks to the Washington Trails Association. The way starts off easy and immediately enters magnificent old-growth forest. In 0.25 mile cross the wilderness boundary, and soon afterward reach an impressive bridge spanning Deception Creek. Sun-kissed granite ledges granting captivating views of frothy rapids may tempt you to linger, while giant boulders may entice young hikers to scout for gnomes and hobbits.

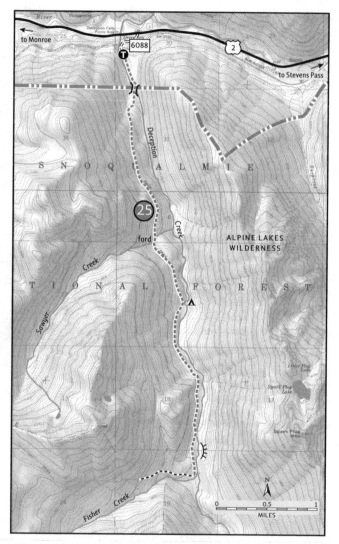

Now pulling away from the creek, the trail crosses an amazing stand of giant cedars before beginning to climb. As the trail steeply gains nearly 1000 feet in 1 mile, Deception Creek fades from sight, but not from sound. Crashing Sawyer Creek (elev. 2900 ft) soon becomes audible, and the trail descends slightly to cross it. In 2007 the footlog spanning it collapsed, but the Washington Trails Association replaced it with an even sturdier bridge.

Once beyond Sawyer Creek, the trail continues on a more leisurely course. Nearly level and traversing more spectacular old growth, at 3.3 miles the trail reacquaints itself with Deception Creek. A quiet campsite invites lunchtime lounging or is a good place to call it quits if time and energy come up short. But some spectacular terrain lies ahead.

After traversing lush flats, come upon a rocky chasm where Deception Creek tumbles into tiered pools and pothole basins. Farther up the valley, transition from dark ravine to an avalanche-opened area providing views of surrounding slopes and peaks.

Resuming a mellow mood, the trail traverses more lush flats complete with impressive primeval trees, before reaching a junction at 5.5 miles (elev. 3150 ft). The trail right climbs steeply, heading 0.7 mile to FR 6830. Continue left on the main trail for a few more hundred feet, finishing out at the confluence of Deception and Fisher creeks. Sunny gravel bars invite the weary to kick back and listen to soothing aquatic melodies before making the journey back to the trailhead.

EXTENDING YOUR TRIP

If Fisher Creek can safely be forded, strong hikers may want to carry on farther up the valley for either 4 miles to the Deception Lakes or 6.2 miles to Deception Pass. However, most backcountry travelers contemplating these destinations will be better off spending a night or two.

26 Evergreen Mountain Lookout

RATING/ DIFFICULTY	ROUND-TRIP	ELEV GAIN/ HIGH POINT	SEASON
★★★★/3	3 miles	1425 feet/ 5587 feet	July–Oct

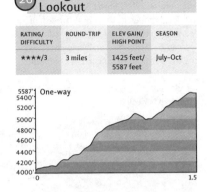

One-way

Map: Green Trails Monte Cristo No. 143; **Contact:** Mount Baker–Snoqualmie National Forest, Skykomish Ranger District, (360) 677-2414, www.fs.fed.us/r6/mbs; **Note:** NW Forest Pass required. **GPS:** N 47 49.582, W 121 16.624

A short and steep hike to a restored lookout provides views long and sweet. From this outpost high above the Beckler River valley feast on alpine views in every direction. Savor Rainier, Glacier Peak, the serrated summits of the Wild Sky, and the massive Monte Cristo massif. And if the views don't spin your senses, the dazzling array of wildflowers carpeting the way most certainly will!

GETTING THERE

From Everett head east on US 2 for 49 miles to the small town of Skykomish. Continue east for 1 more mile, turning left onto Beckler River Road (Forest Road 65). The pavement ends at 6.9 miles. Continue north for another 5.7 miles to a five-way junction at Jack Pass. Take the road to your immediate right (FR 6550) for 0.9 mile to a junction. Turn left onto FR 6554 and drive 8.7 scenic miles to its end at the trailhead (elev. 4175 ft). Note: FR 6550 is subject to frequent washouts, so always check with the Ranger Station for current conditions.

ON THE TRAIL

Starting in an old burn surrounded by old cuts (that will take quite some time to recover due to the high elevation here), the well-built trail takes off steeply up Evergreen Mountain's southwest shoulder.

Big views north toward West Cady Ridge, Kyes Peak, and Columbia Peak from the Evergreen Mountain Lookout.

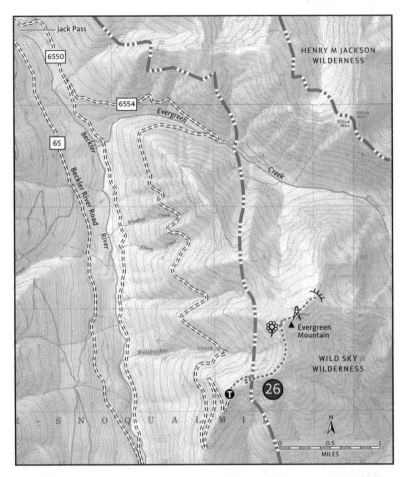

It's a tough start, and the immediate views and, in season, abundant berries may slow you down further. But the verdant meadow-top of Evergreen looming above should help provide stimulus to pick up the pace.

Between switchbacks take in the sweeping view south of the broad U-shaped (evidence of past glaciations) Beckler River valley. At 0.6 mile enter the Wild Sky Wilderness, leaving young regenerating forest for groves of old-growth mountain hemlock. Now on a gentler grade, traverse the ridge, reaching a small gap at about 0.9 mile (elev. 5100 feet).

Almost there! Continuing along the ridge crest, leave forest for glorious meadows.

Purple, red, yellow, white—evergreen it most certainly isn't. Swing around the north side of the mountain, and after one final push reach the 5587-foot summit with its restored fire lookout at 1.4 miles. The trail continues along the ridge for another 0.1 mile or so, and you are encouraged to follow it, taking in excellent views all along the way.

Look south to Stuart, Daniel, Hinman, the Snoqualmie Pass peaks, and big, beautiful Rainier hovering above them all. West it's Merchant, Gunn, Spire, and Bear, jewels of the Wild Sky. Look north to the Monte Cristo peaks, Sloan, and White Horse. East it's the meadow country of Fortune and Grizzly, with a backdrop of the Poet Peaks, White Mountains, Nason Ridge, and the Chiwaukums. This is without a doubt one of the finest viewing posts in the Central Cascades.

And the lookout? It was built in 1935 and revived by the Seattle Explorer Search and Rescue in the 1990s. It's available through the Forest Service for nightly rentals. Just imagine the sunsets, sunrises, and night skies from this lofty perch.

27 Fortune Ponds

RATING/ DIFFICULTY	ROUND-TRIP	ELEV GAIN/ HIGH POINT	SEASON
★★★/4	13 miles	2700 feet/ 4700 feet	July–Oct

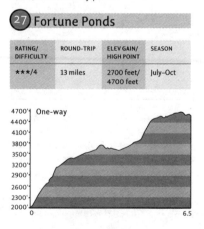

Map: Green Trails Benchmark Mtn No. 144; **Contact:** Mount Baker–Snoqualmie National Forest, Skykomish Ranger District, (360) 677-2414, www.fs.fed.us/r6/mbs; **GPS:** N 47 49.380, W 121 12.320

These two little ponds are snuggled deep in old-growth forest on the Cascade crest. Part of a string of alpine lakes in the heart of the Henry M. Jackson Wilderness, Fortune Ponds are often overlooked in favor of their larger neighbors. The trail in is long, but gentle; the valley, wild and quiet. If it's crowds you shun and remoteness you seek, the Fortunes will reward you well.

GETTING THERE
From Everett head east on US 2 for 49 miles to the small town of Skykomish. Continue east for 1 more mile, turning left onto Beckler River Road (Forest Road 65). Continue north for 6.9 miles to the pavement's end and a three-way junction (just before a bridge over Rapid River). Turn right onto FR 6530 (the road closest to the river) and continue for 4.5 miles to the trailhead (elev. 2000 ft).

ON THE TRAIL
The Fortunes are just two of the many riches to be found in the Henry M. Jackson Wilderness, an area encompassing over 100,000 acres of prime Central Cascades backcountry. Named for Everett native Senator "Scoop" Jackson, this region of old-growth forests, alpine lakes, and sprawling meadows was one of his favorite places in the Washington backcountry. It's one of my favorites too, and the hike to Fortune Ponds via the Meadow Creek Trail allows you to savor this special section of the Cascades in relative solitude.

Beginning in a less-than-attractive forest of stumps and new growth, start climbing.

Old-growth trees along the Meadow Creek valley

Now part of the new Wild Sky Wilderness, the surrounding forest went up in flames in 1967. It continues to recover, and after about 2 miles you can recover from the 1500 feet you just ascended. Upon entering the Jackson Wilderness, the grade eases and the surrounding forest transforms into magnificent old growth.

Marching up the Meadow Creek valley, the trail is embraced by thickly forested eastern slopes. The valley's western slopes bear countless avalanche scars, and snow often lingers long along the creek's west banks. At about 3.5 miles trail and creek meet. Here you'll need to fashion a crossing, often a wet endeavor. Continue upvalley alongside the gurgling creek. At about 4.5 miles cross the creek once more in a marshy low pass (elev. 4000 ft). A trail once continued north through the wet draw. An old sign enveloped in bark and sap attests to this.

Your trail, however, turns east to climb steeply out of the valley. A thick canopy of western hemlock eventually yields to thinning stands of subalpine fir and mountain hemlock. The grade once again relaxes, the trail now traversing huckleberry patches and heather meadows. Views open up north to miles of sprawling alpine meadows draping the Cascade crest and Benchmark Mountain (Hike 38). At 6.5 miles your long journey into the wilderness nears its end at Lower Fortune Pond (elev. 4700 ft).

Perched in a small bowl, waterfall-fed and surrounded by parkland meadow, the ambience at Lower Fortune is quite serene. Remove boots, soak feet, lie back, and let the soothing and healing powers of nature caress you.

EXTENDING YOUR TRIP

As delightful a body of water as Lower Fortune is, the upper pond is more attractive. To reach it, continue up the trail for another 0.25 mile. Then leave the trail in a southwesterly direction through semi-open forest, and after a little brush crashing arrive at Upper Fortune Pond. If time and energy are on your side, consider scrambling up Fortune Mountain. You can also reach Pear Lake (Hike 72) by continuing up the Meadow Creek Trail for another 1.25 miles, crossing a 5200-foot pass, and then dropping 400 feet to the shaped-like-its-name lake.

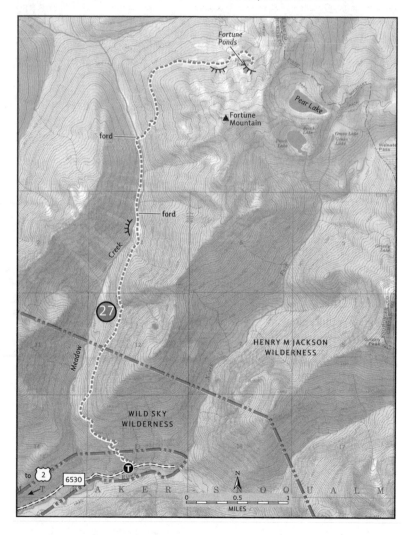

UNTRAMMELED CENTRAL CASCADES

While much of the Central Cascades lies within national forest, that doesn't necessarily mean the area is all protected. National forests are managed for "multiple use." While some uses (like hiking) are fairly compatible with land preservation, other uses (like mining, logging, and off-road vehicle use) are not.

Recognizing that parts of our natural heritage should be altered as little as possible, with bipartisan support Congress overwhelmingly passed the Wilderness Act in 1964 (the House vote was 373-1). One of the strongest and most important pieces of environmental legislation in our nation's history, the Wilderness Act granted precious wild landscapes a reprieve from exploitation, development, and harmful activities such as motorized recreation. Even bicycles are banned from federal wilderness areas. Wilderness is "an area where the earth and community of life are untrammeled by man," states the act, "where man himself is a visitor who does not remain."

While the Central Cascades had no shortage of qualifying wilderness lands back in 1964, only one area, Glacier Peak, was designated under the legislation. In 1976 however, the Alpine Lakes was added. The federal wilderness system would eventually include wilderness areas in national parks, as well as wildlife refuges and other federal lands. In 1984, a sweeping statewide wilderness bill was signed into law, creating the Henry M. Jackson Wilderness in the region. And in 2008, after years of being held up by political wrangling, a bill was signed into law creating Washington's and the Central Cascades' newest wilderness area: the Wild Sky.

Current wilderness acreage in the Central Cascades is as follows:

Alpine Lakes 393,360 acres
Glacier Peak 570,573 acres
Henry M. Jackson 102,673 acres
Wild Sky 106,577 acres

While those numbers seem impressive (in fact, Washington ranks fourth among the states for total wilderness acres), many conservationists (and this author) feel that it's not enough. The vast majority of our national forest lands still remain under threat from development and motorized recreation, especially the latter. And while some of our public land base should be turned over for those uses, our last remaining unprotected roadless tracts of pristine wild country should not be! They should be designated wilderness. Republican congressman Dave Reichert introduced a bill in 2007 to expand the Alpine Lakes Wilderness by 22,000 acres—a great start. These other large roadless areas in the Central Cascades should also be designated wilderness:

Nason Ridge (US 2, Nason Creek Valley) 19,500 acres
South Entiat Mountains (Mad River high country) 95,000 acres
North Fork Entiat River (Entiat River valley) 40,000 acres
Devils Gulch (Wenatchee River valley) 25,000 acres
South Sawtooth Range (Lake Chelan) 96,000 acres

Whether these lands remain untrammeled and wild for future generations is a matter of public opinion and political will.

28 Johnson Ridge

RATING/ DIFFICULTY	ROUND-TRIP	ELEV GAIN/ HIGH POINT	SEASON
★★★★/4	9 miles	2650 feet/ 5540 feet	July–Oct

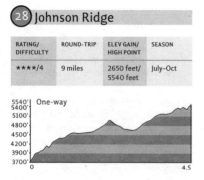

Maps: Green Trails Monte Cristo No. 143, Benchmark Mtn No. 144; **Contact:** Mount Baker–Snoqualmie National Forest, Skykomish Ranger District, (360) 677-2414, www.fs.fed .us/r6/mbs; **GPS:** N 47 47.798, W 121 15.735

🔲 *One of the best meadow-traversing, ridge-walking, view-granting trails in the Skykomish Valley, Johnson Ridge is also surprisingly one of the quieter trails in the region. Sure, it's a long gravel road to the trailhead. And yes, the trail has some steep ups and downs. But the tread is good and the vertical suffering short-lived. Culminating on a peak named Scorpion, the hike gives a panoramic payoff of jagged peaks and emerald ridges that will leave you momentarily paralyzed.*

GETTING THERE
From Everett head east on US 2 for 49 miles to the small town of Skykomish. Continue east for 1 more mile, turning left onto Beckler River Road (Forest Road 65). Continue north for 6.9 miles to the pavement's end and a three-way junction (just before a bridge over Rapid River). Make a sharp right turn onto FR 6520. In 2.7 miles bear left at an unmarked junction, continuing on FR 6520 for another 4.2 miles to the road's end and trailhead (elev. 3700 ft).

ON THE TRAIL
Begin by following an old road-turned-trail through an old cut turning back to forest. While it's a steep start, delectable views of nearby peaks, especially of the serrated summits surrounding Spire Mountain and El Capitan, offer nice diversions. Those impressive peaks across the Beckler River valley, along with the ridge you're now traipsing on, are all part of Washington's newest federal wilderness area, the Wild Sky (see "Untrammeled Central Cascades" in this section).

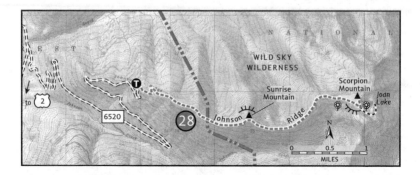

After 0.75 mile the grade eases and the way becomes real trail. Through mature forest flush with huckleberries, the way gently marches along Johnson Ridge. Climbing, however, resumes—and steeply. At 2 miles round the heather-graced 5050-foot summit of Sunrise Mountain. Enjoy outstanding views east of the meadow-cloaked high country that embraces the Cascade crest, with snowy sentinel Glacier Peak watching over. Cherish, too, the view north of the Monte Cristo peaks, an impressive wall of ice and rock. Sunrise Mountain makes a perfectly fine destination for those seeking a shorter hike.

But if it's Scorpion Mountain you wish to strike out for, continue on, steeply dropping more than 300 feet to a narrow saddle. Commence climbing again through patchy meadows and thinning forest. At about 3.5 miles enter a full-blown meadow replete with resplendent wildflowers. Retreating momentarily from the emerald lawns, the trail creeps up the steep ridge crest before traversing flower-studded fields just below Scorpion's summit.

At an unmarked junction, head left, making one final hurrah to subdue Scorpion's 5540-foot rounded summit and reap the spoils of 360-degree Central Cascades viewing: East to Poet Ridge, Grizzly, McCausland, and the Chiwaukums. South to Captain Point, Fernow, Daniel, Hinman, and Cathedral Rock. North it's Evergreen, Sloan, Benchmark and Fortune, while west it's Baring, Spire, and Troublesome. One thing that isn't clear from here is why more hikers don't find their way to this outstanding destination

EXTENDING YOUR TRIP

From Scorpion's summit you probably noticed twinkling and enticing Joan Lake lying

Tiger lilies, asters, lupine, and other wildflowers highlight Johnson Ridge.

below. To reach this serene and secluded lake, retreat to the unmarked junction for a brushy trail that takes off south. On slick tread reach the lake basin after 0.5 mile and 500 feet of elevation loss. The fishing is good at Joan and so are the prospects of being mosquito bait. Visit late in summer or on a breezy day. To enjoy more of the area for more days, make use of the good family-friendly car camping a few miles back from the trailhead at the Forest Service's Beckler River Campground.

㉙ Iron Goat Loop

RATING/ DIFFICULTY	LOOP	ELEV GAIN/ HIGH POINT	SEASON
★★★/2	5.7 miles	700 feet/ 2800 feet	Late May–Nov

Map: Green Trails Stevens Pass No. 176; **Contact:** Mount Baker–Snoqualmie National Forest, Skykomish Ranger District, (360) 677-2414, www.fs.fed.us/r6/mbs; **Note:** NW Forest Pass required; **GPS:** N 47 42.683 W 121 09.704

This is a delightful loop back into history, full of scenic surprises. Thanks to the Volunteers for Outdoor Washington (VOW) this historic rail line through the Cascades has been rescued from oblivion and transformed into a top-notch trail ideal for hikers of all ages and abilities, as well as for lovers of Northwest and railroad history. So get your caboose in gear and, with all due respect to the Man in Black, walk the line!

GETTING THERE

Drive US 2 east to the small town of Skykomish. Continue for another 9 miles, turning left into the Iron Goat Interpretive Site (elev. 2100 ft). Privy available. If the lot is gated, park

Windy Point Tunnel along the Iron Goat Trail

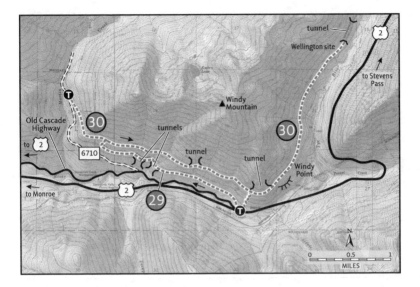

across US 2, using caution when crossing the busy highway.

ON THE TRAIL

The focal point of the Stevens Pass Historic District, the Iron Goat Trail retraces part of the Great Northern Railway, northernmost of the nineteenth-century U.S. transcontinental rail lines. The creation of Minnesota tycoon James J. Hill ("The Empire Builder"), the Great Northern reached Seattle in 1893, greatly stimulating commerce and settlement in the region. Iron Goat, the name chosen for the trail, comes from the railroad's logo, a mountain goat.

Before beginning, check out the 1951 caboose and informative kiosk dedicated to Ruth Ittner, the driving force behind the trail and one of the founders of VOW. And before arriving, check out the trail's website (www .irongoat.org) or the *Iron Goat Trail* guidebook (The Mountaineers Books, 1999) to get the most out of your visit.

This hike makes a loop, following the original rail grade (in use 1893–1929) for a little over 4 miles and using two crossover trails built by VOW. Beginning on pavement, come to a junction in 500 feet. Continue straight; you'll be returning on the right-hand trail. A large milepost sign soon greets you. The number, 1720, denotes the mileage from St. Paul, Minnesota, the Great Northern's originating city.

Climbing on a grade made for trains (easy), the trail begins a long switchback toward Stevens Pass. Although this area is now pleasantly shaded and thickly forested, try to imagine it 100 years ago with tree-denuded slopes. At 0.25 mile pass the first of many walls that once supported snowsheds protecting the line from avalanches (see "Train Wreck Waiting to Happen" in this section). After another mile the trail swings around a twin set of tunnels. The tunnels, as well as many of the trestles along the Iron Goat, have collapsed and are now unsafe. Trail builders bypassed the tunnels and replaced the trestles with new bridges.

At 1.7 miles take a break from all of the history to enjoy a nice view up the Deception Creek valley (Hike 25). At 2.1 miles, just past milepost 1718, reach a junction with the Corea Crossover Trail (elev. 2375 ft). The Iron Goat continues straight to the Martin Creek trailhead (Hike 30). Take the crossover path right, climbing back to the rail grade at milepost 1716 (elev. 2600 ft).

Then turn right and head toward St. Paul. Pass the Spillway Spur, an interesting side trip to an old reservoir. Pass more shed walls, some now sporting waterfalls, and excellent overlooks of nearby mountains and the valley below. At 4.4 miles, just past milepost 1714 and at the beginning of the Windy Point Tunnel, come to a junction with the Windy Point Crossover Trail (elev. 2800 ft).

Remaining on the Iron Goat Trail, make the short 0.25-mile trip to Windy Point for excellent views out toward Stevens Pass and the Surprise Creek valley. Then return to your vehicle via the Windy Point Crossover Trail, steeply descending sunny slopes back to the parking lot.

EXTENDING YOUR TRIP

Explore more of the Iron Goat Trail on the hike to Wellington (Hike 30). Explore more of the Great Northern Railway by hiking the 0.5-mile Bygone Byways Interpretive Trail at milepost 71 on US 2 and the 1.2-mile Tumwater Pipeline Trail (Hike 52)

near Leavenworth. And for the near future: VOW is in the process of extending the Iron Goat by 1.5 miles to the Horseshoe Tunnel, as well as constructing a link to the Kelley Creek Trail (Hike 31).

30 Iron Goat Trail to Wellington

RATING/ DIFFICULTY	ROUND-TRIP	ELEV GAIN/ HIGH POINT	SEASON
★★★★/3	12 miles	650 feet/ 3100 feet	June–Nov

Map: Green Trails Stevens Pass No. 176; **Contact:** Mount Baker–Snoqualmie National Forest, Skykomish Ranger District, (360) 677-2414, www.fs.fed.us/r6/mbs; **Note:** NW Forest Pass required; **GPS:** N 47 43.762 W 121 12.401

Follow an old rail line back into time to the no longer town of Wellington, site of the worst avalanche disaster in American history. Enjoy excellent views of the Tye and Surprise river valleys while marveling at engineering feats required to build the Great Northern Railway across this rugged terrain over a century ago. Admire the tenacity of tycoon James J. Hill and the backbreaking work of the thousands of laborers who constructed this transcontinental railroad. And praise the hundreds of Volunteers for Outdoor Washington (VOW) who converted miles of this line into top-notch trail.

GETTING THERE

Drive US 2 east to the small town of Skykomish. Continue for another 6.3 miles, turning left onto the Old Cascade Highway at milepost 55. Proceed for 2.3 miles, turning left onto Forest Road 6710. Continue for 1.4 miles to the trailhead (elev. 2450 ft). Privy available.

ON THE TRAIL

Before arriving you may want to check out this trail's website (www.irongoat.org) or the *Iron Goat Trail* guidebook (The Mountaineers Books, 1999) to get the most out of your visit. While the focal point of this trail is definitely historic, there's plenty of great scenery to be enjoyed along the way too.

Lined with ferns and alders, the trail takes off east, which is actually westward on the old rail line due to switchbacking. At 0.2 mile, come to a junction with the Martin Creek Crossover Trail. The original rail line continues straight (Hike 29). Take the trail left, climbing stone steps to reach the upper grade of the old rail line (elev. 2550 ft). Then head right, following what was the Great Northern Railway line from 1893 to 1929, since resurrected in the 1990s as the Iron Goat Trail.

Soon pass the remains of one of the many snowsheds that helped protect the line from frequent avalanches. Soon after that, pass one of the many tunnels along the way. Unsafe for passage, the tunnels along the way are bypassed by the trail, and you'd be prudent to not venture into them. Next pass the first of several handsome rail line milepost replicas. The numbers represent miles from St. Paul, Minnesota, the line's eastern terminus.

At 0.7 mile come to a junction with the

The Iron Goat Trail passes through an impressive snowshed tunnel near Wellington.

Corea Crossover Trail, which leads back to the lower grade (Hike 29). Continuing on the main trail, enjoy interpretive displays as well as a few displays of the valley below at scenic overlooks. At 1.7 miles the 0.1 mile Spillway Spur, a mandatory side trip, heads left to an old reservoir.

At 2.8 miles reach the western end of the quarter-mile-long Windy Point Tunnel. Shortly afterward come to the junction with the Windy Point Crossover Trail which steeply descends 700 feet to the US 2 trailhead and interpretive site (Hike 29). Continue walking the line instead, soon reaching the Windy Point viewpoint (elev. 2800 ft) with its excellent viewing toward Stevens Pass and the Surprise Creek valley.

Heading east the terrain gets more interesting as the trail crosses dark forest groves and brushy avalanche slopes, with lots of maples and cottonwoods that add vibrant colors in autumn. Catch glimpses of the Old Stevens Pass Highway winding below. At 5.25 miles reach one of the trail's coolest features (literally: because it traps cool air), a half-mile intact, all-concrete snowshed, which the trail chugs through. Be sure to stop at the avalanche disaster viewpoint halfway through the shed. It was here in 1910 that the worst avalanche disaster in American history occurred (see "Train Wreck Waiting to Happen" in this section).

At 6 miles reach the former site of the railroad town of Wellington. Abandoned when the rail line was rerouted to a new tunnel in 1929, nothing remains of this once bustling community. Wellington now serves as the eastern trailhead to the Iron Goat, and the old tunnel through the Cascade crest still survives. But it's closed to entry because it is extremely dangerous. You may, however, still hear trains echoing from its depths, as well as voices from the past blowing across the trail.

TRAIN WRECK WAITING TO HAPPEN: THE WELLINGTON AVALANCHE

Wellington was named by Great Northern Railway officials for England's Duke of Wellington, who defeated Napoleon at Waterloo in 1815, but after the winter of 1910 this former railroad town would forever be associated with one of the greatest natural disasters in American history. It was in February of that year, during a blizzard that lasted for nine days, that a passenger and mail train became trapped, dooming ninety-six people to a terrible fate.

After the heavy snowfall, the temperature warmed, bringing heavy rains. Then on March 1 a half-mile-wide slab of snow 10 feet deep came barreling down Windy Mountain. The avalanche hit Wellington's depot and the two trains, sending them 150 feet into the Tye River below. Ninety-six people (thirty-five passengers and sixty-one Great Northern employees) lost their lives in this, the worst avalanche disaster (in terms of human lives lost) on American soil. Remarkably, there were twenty-three survivors.

In the following autumn the town was renamed Tye (to disassociate the area from the avalanche), and construction began on concrete snow sheds to prevent this from occurring again. The town of Wellington, which once bustled with travelers from around America and workers from Austria, Canada, China, Finland, France, Germany, Great Britain, Italy, Japan, Norway, Russia, Sweden, and Switzerland, disappeared from maps in 1929 when this section of rail line was relocated to a new tunnel. Gary Krist's book *The White Cascade* (Henry Holt, 2007) does an excellent job of recapturing this tragic moment in Northwest history.

31 Kelley Creek

RATING/ DIFFICULTY	ROUND-TRIP	ELEV GAIN/ HIGH POINT	SEASON
★★★/4	7 miles	2100 feet/ 5100 feet	July–Oct

Maps: Green Trails Stevens Pass No. 176, Benchmark Mtn No. 144 (trail not shown); **Contact:** Mount Baker–Snoqualmie National Forest, Skykomish Ranger District, (360) 677-2414, www.fs.fed.us/r6/mbs; **Note:** Trail is currently impassable at 2.7 miles due to an extensive blowdown. **GPS:** N 47 44.935 W 121 10.939

❌ 🔪 *You want spectacular old growth? Solitude? Adventure? Head to Kelley Creek, a trail long abandoned by the Forest Service (why?), kept on life support by a few hikers who refuse to see it fade away, and soon to be resuscitated by the Volunteers for Outdoor Washington (VOW). For now, however, it remains a lightly traveled path, surprisingly in remarkably good shape. Expect a little brush, a little slumping, and a few obstacles, but overall this is a pleasant path with no major route-finding problems.*

GETTING THERE

Drive US 2 east to the small town of Skykomish. Continue for another 6.3 miles, turning left onto the Old Cascade Highway at milepost 55. Proceed for 2.3 miles, turning left onto Forest Road 6710. Continue for 2.8 miles (passing the Iron Goat trailhead) and bear left at a junction. In another 0.3 mile bear left again, coming to a bridge over Martin Creek in 0.1 mile. Park here near the bridge. Walk across it, locating a brushy old logging road on your left. This is the trailhead (elev. 3000 ft).

ON THE TRAIL

Don't let the uninspiring beginning of this hike set your mood. Despite following an old, grown-in logging road for the first mile, it's not that rough. For one thing, it's nearly level. For another, the unsung heroes of Kelley Creek (I met one of them while scouting the trail—thanks Bruce!) periodically brush it back. So carry on, it gets much better.

After following the old skid road for nearly a mile, scrappy alder and hemlock yield to beautiful primeval forest as you enter the new Wild Sky Wilderness. Shortly afterward reach a sign pointing right to Johnson Ridge. Look down at your feet too: you're now on the old trail! Once VOW gets around to officially reopening this trail, the brushy logging road approach will be history. The dedicated trail builders plan on extending the path to the Martin Creek trailhead of the Iron Goat Trail by roughly following the original route of the trail. It'll be a much nicer and more interesting approach.

Now under an ancient forest canopy alongside crashing Kelley Creek, head up the original trail. While much of the tread is covered in soft mosses and ground pines, it is well defined. Remarkable too is that few of the old-growth giants lining the way have fallen across the path when nature has called them back to nourish the forest floor. Marvel at the big cedars and hemlocks. Now protected within federal wilderness, this forest stands free of threats from the modern world.

Soon begin climbing, angling upward out of the creek valley onto the western slopes of Captain Point. At 1.9 miles cross a creek in a deep gully (elev. 3800 ft). Once a tricky spot to negotiate, this crossing was recently re-engineered by a trail crew. Now traverse a couple of moist herbaceous openings, coming to a massive blowdown at 2.7 miles. The

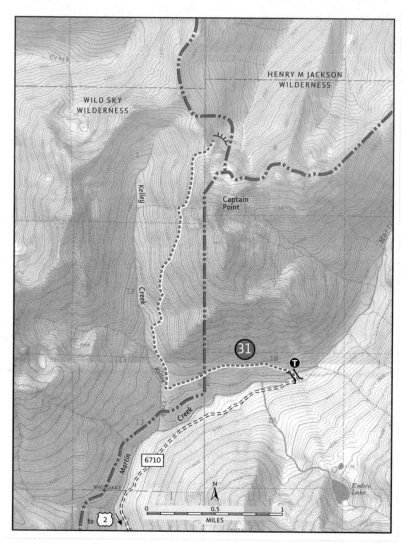

The Kelley Creek Trail passes through a stunning old-growth fir and hemlock forest.

Forest Service hopes to clear a way through this mangled mess sometime in the future. As you continue to gain elevation, Kelley Creek's crashing fades into the distance. With the forest now thinning, catch glimpses of 6190-foot Mount Fernow across the valley.

After one final steep push around some ledges, reach the ridge crest (elev. 5100 ft), where at 3.5 miles the trail ends in a flat of heather. Being careful not to crush delicate vegetation, roam the area for good views north across the Rapid River valley out to the emerald-draped Cascade crest.

EXTENDING YOUR TRIP

Experienced off-trail travelers can continue left, following remnants of the old Johnson Ridge Trail for 1.75 miles, intersecting the remaining Johnson Ridge Trail in a meadow just below Scorpion Mountain. Or head right and locate tread to a shoulder high upon Captain Point. Both routes are difficult to follow in spots, but both promise plenty of scenic rewards for those who persevere.

32 Surprise and Glacier Lakes

RATING/ DIFFICULTY	ROUND-TRIP	ELEV GAIN/ HIGH POINT	SEASON
★★★★/4	11 miles	2800 feet/ 4900 feet	Late June– Oct

Map: Green Trails Stevens Pass No. 176; **Contact:** Mount Baker–Snoqualmie National Forest, Skykomish Ranger District, (360) 677-2414, www.fs.fed.us/r6/mbs; **Notes:** NW

Forest Pass required. Free day-use permit required, available at trailhead. Dogs must be leashed; **GPS:** N 47 42.468, W 121 09.402

Wedged between craggy Thunder and Spark Plug mountains, these two lakes are set in a truly electrifying environment, flanked by towering evergreens and slopes of shiny granite ledges and talus. But even more stimulating than these aquatic gems is the forest that lines the trail leading to them. It's one of the finest tracts of old growth along the US 2 corridor.

GETTING THERE

Drive US 2 east to the small town of Skykomish. Continue for another 10 miles, turning right (just after passing the Iron Goat Interpretive Site) into the old railroad community of Scenic. Cross the railroad tracks and turn right, following a narrow and bumpy dirt road 0.3 mile to the trailhead (elev. 2200 ft).

ON THE TRAIL

Begin by walking a short distance up a powerline service road. In 0.2 mile turn left onto real trail, and real nice trail at that. On good tread, sturdy stairs, and solid planking, head up the narrow Surprise Creek valley through a magnificent forest of ancient cedars and giant hemlocks. Soon enter the Alpine Lakes Wilderness, its designation guaranteeing that those giant arboreal elders' lives won't be cut short.

At about 1.3 miles the trail crosses cascading Surprise Creek on a big log. Note previous log crossings strewn about in the creek's bed. Then skirt beneath avalanche slopes and undulate between patches of brush and groves of majestic primeval forest as the trail continues upvalley. Tumbling Surprise Creek, always nearby, provides constant visual and audio delights.

At about 3 miles begin climbing more steeply. At 4.5 miles, after winding around talus and ascending steep forested slopes, reach a trail junction just shy of Surprise Lake. The trail left climbs briskly toward Trap Pass to connect with the Pacific Crest Trail (PCT). Continue right, traversing a marshy meadow and a precarious creek crossing to reach Surprise Lake.

A popular backpacking destination with

Spark Plug Mountain rises behind Surprise Lake.

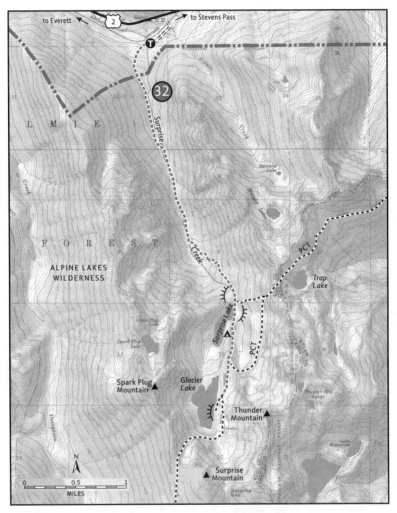

its numerous designated campsites, the lake is well-loved by day hikers too. Treat it well. Find a quiet shoreline ledge or boulder to soak rays or feet. While away the afternoon here, or continue farther to bigger and prettier Glacier Lake by continuing south along the trail, climbing a rib between Surprise Lake on the right and a cascading creek on the left.

About 0.5 mile beyond Surprise Lake, reach a junction with the PCT (elev. 4900 ft). Left goes to Trap Pass. Continue straight. Come to a big granite talus slope just after passing a tarn tucked below on the left. Locate an unmarked but obvious trail heading right. Take it, passing an old Snoqualmie National Forest sign and dropping steeply 50 feet or so to granite-bound Glacier Lake (elev. 4800 ft).

No glaciers, lots of granite, this lake along with Surprise are also known as the Scenic Lakes. Can't argue with that moniker.

EXTENDING YOUR TRIP

Strong day hikers can continue south on the PCT past Glacier Lake to either 5900-foot Pieper Pass or the old Cascade Crest Trail (veering left from the PCT in the open basin just south of the lake) leading to Surprise Gap and 6330-foot Surprise Mountain. From this old fire lookout the views are superb, especially north over the Scenic Lakes to Glacier Peak and southwest to the glistening glaciers of Mount Daniel.

33 Hope and Mig Lakes

RATING/ DIFFICULTY	ROUND-TRIP	ELEV GAIN/ HIGH POINT	SEASON
★★/3	4.6 miles	1550 feet/ 4650 feet	July–Oct

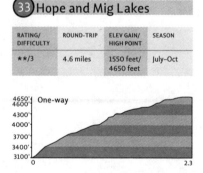

Map: Green Trails Stevens Pass No. 176; **Contact:** Mount Baker–Snoqualmie National Forest, Skykomish Ranger District, (360) 677-2414, www.fs.fed.us/r6/mbs; **Note:** NW Forest Pass required; **GPS:** N 47 42.768, W 121 06.439

These are Hope and Mig ponds, actually—but what these two little lakes lack in surface area they make up for in setting. Especially if it's flowers or berries you seek. Set in parkland meadows amid groves of hardy mountain hemlock along the Cascade crest, the lakes and surrounding area invite further exploring. But first you'll need to get there via the Tunnel Creek Trail, an at times steep, at times rocky approach.

GETTING THERE

Drive US 2 east to the small town of Skykomish. Continue for another 12 miles, turning right onto Forest Road 6095 located just after crossing the Tunnel Creek Bridge at a hairpin turn. (If you're coming from the east, a barrier makes it impossible to turn left onto FR 6095.) Follow FR 6095 for 1.2 miles (avoiding side roads) to a Y intersection. Bear left, coming to the trailhead in 0.1 mile (elev. 3100 ft).

ON THE TRAIL

Start climbing in an old cut on a recently reconstructed section of trail. Tread eventually degrades to roots and rocks in places, while stumps and second growth yield to beautiful old growth. While this trail is named for Tunnel Creek, it travels nowhere near it, although it does tag above one of its small tributaries.

Working its way upward, the trail traverses steep slopes, crossing several small cascading side creeks. Occasionally the trail leaves the cover of the primeval canopy to cross a small opening, granting limited views to the tumbling tributary below.

At 1.5 miles enter the Alpine Lakes Wilderness at a broad ridge crest. The valley behind with all of its magnificent old trees was left out of wilderness and slated to be logged before globalization shifted the emphasis to cheaper (but just as ecologically rich and important) timber from the ancient forests of Russia, Chile, and other nations.

Just beyond the wilderness border reach a junction with the Pacific Crest Trail (PCT) at little Hope Lake (elev. 4400 ft). Primarily

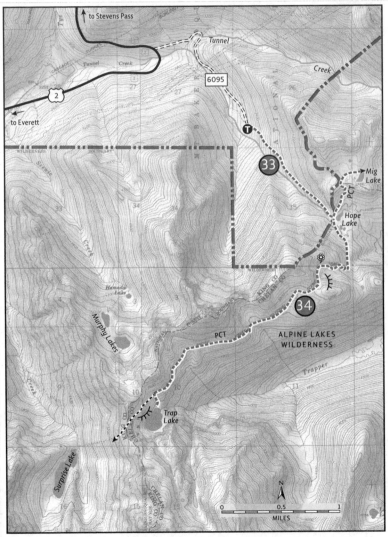

A hiker pauses along the Pacific Crest Trail at Hope Lake.

wooded with pockets of meadows, the shores of this small lake have been heavily trampled by campers, anglers, and berry pickers. Go easy on this landscape.

Turn left, traveling north on the PCT to reach Mig Lake. After winding through groves of mountain hemlock and heather meadows for 0.7 mile, reach the small lake (elev. 4650 ft). Surrounded by marshy meadow, berry patches, and clumps of subalpine forest, Mig's setting is serene. Come in early summer for the floral show, including lawns of flowering cotton grass, which is actually a sedge that sprouts cottony seed clusters.

EXTENDING YOUR TRIP

Stretch your legs further by continuing north on the PCT toward Lake Susan Jane (Hike 39). At about 2.5 miles from Mig Lake, look down into a small cirque housing lonely Swimming Deer Lake.

③④ Trap Lake

RATING/ DIFFICULTY	ROUND-TRIP	ELEV GAIN/ HIGH POINT	SEASON
★★★★/4	11 miles	2600 feet/ 5300 feet	July–Oct

Map: Green Trails Stevens Pass No. 176; **Contact:** Mount Baker–Snoqualmie National Forest, Skykomish Ranger District, (360) 677-2414, www.fs.fed.us/r6/mbs; **Note:** NW Forest Pass required; **GPS:** N 47 42.768, W 121 06.439

This beautiful alpine lake is set in a rocky cirque along the Cascade crest beneath a cluster of craggy summits—a gorgeous destination, but the journey in its own right is just as visually stimulating. Follow the Pacific Crest Trail for several miles through flowering fields and weathered stands of subalpine forest, by snowmelt pools and creeklets, and along open slopes providing sweeping views.

GETTING THERE

Drive US 2 east to the small town of Skykomish. Continue for another 12 miles, turning right onto Forest Road 6095 located just after crossing the Tunnel Creek Bridge at a hairpin turn. (If you're coming from the east, a barrier makes it impossible to turn left onto FR 6095.) Follow FR 6095 for 1.2 miles (avoiding side roads) to a Y intersection. Bear left, coming to the trailhead in 0.1 mile (elev. 3100 ft).

ON THE TRAIL

Starting on the Tunnel Creek Trail (Hike 33) hike 1.6 at times steep, at times rocky miles to the Pacific Crest Trail (PCT) at Hope Lake (elev. 4400 ft), just within the Alpine Lakes Wilderness. Then turn right, hiking south along the Canada to Mexico hiker throughway, winding upward through marshy meadow, subalpine forest, berry patches, and heather fields. Round a basin—home to marmots—to crest a small rib (elev. 5200 ft) that provides nice views north.

The trail now gently descends, weaving through clusters of old hemlocks and brilliant meadows that shout purple and gold. There are views too—out over the Icicle

Looking down at Trap Lake from the Pacific Crest Trail

Creek drainage and the cluster of peaks surrounding the Bulls Tooth. At about 4 miles cross a snowfield-fed creek below a rocky basin (elev. 4950 ft), and then begin to gradually climb.

Pass pothole ponds, charming in autumn with colorful reflections, but annoying in July when incubating pesky mosquitoes. Enjoy views east to Lake Lorraine Point and down below into the Trapper Creek valley housing tiny Grass Lake.

At about 5 miles, just before the trail crosses a wide-open slope of talus, locate an unsigned but obvious trail left (elev. 5300 ft). Follow this path through heather and hemlock for 0.25 mile, dropping 150 feet to Trap Lake (elev. 5150 ft). Break out lunch on an inviting shoreline meadow, staring out at the rocky wall that nearly encircles the lake.

Or mosey around, scouting for views by the lake's cascading outlet creek.

EXTENDING YOUR TRIP

Continue south along the PCT for another 0.7 mile, climbing slopes of talus and meadow to 5800-foot Trap Pass, a small gap on the northern ridge of Thunder Mountain. Views east from here are explosive! If you can arrange a car shuttle, continue another 1.5 miles to Surprise Lake or 1.6 miles to Glacier Lake (Hike 32), returning to civilization via the Surprise Creek Trail.

35 Skyline Lake

RATING/ DIFFICULTY	ROUND-TRIP	ELEV GAIN/ HIGH POINT	SEASON
★/3	2.5 miles	1050 feet/ 5100 feet	July–Oct

Skyline Lake high above Stevens Pass

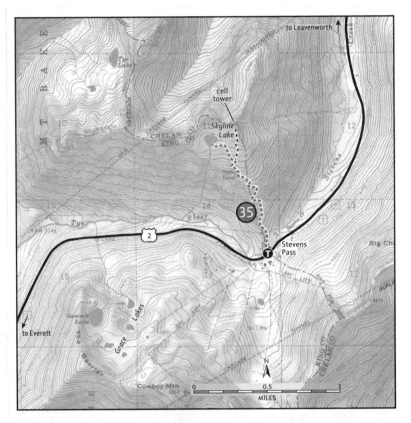

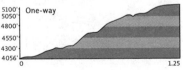

Maps: Green Trails Stevens Pass No. 176, Benchmark Mtn No. 144; **Contact:** Mount Baker–Snoqualmie National Forest, Skykomish Ranger District, (360) 677-2414, www.fs.fed .us/r6/mbs; **GPS:** N 47 44.836, W 121 05.308

This quiet little tarn is tucked in a ridge high above the hustle and bustle of Stevens Pass. Following a steep jeep track, the hike is not exactly a nice trail experience. But the views of the busy pass are good, and Skyline makes a nice leg stretcher if you're passing through. In summer, wildflowers brighten the way, and huckleberries add an incentive to visit in fall. And if you follow the jeep track beyond the lake, you'll add good views of Nason Ridge to your hike.

GETTING THERE

From Everett head east on US 2 for 65 miles to Stevens Pass (elev. 4056 ft). Park on the north side of the pass, careful not to block any driveways or access roads.

ON THE TRAIL

Locate a gravel road left of a residence and electric substation. Walk it, passing more residences and ski area buildings. At about 0.2 mile come to a gated road beside a power pole. This is your route to Skyline. Climbing steeply, the way passes more utility buildings, occasionally breaking out of forest to open slopes covered in wildflowers and granting views south to ski slopes and west to the avalanche slopes of Windy Mountain.

At 0.75 mile pass an interesting utility tower (elev. 4875 ft). Continue up the road another 0.25 mile to a Y junction (elev. 5050 ft). The main road travels right, ending at a cell tower. A good view east to Nason Ridge makes it a worthy side trip. The way to Skyline, however, is left, on a lighter jeep track that eventually becomes a single-track trail. A final easy push through heather meadows delivers you to tiny Skyline Lake (elev. 5100 ft).

The shallow tarn makes for good foot soaking in late summer. It is then too, that you can easily walk around this alpine lake. Otherwise, admire it from where you are resisting temptation to crash through (subsequently killing) fragile heather to explore the shoreline.

EXTENDING YOUR TRIP

If you don't mind walking up a ski area service road, you can reach the Grace Lakes on the south side of Stevens Pass. Follow the Brooks Chair Service Road to its end and pick up trail from there. It's about a 3.6-mile round-trip.

North Fork Skykomish River Valley

An area of immense rugged beauty surrounded by the Henry M. Jackson Wilderness and the new Wild Sky Wilderness, the North Fork Skykomish River valley allows access to some of the finest backcountry on the west slopes of the Central Cascades. Trampled in the past by seekers of mineral wealth and traversed over the ages by Native peoples, surveyors, and prospectors, today much of the area is void of human activity. And that goes for hikers too, due to the storms of autumn 2006 that laid waste to the main access road into the area. Until this road is repaired, hikers wishing to explore parts of this spectacular region will have to access it via Jack Pass.

36 Blanca Lake

RATING/ DIFFICULTY	ROUND-TRIP	ELEV GAIN/ HIGH POINT	SEASON
★★★★/4	8.4 miles	3300 feet/ 4650 feet	July–Oct

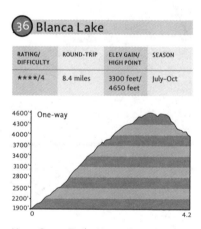

Map: Green Trails Monte Cristo No. 143; **Contact:** Mount Baker–Snoqualmie National Forest, Skykomish Ranger District, (360) 677-2414, www.fs.fed.us/r6/mbs; **Notes:** NW Forest Pass required; **GPS:** N 47 54.922 W 121 18.742

Blanca Lake and the Columbia Glacier

Set in a large cirque in the rugged Monte Cristo peaks and fed by the Columbia Glacier and icy snowfields hanging and clinging to the surrounding steep slopes, Blanca's location is as dramatic as any in the Cascades. But what really strikes all who toil up the steep trail to witness this marvel is the lake's cobalt blue water. Its sheen and tone constantly change, depending on the amount and angle of sunlight shining down on it.

GETTING THERE

The North Fork Skykomish River Road from Index, the normal approach for this hike, sustained considerable flood damage in fall 2006. It will be years before this road is repaired. Until then, the trail can be accessed from Skykomish via Jack Pass. From Everett head east on US 2 for 49 miles to the small town of Skykomish. Continue

east for 1 more mile, turning left onto Beckler River Road (Forest Road 65). The pavement ends at 6.9 miles. Continue north for another 8 miles, and just after crossing the North Fork Skykomish River, come to pavement and a junction. Turn right onto FR 63 and drive 1.8 miles, turning left into the trailhead parking area (elev. 2000 ft).

ON THE TRAIL

The hike to Blanca Lake isn't long, but it's not easy. For the first 3 miles the trail ruthlessly climbs 2650 feet. Then on rough tread it drops 650 feet. *Oy vey!* But at least while you're grunting up from the deep valley you'll have the luxury of shade. The trail advances up a slope of luxuriant old-growth Douglas-fir and hemlock forests. Left out of the 1984 Washington Wilderness Act (the timber industry had its eyes on these trees), they are now permanently protected from the ax, having been included in the 2008 Wild Sky Wilderness designation.

After 3 miles of incessant switchbacking and climbing, enter the Henry M. Jackson Wilderness upon reaching a small gap (elev. 4600 ft). Here, amid heather fields and open forest, find tiny Virgin Lake. Then start dropping 650 vertical feet, following rough-at-times tread 1.2 miles to the big cirque housing big Blanca Lake.

While the snowfields and glaciers above can accurately be described as blanca, turquoise or aquamarine would be a more fitting description for this backcountry lake.

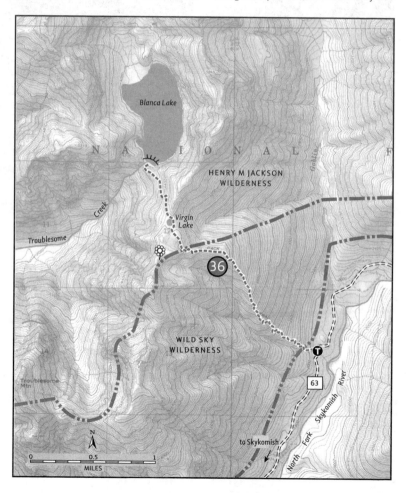

Feel free to explore this rugged environment by following a rough path along the lake's western shoreline. Feel the icy breeze blowing down from the Columbia Glacier, one of the larger ice fields in these parts.

EXTENDING YOUR TRIP
If you're itching for some alpine viewing, head back to the gap above Virgin Lake and locate a way path taking off west toward Troublesome Mountain. Follow this sometimes steep primitive path 0.5 mile to a 5128-foot knoll for excellent viewing of the massive Monte Cristo mountains soaring above Blanca.

37 Quartz Creek

RATING/ DIFFICULTY	ROUND-TRIP	ELEV GAIN/ HIGH POINT	SEASON
★★★/2	8.4 miles	1450 feet/ 3950 feet	July–Oct

Map: Green Trails Monte Cristo No. 143; **Contact:** Mount Baker–Snoqualmie National Forest, Skykomish Ranger District, (360) 677-2414, www.fs.fed.us/r6/mbs; **Note:** NW Forest Pass required; **GPS:** N 47 55.604 W 121 16.623

Enjoy a lonely walk on a charming trail through one of the finest stretches of old-growth forest anywhere in the Cascades. Marvel at magnificent trees many stories high and many centuries old. Let Quartz Creek soothe you

Old tree snags punctuate lush green forest along Quartz Creek.

with its water music. Delight at a side creek cascading into a deep, cool pool. And catch a few good glimpses of the awesome Monte Cristo peaks through all those big trees.

GETTING THERE
The North Fork Skykomish River Road from Index, the normal approach for this hike, sustained considerable flood damage in fall 2006. It will be years before this road is repaired. Until then, the trail can be accessed from Skykomish via Jack Pass. From Everett head east on US 2 for 49 miles to the small town of Skykomish. Continue east for 1 more mile, turning left onto Beckler River Road (Forest Road 65). The pavement ends at 6.9

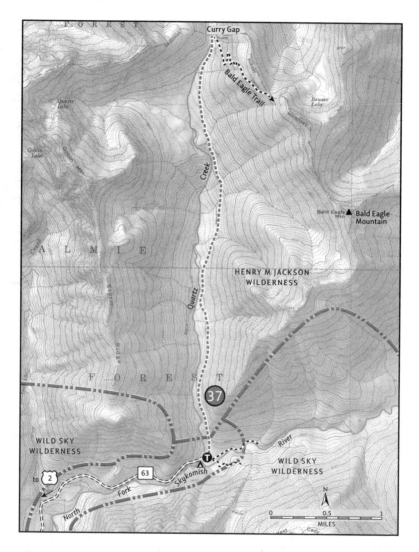

miles. Continue north for another 8 miles, and just after crossing the North Fork Skykomish River, come to pavement and a junction.

Turn right onto FR 63 and drive 4.3 miles to the road's end and trailhead (elev. 2500 ft). Primitive camping and privy available.

ON THE TRAIL

Lightly traveled but lovingly maintained thanks to the Backcountry Horsemen of Washington, the Quartz Creek Trail is one of the easiest to hike in the North Fork Skokomish Valley. And on its little more than 4-mile journey to Curry Gap, you'll gain only a measly 1450 feet of elevation, making this trail easy on the lungs as well as the feet.

Immediately enter a forest of primeval glory, one that was old before Washington's first permanent non-Native settlement was established in 1824 at Fort Vancouver on the Columbia River. Gently winding up the valley beneath a canopy of ancient Doug-firs, western red cedars, and western hemlocks, the trail soon enters the Henry M. Jackson Wilderness. Dwarf dogwood (a.k.a. bunchberry) carpets the forest floor, while huckleberry adds a tasty element to the understory.

While not always visible, Quartz Creek remains audible along the way, crooning soothing arias in this sacred natural cathedral. Side creeks add their harmonies. At about 2.5 miles the trail crosses a creek (tricky in high water) beside a deep pool fed by a tumbling cascade.

Now continuing upvalley, the trail begins to gain elevation more steadily. Traverse an open boggy area hopping with frogs and in early summer graced with marsh marigolds and shooting stars. Gaps in the forest begin to provide nice views west of the awesome Monte Cristo block of peaks. Entering Curry Gap (elev. 3950 ft), a low-lying notch of meadow and mountain hemlock, the trail ends at a junction 4.2 miles from the trailhead. If mosquitoes permit, linger for a while.

EXTENDING YOUR TRIP

Strong day hikers can continue from Curry Gap, taking the Bald Eagle Trail right. After some steep climbing, the trail rounds a high northern slope (elev. 5100 ft) beneath Bald Eagle Mountain at 2.5 miles. Steep, dangerous snowfields linger here well into August. Stop and enjoy the limited but good views north out to Pilot Ridge and beyond.

38 Benchmark Mountain

RATING/ DIFFICULTY	ROUND-TRIP	ELEV GAIN/ HIGH POINT	SEASON
★★★★★/5	14.4 miles	3700 feet/ 5816 feet	July–Oct

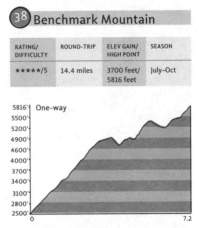

Map: Green Trails Monte Cristo No. 143; **Contact:** Mount Baker–Snoqualmie National Forest, Skykomish Ranger District, (360) 677-2414, www.fs.fed.us/r6/mbs; **Note:** NW Forest Pass required; **GPS:** N 47 55.604 W 121 16.623

Benchmark is the benchmark in the Central Cascades when it comes to supreme alpine meadows. At this high point on West Cady Ridge, one of the most spectacular ridgeline hikes in this guidebook, the only thing superseding the flowers is the views. The hike is long and there's quite a climb involved, but excellent views begin at 4 miles, making a shorter trip a satisfying option.

GETTING THERE

The North Fork Skykomish River Road from Index, the normal approach for this hike,

Kyes Peak from the flower-filled meadows along West Cady Ridge

sustained considerable flood damage in fall 2006. It will be years before this road is repaired. Until then, the trail can be accessed from Skykomish via Jack Pass. From Everett head east on US 2 for 49 miles to the small town of Skykomish. Continue east for 1 more mile, turning left onto Beckler River Road (Forest Road 65). The pavement ends at 6.9 miles. Continue north for another 8 miles, and just after crossing the North Fork Skykomish River, come to pavement and a junction. Turn right onto FR 63 and drive 4.3 miles to the road's end and trailhead (elev. 2500 ft). Primitive camping and privy available.

ON THE TRAIL

From the south end of the parking lot, locate the West Cady Ridge Trail heading off into luxurious ancient forest. After 0.25 mile cross the North Fork Skykomish on a bridge above a small gorge, and then begin climbing—gently at first. The trail winds through some of the biggest and oldest trees in the Skykomish Ranger District. Left out of the 1984 Washington Wilderness Act, permanent protection was afforded these trees when President Bush signed the Wild Sky Wilderness into law on May 8, 2008 (see "Untrammeled Central Cascades" in this section).

Much of this trail was rebuilt in the early 1990s when the Forest Service actually had a budget for trails. The tread is good, and solid boardwalks and puncheon traverse wet draws choked in devil's club. At approximately 2 miles reach a densely forested gap (elev. 3500 ft) between West Cady Ridge and Excelsior Mountain. Real climbing now begins as the trail steeply marches up the spine of West Cady.

Huckleberry (allot time for harvesting) and mountain ash become more profuse as the forest canopy thins. Views out to surrounding peaks grow as you continue upward through heather meadows. At 3.8 miles crest a 4750-foot knoll, a good spot to call it a day if you don't feel like more climbing. Enjoy views north across the valley to Columbia and Monte Cristo peaks and west across Jack Pass to snow-faced Spire Mountain.

The views and the meadows only get

better, so carry on if you've got the drive. Continuing along the high ridge the trail dips 100 feet to a small saddle before cresting a 4825-foot knoll. Enjoy excellent views of Bald Eagle Mountain and Glacier Peak to the north, Fortune and Evergreen mountains to the south. Drop 200 feet into a berried flat, then up another knoll, down a little again, then up, up, and away up a 5350-foot knoll. Behold the view west over the North Fork Skykomish Valley and the peaks and slopes north and south, now part of the Wild Sky Wilderness.

Enter the Henry M. Jackson Wilderness and traverse parkland meadows blotched with small tarns. Keep your senses keen for bears; this area is crawling with them and signs of their presence are everywhere. After dropping 200 feet by a small tarn, climb a steep, flower-bursting slope before coming to an easy-to-miss junction (elev. 5550 ft) near a cluster of mountain hemlock and just after a pyramid-shaped boulder. Veer left and after 0.3 mile pop up on Benchmark Mountain's elongated summit.

Flowers! Views! South along the Cascade crest. North to Skykomish, Johnson, Tenpeak, and Glacier. East to the Poets. West to the heart of the Wild Sky. And from here you can see Cady Pass, the Cady Creek and West Cady Creek valleys, all named for an employee of the Northern Pacific Railway who was looking for a feasible crossing through the Cascades. That honor went to Stevens Pass to the south, leaving Cady country wild and untrammeled by modern man.

EXTENDING YOUR TRIP

Very strong hikers can make a 17-mile loop by continuing east to Saddle Gap. Then head north on the Pacific Crest Trail, taking the Pass Creek Trail to the North Fork Skykomish Trail back to the trailhead. But be aware that this requires a ford of the North Fork—dangerous in high water. The loop should be attempted clockwise to avoid a long backtrack if the river can't be forded.

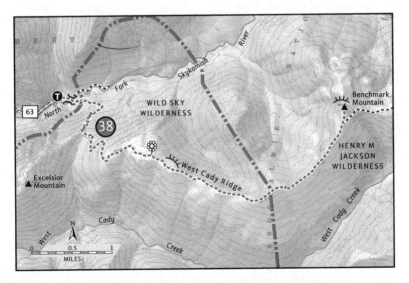

WHEN A RIVER RUNS WILD

One thing that can be said about the Central Cascades is that like all ecosystems they are in a state of constant flux. Life. Death. Rebirth. Decay. It's all part of the circle of life. Sometimes flux comes slowly, and change is subtle. Other times its pace is swift, leaving in its wake a totally altered state. Such was the case of the violent wind and rain storms of November 2006.

Mother Nature apparently was in the mood for a little rearranging. She unleashed a fury of storms, causing rivers to jump their banks, stands of ancient trees to uproot, and tons of rock and soil to come crashing down from the mountains. Not only did these storms inflict some major changes on the landscape, they wreaked record damage upon the trails and roads traversing it.

The storms of November 2006 were unprecedented. In some areas of Mount Rainier National Park more than 18 inches of rain fell in a 36-hour period. June Lake in the Mount St. Helens National Monument set the state's rainfall record for a 24-hour period, receiving 15.2 inches. And throughout much of the west slopes of the Central Cascades, a similar story unfolded. Road and trail damage from these deluges was both grand in scope and in the amount of money needed for repairs. In all, over $70 million worth of damage was assessed by national parks and forest officials in western Washington.

While Mount Rainier sustained the brunt of the damage, the Skykomish Ranger District in the Mount Baker–Snoqualmie National Forest was also severely affected. The storms left a good portion of the district's trails damaged or inaccessible due to washed-out access roads. Among trails affected were popular destinations like the West Fork Foss Lakes, Troublesome Creek, and Evergreen Mountain. It's uncertain when these trails and the roads leading to them will be repaired. The problem now is money—or lack of it.

Since the end of major timber harvesting in western Washington national forests in the early 1990s, Congress has practically starved the U.S. Forest Service of any monies for trail and road maintenance. To many in the hiking community, the storms of 2006 looked like a death knell for many of our trails and roads. Concerned hikers must make their voices heard, telling our elected officials to adequately fund *our* Forest Service and to release funding to repair this unprecedented damage. But hikers need to do more than write letters. We need to get involved with trail advocacy groups like the Washington Trails Association to assist in trail repairs, and pick up where the government leaves off.

And as far as hiking to your favorite destinations goes, it is imperative that you contact the appropriate park or forest ranger districts to inquire about trail and road status before setting out.

Opposite: Lake Valhalla and Lichtenberg Mountain from Mount McCausland

nason creek and wenatchee river valleys

US 2 East

Easily accessible trails to a wide array of lakes, peaks, and ridges line US 2 from Stevens Pass to Cashmere. Nason Creek and the Wenatchee River cut deep gorges into the Cascades, resulting in dramatic relief. Several of the trails originating in these valleys pack plenty of vertical rise, but there are plenty that don't, offering easy options and pleasant wanderings. And if bad weather is blowing in from the west, keep heading east along US 2, where chances are good you'll eventually come to a sunny trailhead.

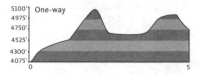

39 Josephine Lake

RATING/ DIFFICULTY	ROUND-TRIP	ELEV GAIN/ HIGH POINT	SEASON
★★★/3	10 miles	2150 feet/ 5100 feet	Mid-July– Oct

Map: Green Trails Stevens Pass No. 176; **Contact:** Okanogan-Wenatchee National Forest, Wenatchee River Ranger District, Leavenworth, (509) 548-6977, www.fs.fed .us/r6/wenatchee; **Note:** NW Forest Pass required; **GPS:** N 47 44.788, W 121 05.191

Sure you have to cross ski slopes and a powerline swath, not exactly wild country. But views are good and at the end of the disturbances is true wilderness. You'll get to explore a quiet little tarn and a big sparkling lake set in a cirque at the head of the Icicle Creek valley. And

Lake Susan Jane along the Pacific Crest Trail

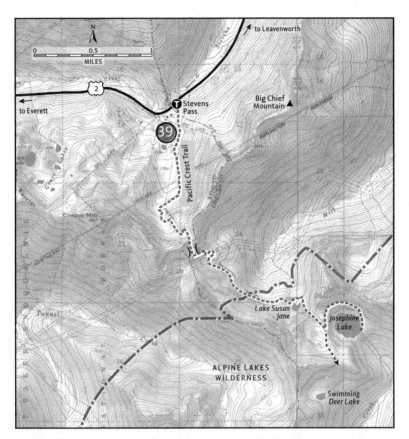

most of the way is along the Pacific Crest Trail, allowing you to sample one of the most famous long-distance hiking trails in the country.

GETTING THERE

From Everett head east on US 2 for 65 miles to Stevens Pass. Turn right into a large parking area on the south side of the highway, just east of the main Stevens Pass Ski Area buildings (elev. 4075 ft). Privy available.

ON THE TRAIL

Pick up the Pacific Crest Trail (PCT) and head south. You're sure to pass a handful of backpackers along the way, for this section of the Mexico-to-Canada long-distance trail from Stevens to Snoqualmie passes is among its most popular. Soon begin traversing a handful of ski slopes and lift lines. Not the most aesthetic hiking terrain, but the open slopes do offer good views.

After fairly gentle going, the trail begins

switchbacking to reach a 5100-foot ridge crest in about 2 miles. The way then begins to descend, crossing more ski slopes as well as a big powerline swath complete with a rough service road. Now contouring along a ridge, the way finally leaves civilization behind and enters the Alpine Lakes Wilderness at about 3.5 miles. A half mile farther, reach pretty little Lake Susan Jane (elev. 4600 ft) perched in a rocky cirque, an excellent spot to call it a day if you're not inclined to travel farther.

Otherwise, continue on the PCT through meadows, climbing a little to reach a junction (elev. 4950 ft) on a tarn-blotched bench. The PCT proceeds right, passing high above Swimming Deer Lake on its way to Mig Lake (Hike 33). To reach Josephine Lake (elev. 4680 ft), head left on the Icicle Creek Trail, gently dropping down into the big basin. En route enjoy views of the verdant Icicle Creek valley and the gray Stuart Range hovering in the distance.

EXTENDING YOUR TRIP

It's a nice 3.5-mile hike along the PCT to Hope Lake (Hike 33) from the Icicle Creek Trail junction. If you can arrange a car shuttle, hike out via the Tunnel Creek Trail.

40 Lake Valhalla

RATING/ DIFFICULTY	ROUND-TRIP	ELEV GAIN/ HIGH POINT	SEASON
★★★/3	12 miles	1500 feet/ 5050 feet	July–Oct

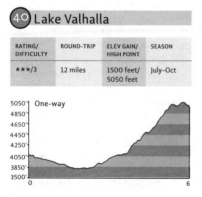

Maps: Green Trails Stevens Pass No. 176, Benchmark Mtn No. 144; **Contact:** Okanogan-Wenatchee National Forest, Wenatchee River Ranger District, Leavenworth, (509) 548-6977, www.fs.fed.us/r6/wenatchee; **GPS:** N 47 44.875, W 121 05.298

You won't find any slain warriors at Lake Valhalla, nor will maidens escort you here, but ancient conifers line the gallant shores and boisterous chickarees usher you along the backbone of the Cascades. Unlike Odin's Valhalla, this one is very real and attainable by all willing to expend a little energy and expunge the outside world for a little while. On this inspiring march through a corridor of majestic tress, you may end up humming a little Wagner en route.

GETTING THERE

From Everett head east on US 2 for 65 miles to Stevens Pass. Park on the north side of the highway (across from the ski area) and locate the Pacific Crest Trail trailhead to the right of an electric substation (elev. 4050 ft). Privy available.

ON THE TRAIL

Head north on the Pacific Crest Trail (PCT), a 2650-mile alpine odyssey from Mexico to Canada along the spine of the Sierra and Cascade ranges (see "Mexico to Canada" in this section). Don't get too anxious, though—your objective lies just 6 moderate miles away. Traversing open forest periodically thinned by avalanche fall (avoid in early season), the way follows the original grade of the Great Northern Railway surveyed by engineer John F. Stevens. The route over the pass bearing Stevens's name was abandoned in 1900 upon completion of the Cascade Tunnel.

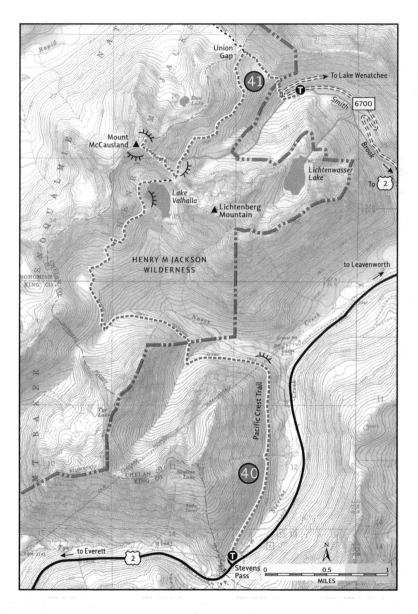

Union Gap

To Lake Wenatchee

41

Smith 6700

To 2

Lichtenwasser Lake

Mount McCausland

Lake Valhalla

Lichtenberg Mountain

HENRY M JACKSON WILDERNESS

Nason

to Leavenworth

Pacific Crest Trail

40

to Everett

2

Stevens Pass

N

0   0.5   1
MILES

Lichtenberg Mountain stands watch over Lake Valhalla.

and camps. Locate a spur trail right to deliver you to the lake's northern shore. There's a shorter "backdoor" way to Valhalla (3.4 miles via Hike 41), so chances are you won't be alone. Share your lunch spot and treat this popular backcountry destination kindly.

EXTENDING YOUR TRIP

Continue north on the PCT another 0.5 mile to a small gap above the lake. Locate a steep side trail taking off for Mount McCausland (Hike 41). Views of and over the lake from this peak are superb. Experienced scramblers may want to set their sights on Lichtenberg Mountain's open slopes. The "backdoor" approach to Valhalla is from the north via the Smith Brook Trail (Hike 41), a journey roughly half the distance.

41 Mount McCausland

RATING/ DIFFICULTY	ROUND-TRIP	ELEV GAIN/ HIGH POINT	SEASON
★★★/3	7 miles	1800 feet/ 5747 feet	July–Oct

Map: Green Trails Benchmark Mtn No. 144; **Contact:** Okanogan-Wenatchee National Forest, Wenatchee River Ranger District, Leavenworth, (509) 548-6977, www.fs.fed .us/r6/wenatchee; **Note:** NW Forest Pass required; **GPS:** N 47 48.140, W 121 04.634

The trail parallels above Stevens Creek and US 2 for 1.5 miles, providing good albeit noisy viewing of Lichtenberg Mountain and Nason Ridge. Losing about 300 feet on very gentle grade, the trail bends westward to cross a creek and finally leaves the old railbed. Now gradually climbing, enter the 100,000-plus-acre Henry M. Jackson Wilderness.

At about 3.5 miles cross another creek and begin ascending moderately through cool mature timber. Boggy meadows provide opportunities to momentarily snag some sunlight. At about 5.5 miles the trail rounds a 5050-foot shoulder. Valhalla's rippling waters lie in a basin below. To reach them, carry on, quickly losing 200 feet to reach a meadow

Rising above sparkling Lake Valhalla, Mount McCausland provides out-standing viewing in the midst of bountiful

berry patches. Come in September and gaze while you graze. As you dye your hands and lips blue, set your sights all around, north to Glacier Peak, south to the Chiwaukums, east to Nason Ridge, and west to the peaks of the Wild Sky. But it's the gleaming body of water below that'll command most of your attention.

GETTING THERE

From Everett head east on US 2 for 65 miles to Stevens Pass. Continue east for another 4 miles. Just after the highway divides, turn left (exercising caution crossing the westbound lanes) onto Smith Brook Road (Forest Road 6700). (From Leavenworth reach the turnoff in 30 miles.) Follow FR 6700 for 2.8 miles to a large parking area on your left (elev. 3950 ft).

ON THE TRAIL

Smith Brook Trail No. 1590 is a busy portal to Lakes Valhalla and Janus. Offering short and easy access to these two fine backcountry bodies of water, why wouldn't it be? A lot of boots can raise havoc on a trail, and that was the story here until about a decade ago. The trail has been upgraded to withstand the pounding of the masses, and the mud holes that used to feed on boots of unwitting hikers have been detoured. The Smith Brook Trail is now a joy to walk.

The trail starts by traversing a marshy flat where mosquitoes often see to it that you move swiftly. In 0.2 mile pass the old trailhead, where parking was always at a premium. Now on gentle switchbacks, ascend through mature timber. Smith Brook softly gurgles in the background. Enter the protected shrine of the Henry M. Jackson Wilderness, leaving the hurried and mechanized world behind.

After skirting beneath some impressive boulders, the Smith Brook Trail ends its 1.4-mile run at an intersection with the Pacific Crest Trail (PCT) at Union Gap (elev. 4700 ft). Turn left, heading south on the long-distance trail that spans the spine of the Cascades and Sierras. For close to a mile the way is nearly level. Then come to another gentle ascent. At about 1.6 miles from Union Gap reach a 5100-foot unnamed gap above Lake Valhalla.

Look for an unmarked and unmaintained but obvious trail heading north from the gap. This is your ticket to the sights and delights that await you on top of Mount McCausland.

Glacier Peak as seen from the rocky summit of Mount McCausland

It's a steep grunt of about 0.5 mile through brush and around ledges to the 5747-foot summit. Now enjoy bird's-eye views of Valhalla and Stevens Pass and the precipitous thumb of Lichtenberg Mountain sticking out directly to the south. Autumn is an especially nice time to visit, when carpeting blueberry bushes set the slopes afire in red.

EXTENDING YOUR TRIP

From the 5100-foot unnamed gap it's a half-mile and 250-foot drop on the PCT to Lake Valhalla. Lovers of abandoned trails may want to hike south along the PCT for another mile or so from the gap in search of the old Johnson Ridge Trail. If you can locate it and are skilled in off-trail travel, a handful of scenic rewards await you.

42 Lake Janus and Grizzly Peak

Lake Janus

RATING/ DIFFICULTY	ROUND-TRIP	ELEV GAIN/ HIGH POINT	SEASON
★★★/2	7.2 miles	1550 feet/ 4700 feet	July–Oct

Grizzly Peak

RATING/ DIFFICULTY	ROUND-TRIP	ELEV GAIN/ HIGH POINT	SEASON
★★★★/5	16.8 miles	3400 feet/ 5597 feet	July–Oct

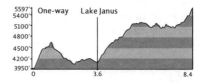

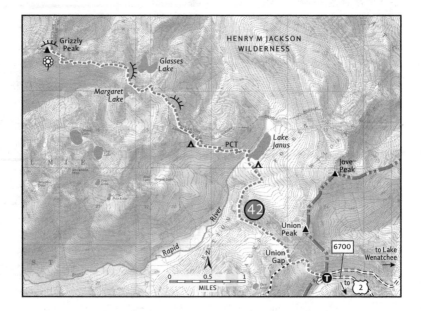

The PCT winds across sprawling meadows on its way to crossing Grizzly Peak.

Map: Green Trails Benchmark Mtn No. 144;
Contact: Okanogan-Wenatchee National
Forest, Wenatchee River Ranger District,
Leavenworth, (509) 548-6977, www.fs.fed
.us/r6/wenatchee; **Note:** NW Forest Pass
required; **GPS:** N 47 48.140, W 121 04.634

A warm, inviting lake, a
gentle summit carpeted
*in flowering meadows, entrancing views, and
deep, soothing wilderness are all yours on
this hike. Easy to reach, Lake Janus beckons
its fair share of anglers and beginning back-*

*packers, while Grizzly's bear of a distance
culls all but the strongest hikers. Those who
do push on, however, will be rewarded with
continuous panoramic viewing, all while
under the watchful guise of majestic snow-
and ice-crowned Glacier Peak.*

GETTING THERE

From Everett head east on US 2 for 65 miles
to Stevens Pass. Continue east for another 4
miles. Just after the highway divides, turn left
(exercising caution crossing the westbound
lanes) onto Smith Brook Road (Forest Road

6700). (From Leavenworth, reach the turnoff in 30 miles.) Follow FR 6700 for 2.8 miles to a large parking area on your left (elev. 3950 ft).

ON THE TRAIL

Start by following the well-groomed delight-to-hike Smith Brook Trail for 1.4 miles, coming to a junction with the Pacific Crest Trail (PCT) at 4700-foot Union Gap. Left, the PCT heads south to Lake Valhalla and Mexico. Head right instead toward Janus, Grizzly, and Canada. Avoiding Union Peak's steep boulder-bound slopes, the trail descends, losing 700 feet in about a mile.

Skirt boggy meadows, with glimpses down into the Rapid River valley, then begin climbing again. After traversing a brushy boulder field, cross a small creek beneath a little cascade and emerge onto a forested flat that harbors patches of blueberries. Lake Janus lies just ahead: find a short spur trail leading to the right to its grassy and welcoming shores. Children will enjoy tadpole tallying while you'll enjoy soaking your tootsies in the warm, shallow waters. Cast a lure into the emerald meadows of Jove Peak that are reflected on the placid lake surface.

The 3.6-mile hike to Janus is satisfying to most people, but if you came for maximum viewing and aerobic exercise, carry on. Continue north on the PCT, rock-hopping across Janus's outlet creek. Be sure water bottles are filled here, for beyond, the life-sustaining liquid isn't always readily available.

Climbing steadily but gently, the way weaves back and forth in pursuit of the Cascade crest. About 1 mile from the lake, arrive at a heathered swale complete with campsites along a sometimes flowing creek. A 5650-foot open knoll just to the west makes a good viewing and quitting spot. Otherwise carry on, reaching a 5200-foot gap in

another 0.5 mile with a mouthwatering preview of the spectacular alpine scenery lying ahead. Bust out of the forest into a granite sculpture garden. Views! Labyrinth, Poet Ridge, and the White Mountains vie for your attention to the east. But the snowy volcanic monolith that is Glacier Peak, Washington's fourth-loftiest summit, draws and holds your gaze northward.

In 0.5 mile beyond the gap, an overhanging ledge offers clear viewing straight down to Glasses Lake. A little farther, gaps in the forest reveal little Margaret Lake lying beneath the west side of the crest. After a slight drop, reach a 5000-foot low point where two steep, boot-beaten side paths take off for those lakes.

Now gently climbing again, the trail hugs the west side of the Cascade crest, revealing nice glimpses of Mounts Hinman and Daniel. Undulating between sun-kissed heather meadows and cool groves of mountain hemlock, the trail continues along the vibrant vertebrae of Washington State.

Perched in a wide cirque 1200 feet below, Heather Lake (Hike 71) comes into view. Against an emerald backdrop with Glacier Peak hovering above, the shimmering backcountry lake looks stunning from high above. Using switchbacks, the trail then climbs steeply up open slopes, providing striking views southward all the way to Rainier.

Finally, after 8 long but scenically satisfying miles, reach the unassuming 5597-foot summit of Grizzly Peak. A carpet of flowering meadows unrolls northward and entices you to keep going all the way to Glacier Peak. But your tired calves and better judgment lead you instead to lie back in the soft grasses and contemplate the beauty before you. And here in the heart of the Henry M. Jackson Wilderness it's bountiful.

MEXICO TO CANADA

Putting in a long and hard day on the trail can certainly be challenging, but most likely rewarding as well. Imagine putting three, four, or five months on the trail. A small but growing group of hikers from coast to coast do just that each year on one of America's eight long-distance National Scenic Trails. The granddaddy of them all, the 2175-mile Appalachian Trail (AT), is the most popular. Completed in 1937, it winds its way from Georgia to Maine.

Here in the Central Cascades, the Pacific Crest Trail works some of its 2650 miles from the Mexican to the Canadian border. Officially completed in 1993, the Pacific Crest Trail—or PCT as it's lovingly called—became the first of America's designated national trails in 1968, along with the AT. Administered by the National Park Service, the National Trails System consists of congressionally designated trails. Inclusion in the system is based on a trail's cultural, historic, and scenic attributes as well as its draw for outdoor recreation.

The PCT, like most of the national trails, actually consists of many trails woven together to form one continuous corridor. While much of the PCT traverses deep wilderness far from population centers and roads, many good day-hiking opportunities do exist on the trail where it crosses or comes close to road corridors.

The trail is well maintained and cared for and is looked after by several citizen groups like the Pacific Crest Trail Association (PCTA). In the Central Cascades, take a day hike on this grand trail at Hope and Mig Lakes (Hike 33), Trap Lake (Hike 34), Josephine Lake (Hike 39), Lake Valhalla (Hike 40), Mount McCausland (Hike 41), Lake Janus and Grizzly Peak (Hike 42), Pear Lake (Hike 72), and Howard Lake (Hike 114).

43 Lanham Lake

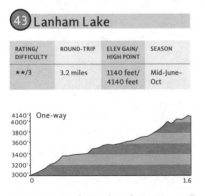

RATING/ DIFFICULTY	ROUND-TRIP	ELEV GAIN/ HIGH POINT	SEASON
★★/3	3.2 miles	1140 feet/ 4140 feet	Mid-June– Oct

Map: Green Trails Benchmark Mtn No. 144;
Contact: Okanogan-Wenatchee National Forest, Wenatchee River Ranger District, Leavenworth, (509) 548-6977, www.fs.fed.us/r6/wenatchee; **GPS:** N 47 46.298, W 121 00.818

A small lake under a big mountain, reached by a short trail alongside a pretty creek shaded by old trees—Lanham makes for a good afternoon hike or a nice break from traveling busy US 2. A popular winter snowshoe destination, the lake is fairly peaceful during the summer. Visit in June when lake and creek levels are high and the forest is alive with avian arias.

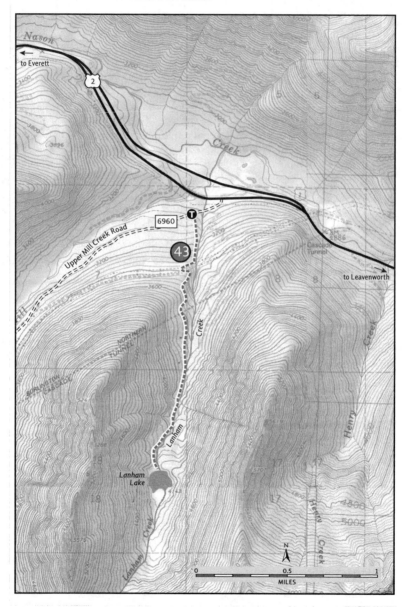

GETTING THERE

From Everett head east on US 2 for 65 miles to Stevens Pass. Continue east for another 5.5 miles, turning right onto Upper Mill Creek Road (Forest Road 6960, signed for Stevens Pass Nordic Center). (From Leavenworth reach the turnoff in 29 miles, 0.5 mile after US 2 divides.) The trail begins on the far east side of the lower parking area (elev. 3000 ft).

ON THE TRAIL

Starting from the base of what is the Nordic Center in winter, the trail immediately enters thick forest and commences climbing aside tumbling Lanham Creek. The way soon pops out from under the cool canopy to cross beneath buzzing high-tension wires. It then reenters forest and shortly afterwards passes over the Burlington Northern Railroad Tunnel, but you'll never notice it.

Now climbing steadily, the trail intersects some old logging spurs as it traverses newer growth. In no time it's back to impressive old growth and a little reprieve from steep climbing. With Lanham Creek always within eyesight and earshot, the trail continues up the narrow valley. One final steep section awaits before emerging at little Lanham Lake near its outlet.

Scout the sunny northern shoreline for a good place to plop down and enjoy the serenity of the lake basin. Stare up at impressive 6765-foot Jim Hill Mountain, named by A. H. Sylvester (see "Sly Sylvester" in the Lake Wenatchee section) for James J. Hill, "The Empire Builder." It was Hill who was responsible for constructing the Great Northern Railway that helped open up the Pacific Northwest to pioneer settlement. One of Mr. Hill's most notable quotes was, "Give me snuff, whiskey, and Swedes, and I will build a railroad to hell." He reached Seattle!

Sizable Jim Hill Mountain rises above tiny Lanham Lake.

44 Rock Mountain via Rock Lake

Rock Mountain

RATING/ DIFFICULTY	ROUND-TRIP	ELEV GAIN/ HIGH POINT	SEASON
★★★★/5	11 miles	4175 feet/ 6852 feet	July–Oct

Rock Lake

RATING/ DIFFICULTY	ROUND-TRIP	ELEV GAIN/ HIGH POINT	SEASON
★★★★/5	9.5 miles	3625 feet/ 6100 feet	July–Oct

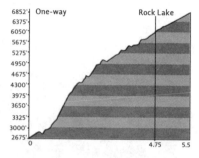

Map: Green Trails Wenatchee Lake No. 145; **Contact:** Okanogan-Wenatchee National Forest, Wenatchee River Ranger District, Leavenworth, (509) 548-6977, www.fs.fed.us/r6/wenatchee; **GPS:** N 47 46.544 W 120 57.486

What are you up for today? One of Nason Ridge's prominent peaks or dramatic lakes? Either way it's going to cost you big time in sweat expended and calories burned to reach them. The way is steep, hot, and entails a whole lot of vertical rise. But the trailhead is easy to reach, the trail is in good shape, and views are practically non-stop. And did I mention all the flowers?

GETTING THERE

From Everett head east on US 2 for 65 miles to Stevens Pass. Continue east for another 8.5 miles, turning left onto an inconspicuous dirt road leading almost immediately to the trailhead (elev. 2675 ft). The turnoff is just after milepost 73, approximately 0.4 mile east of the Washington Department of Transportation buildings. (From Leavenworth follow US 2 west for 26 miles.)

ON THE TRAIL

If your intent is solely to summit Rock Mountain, it's a much easier pursuit via the Snowy

Rock Lake sits in a rocky fold on Nason Ridge.

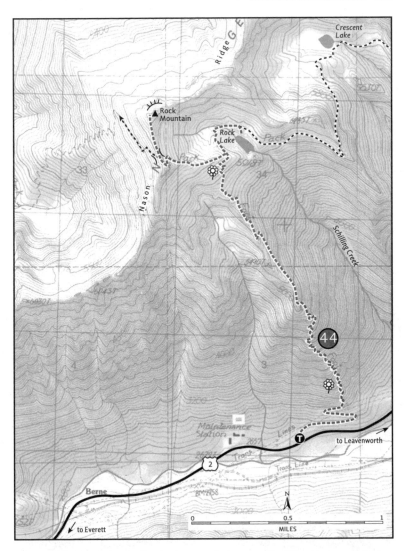

Creek Trail (Hike 70). Via Rock Lake there are over 4000 feet of vertical to subdue, on lightly forested southern slopes. In summer the heat can be stifling. However, that same heat melts snow fast, often providing an early season high-country probe. The snow in the basin just below Rock's summit, where Rock Lake sits, often doesn't melt out until well into July. These snowfields can be dangerous and are best avoided unless you're experienced with an ice ax.

Starting beneath high-tension wires, follow a service road. At 0.3 mile make a sharp turn left onto another service road and follow it to its end at 0.6 mile, where real trail begins (elev. 3000 ft). On brushy-at-times but decent tread, climb! My guidebook predecessor Harvey Manning says there are ninety-five switchbacks along the way. I didn't count them but I'm not discounting his claim.

Up and around ledges and across grassy slopes, be sure while you're catching your breath to look down to admire a myriad of blossoms, and look out to take in the beauty of the Chiwaukum Mountains. At 4000 feet Douglas-firs offer some shady relief. At 4800 feet the grade eases. Now in cool subalpine forest, the way marches up a rib. Don't be alarmed by the artillery warning sign—just don't venture off the trail here.

Thinning forest soon yields to heather meadows and striated slabs of rock. Views to the south are now awesome. Arrowhead, Jim Hill, Daniel, Hinman, and the Chiwaukums! After 4.3 endurance-testing miles, reach a junction with the Nason Ridge Trail (elev. 6100 ft).

For Rock Mountain, head left climbing another 600 feet up steep meadows, cresting a ridge, and turning right at a junction to follow a short spur to the 6852-foot summit. Views are simply sublime from this former fire lookout post. From Glacier Peak to Rainier to Howard along Nason Ridge to hundreds of other summits near and far—wow!

For Rock Lake, head right. Upon rounding a ridge you'll see the alpine lake revealed in a rugged basin 200 feet below. To reach it descend through rock, meadow, and snow. Take care not to trample fragile shoreline vegetation. If mosquitoes are in full force (which they usually are throughout the summer), retreat to a windy ledge back above the lake.

EXTENDING YOUR TRIP

Crescent Lake (elev. 5450 ft), perhaps the prettiest body of water on Nason Ridge, can be reached by following the Nason Ridge Trail east for 2 adventurous miles. Most of the way is along steep open slopes bursting with flowers and views. The trail, however, is slumping in spots and may be unnerving for those uncomfortable with heights.

45 Merritt Lake and Lost Lake

Merritt Lake

RATING/ DIFFICULTY	ROUND-TRIP	ELEV GAIN/ HIGH POINT	SEASON
★★/3	6 miles	1900 feet/ 5000 feet	June–Oct

Lost Lake

RATING/ DIFFICULTY	ROUND-TRIP	ELEV GAIN/ HIGH POINT	SEASON
★★/4	9 miles	3200 feet/ 5600 feet	June–Oct

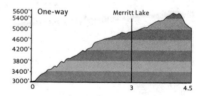

Map: Green Trails Wenatchee Lake No. 145; **Contact:** Okanogan-Wenatchee National Forest, Wenatchee River Ranger District, Leavenworth, (509) 548-6977, www.fs.fed .us/r6/wenatchee; **Note:** NW Forest Pass required; **GPS:** N 47 47.474, W 120 53.089

Merritt Lake from the trail to Lost Lake

Merritt is a popular lake—in fact crowded at times—but not much of a lake. The trail is good and the old-growth forest appealing, but the lake itself is swarming with mosquitoes, shallow and grassy, and with a shoreline trampled by overuse. Merritt appears to lack much merit. A trip in fall, however, when the buzzing buggers are absent and deciduous shrubs streak the lake basin red and yellow, has its charms. And if you want adventure, find Lost Lake, the largest lake on Nason Ridge and one whose tough approach keeps visitation down.

GETTING THERE

From Everett head east on US 2 for 65 miles to Stevens Pass. Continue east for another 11.3 miles turning left onto Forest Road 657. (From Leavenworth head west on US 2 for 23 miles.) Proceed 1.6 miles on FR 657, reaching the trailhead at the road's end (elev. 3100 ft).

ON THE TRAIL

Like Lower Lena Lake in the Olympics, Merritt attracts throngs of hikers from all walks of life. And like Lena the trail shows scars from the less enlightened. Set a good example by not cutting switchbacks and help educate those tempted to do so.

In mature timber, head off on a dusty and brushy-at-times but generally good trail. Steadily climbing along a rib, the trail winds through small openings and beneath a canopy made up in part of impressive giant ponderosa pines. Big Doug-firs begin to add to the old-growth mix. As you ascend steeply at times and with aid of switchbacks, Mahar Creek can be heard tumbling in the distance.

Traverse above cliff and talus and enjoy

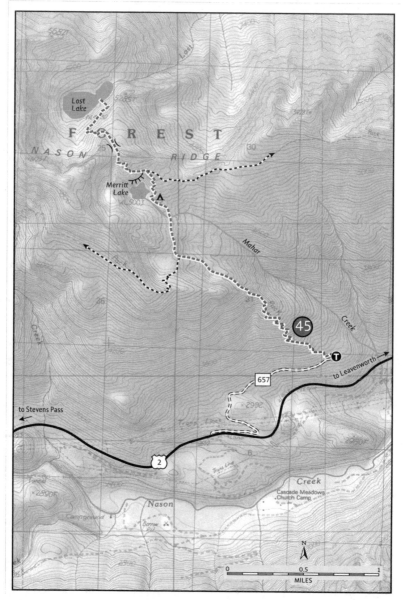

a window view east out to Alpine Lookout (Hike 48). At 2.5 miles, shortly after crossing a small creek, reach a junction with the Nason Ridge Trail (elev. 4850 ft). Follow this trail, the more beaten way, to the right on a gentle 0.5-mile journey, passing a small bog and crossing Mahar Creek before reaching Merritt Lake (elev. 5000 ft). Set in a forested cirque beneath craggy ridges, the lake does not have a shoreline with many good spots for lounging.

To find Lost Lake, continue on the Nason Ridge Trail for another 0.5 mile, climbing 300 feet to an unmarked junction. Follow an unmaintained but very obvious and used trail left, climbing another 250 feet to a forested saddle. Enjoy excellent views of Merritt Lake along the way. Ignore side trails (unless you want to explore view-providing knolls). Continue straight through heather meadows, and then drop steeply 600 feet to Lost Lake (elev. 4930 ft), set in a cirque beneath Mount Mastiff. You'll find a lot fewer people here, but probably the same quantity of swarming mosquitoes.

EXTENDING YOUR TRIP

Follow the Nason Ridge Trail west from the Merritt Lake Trail junction for 3.8 sometimes rough miles to pretty little Crescent Lake set beneath emerald slopes between Rock Mountain and Mount Howard, the highest summit on Nason Ridge. Like other lakes along Nason, the mosquitoes can be brutal, so best to explore late in the season.

46 Whitepine Creek

RATING/ DIFFICULTY	ROUND-TRIP	ELEV GAIN/ HIGH POINT	SEASON
★★/2	5 miles	400 feet/ 3200 feet	June– mid-Oct

Maps: Green Trails Wenatchee Lake No. 145,

Chiwaukum Mtns No. 177; **Contact:** Okanogan-Wenatchee National Forest, Wenatchee River Ranger District, Leavenworth, (509) 548-6977, www.fs.fed.us/r6/wenatchee; **Note:** NW Forest Pass required. Free wilderness permit required, available at trailhead; **GPS:** N 47 46.238; W 120 55.632

No lakes wait for you on this quiet trail in the Alpine Lakes Wilderness, just a tumbling frothy creek slicing through a deep valley flanked by pyramidal peaks. Absent are the crowds. Plentiful is the solitude. Visit in early summer to an awakening valley while the surrounding high country still lies dormant. Or come in late fall while much of nature prepares to close for the season. But no matter the season, Whitepine Creek will be busy lulling you with its soothing sonatas.

GETTING THERE

From Everett head east on US 2 for 65 miles to Stevens Pass. Continue east for another 13.5 miles. Just after passing milepost 78, turn right onto Whitepine Road (Forest Road 6950, signed "Cascade Meadows"). (From Leavenworth the turnoff is 6.5 miles west of Coles Corner.) In 0.6 mile pass a rundown Forest Service campground. At 2.1 miles pass a church camp. At 2.7 miles bear left at a Y-junction. Continue for just over a mile, reaching the trailhead at the road's end (elev. 2800 ft).

ON THE TRAIL

On good, wide tread, head into dark forest. Making your way toward Whitepine Creek, cross numerous side creeks also eager to meet it. Pass by big burnt snags and a few remnant giant firs. A few white pines line the way too. Once abundant throughout the Cascades and Northern Rockies, this elegant evergreen has been decimated by a blister rot (a type of fungus) accidentally introduced from Europe a century ago. But maybe someday these beautiful trees will once again dominate Washington hillsides. Forest Service scientists have recently been successful breeding rust-resistant specimens.

Continue up the valley, breaking out of forest to cross brush- and shrub-choked

An impressive triple-trunk western red cedar along Whitepine Creek

avalanche chutes. Enjoy close-ups of cliffy Arrowhead Mountain and views downvalley to bulky Nason Ridge. At about 1 mile enter the Alpine Lakes Wilderness. Not far beyond, take a break on a sunny ledge above a small cascade on the creek.

Head through another brushy avalanche zone and pass by a second wilderness boundary sign (yeah, I'm confused too about why it's there). At just shy of 2.5 miles come to a junction with the Wildhorse Creek Trail (elev. 3200 ft). Continue a short distance to the right on light tread to a lush bottomland of giant cedars, black cottonwoods, and Engelmann spruce. One particular tree, a triple-trunked monster cedar, is especially impressive. Most day hikers will want to call it quits here. To go farther requires a ford of the Whitepine, a crossing that can be tricky at times.

EXTENDING YOUR TRIP

If you can safely ford the creek, continue upvalley for a couple more miles. The trail beyond the ford receives very little maintenance. It is often choked with brush. Between the jungled avalanche slopes, however, are nice stretches of tread through gorgeous groves of old growth. An easier option for extending your hike is to continue up the Wildhorse Creek Trail. Expect some climbing as the trail quickly leaves the valley to ascend high slopes of the Chiwaukum Mountains. Good views open up in about 2 miles, just rewards for your effort.

47 Lake Ethel

RATING/ DIFFICULTY	ROUND-TRIP	ELEV GAIN/ HIGH POINT	SEASON
★★★/4	10 miles	3500 feet/ 5750 feet	July–Oct

Map: Green Trails Wenatchee Lake No. 145;

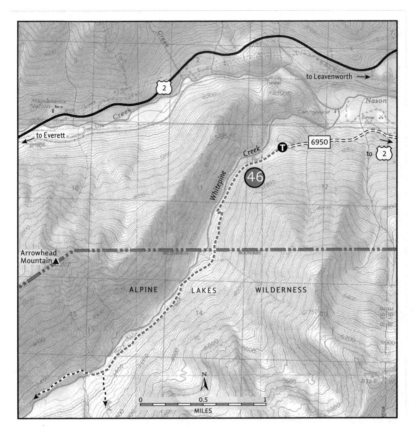

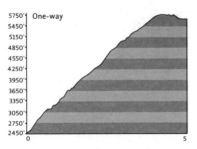

One-way

Contact: Okanogan-Wenatchee National Forest, Wenatchee River Ranger District, Leavenworth, (509) 548-6977, www.fs.fed.us/r6 /wenatchee; **GPS:** N 47 46.364, W 120 49.951

🔲 *A pretty alpine lake tucked in a cirque high in the Chiwaukum Mountains, Ethel is a fine destination for lazy summer days and cool, crisp autumn afternoons. Unfortunately, the trail leading to this Scottish Lakes gem is tarnished with clear-cuts and*

A male blue grouse "Sooty" subspecies struts his stuff.

logging-road crossings. And it's a bear of a hike too. Steep in sections with lots of elevation to gain, it'll leave you spent upon your arrival at the lake. Fortunately, Ethel's shimmering waters and sublime surroundings should help you rest and recover just fine.

GETTING THERE

From Everett head east on US 2 for 65 miles to Stevens Pass. Continue east for another 15 miles. Just before milepost 79 turn right onto Forest Road 6940 (signed "Gill Creek, Merritt, Lake Ethel Trailhead"). (From Leavenworth the turnoff is 5.2 miles west of Coles Corner.) Cross Nason Creek, turn left, and continue on a rough-at-times gravel road for 1.4 miles to the trailhead (elev. 2450 ft).

ON THE TRAIL

Several good trails once led from the Nason Creek valley to the high lakes tucked in the northern reaches of the lofty Chiwaukum

Range. Unfortunately, those trails traversed large checkerboard tracts of private land (legacies of the nineteenth-century railroad grants) that were heavily logged in the 1980s and '90s. The Roaring Creek Trail was obliterated and remains primarily a memory among many an old-timer. The Ethel Lake Trail's fate was not as grim. But while restored and rerouted, it still travels across several large clear-cuts—not exactly the most pleasant journey now, and one that can be quite hot when the eastern-slope sun is shining. On the positive side there are more views now, and you can still day hike to Lake Ethel, a most worthy objective.

The way starts off in a grove of big ponderosa pines and wastes little time gaining elevation. Switchbacking steeply along a small creek, the trail skirts a few ledges with nice views of the Nason Creek valley. Just shy of 2 miles the climb eases as the trail leaves Forest Service property. Shortly afterward the first of four road crossings is encountered (elev. 4050 ft). Traversing open pine forest and cuts new and old, the way marches onward and upward. Take in growing views of Nason Ridge, Glacier Peak, and the Chiwaukums along the way.

After passing through the last cut (elev. 5000 ft) the trail continues its stiff climb, taking you to a ridge crest. After reaching an elevation of 5750 feet you're granted a reprieve. The way then heads downward, crosses a small creek, and levels out in a beautiful grove of old-growth fir, spruce, and hemlock. Here intersect the original trail. Make a sharp right. Don't bother exploring the vintage tread that heads left—it soon ends in an old clear-cut.

Following Gill Creek, soon enter the Alpine Lakes Wilderness and come to a junction with the Roaring Creek Trail. Lake Ethel lies

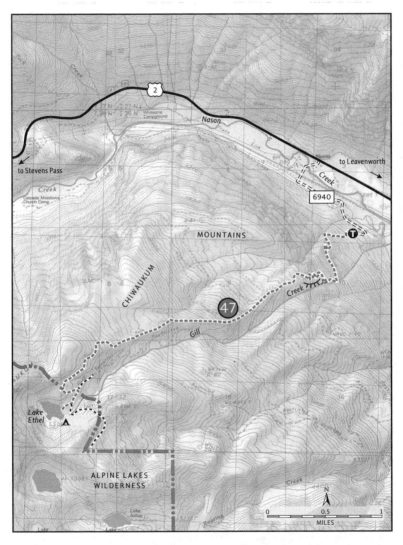

0.1 mile straight ahead. Go for it. You deserve to take in its beauty. Sitting in a deep cirque, the lake is flanked by old-growth forest on its northern shoreline, while meadows, talus, and big boulders grace its southern shore. In early summer small cascades trickle down from lingering snows high above. In autumn patches of blueberry bushes streak the cirque crimson.

EXTENDING YOUR TRIP

If the hike to Ethel didn't totally beat you up, consider wandering up the Roaring Creek Trail for a mile or 2. After an initial climb that is quite steep, the trail breaks out onto gentle, open slopes rife with wildflowers, berries, and splendid far-reaching views north and east.

48 Alpine Lookout

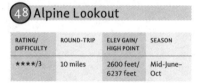

RATING/ DIFFICULTY	ROUND-TRIP	ELEV GAIN/ HIGH POINT	SEASON
★★★★/3	10 miles	2600 feet/ 6237 feet	Mid-June– Oct

Map: Green Trails Wenatchee Lake No. 145;

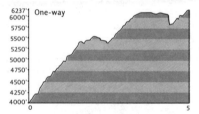

Contact: Okanogan-Wenatchee National Forest, Wenatchee River Ranger District, Leavenworth, (509) 548-6977, www.fs.fed .us/r6/wenatchee; **Notes:** NW Forest Pass required. Three miles open to motorcycles; **GPS:** N 47 47.536, W 120 47.667

❌ ⚙ 🏠 *This is one of the most popular hikes along the US 2 corridor, and it's easy to understand why: a historic and active fire lookout, an enclave for mountain goats, miles of flower-blooming meadows, jaw-slacking views of Lake Wenatchee, Glacier Peak, and*

hundreds of other peaks. It's amazing there aren't more hikers sunning themselves on this Nason Ridge summit. And being on one of the area's first high peaks to shed its winter snows, Alpine Lookout makes for an excellent early summer adventure. But a few blemishes make this well-esteemed hike less than perfect. The first 1.6 miles are quite steep. The next 3 miles are open to motorcycles. And the entire 5 miles is bone dry for much of the season. Get an early start, pack plenty of water, and avoid busy weekends.

GETTING THERE

From Everett head east on US 2 for 65 miles to Stevens Pass. Continue east for another 17 miles to the Nason Creek Rest Area. A quarter mile beyond, turn left onto unsigned and easy-to-miss Forest Road 6910 (look for a row of mailboxes). (From Leavenworth reach the turnoff in 16.75 miles.) Cross Nason Creek after 0.2 mile and a powerline corridor after another 0.3 mile. Follow the main road, avoiding side spurs. At 4.5 miles from US 2 bear right onto a narrow, brushy, somewhat rough road. Reach the trailhead in 0.2 mile (elev. 4000 ft). Privy available.

ON THE TRAIL

Start hiking via the Round Mountain Trail, immediately climbing, and steeply. In 0.5 mile enter the edge of a 1990s burn (elev. 4600 ft). The scorched forest is recovering nicely. Silver snags stand surrounded by swaying strands of fireweed. Nuthatches and woodpeckers busily grocery shop up and down their weathered and withered trunks.

Enjoy views southeast over waves of forested ridges resembling the Blue Ridge Mountains of the American Southeast. The

A hiker relaxes while taking in views at the Alpine Lookout.

grade eases somewhat as the way reenters green forest after about 0.5 mile. Traverse pocket meadows before reaching the Nason Ridge Trail at 1.6 miles (elev. 5200 ft).

Turn left, following wheel-beaten tread along the high crest of Nason Ridge. Note that while most motorcyclists stick to the trail, a few renegades have veered off, leaving ugly scars in the fragile forest floor. Frustrating and disheartening. Best to cast your attention to the upcoming series of excellent window views to Glacier Peak and over Lake Wenatchee to set your mood back in positive territory.

Skirting the 5700-foot summit of Round Mountain, the trail moseys along, breaking out into open meadows (elev. 5500 ft) that provide splendid viewing west along Nason Ridge and south to the Chiwaukums. Undu-

lating between forest and meadow, the trail reaches an elevation of 5600 feet before dipping to a small saddle (elev. 5450 ft).

Regain elevation lost and then some, following tread that at times is deeply eroded (blame the motorcycles). At 3.7 miles reach another small saddle, and then round a small knoll before emerging on a broad ridge. More meadows! More views! Gently climbing, the trail rounds yet another knoll (elev. 6100 ft) before dropping a couple hundred feet to rocky Ninemile Saddle at 4.5 miles. Overhanging and balancing rocks add intrigue to this rugged spot. Motorcycles are barred from continuing farther, but you aren't. Carry on, making one last climb.

Come to a signed junction. The main trail heads left to the high hinterlands of Nason Ridge. Take the spur right, reaching

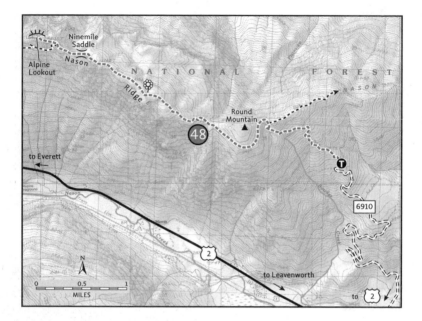

the Alpine Lookout after 0.3 mile. One of only a handful of lookouts still staffed in the Cascades, there's a good chance a real live lookout may be present.

But you have some looking out to do too. The views are amazing from this 6237-foot knob: Straight down to Lake Wenatchee and the oxbowing White River flowing into it. South to Big Jim, Snowgrass, Rainier, and Stuart. West to Hinman, Daniel, Jim Hill, Rock, Mastiff, and Howard. North to Sloan, the Poet Ridge, Buck, and Glacier. And east to the Entiat and Chelan ranges and the "rock chimneys" of Chiwawa Ridge. What a panorama! Hang around late in the day or arrive early in the morning, and perhaps you'll share this alpine splendor with the resident mountain goats.

EXTENDING YOUR TRIP

For a motor-free, less-traveled, but slightly longer hike to Alpine Lookout, approach from the west. Follow the Merritt Lake Trail for 2 miles to the Nason Ridge Trail (Hike 45), and then continue east for 4.4 miles to the lookout.

49 Larch Lake

RATING/ DIFFICULTY	ROUND-TRIP	ELEV GAIN/ HIGH POINT	SEASON
★★★★★/4	12 miles	2450 feet/ 6078 feet	Mid-Aug– mid-Oct

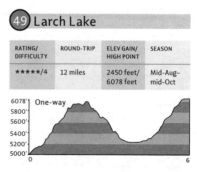

Map: Green Trails Chiwaukum Mtns No. 177; **Contact:** Okanogan-Wenatchee National Forest, Wenatchee River Ranger District, Leavenworth, (509) 548-6977, www.fs.fed.us/r6/wenatchee; **Note:** Trailhead accessible via private logging road gated to vehicles. Mountain bike 7 miles and 3000 vertical feet to trailhead (tough!), or stay at the Scottish Lakes High Camp (rustic backcountry cabins open mid-Aug to mid-Oct) and take their shuttle (recommended), (425) 844-2000, www.scottishlakes.com; **GPS:** N 47 43.697, W 120 50.620

Tucked in the heart of the rugged Chiwaukum Range, Larch Lake is a spectacular high-country lake flanked by rocky spires and ringed with its soft-needled namesakes. Remote and breathtakingly beautiful, getting there is quite a jaunt. It requires a slog up and over McCue Ridge and an up-and-over McCue slog again on the return. But the sweeping alpine views . . . and big, shimmering Chiwaukum Lake . . . and wide-open Ewing Basin along the way all help ease the pain.

GETTING THERE

From Everett head east on US 2 for 65 miles to Stevens Pass. Continue east for another 17 miles to Nason Creek Rest Area. (From Leavenworth reach the rest area in 17 miles.) Directly across from the rest area, turn right onto Coulter Creek Road. Cross railroad tracks and turn right into the parking lot for Scottish Lakes High Camp. Take the shuttle to the trailhead located at High Camp (elev. 5000 ft). The shuttle and a cabin stay require advance reservations.

ON THE TRAIL

Locate the Summer Trail that takes off from behind the main lodge at High Camp. Built by camp staff, the trail is a nice forested connection to the McCue Ridge Trail. Immediately enter national forest land. At 0.2 mile, just after crossing a creek, come to a junction with the Sunset Trail. Another High Camp–built trail, Sunset offers a longer and more scenic alternative to McCue Ridge.

Winding through cool forest, the Summer Trail quickly gains elevation. At 0.5 mile veer right onto the Low Road Trail and follow it for 0.5 mile to its end at the McCue Ridge Trail (elev. 5600 ft). Right heads to the famed Scottish Lakes (Hikes 47 and 50). Hang a left instead, ascending McCue Ridge (elev. 5950 ft) and entering the Alpine Lakes Wilderness. The forest

Golden larches surround appropriately named Larch Lake.

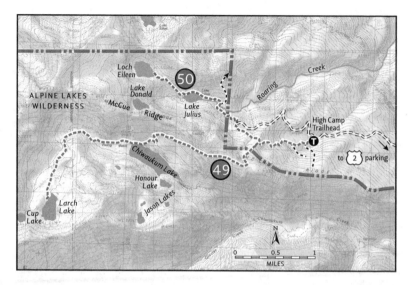

thins and good views of the Chiwaukums and Big Jim Mountain are to be had from this long broad ridge once used as pasture for William McCue's sheep flocks.

After ambling easily along the ridge, begin a long descent, dropping 700 feet to a junction on the wooded shores of Chiwaukum Lake (elev. 5250 ft). One mile long and perched at the head of a hanging valley, the lake is a favorite destination for backpackers, anglers, and day hikers abandoning plans to pursue Larch Lake.

For the Larch-bound, carry on to the right, entering the stunning Ewing Basin in a short mile. The word Chiwaukum is derived from the Wenatchee dialect meaning "many little creeks running into one big one." Look around—a most appropriate name indeed for these mountains. After rock-hopping over a couple of those creeks, leave the basin to climb a small rib rife with larch.

At 6 miles enter a glorious high meadow

spread out before sparkling Larch Lake (elev. 6078 ft). Beautiful in summer, the lake and its environs are resplendent in autumn when low-lying blueberry bushes carpet the basin crimson and crag-clinging larches illuminate it with a golden glow.

EXTENDING YOUR TRIP

Adventurous souls can follow a path of sorts to Cup Lake, set in a rocky cirque 400 feet above Larch Lake and frozen most of the year. The route involves a tricky traverse over a scree slope, so proceed with caution. McCue Ridge makes for an interesting side trip with easy wanderings east and west.

50 Lake Julius and Loch Eileen

RATING/ DIFFICULTY	ROUND-TRIP	ELEV GAIN/ HIGH POINT	SEASON
★★★/3	7 miles	1400 feet/ 5508 feet	Mid-Aug– mid-Oct

Map: Green Trails Chiwaukum Mtns No. 177; **Contact:** Okanogan-Wenatchee National Forest, Wenatchee River Ranger District, Leavenworth, (509) 548-6977, www.fs.fed .us/r6/wenatchee; **Note:** Trailhead accessible via private logging road gated to vehicles. Mountain bike 7 miles and 3000 vertical feet to trailhead (tough!), or stay at Scottish Lakes High Camp (rustic backcountry cabins open mid-Aug to mid-Oct) and take their shuttle (recommended), (425) 844-2000, www .scottishlakes.com; **GPS:** N 47 43.697, W 120 50.620

Lake Julius and Loch Eileen, along with nearby Lakes Ethel and Donald, comprise Washington's famed Scottish Lakes. Named by A. H. Sylvester (see "Sly Sylvester" in the Lake Wenatchee section) for various acquaintances, none of whom hailed from Scotland, the surrounding boggy and meadowed high slopes do, however, bear a slight resemblance to the Scottish moors. Easily reached from High Camp, Julius and Eileen extend a hearty fáilte to all hikers, young and old alike.

GETTING THERE

From Everett head east on US 2 for 65 miles to Stevens Pass. Continue east for another 17 miles to Nason Creek Rest Area. Directly across from the rest area, turn right onto Coulter Creek Road. Cross railroad tracks and turn right into the parking lot for Scottish Lakes High Camp. Take the shuttle to the trailhead located at High Camp (elev. 5000 ft). The shuttle and a cabin stay require advance reservations.

Snow shrouds Lake Julius in early spring.

ON THE TRAIL

From High Camp take the Summer Trail, which takes off from behind the main lodge and immediately enters national forest land. Come to a junction with the Sunset Trail at 0.2 mile and continue right. Through cool forest, the Summer Trail quickly gains elevation. At 0.5 mile veer right onto the Low Road Trail and follow it for 0.5 mile to its end at the McCue Ridge Trail (elev. 5600 ft). Left heads up and over McCue to Chiwaukum and Larch lakes (Hike 49). Go right.

Soon come to a signed junction. The way right is the old Roaring Creek Trail that once traveled for miles through unbroken forest to the Nason Creek valley. It became a logging casualty in the 1980s. Continue left through pleasant old growth. Cross a small creek and slowly descend, coming to the end of a logging road at 1.75 miles (elev. 5350 ft). The logging road offers a 1.5-mile, slightly easier alternative route back to High Camp.

The trail veers back into the forest, where it continues to descend. Soon after entering the Alpine Lakes Wilderness, the way bottoms out along Roaring Creek, which lets out nary a growl here within a peaceful flat (elev. 5150 ft). After carefully crossing the creek on a set of logs that shift each year, reach a junction. The trail right leads 2.5 lonely and scenic miles to Lake Ethel (Hike 47).

Take the more boot-beaten path left, reaching Lake Julius (elev. 5200 ft) in a mere 0.25 mile (2.5 miles from your start). A shallow lake ringed with handsome forest and a rugged backdrop of McCue Ridge, it's a pleasant destination for picnicking or for calling it a day. If intent on seeing Eileen, however, continue. Skirt Julius's shoreline, and then climb a series of ledges to reach the bowl-bound Loch Eileen at 3.5 miles (elev. 5508 ft).

Fed by waterfalls tumbling over steep headwalls and surrounded by rocky slopes and groves of larches, Eileen sits in a dramatically different environment than its lower cousin Julius. Particularly striking in autumn, Eileen also has a nice appeal during hot summer days, when shoreline ledges invite foot-soaking.

EXTENDING YOUR TRIP

Experienced off-trail hikers can follow a very steep trail of sorts (some ledges, but no exposure) for 0.5 mile to Lake Donald, set in a rocky basin. High-country meadows above Lake Donald invite adventurous souls to miles of spectacular alpine wandering.

51 Chiwaukum Creek

RATING/ DIFFICULTY	ROUND-TRIP	ELEV GAIN/ HIGH POINT	SEASON
★★★/3	12 miles	1550 feet/ 3350 feet	May–Nov

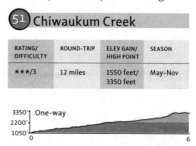

Map: Green Trails Chiwaukum Mtns No. 177; **Contact:** Okanogan-Wenatchee National Forest, Wenatchee River Ranger District, Leavenworth, (509) 548-6977, www.fs.fed .us/r6/wenatchee; **Notes:** NW Forest Pass required. Free day-use permit required, available at trailhead. Be alert for rattlesnakes; **GPS:** N 47 41.336, W 120 44.449

Hike along a raucous waterway into a quiet corner of the Alpine Lakes Wilderness. Amble aimlessly through groves of cedar, cottonwood, and towering ponderosa pines resembling pillars holding up the sky. Always within sight and sound of the crashing creek, you will find no dearth of great lounging-away-the-afternoon spots along the Chiwaukum.

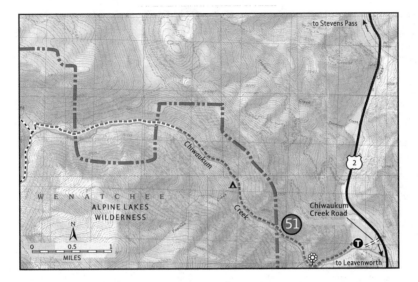

GETTING THERE

From Everett head east on US 2 for 85 miles to Coles Corner. Continue east on US 2 for 4.8 miles, turning right on Chiwaukum Creek Road (the turnoff is 0.75 mile before Tumwater Campground between mileposts 89 and 90). (From Leavenworth follow US 2 west for 10 miles to the turnoff.) Follow Chiwaukum Creek Road for 0.2 mile to the trailhead (elev. 1850 ft). Privy available.

ON THE TRAIL

From the trailhead kiosk, begin your walk by heading for a gated road that traverses private property. Hikers and horseback riders are allowed to walk this road to reach the actual trailhead. Hugging the creek in deep timber and passing just a couple of structures, the road walk is actually quite pleasant.

At 1.25 miles reach true trail (elev. 2000 ft), and after another 0.25 mile enter the Alpine Lakes Wilderness. Traveling at first on a bench above the chattering (and in spring,

roaring) Chiwaukum Creek, the trail soon comes down to creek level, where the water has tried to level the trail! Then it's back to higher ground. In spring and early summer the trail is lined with blooming calypso orchids, groundsel, trilliums, paintbrush, and the fun-to-say ballhead waterleaf. Look too for Tweedy's lewisia, a showy, somewhat rare blossom.

At 2.5 miles pass a nice creekside campsite (perfectly suitable for lunchtime napping as well) in a grove of western white pines. Farther upriver the trail meanders through pleasant flats of ponderosa pines, occasionally passing by a gargantuan specimen.

At 4.5 miles enter a forested area lacking old-growth giants, rife instead with cherry and aspen, species indicative of disturbance. Part of a private inholding (legacy of the railroad grants), the ancient pine forest here was "disturbed" by chain saws in the 1980s. Public outcry and protests from guidebook pioneers Harvey Manning and Ira Spring

The rare and showy Tweedy's lewisia flourishes along the Chiwaukum Creek Trail.

couldn't stop it. The parcel was eventually added to the Alpine Wilderness, but with substantially less board footage.

Reenter mature forest and, with the creek crashing beneath a formidable wall of rock, begin a short and steep climb of about 400 feet in 0.5 mile. Round a small knoll, and then descend slightly under a cool canopy of cedars to a precarious log crossing of Chiwaukum Creek (elev. 3300 ft). Here, 6 miles from your vehicle, is a good place to call it quits. Enjoy the creek chatter and the quiet of the surrounding wilderness.

EXTENDING YOUR TRIP

Sure-footed hikers can cross the Chiwaukum, coming to a junction just above its confluence with its South Fork. Head left along the South Fork for 2 miles to Timothy Meadows. Or continue right for another 1.6 miles to yet another junction and confluence. Go left along Glacier Creek for 1.7 miles into a lonely valley or right 2 miles, climbing 1400 feet to reach big Chiwaukum Lake (Hike 49).

52 Tumwater Pipeline Trail

RATING/ DIFFICULTY	ROUND-TRIP	ELEV GAIN/ HIGH POINT	SEASON
★★/1	2.4 miles	100 feet/ 1400 feet	Apr–late Nov

Map: Green Trails Leavenworth No. 178; **Contact:** Okanogan-Wenatchee National Forest, Wenatchee River Ranger District, Leavenworth, (509) 548-6977, www.fs.fed .us/r6/wenatchee; **Note:** While not a major concern, be alert for rattlesnakes; **GPS:** N 47 35.224, W 120 42.456

Walk on an old pipeline right-of-way along the crashing Wenatchee River in a deep and impressive canyon. The hike is easy and the scenery is breathtaking. Come in spring for flowers, fall for color, and anytime to take a short trip back into time. For railroad and history buffs, the Tumwater Pipeline Trail is an outdoor museum.

GETTING THERE

From Everett head east on US 2 for 85 miles to Coles Corner. Continue east on US 2 for 12.7 miles to the trailhead (elev. 1300 ft), located on your right between mileposts 97 and 98. (From Leavenworth follow US 2 west for 2 miles to the trailhead, on your left.) Privy available.

ON THE TRAIL

When the Great Northern Railway abandoned its route over Stevens Pass and opted to go under the pass instead, its exhaust-emitting steam engines proved problematic in the long tunnel. So the line switched over to electric engines between Skykomish and Leavenworth. The railroad built a dam on the Wenatchee River (the dam is still there about 3 miles upriver from the trailhead) and ran a pipeline (penstock) down to a generating plant to produce electricity for the locomotives. In 1956 the railroad switched to diesel, abandoning the pipeline and power plant.

The trail starts at the site of the power plant, where parts of the foundation remain. Head off through a pine grove graced with big boulders and soon come to what no doubt will be the most popular feature on this hike for many, an old iron bridge spanning the river. Built to carry the pipeline across the water, the bridge offers exhilarating viewing of the Wenatchee River. Come in spring to watch kayakers and rafters riding the rapids. But be prepared for a wet crossing early in the season, when deep pools of water collect on the bridge.

Once across, follow the gentle trail along the river through Tumwater Canyon. Cottonwoods and maples adorn the trail and add touches of gold and crimson come October. At about 0.5 mile rock-hop across a side creek. Pass by big boulders and nice sandy beaches on the river. But before you're tempted to soak in the crystal waters, be forewarned. The word Tumwater is derived from Chinook Jargon, meaning strong or falling water. This is not an understatement here. In the summer of 2006 two teenagers swimming in the river were swept away and drowned. It's best not to soak more than feet in the powerful Wenatchee.

As you continue upriver, pass through pleasant pine groves—peaceful if not for the churn of the river and the hum of zooming vehicles on the opposite bank. Across the river, Castle Rock, a craggy protruding thumb favored by rock climbers, soon comes

Views up the Wenatchee River from the Tumwater Pipeline Trail

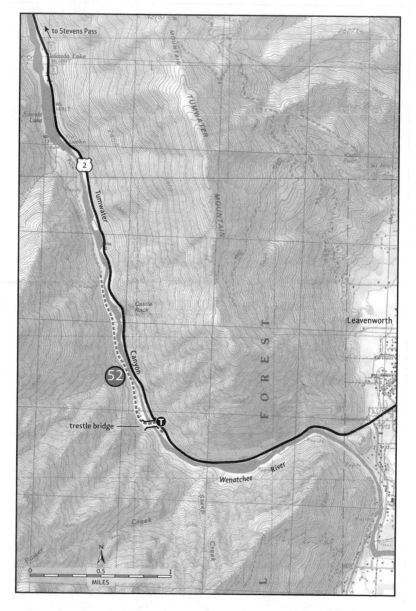

into view. Admire it and the clambering souls trying to subdue it. At 1.2 miles the trail abruptly ends where once a tunnel bore through the jumbled rocks and ledges that now impede further travel.

EXTENDING YOUR TRIP

If it's springtime why not consider visiting the nearby Tumwater Botanical Area for an outstanding floral show, including Tweedy's lewisia and many other blossoms both rare and common. Access to the botanical area is via an old logging road, Forest Road 7903. From the Tumwater Pipeline trailhead, find the gated road 5 miles west on US 2 (0.25 mile east of the Swiftwater Picnic Area).

(53) Peshastin Pinnacles

RATING/ DIFFICULTY	LOOP	ELEV GAIN/ HIGH POINT	SEASON
★★★/2	1.5 miles	400 feet/ 1450 feet	Mar–Nov

Loop
1450'
1250'
1050'
0   1.5

Map: Green Trails Leavenworth No. 178; **Contact:** Peshastin Pinnacles State Park, (509) 664-6373, www.parks.wa.gov; **Notes:** Dogs must be leashed; Discover Pass required; park is closed Nov 1–Mar 14. **GPS:** N 47 32.402, W 120 31.213

Long a favorite haunt among the carabiner-carrying crowd, the Pinnacles attract many a hiker too. Well-built trails weave through the 200-foot-high sandstone spires that perch on a sun-kissed hillside above the fruited Wenatchee River valley. When not fixated on the striking outcrops and sculptured slabs that surround you, peer out over orchards and a backdrop

Hikers enjoying the trails of Peshastin Pinnacles State Park

of lofty ridges and peaks. Come in spring for fabulous floral blooms, and come all year to watch climbers clinging and clambering.

GETTING THERE

From Leavenworth head east on US 2 for 9 miles, turning left on North Dryden Road. (From Wenatchee travel west on US 2 for 10 miles.) Continue for 0.5 mile, turning right into Peshastin Pinnacles State Park and parking at the trailhead (elev. 1050 ft). Privy available.

ON THE TRAIL

This little 34.5-acre park packs quite a varied landscape within its tight boundaries. Pass through a gate and immediately enter a magical kingdom of sandstone spires resembling rows of shark teeth protruding from a golden hillside. Trails quickly diverge from the Pinnacles' portal. It doesn't really matter which direction you choose to set off in to explore this land of wind-sculpted spires. Walk willy-nilly, amble aimlessly, or promenade along the periphery as suggested here for a nice 1.5-mile hike.

Head left, skirting the Pinnacles to enter a big dry draw. While this landscape is dull brown most of the year, from March

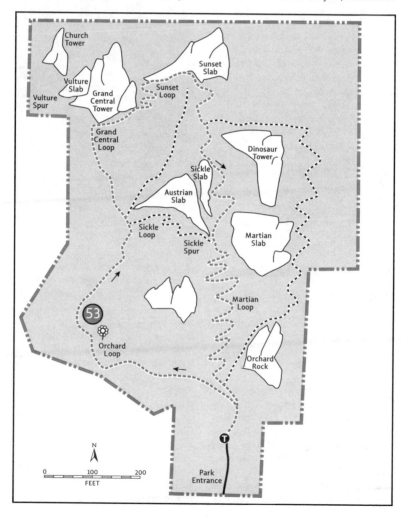

through May desert buttercups, avalanche lilies, and arrowleaf balsamroot add brilliant touches of gold to the surrounding slopes. Staying on the main tread, pass a side trail diverging right, and soon come to another junction. Now head to the right up a series of tight switchbacks under and beside the Grand Central Tower, one of the more prominent of the Pinnacles. Bending east, the way then traverses beneath Sunset Slab. Passing a junction, head up to a small ridge crest where some lonely pines extend a welcome.

Here beneath the Dinosaur Tower, views are grand close and far. This is a good spot too for observing falcons and hawks riding thermals above the serrated surroundings. The Pinnacles provide plenty of brooding spots for rock doves, otherwise known as pigeons, a raptor's delight! Now beside the more colorfully named Martian Slab, work your way off of the crest on switchbacks dropping steeply back to the gate. And if this loop wasn't enough to satisfy your wandering lust, feel free to repeat, exploring side trails.

54 Mission Ridge

RATING/ DIFFICULTY	ROUND-TRIP	ELEV GAIN/ HIGH POINT	SEASON
★★★/4	14 miles	3200 feet/ 4700 feet	Apr– mid-Nov

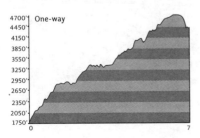

Map: Green Trails Wenatchee/Mission Ridge No. 211S; **Contact:** Okanogan-Wenatchee National Forest, Wenatchee River Ranger District, Leavenworth, (509) 548-6977, www .fs.fed.us/r6/wenatchee; **Notes:** NW Forest Pass required. Trail open to motorcycles from June 15 to Oct 1; **GPS:** N 47 23.878, W 120 30.072

❌ ⚙ *Dry, dusty, deeply rutted, and dominated by motorcycles—why bother, right? How about knockout views from Glacier Peak to the Columbia River? One of the largest and finest old-growth ponderosa pine forests in the entire state? An amazing array of dazzling wildflowers? And wildlife—this is the only hike in Washington where I've encountered a bobcat! Just come on a weekday, or early in the season when patches of snow prohibit the trail from becoming a motorway.*

GETTING THERE

From Leavenworth head east on US 2 for 11 miles, turning right 6.4 miles east of the US 97 junction onto Aplets Way into Cashmere. (From Wenatchee travel west on US 2 for 8 miles.) Cross the Wenatchee River and proceed south through downtown Cashmere. In 0.6 mile Aplets Way veers right, becoming Division Street. Continue for 0.1 mile, and then turn left onto Mission Creek Road. In 0.5 mile turn right at a stop sign. Cross the creek and in 500 feet turn left, continuing on Mission Creek Road. Follow it for 6.2 miles to the pavement's end at an auto graveyard and junction. Continue left on Forest Road 7100 for 2.5 miles to the trailhead (elev. 1750 ft). Privy available.

ON THE TRAIL

Despite being a popular motorcycle and mountain-biking destination, Mission Ridge makes a good early season hike. But do avoid it in the height of summer—not just because of motors and fat tires, but also for the stifling heat. Remember to pack plenty of water anytime on this trail—it's bone dry.

Start by crossing Mission Creek on a sturdy bridge. Come to a junction and head left. The trail right, Red Devil, holds little interest for pedestrians. In lush bottomland soon come to another junction. The trail right continues along Mission Creek heading up Devils Gulch (Hike 55). Head left to cross Mission Creek and immediately begin ascending Mission Ridge, within minutes rounding a knoll that grants good viewing into the Devil's lair.

The trail switchbacks and climbs, sometimes gently, sometimes not so gently. Pause along the way to take in good views northeast over the East Fork Mission Creek valley to ledgy Sheep Rock and forested Twin Peaks

a.k.a. Horse Lake Mountain (Hike 124). At about 1.5 miles the way steepens after crossing a small meadow, providing good viewing south along the long spine of Mission Ridge.

At 2 miles crest a small knoll (elev. 2900), and then drop into a small saddle, a pattern that will be repeated several times on this hike. After some minor ups and downs, come to a steep section made worse by ruts and some errant motorcycle riding. Question if this is good land stewardship. Continue climbing steeply, traversing pleasant parklands of ponderosa pine to a 3400-foot knoll. More ups and downs; another attractive piney knoll; then an open rocky slope that in late spring sports showy blossoms of bitterroot, one of our more striking wildflowers.

Drop. Climb. Traverse pine parkland. Then, at about 4.5 miles, reach the first of several open areas (elev. 3500 ft), this one

The Twin Peaks from Mission Ridge

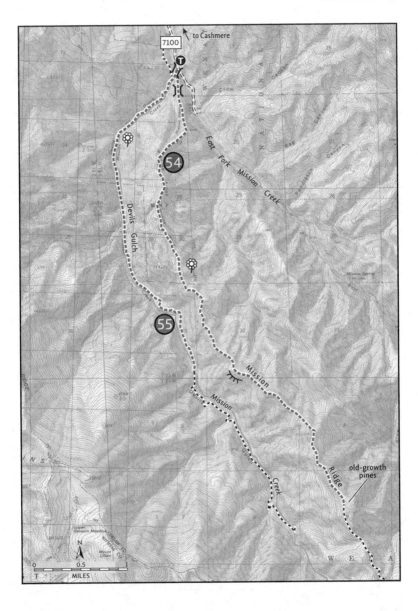

to Cashmere

7100

East Fork Mission Creek

54

Devils Gulch

55

Mission

Mission

Creek

Ridge

old-growth
pines

N

0   0.5   1

MILES

with exceptional views over Devils Gulch and to the cliffs and scoured slopes of Tronsen Ridge and Mount Lillian (Hike 120). More steep climbing; then a nice ridge walk with good views north to Glacier Peak and the Entiat Range. This is a good place to quit if you're spent. Otherwise, the views get better, but you'll need to keep working for them.

Crest a 4500-foot knoll, drop into a pine-studded gap, and then ascend a 4700-foot wide-open narrow ridgeline. Here, roughly 7 long miles from the trailhead, sit and relax and take in sweeping views in all directions: West to Icicle Ridge and the Stuart Range. East to Badger Mountain and the Columbia Plateau. South into the gulch. And north to Chelan Butte and the Columbia River. You've earned all of this.

EXTENDING YOUR TRIP

The trail climbs another 150 feet to round a 4963-foot knoll before dropping 450 feet to reach a gap set in a spectacular ancient pine forest. From here, 8 miles from the trailhead, you can make a 17-mile loop by following the Devils Gulch Trail back to your vehicle. Or if you can arrange a car shuttle, continue on the Mission Ridge Trail for another 2.7 miles and 1300 vertical feet to FR 9712.

55 Devils Gulch

RATING/ DIFFICULTY	ROUND-TRIP	ELEV GAIN/ HIGH POINT	SEASON
★★/2	9 miles	1100 feet/ 2800 feet	Apr– late Nov

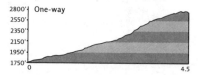

Map: Green Trails Wenatchee/Mission Ridge No. 211S; **Contact:** Okanogan-Wenatchee National Forest, Wenatchee River Ranger District, Leavenworth, (509) 548-6977, www.fs.fed.us/r6/wenatchee; **Notes:** NW Forest Pass required. Trail open to motorcycles and popular with mountain bikers. Be alert for rattlesnakes; **GPS:** N 47 23.878, W 120 30.072

Shadowed by sheer cliffs and decorated with sandstone spires, Devils Gulch is a deep valley rich in birdlife and diverse in vegetation. The heart of a 25,000-acre roadless area containing large tracts of primeval pines and exceptional wildlife habitat, the devil is in the details. The trail is open to dirt bikes and revered by fat-tire aficionados. Steer clear on weekends, and avoid this hike altogether in summer when Devils Gulch can get as hot as hell.

GETTING THERE

From Leavenworth head east on US 2 for 11 miles, turning right 6.4 miles east of the US 97 junction onto Aplets Way into Cashmere. (From Wenatchee travel west on US 2 for 8 miles.) Cross the Wenatchee River and proceed south through downtown Cashmere. In 0.6 mile Aplets Way veers right, becoming Division Street. Continue for 0.1 mile, and then turn left onto Mission Creek Road. In 0.5 mile turn right at a stop sign. Cross the creek and in 500 feet turn left, continuing on Mission Creek Road. Follow it for 6.2 miles to the pavement's end at an auto graveyard and junction. Continue left on Forest Road 71 for 2.5 miles to the trailhead (elev. 1750 ft). Privy available.

ON THE TRAIL

Devils Gulch makes for good early season wanderings while the high country is still

Ponderosa pines and even a few Douglas-firs grow among the rock formations along Devils Gulch.

blanketed white and the rattlesnakes haven't yet come out of their sleeping bags. However, the trail crosses Mission Creek four times, three of those times *sans pont*. During periods of heavy runoff, be prepared to cut your hike short at 3 miles.

Begin by immediately crossing Mission Creek on a solid bridge. Come to a junction and go left. The trail right is the start of a 15-mile loop of interest mostly to the wheeled set. In 0.2 mile come to another junction. The trail left leaves the valley for Mission Ridge (Hike 54). Stay right, following Mission Creek upstream to enter Devils Gulch.

Jesuit missionaries established a post at the mouth of Mission Creek back in the 1860s. Did the black robes shy away from the upper reaches of the creek? The demonic moniker for the canyon probably had more to do with the forbidding walls

and cliffs and the gargoyle-like outcroppings peering down from them.

In spring the gulch is quite heavenly, brushed with purples and yellows thanks to blossoming balsamroot, penstemon, and larkspur—somewhat Southwestern in appearance, but with a fraction of the lizards. At 1 mile reach a junction (elev. 1900 ft) with the trail to Red Hill, part of the aforementioned motor-happy loop. Continue left in cool forest, dropping down to creek level. Crossing side creeks and pulling away from Mission Creek upvalley, the trail carries on.

At 3 miles the trail crosses the creek (elev. 2300 ft) where there may or may not be a foot log. Once across, the trail climbs above the creek, traversing the gulch's sunny southern slopes. Descending slightly, enter a grove of big ponderosa pines before coming to the second ford of Mission Creek (elev. 2700 ft). Here, 4.5 miles from the trailhead, is a good place to have lunch and call it a hike.

EXTENDING YOUR TRIP
The best part of this trail lies farther along, and strong hikers should consider continuing. After fording the creek, carry on for 2.6 miles, darting into side gulches and traveling high above the creek before once again fording it (elev. 3500 ft). The trail then climbs 900 feet in 1.9 miles to Mission Ridge. En route the way passes spectacular vistas of the gulch and meanders through some of the finest groves of towering ancient ponderosa pines in the Cascades. Follow the Mission Ridge Trail back to your vehicle for a 17-mile loop.

Icicle River Valley
A major tributary to the Wenatchee River, the Icicle River starts high on the Cascade crest at Lake Josephine before flowing through a dramatic gorge. Much of the backcountry that fronts the Icicle River is protected within the Alpine Lakes Wilderness. The river acts as a portal into this land of lofty, jagged peaks and sparkling alpine lakes. Though this region is a ways from the population centers of Puget Sound, the bustling four-season resort town of Leavenworth sits at the confluence of the Wenatchee and Icicle rivers, providing a constant flow of hikers onto the area's spectacular trails.

56 Snow Lakes

RATING/ DIFFICULTY	ROUND-TRIP	ELEV GAIN/ HIGH POINT	SEASON
★★★★/5	13 miles	4185 feet/ 5500 feet	July–Oct

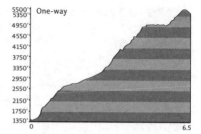

Map: Green Trails the Enchantments No. 209S; **Contact:** Okanogan-Wenatchee National Forest, Wenatchee River Ranger District, Leavenworth, (509) 548-6977, www.fs.fed .us/r6/wenatchee; **Notes:** NW Forest Pass required. Free day-use permit required, available at trailhead. Enchantment Permit required for overnight visits, available at Leavenworth Ranger Station. Dogs prohibited. Be aware of rattlesnakes at lower elevations; **GPS:** N 47 32.648, W 120 42.582

The Snow Lakes sit in one of the most spectacular basins within the entire Cascade Range—the largest of the legendary Enchantment Lakes, sparkling gems surrounded by spiraling walls of rock adorned with jagged turrets. Mostly the domain of backpackers, the Snows can be reached by strong day hikers. The Enchantments are popular, however, and in order to limit impact on this fragile and special environment the Forest Service has implemented a strict set of rules for visitation, including a quota system for overnighters. Day hikers limit themselves, primarily because of the long approach and stiff climb.

GETTING THERE
From milepost 99 on US 2, on the western edge of Leavenworth, follow the paved Icicle

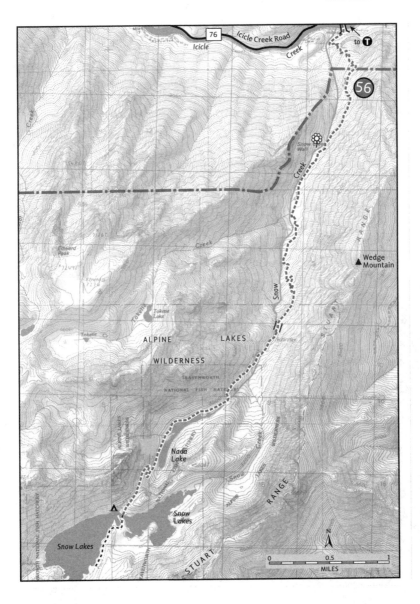

Creek Road (Forest Road 76) for 4.2 miles, turning left into a large parking lot at the trailhead (elev. 1350 ft). Privy available.

ON THE TRAIL

Start by dropping 50 feet to cross Icicle Creek on a big bridge. Follow an old road to the right to an irrigation canal. Take a minute or two here to scope for birds. The brushy creek banks provide excellent habitat for warblers and tanagers. Then on real trail, begin some real hiking! Climbing out of the Icicle Gorge, the trail switchbacks up hot and dusty rocky slopes denuded of shade thanks to wildfires in 1994 that burned more than 180,000 surrounding acres. Best to get an early start.

Lack of forest canopy also translates to views. Enjoy good ones west up the Icicle

Enchanting Upper Snow Lake and McClellan Peak (Craig Romano photo)

Gorge and north to Sugarloaf Mountain. Enjoy, too, the occasional residual groves of shade-providing green pines. At 1.2 miles enter the Alpine Lakes Wilderness (elev. 2200 ft). Now on a considerably easier grade, traverse the lower reaches of Wedge Mountain. With the impressive favored-by-climbers Snow Creek Wall across the way, the trail heads up a tight slot of a valley. Snow Creek crashes below, while heat radiates off of surrounding granite ledges and boulders.

At about 2.25 miles enter a cool grove of old cedars, a welcome relief from the heat. Pleasantly amble a ways creekside through refreshing forest before beginning another round of switchbacks. This time, however, they're much rougher and steeper as the trail heads up rocky gullies and across slides, working its way to a hanging valley.

At about 4.25 miles pass a showy cascade, and shortly afterward cross Snow Creek on a reliable bridge (elev. 4100 ft). Pleasant walking resumes as the trail passes a lot of nice spots along the creek for snacking and napping (or calling it quits). Farther along, the trail breaks out of forest to traverse a talus slope before arriving at Nada Lake at 5.5 miles (elev. 4900 ft), which is really quite a pleasant lake.

Take a break along the shallow finger lake, admiring its mountain reflections, or push on another mile, climbing up a hot talus slope to a forested gap (elev. 5450 ft) before dropping a tad to the Snow Lakes (elev. 5415 ft). Set in a wide-open basin beneath jagged and spiraling peaks, and separated by a small irrigation dam, these two lakes are among the largest in the Enchantments.

For the best viewing, napping, and feet-soaking spots, you'll need to walk across the dam. But with water cascading over it, it may appear intimidating. If the flow is low, just take it slow and you'll be good to go. Views of the 8292-foot Temple and the large, rocky, snow-blotched cirque beneath 8364-foot McClellan Peak from the pined shoreline of Upper Snow are awesome. The lower lake, with its shoreline of granite ledges, looks like it's right out of the Canadian Shield. You can spend days up here, and it's easy to see why most hikers do. Perhaps a return trip is in order with tent and sleeping bag. Just don't forget to apply for the permit.

WATER, WATER EVERYWHERE!

Within an approximately 50-mile-long rugged tract of the Cascades, tucked between US 2 and I-90, are more than 700 alpine lakes—one of the highest concentrations of mountain lakes anywhere. And because the area is wedged between two of the state's busiest highways, within an hour or two's drive for over half the state's population, it should come as no surprise that many of these beautiful high-country lakes are among the most popular in the Cascades.

In 1968 a group of concerned citizens formed the Alpine Lakes Protection Society (ALPS) to help protect this special area from logging, off-road vehicles, and other threatening activities. After nearly a decade of hard work by citizens, legislation spearheaded by Democratic congressman Lloyd Meeds was passed by Congress in 1976, creating the 393,360-acre Alpine Lakes Wilderness Area.

Now, due to the area's overwhelming popularity, the Alpine Lakes need protection from the very people who sought to protect them. In essence, large numbers of hikers and equestrians are loving the Alpine Lakes Wilderness to death. To protect this fragile area from overuse, the Forest Service has implemented additional rules along with the usual regulations that apply to all wilderness areas (such as party size limits and prohibition of bicycles and motorized equipment). Most of the more restrictive rules apply to trails and lakes along the I-90 corridor in the Snoqualmie Pass region. But several areas of the Alpine Lakes Wilderness within the Central Cascades also carry additional regulations.

Many of these rules apply to overnight visits, especially in the Enchantment Basin, where numbers are limited through a permit lottery. Dogs are restricted too in much of the Alpine Lakes. In the Enchantments they are prohibited. In other areas, such as most of the trails along US 2 west of Stevens Pass, they must be on-leash. And unlike many other national forest areas, the rules are strictly enforced here. Backcountry rangers patrol and will issue citations for camping and dog violations.

Throughout most of the Alpine Lakes, day-use permits are also required. They are available free at trailheads. The intent is mostly for you to become familiar with wilderness rules and with Leave No Trace backcountry travel and camping principles. Be sure you take the time to familiarize yourself with these principles. If ever in doubt about regulations, call the appropriate ranger district.

The regulations aren't meant to restrict your freedom within the Alpine Lakes Wilderness—they're meant to ensure that a healthy and wild landscape remains for you to visit. Do your part to help maintain the ecological integrity of this spectacular and special place by practicing good stewardship and responsible hiking.

57 Colchuck Lake

RATING/ DIFFICULTY	ROUND-TRIP	ELEV GAIN/ HIGH POINT	SEASON
★★★★★/4	8.4 miles	2200 feet/ 5600 feet	July– mid-Oct

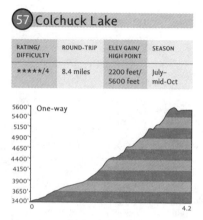

Map: Green Trails the Enchantments No. 209S; **Contact:** Okanogan-Wenatchee National Forest, Wenatchee River Ranger District, Leavenworth, (509) 548-6977, www .fs.fed.us/r6/wenatchee; **Notes:** NW Forest Pass required. Free day-use permit required, available at trailhead. Enchantment Permit required for overnight visits, available at Leavenworth Ranger Station. Dogs prohibited; **GPS:** N 47 31.662, W 120 49.259

Set in a granite bathtub beneath spiraling peaks dabbed with shimmering strings of glacial ice, Colchuck ranks as one of the most beautiful alpine lakes in all of Washington. And one of the most popular too! Can you resist the lure of Colchuck's sparkling cobalt waters? Or being mesmerized by her glacial-scoured surroundings that appear right out of the High Sierra? I didn't think so. But before joining the boot-beating brigade, be forewarned. The hike isn't easy. It involves a knee knocking ascent over some pretty steep and rocky terrain.

GETTING THERE

From milepost 99 on US 2, on the western edge of Leavenworth, follow the paved Icicle Creek Road (Forest Road 76) for 8.4 miles,

Dragontail and Colchuck peaks tower above Colchuck Lake.

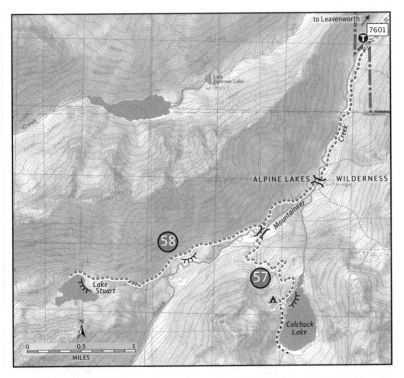

turning left onto Eightmile Road (FR 7601). Continue on this washboarded dirt road for 3.8 miles to a large parking lot and the trailhead (elev. 3400 ft). Privy available.

ON THE TRAIL

Immediately entering cool, dark forest, the trail starts off easy enough, following alongside sensory-pleasing Mountaineer Creek. Soon after crossing into the Alpine Lakes Wilderness, transition into open lodgepole pine forest.

On decent tread and good grade, weave through big boulders and cross bubbling side creeks, all while staying within constant eyesight and earshot of tumbling Mountaineer Creek. At about 1.75 miles (elev. 4000 ft) cross Mountaineer Creek on an attractive log bridge spanning deep pools fed by crashing rapids. The trail now begins to climb in earnest—through fields of big boulders, up and around granite ledges, and through open forest granting views of the craggy Enchantment peaks. You'll notice a considerable increase in temperature too on these sun-kissed slopes.

The way eases before coming to a junction at 2.5 miles (elev. 4500 ft). The main trail continues straight for a fairly easy amble to Lake Stuart (Hike 58). Hang left instead for the more challenging and more scenic journey. Cross Mountaineer Creek once again, and then work your way through a boulder field alongside the creek, maintaining balance and dry boots. The trail reenters forest to cross a devil's club–cloaked creek, makes a big sweep up ledges, recrosses the creek, and then heads up a steep rocky stretch, passing a small cascade.

Now ascending a series of granite ledges between steep stretches of rocky and rooty tread, the way continues its abrupt climb. A short drop of 50 feet or so may dampen spirits. But growing views of the valley and surrounding peaks should help recharge them. The sheer volume of scoured granite above and below may give California transplants a Yosemite flashback or two.

But all will rejoice upon reaching the deep rocky pocket cradling the lake. A short spur takes off left 0.1 mile to a small lagoon on Colchuck's south end, where breathtaking views of the backdrop spires Dragontail and Colchuck peaks can be enjoyed. Tucked between that pair of precipitous peaks is the Colchuck Glacier, one of the many icy sources feeding the chilling waters of the lake. Colchuck is derived from the Chinook Jargon meaning "cold water."

Feel free to explore the lakeshore, looking for sunny slabs, perfect for snacking and napping. But treat this area with care. Despite the durable appearance, plants have a tough time surviving in this harsh environment. Keep to rock and use the available backcountry privy if nature calls.

EXTENDING YOUR TRIP

The trail continues for another mile along Colchuck's western and southern shore, passing by backcountry campsites and through stunning lakeside scenery. Beyond,

the way continues as a climber's route to 7800-foot Aasgard Pass. Only experienced and extremely fit off-trail travelers should consider attempting this taxing and potentially dangerous climb involving 2200 feet of elevation gain in less than a mile.

58 Lake Stuart

RATING/ DIFFICULTY	ROUND-TRIP	ELEV GAIN/ HIGH POINT	SEASON
★★★/3	10 miles	1665 feet/ 5065 feet	July–Oct

Map: Green Trails the Enchantments No. 209S; **Contact:** Okanogan-Wenatchee National Forest, Wenatchee River Ranger District, Leavenworth, (509) 548-6977, www.fs.fed.us/r6/wenatchee; **Notes:** NW Forest Pass required. Free day-use permit required, available at trailhead. Enchantment Permit required for overnight visits, available at Leavenworth Ranger Station. Dogs prohibited; **GPS:** N 47 31.662, W 120 49.259

Lake Stuart is an inviting lake beneath the fearsome north face of one of Washington's highest and most imposing peaks. Though not as dramatic as nearby Colchuck Lake, Stuart still serves up plenty of nice scenery, including a close-up of the 9415-foot peak that shares its name. The journey is longer than to Colchuck, but much easier due to Stuart's lower elevation and the gentler topography on the way. Stuart is smaller and shallower than Colchuck, too, but warmer—by late summer, warm enough to even splash in. Try that in nearby Colchuck, whose name means "cold water!"

GETTING THERE

From milepost 99 on US 2, on the western edge of Leavenworth, follow the paved Icicle Creek Road (Forest Road 76) for 8.4 miles, turning left onto Eightmile Road (FR 7601). Continue on this washboarded dirt road for 3.8 miles to a large parking lot and the trailhead (elev. 3400 ft). Privy available.

ON THE TRAIL

The Lake Stuart Trail starts easy, kicks up a little dust, settles down, then makes one last push, albeit moderate, before emerging in the forested basin housing the aquatic object of your desire. Begin your hike in cool forest, soon entering the Alpine Lakes Wilderness. Follow alongside the tumbling and chattering Mountaineer Creek and enjoy an air-conditioning effect thanks to flows of heavy cool air constantly funneling down this tight valley. At about 1.75 miles (elev. 4000 ft) cross Mountaineer Creek on an attractive log bridge. Then begin a short but grueling grunt up sun-kissed slopes of open forest interspersed with slabs of granite.

At 2.5 miles the grade relaxes and a junction is reached (elev. 4500 ft). The trail left leads to Colchuck Lake (Hike 57) and is where the majority of hikers heading up this valley end up. Good. Now, you can enjoy your trip to Stuart even more. The way continues up the Mountaineer Creek valley on a near-level course. Soon break out of the cool forest into a brushy meadow, affording a splendid view of an almost-dead-ringer for Mount Stuart, its smaller twin, 8453-foot Argonaut Peak.

Cross the base of a boulder field, return-

Argonaut Peak and the Stuart Range hover above meadows on the hike to Lake Stuart.

ing to forest, this time of the lodgepole pine persuasion. The trail pulls away from the creek, continuing up the wide valley, undulating between forest and meadow, gaining very little elevation en route. Meeting up again with Mountaineer Creek at about 4.5 miles, the way commences a short climb via a series of short switchbacks. With the creek now tumbling beside you, pass through groves of aspen that warrant a return trip in autumn for a golden showing.

At 5 miles reach Lake Stuart (elev. 5065), surrounded by tall timber and tall peaks. Much of the shoreline is rocky and forested, but you can find grassy and sandy spots perfect for sunning and wading. Find a nice spot on the north shore for staring out across the placid waters to imposing Mount Stuart with its hanging glaciers. Consider bringing your fishing pole—the cutthroat are jumping.

59 Eightmile Lake

RATING/ DIFFICULTY	ROUND-TRIP	ELEV GAIN/ HIGH POINT	SEASON
★★★/2	6.6 miles	1300 feet/ 4650 feet	Late June– Oct

Map: Green Trails the Enchantments No. 209S; **Contact:** Okanogan-Wenatchee National Forest, Wenatchee River Ranger District, Leavenworth, (509) 548-6977, www.fs.fed .us/r6/wenatchee; **Notes:** NW Forest Pass required. Free day-use permit required, available at trailhead. Enchantment Permit required for overnight visits, available at Leavenworth Ranger Station. Dogs prohibited; **GPS:** N 47 32.158, W 120 48.834

Eightmile is a gorgeous, big back-country lake ideal for quick escapes when the thermometer is pushing 100 in the Wenatchee Valley. But get an early start to beat the heat. The first half of this hike traverses an open burn zone that'll leave you scorched by the sun. Plop yourself down on a shoreline rock and soak up the soothing backdrop of Eightmile Mountain, which is oft-reflected in the lake's placid waters.

GETTING THERE

From milepost 99 on US 2, on the western edge of Leavenworth, follow the paved Icicle Creek Road (Forest Road 76) for 8.4 miles, turning left onto Eightmile Road (FR 7601). Continue on this washboarded dirt road for

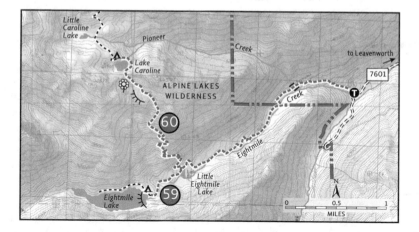

Eightmile Mountain forms a backdrop for Eightmile Lake.

3.1 miles to the trailhead. Park opposite the trailhead, on the left side of the road (elev. 3300 ft). Privy available.

ON THE TRAIL

The way starts off with a steady climb up open slopes punctuated with ponderosa pine. Roaring Eightmile Creek nearby provides a deafening score, drowning out birdsong and insect buzz. Heading into the heart of a massive burn zone from a 1990s forest fire, the trail and its environs warms up rapidly once the sun casts its rays. Pioneering fireweed growing head high flourishes along the trail.

After crossing a side creek, intersect an old logging road, once used as the trail's approach. At 0.75 mile cross tumbling Pioneer Creek on a steady foot log (elev. 3800 ft). Shortly afterward enter the Alpine Lakes Wilderness, following Eightmile Creek up the broad valley. Most of the way, the going is fairly easy. At 2.8 miles reach a junction with the trail to Lake Caroline (Hike 60) at the mud hole of a pond, Little Eightmile Lake (elev. 4450 ft).

Continue straight, crossing a massive rock slide peeping with pikas. Giant sandstone boulders litter the way, and hiking tykes will probably enjoy flitting about them. Brush up against maddening Eightmile Creek, making a short, steep ascent to its source, Eightmile Lake. Like many of the lakes in the Leavenworth area, this one sports an irrigation dam and a "washtub ring" from its fluctuating levels.

Scout the shoreline for good sunning and swimming spots. A trail continues along the north shore for nearly a mile to the lake's inlet creek. Check it out, or just settle down on a nearby ledge and gaze out at a jagged ridgeline reflected in crystal waters.

60 Lake Caroline

RATING/ DIFFICULTY	ROUND-TRIP	ELEV GAIN/ HIGH POINT	SEASON
★★★/4	11.5 miles	3100 feet/ 6300 feet	July–Oct

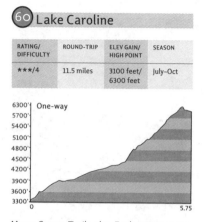

Map: Green Trails the Enchantments No. 209S; **Contact:** Okanogan-Wenatchee National Forest, Wenatchee River Ranger District, Leavenworth, (509) 548-6977, www .fs.fed.us/r6/wenatchee; **Notes:** NW Forest Pass required. Free day-use permit required, available at trailhead. Enchantment Permit required for overnight visits, available at Leavenworth Ranger Station. Dogs prohibited; **GPS:** N 47 32.158, W 120 48.834

⚙️ *Sweet Caroline, set high in a hidden basin between 7996-foot Eightmile Mountain and 8501-foot Cashmere Mountain, will no doubt have you singing (Neil Diamond or other) tunes from its peaceful shoreline. But you'll probably be muttering some not-so-sweet things as you toil up the steep and hot trail to reach it. There's a reason why Lake Caroline receives only a fraction of the visitors that the nearby alpine lakes do. Such is the price for solitude in the land of the Enchantments.*

GETTING THERE

From milepost 99 on US 2, on the western edge of Leavenworth, follow the paved Icicle

View across Lake Caroline to Windy Pass

Creek Road (Forest Road 76) for 8.4 miles, turning left onto Eightmile Road (FR 7601). Continue on this washboarded dirt road for 3.1 miles to the trailhead. Park opposite the trailhead, on the left side of the road (elev. 3300 ft). Privy available.

ON THE TRAIL

Start on the Eightmile Lake Trail (Hike 59), climbing steadily at first up open slopes scorched by forest fire in the 1990s. At 1 mile or so enter the Alpine Lakes Wilderness and continue on a more gentle incline, paralleling Eightmile Creek. At 2.8 miles, just after passing the fraction of a pond, Little Eightmile Lake, come to a signed junction (elev. 4450 ft). The trail straight ahead continues 0.5 mile to beautiful, big Eightmile Lake. Take the trail right, the one less traveled.

Brushy at times and sizzling when the sun is shining, the way climbs steeply, switchbacking up slopes that are slowly recovering from the big burn of 1994. Views increase with elevation gain: Little Eightmile Lake, then Eightmile Lake, then the Stuart Range and Enchantment peaks.

At about 4 miles cross a few small creeks (elev. 5350 ft) before traversing a grove of silver snags. After passing by some sandstone boulders, the grade eases and the way slowly transitions into unburnt territory. A series of meadows teeming with birdlife and more than likely a few mammals too is a welcome sight. Pass patches of whitebark pine, and where there's *Pinus albicaulis* there are Clark's nutcrackers.

At about 5.5 miles reach a small "pass" (elev. 6300 ft). Then drop quickly and steeply under a cool forest canopy, reaching Caroline Lake (elev. 6190 ft) in about 0.25 mile. Set in a semi-open bowl, the lake sports big sun-kissed logs on its shallow north shore—good

posts for gazing and grazing. Watch the fish jump. They're loving the bugs you're not!

EXTENDING YOUR TRIP

There is plenty of spectacular high country ahead, beckoning you to explore. Continue on the trail, passing backcountry campsites near Caroline's outlet, and ascend a ledgy meadow providing a nice view of Caroline's greenish waters reflecting craggy knolls. About 0.6 mile from Caroline is Little Caroline Lake, flanked by verdant slopes. Very strong hikers can continue for another 1.7 miles to 7200-foot Windy Pass on the shoulder of Cashmere Mountain for supreme viewing of peaks and plateaus near and far.

61 Icicle Ridge via Fourth of July Creek

RATING/ DIFFICULTY	ROUND-TRIP	ELEV GAIN/ HIGH POINT	SEASON
★★★★/5	12 miles	4370 feet/ 7020 feet	June–Oct

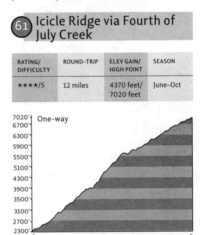

Map: Green Trails Chiwaukum Mtns No. 177; **Contact:** Okanogan-Wenatchee National Forest, Wenatchee River Ranger District, Leavenworth, (509) 548-6977, www.fs.fed.us/r6/wenatchee; **Notes:** NW Forest Pass required. Free day-use permit required, available at trailhead. Rattlesnakes common along lower portions of trail; **GPS:** N 47 34.696, W 120 47.811

A hiker crests Icicle Ridge from the Fourth of July Creek Trail, with Cashmere Mountain rising to the south. (Craig Romano photo)

🔧 🏠 *Don't let this hike's bad reputation dissuade you from reaping its good views. Sure, it's one of the snakiest trails in the Icicle Valley—save it for a cool day. And yeah, it's one of the steepest trails in the valley—hottest too—best to save it for a cool day. And total vertical feet—oh boy, you'll gain plenty—so save it for a cool day when the serpents are sedate. Are you getting the picture? But the views are amazing: from the Chiwaukum to the Entiat to the Stuart ranges and beyond—savor the panorama on any day!*

GETTING THERE

From milepost 99 on US 2, on the western edge of Leavenworth, follow the paved Icicle Creek Road (Forest Road 76) for 9.4 miles to the trailhead, located on your right (elev. 2300 ft).

ON THE TRAIL

There's no easy way up Icicle Ridge. The Fourth of July Creek Trail provides one of the shorter routes, but though it reaches the ridge crest in a little more than a mile, it climbs nearly a vertical mile in the process. The switchbacks are relentless, and for most of the season so is the heat. Traversing south-facing slopes, the trail takes the full brunt of the east-side-of-the-Cascade-crest sun. But there's a bonus to that aspect. This trail often melts out by mid-May, providing early season high-country probing while surrounding trails remain buried in winter's white. In any season, though, take plenty of water along.

Start amid some big pines and firs. Cross Fourth of July Creek at 0.25 mile and start shooting for the stars. Through pine parklands and aspen groves, the fern- and bitterbrush-lined trail winds upward. Cross the creek once more and then begin to switchback like there's no tomorrow.

Up open slopes punctuated by massive ponderosa pines—climb! In early season marvel at the floral show spread out before you. In any season cherish the views expanding before you. At about 2 miles a spring (elev. 4700 ft) may be bubbling—but don't count on it. A little farther come upon one of the biggest ponderosas this side of the Black Hills. At about 3.5 miles the grade eases and the trail makes a long traverse before resuming its switchbacks.

At about 4.3 miles is another possibly flowing spring (elev. 5750 ft). Continue climbing through silver forest and rock gardens before making another long traverse. Across grassy slopes graced with whitebark pine, make one final slog, coming to the 6775-foot crest of Icicle Ridge and a trail junction at 5.7 miles.

Muster up what little energy you have left and head left on the Icicle Ridge Trail

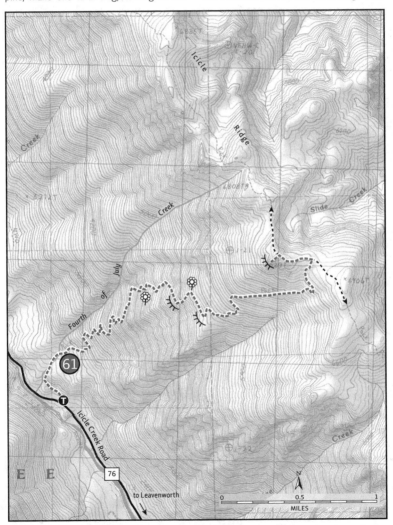

for 0.2 mile to a junction signed "lookout site." Hang left once more and scramble 500 feet to within 10 feet of the 7029-foot former fire lookout site. The 1929-built lookout actually sat right on the rocky thumb. The steps and railings are now gone and so should be any desire to attain the true summit. Stay safe and enjoy the amazing panoramic views right before you. East it's Mission Ridge and the Entiat Range. North it's the Chelan Range, Glacier Peak, Poet Ridge, and the White Mountains. To the west, scan Icicle Ridge to Big Jim, Grindstone, and out to Daniel. And south it's the Stuart Range and that big mountain right in front of you, Cashmere. What a view! Worth every step.

EXTENDING YOUR TRIP

You've worked hard to get here, so feel free to just hang out at the lookout site. But if you're itchy to explore, fairly easy wanderings can be had by following the Icicle Ridge Trail for a mile or so in either direction.

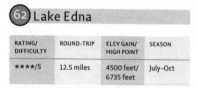

62 Lake Edna

RATING/ DIFFICULTY	ROUND-TRIP	ELEV GAIN/ HIGH POINT	SEASON
★★★★/5	12.5 miles	4500 feet/ 6735 feet	July–Oct

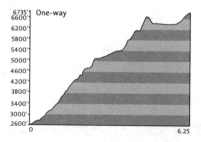

Map: Green Trails Chiwaukum Mtns No. 177; **Contact:** Okanogan-Wenatchee National Forest, Wenatchee River Ranger District, Leavenworth, (509) 548-6977, www.fs.fed. us/r6/wenatchee; **Notes:** NW Forest Pass required. Free day-use permit required, available at trailhead. **GPS:** N 47 36.513, W 120 52.922

❌ ⚙ *Reaching this alpine gem high on Icicle Ridge requires tenacity and determination. The trail along Chatter Creek is steep, hot, rocky, brushy, and eroded. And just when you think you're done climbing, you'll drop a few hundred feet and then climb some more. But the flowered meadows, and tundra slopes, and precariously perched larches, and the awesome views of nearby lofty peaks . . . make it all worth it!*

GETTING THERE

From milepost 99 on US 2, at the western edge of Leavenworth, follow the Icicle Creek Road (Forest Road 76) for 14.5 miles (the pavement ends at 12.3 miles) to the trailhead, just east of the Chatter Creek Guard Station (elev. 2600 ft).

ON THE TRAIL

The trail starts off easy enough, winding gently through ponderosa pine groves on good tread. But after crossing Chatter Creek on a bridge at 1 mile (elev. 3000 ft), the grade stiffens, the tread deteriorates, and brush moves in (when was the last time this trail saw a pair of loppers?). Enter wilderness and begin to wildly climb.

At about 1.7 miles (elev. 4100 ft), catch a view south of the slide responsible for forcing Icicle Creek to jump its bed. Notice that it originated from an old clear-cut (draw your own conclusions). At 2 miles, just after skirting a talus slope, recross Chatter Creek, this time without aid of a bridge. Old fir forest soon yields to brushy willow, while the tread gets rockier.

A reprieve from climbing comes at 2.5 miles as the trail eases into a hanging valley (elev. 5000 ft). Forest cover gives way to rock gardens, with views limited to the great northern rocky face of Grindstone Mountain.

There's more tough going ahead as you start working your way over a headwall where Chatter Creek cascades through heather meadows and over granite ledges. Push on to a small gap along the lofty ridge crest (elev. 6680 ft). Here, 4.5 miles from the trailhead, enjoy a breathtaking view of Cashmere Mountain to the south, Big Jim and Icicle Ridge to the east, and down the Index Valley to the north. And speaking of down, the trail now drops steeply 300 feet into a lonely basin of talus and larch. Snow lingers here well into July and may create a difficult descent and require some routefinding.

Skirt left of campsites and small tarns to traverse a jumbled pile of rocks. Good tread returns as the trail drops into a small basin of gurgling streams and lush meadows (elev. 6275 ft). Come to a post denoting a junction. Ignore the fading tread right, choosing instead the more obvious way left that heads up a gully alongside a cascading creek. Then cross the creek and head up a steep side slope, reaching a junction with the Icicle Ridge Trail at 5.75 miles.

Lake Edna lies 0.5 mile and 300 vertical feet up to the left. A carpet of wildflowers leads the way into the semibarren basin that houses the twinkling alpine lake. Cape Horn looms over the icy cold waters, a stunning backdrop. Tenacious flowers enhance the

Outcrop of pink flowering heather on the shores of Lake Edna

rocky and grassy shores, while a smattering of larches add a soft golden touch later in the season. Despite the rugged nature of this place, it is quite fragile. Explore with care, and if you care to spend the night, do so at least 200 feet from the shoreline.

EXTENDING YOUR TRIP

If you can muster up a little more energy, continue west toward Ladies Pass and locate the

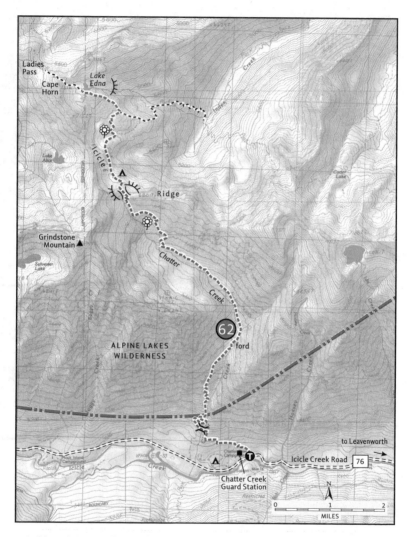

scramble path up 7316-foot Cape Horn. The extra 0.5 mile and 600 feet of climbing yields sweeping views of the Chiwaukums, Icicle Ridge, and the Wenatchee Mountains.

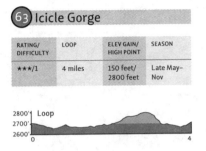

63 Icicle Gorge

RATING/ DIFFICULTY	LOOP	ELEV GAIN/ HIGH POINT	SEASON
★★★/1	4 miles	150 feet/ 2800 feet	Late May– Nov

Map: Green Trails Chiwaukum Mtns No. 177; **Contact:** Okanogan-Wenatchee National Forest, Wenatchee River Ranger District, Leavenworth, (509) 548-6977, www.fs.fed.us/r6/wenatchee; **Notes:** NW Forest Pass required. Free day-use permit required, available at trailhead. **GPS:** N 47 36.513, W 120 53.672

A delightful loop along a tight gorge carved by the Icicle River, this hike makes for a perfect early and late-season leg stretcher. Its good tread and gentle terrain also make it ideal for children, first-time hikers, and those trying to get back into the groove. Leisurely stroll along this major tributary of the Wenatchee River, watching for darting dippers and admiring raucous rapids and swirling pools.

GETTING THERE
From milepost 99 on US 2, at the western edge of Leavenworth, follow the Icicle Creek Road (Forest Road 76) for 15.3 miles (the pavement ends at 12.3 miles), passing the Chatter Creek Guard Station and reaching the trailhead on the left (south) side of the road (elev. 2700 ft). Privy available.

ON THE TRAIL
From the trailhead kiosk, veer right. The trail left leads to the Icicle Gorge View Trail

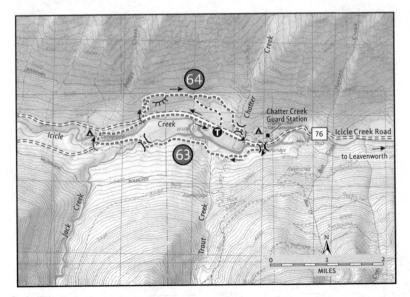

(Hike 64). In 0.1 mile you'll come to the Icicle Gorge River Trail. Left or right, it's your choice. I prefer heading downstream first.

Turning left, follow the good trail through a diverse forest of conifers. Undulate between open pine and cool, dark fir stands. Take time to read the interpretive signs. After crossing Chatter Creek come to a junction with the Gorge View Trail. Continue straight, coming to nice viewing spots of the gorge below. Take a short diversion to check out the old Chatter Creek Guard Station, but respect the privacy of anyone who may be spending the evening there.

The trail drops down to cross the creek (elev. 2650 ft) on a well-photographed bridge at a well-photographed section of the water-sculptured gorge. Now heading upriver, pass great viewpoints of rapids and cascades. Cross a cedar swamp, Trout Creek, and various outwashes and channels and tempting huckleberry patches.

The creek mellows as the trail travels alongside it through open pine and fir forest. Cross Jack Creek and soon after come to FR 76 at the Rock Island Campground at 2.5 miles. Turn right, crossing Icicle Creek (elev. 2800 ft) on the road bridge, picking up the trail once again at the edge of the campground. Then travel downriver to more excellent gorge views.

Pass the junction with the western terminus of the Gorge View Trail. Continue downstream through cedar groves and along scenic bluffs, occasionally brushing up against FR 76. At 3.9 miles arrive back at the spur trail leading to the trailhead. Not a bad little loop, huh?

EXTENDING YOUR TRIP

Increase your mileage by including the Icicle Gorge View Trail (Hike 64). Spend the night at the very nice Chatter Creek or Rock Island campgrounds, and hit this trail after dinner for an excellent evening hike.

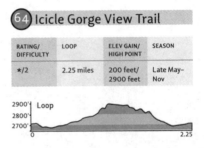

64 Icicle Gorge View Trail

RATING/ DIFFICULTY	LOOP	ELEV GAIN/ HIGH POINT	SEASON
★/2	2.25 miles	200 feet/ 2900 feet	Late May– Nov

Map: Green Trails Chiwaukum Mtns No. 177; **Contact:** Okanogan-Wenatchee National Forest, Wenatchee River Ranger District, Leavenworth, (509) 548-6977, www.fs.fed .us/r6/wenatchee; **Notes:** NW Forest Pass required. Free day-use permit required, available at trailhead. **GPS:** N 47 36.513, W 120 53.672

Can't get enough of the Icicle Gorge? But need to escape the hubbub of the Icicle Gorge River Trail? Venture on this path less chosen, then—the Icicle Gorge View Trail. Here you'll be able to enjoy the river's roar and soak up views of the glacier-created valley cradling it, all by your lonesome. But prepare for some brush, as this trail is yet another in the long line of our trails in danger of vanishing if it doesn't receive some much needed maintenance soon.

Opposite: Icicle Creek Gorge from the main bridge over Icicle Creek

Views down the Icicle Creek valley from the Icicle Gorge View Trail

GETTING THERE

From milepost 99 on US 2, at the western edge of Leavenworth, follow the Icicle Creek Road (Forest Road 76) for 15.3 miles (the pavement ends at 12.3 miles), passing the Chatter Creek Guard Station and reaching the trailhead (elev. 2700 ft). Privy available.

ON THE TRAIL

From the trailhead kiosk, veer right, ignoring the other trail to the left that leads to the Icicle Gorge View Trail. That section of trail is a brushy mess and not worth the scratches you'll endure. In 0.1 mile come to the Icicle Gorge River Trail, which you'll hike a bit to access the Gorge View Trail and make a loop. Turn right (though you can do this in reverse if you prefer), heading upstream along the delightfully beautiful Icicle Creek.

Traversing cedar groves and scenic bluffs, savor the river and all of its beauty. After 0.6 mile or so, come to a junction with the Icicle Gorge View Trail. Turn right, cross FR 76, and then gently start climbing, emerging onto a small bluff with good views of the Icicle Ridge, Bootjack Mountain, and the Jack and Trout Creek valleys.

Continuing along, climb a little more, coming to signed junction (elev. 2900 ft) with the brushy trail I told you earlier to ignore. Proceed straight on the main path, coming to more viewing areas and a couple of overgrown brushy areas. Gently descending, pass through an open grove of ponderosa pines (the old Chatter Creek trailhead), and then enter a cedar grove along Chatter Creek.

Cross the babbling brook into the Chatter Creek Campground, and then follow the trail downstream. Recross FR 76 and return to the Gorge River Trail. Then turn right, heading upstream along Icicle Creek to return to your vehicle in about 0.3 mile.

65 Trout Lake

RATING/ DIFFICULTY	ROUND-TRIP	ELEV GAIN/ HIGH POINT	SEASON
★★★/3	11.5 miles	2000 feet/ 4800 feet	Late June–Oct

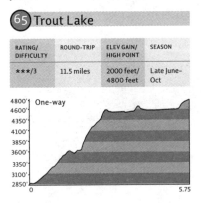

Map: Green Trails Chiwaukum Mtns No. 177; **Contact:** Okanogan-Wenatchee National Forest, Wenatchee River Ranger District, Leavenworth, (509) 548-6977, www.fs.fed .us/r6/wenatchee; **Notes:** NW Forest Pass required. Free day-use permit required, available at trailhead. **GPS:** N 47 36.354, W 120 55.022

In an area of spectacular alpine lakes, Trout rates as so-so. At this lake, tucked in a wooded basin with limited views of Eightmile Mountain's craggy ridges, you won't be oohing and ahhing from its grassy shoreline. But if it's peaceful wanderings you seek, Trout won't let you down. The forest is attractive, and both Jack and Trout creeks add musical scores to it. There are some good views, too, out to Icicle Ridge, and in October stands of western larch stain the slopes bright yellow.

GETTING THERE

From milepost 99 on US 2, at the western edge of Leavenworth, follow the Icicle Creek Road (Forest Road 76) for 16.3 miles (the pavement ends at 12.3 miles) to Rock Island Campground. Turn left, crossing Icicle Creek, and after 0.2 mile turn left onto FR Spur 615 (signed "Jack/Trout Trailhead"). In 0.2 mile bear right to trailhead parking (elev. 2850 ft). Privy available.

ON THE TRAIL

Upon starting off, immediately come to a junction with the Jack Pine Trail coming in from the right, a popular path with the equestrian crowd. Continue left instead on the Jack Creek Trail. After crossing an old clear-cut yielding an excellent view of Grindstone Mountain across the valley, come to a sturdy bridge spanning crashing Jack Creek.

The trail enters the Alpine Lakes Wilderness and in mature timber pulls away from the boisterous waterway to climb a bluff well above it. At 1.2 miles, come to a junction (elev. 3500 ft). The trail straight continues up the Jack Creek valley. Take the path left, ascending a slope that sports attractive groves of larch, cedar, spruce, and fir.

After a few twists and turns, the trail brushes up against a boulder field with a nice view up the Icicle Creek valley. Leaving the Jack Creek drainage, the way gently contours along a ridge and enters the Trout Creek drainage. Then you leave the wilderness area and enter a huge old cut, a legacy of the railroad checkerboard

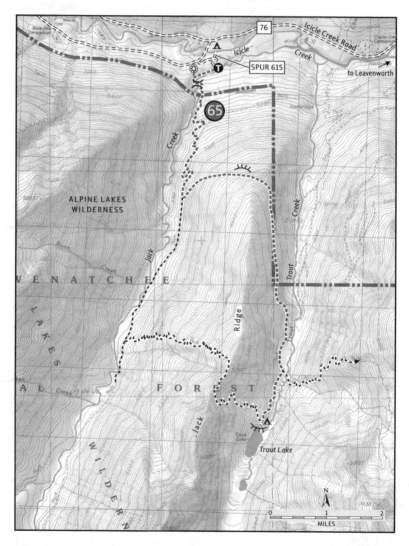

Trout Lake beneath Jack Ridge

grants. Conservationists and government officials weren't able to transfer this area into the national forest before most of its valuable timber was stripped in the 1980s. The silver lining to the stumps and scraggly new growth are the nice views out to Icicle Ridge and Cashmere Mountain.

The way now turns south to traverse the top of the cut, which is nearly a mile long, except for one small interrupting section of forest. Finally reenter wilderness, descending slightly toward Trout Creek and crossing numerous side creeks and gorgeous protected groves of ancient cedars. At 5.25 miles reach a junction (elev. 4575 ft). The trail left leads to Eightmile and Caroline lakes (Hikes 59 and 60) via 7200-foot Windy Pass. It's an arduous and awesome journey.

Carry on forward for another 0.5 mile to Trout Lake (elev. 4800 ft), skirting wetlands and traversing hemlock stands and white pine groves en route. Shallow and surrounded by forest and marshy shoreline, Trout isn't a stunning alpine lake. But its tranquil location in a deep valley beneath rugged, almost 8000-foot Eightmile Mountain should bring some satisfaction.

EXTENDING YOUR TRIP

The Jack Ridge Trail veers from the lake west, rapidly climbing 900 feet before dropping 2000 feet en route to Jack Creek. It used to make for a nice albeit tough 12-mile loop. Unfortunately, this trail currently can't be recommended—another casualty of Forest Service neglect (due to inadequate funding), it's a brushy, windfall nightmare.

66 Bootjack Mountain

RATING/ DIFFICULTY	ROUND-TRIP	ELEV GAIN/ HIGH POINT	SEASON
★★★/5	8 miles	3900 feet/ 6789 feet	July–Oct

One-way

Map: Green Trails Chiwaukum Mtns No. 177; **Contact:** Okanogan-Wenatchee National Forest, Wenatchee River Ranger District, Leavenworth, (509) 548-6977, www.fs.fed.us/r6/wenatchee; **Notes:** NW Forest Pass required. Free day-use permit required, available at trailhead. **GPS:** N 47 36.605, W 120 56.704

⚙ *A brutally steep trail—one of the steepest in the Icicle Creek valley— the way to Bootjack may well have you ripping your boots off once you're down, eager to soak your sore tootsies. But the relentless climb is worth it, delivering you to a high ridge where alpine breezes whistle through silver snags and dazzling wildflowers dance beneath them. Then follow a scramble path to Bootjack's summit, where it's the knockout panoramic views that will knock your boots off.*

GETTING THERE

From milepost 99 on US 2, at the western edge of Leavenworth, follow the Icicle Creek Road (Forest Road 76) for 16.3 miles (the pavement ends at 12.3 miles) to Rock Island Campground. Turn left, crossing Icicle Creek, and after 1.4 miles come to the trailhead (elev. 2850 ft), located just before the Black Pine Creek Horse Camp.

ON THE TRAIL

One positive thing that can be said about this trail's steepness is that it keeps the folks on other trails. You're more apt to greet a bear than a fellow hiker on this lonesome path. Immediately begin in gorgeous old-growth forest that'll have you sounding like you're from Philadelphia as you keep exclaiming, "hey, yews!" The understory is plush with Pacific yews.

Shortly after starting, come to a junction with a spur heading to the horse camp. Turn left and within minutes come to another junction. Turn right, following the Blackjack Ridge Trail to Bootjack. After negotiating a few brushy sections, the trail enters the Alpine Lakes Wilderness and commences to climb on good tread.

At about 3700 feet, pass a small spring, the last reliable water source along the way. Then steepness intensifies. At about 4300 feet, the way takes a short respite from climbing, but then it's back to the grind up

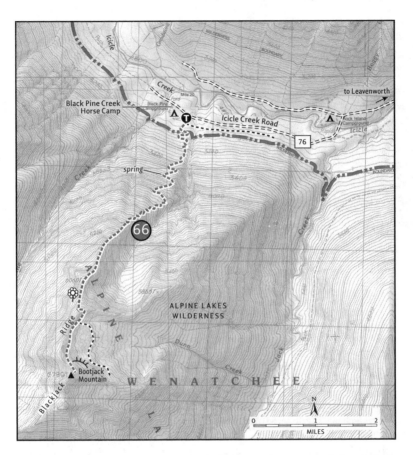

a steep rib. At about 2.75 miles, break out of forest into meadow (elev. 5900 ft). Now begin to reap the scenic rewards that justify all this toil.

Along a ridge awash in yellow and purple blossoms and punctuated with ghostly silver snags, continue gaining elevation. Savor the alpine views along with the flowers. Cashmere Mountain lies directly east across

Jack Creek. Snowgrass, Grindstone, and Icicle Ridge fill the northern sky. Sloan, Pugh, Baker, and Glacier can be seen in the northwest.

The rocky summit of Bootjack Mountain is revealed at 3.25 miles upon rounding a shoulder (elev. 6225 ft). Call it a day here, or continue toward the summit, walking southwest off-trail up the shoulder. You'll soon pick up tread that's quite easy to follow.

An American three-toed woodpecker looking for grubs and other goodies

Tracing the northern ridge of the mountain, the boot-beaten scramble path reaches Bootjack's 6789-foot summit after 0.75 mile. The last 100 feet or so require scrambling up rock and should be skipped if you're not comfortable or experienced on such terrain. The views are just as superb below the summit rocks. Walk around. Stuart, Ingalls, Rainier, and the granite-faced Wenatchee Mountains add to the panorama.

67 Upper Icicle Creek

RATING/ DIFFICULTY	ROUND-TRIP	ELEV GAIN/ HIGH POINT	SEASON
★★★/2	10 miles	400 feet/ 3200 feet	Late May– mid-Nov

3200' One-way
3000'
2800'
0   5

Maps: Green Trails Chiwaukum Mtns No. 177, Stevens Pass No. 176; **Contact:** Okanogan-Wenatchee National Forest, Wenatchee River Ranger District, Leavenworth, (509) 548-6977, www.fs.fed.us/r6/wenatchee; **Notes:** NW Forest Pass required. Free day-use permit required, available at trailhead. **GPS:** N 47 36.748, W 120 56.995

Paralleled by a busy recreational road for much of its length, the frothing, tumbling, spectacularly beautiful Icicle Creek flows unmolested in deep wilderness at its upper reaches. The upper Icicle is more sedate than its canyon run downriver, trading heart-pounding rapids for soul-soothing ripples, steep, stark walls for lush flats of luxuriant old-growth forest, pavement for trail. A great hike for late spring, late fall, or lazy summer days, the upper Icicle invites outdoor adventurers of all levels.

GETTING THERE

From milepost 99 on US 2, at the western edge of Leavenworth, follow the Icicle Creek Road (Forest Road 76) for 16.3 miles (the pavement ends at 12.3 miles) to Rock Island Campground. Turn left, crossing Icicle Creek and continuing for 1.8 miles to the road's end and trailhead (elev. 2800 ft). Privy available.

ON THE TRAIL

In an impressive grove of towering cottonwoods, ancient western cedars, and gigantic Engelmann spruce, the wide and well-trodden path begins its upriver journey. Within five minutes (more if the big trees hold you captive), enter the Alpine Lakes Wilderness. This is one of the busiest trails in this wilderness, and hordes of hikers and horse packers turn it into a dusty thoroughfare by midsummer.

But in spite of the dust, the trail is nearly level, easy to walk, and ideal for fledgling hikers and budding backpackers. Traversing grove after grove of ancient giants and passing one gurgling creek after another, the way lethargically delves deeper into the wilderness. At about 1.5 miles notice a change in forest cover as lodgepole pine replaces spruce, fir, and cedar. Notice too that the creek is more audible. The reason is soon revealed as a pretty set of small falls comes into view. Here, just below the confluence with French Creek, is one of the most popular backcountry sites in the Icicle Valley, a perfect spot to call it a day if hiking with young children. Seek out sunning, snacking, soaking, and snoozing spots.

Beyond the falls and its busy campsites, cross French Creek (elev. 2900 ft) on a big bridge and come to a junction with the French Creek Trail shortly afterward. The way now hugs the Icicle, revealing some appealing swimming holes. At 1.9 miles the French Ridge Trail (Hike 68) takes off left. To the right, Spanish Camp Creek, named for Basque sheepherders who once worked the Chiwaukum high country, tumbles into the Icicle.

Across lush flats the trail continues its easy way up the wilderness valley. At about 2.6 miles Frosty Creek adds its chilly waters to the Icicle. At about 4 miles the trail pulls away from the creek in a wide bottomland. With the

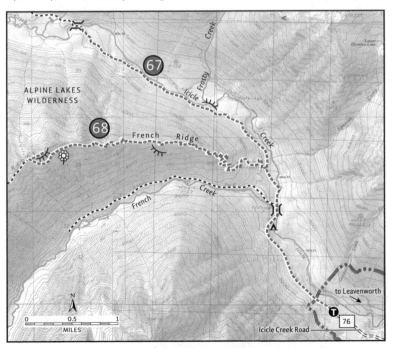

French Creek flowing into Icicle Creek

river's babbling farther in the distance, listen now to soothing melodies from thrushes, wrens, warblers, and flycatchers.

At 5 miles come to a bridge spanning the Icicle just before a junction with the trail to Frosty Pass (elev. 3200 ft). This is a good place to turn around, but not before more lingering and lounging.

EXTENDING YOUR TRIP
Strong hikers may want to continue farther up the valley. The trail remains good and gentle, albeit brushy in spots for another 4 miles. Then, after crossing Chain Creek, it climbs 1400 feet in 2.5 miles to Josephine Lake (Hike 39).

68 French Ridge

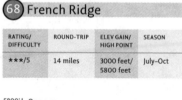

RATING/ DIFFICULTY	ROUND-TRIP	ELEV GAIN/ HIGH POINT	SEASON
★★★/5	14 miles	3000 feet/ 5800 feet	July–Oct

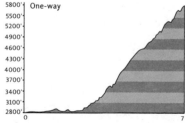

Maps: Green Trails Chiwaukum Mtns No. 177, Stevens Pass No. 176; **Contact:** Okanogan-Wenatchee National Forest, Wenatchee River Ranger District, Leavenworth, (509) 548-6977, www.fs.fed.us/r6/wenatchee; **Notes:** NW Forest Pass required. Free day-use permit required, available at trailhead. **GPS:** N 47 36.748, W 120 56.995

⊗ ✿ *This is a long and lonely trek to a long-gone lookout post. Bone dry, with fading tread and a steep ascent, the hike to French Ridge is trés difficile. But the solitude! Leave the huddled masses down below in the Icicle Creek valley and enjoy a wild ridge in the heart of the Alpine Lakes Wilderness. The views aren't too bad, and neither are the chances of spotting a wild critter or two.*

GETTING THERE

From milepost 99 on US 2, at the western edge of Leavenworth, follow the Icicle Creek Road (Forest Road 76) for 16.3 miles (the pavement ends at 12.3 miles) to Rock Island Campground. Turn left, crossing Icicle Creek and continuing for 1.8 miles to the road's end and trailhead (elev. 2800 ft). Privy available.

ON THE TRAIL

Begin on the boot-beaten busy Icicle Creek Trail (Hike 67), paralleling the lovely waterway through impressive groves of giant cottonwoods and old-growth conifers. At 1.5 miles, at a small picturesque waterfall, cross French Creek on a sturdy bridge. Just beyond, the French Creek Trail takes off left. Stay right on the Icicle Creek Trail, and in an easy 0.4 mile reach the junction with the French Ridge Trail (elev. 2900 ft).

Now on vastly lighter tread that's brushy in places, begin climbing away from the lush Icicle Valley. River music soon fades. Actually, so do any prospects for filling water bottles. Be sure to pack plenty of water on this dry ridge. Through open forest with views out to surrounding peaks, the trail switchbacks up a steep rib. The way is slow going in the best conditions, but numerous blowdowns will slow you further. This trail receives little if any maintenance and is in real danger of fading forever into the Northwest's growing graveyard of abandoned and neglected trails. Sigh.

You reach the ridge crest at about 3.4 miles, but there's still much more climbing to be had. The grade does, however, soon let up as the trail swings a little to the west side of the ridge (elev. 4300 ft). Swinging back to the east side of the ridge, take in excellent views of Cashmere Mountain and the emerald French Creek valley spread below. Then the way once again steepens. At 5.25 miles reach a mile-high knoll granting great views south and east and north to the Bulls Tooth and Chiwaukums.

Traversing meadows flush in blueberries and huckleberries (and in season plenty of birds and critters feasting on them), the sometimes slumping, sometimes brushy trail continues along the ridge, picking up some more elevation in the process.

At about 6.3 miles, look for a fading spur path taking off right for 0.2 mile and 100 vertical feet to a meadowed knoll, the site of a former lookout. Though the lookout has been gone since the 1970s, this 5800-foot perch still offers commanding views of the Wenatchee Mountains, French Creek valley, Cradle Peak, Sixtysix Hundred Ridge, Icicle Ridge, and the Chiwaukums.

EXTENDING YOUR TRIP

The main trail continues another 0.75 mile,

Bridge over French Creek along the Icicle Creek Trail

dropping 350 feet through bountiful berry patches to a small basin. Here, an unmarked way trail takes off right for a rough up and down and up again 2 miles to beautiful Turquoise Lake, set in a rugged cirque. Add 1500 vertical feet to your total if you make this arduous journey. The French Ridge Trail continues another 1.5 miles or so, dropping 1200 steep feet to the French Creek Trail, where it's 3.5 miles back to the Icicle Creek Trail. While it's possible to make a loop, it's not recommended. This section of trail is rocky, insanely steep, badly eroded, and choked in leg- and arm-scratching brush.

Opposite: A weathered sign sits at a trail junction high in the Entiat Mountains.

lake wenatchee

Little Wenatchee and White River Valleys

Sparkling alpine lakes, resplendent alpine meadows, impressive groves of primeval forest, and ridges and peaks providing spectacular panoramic viewing—you'll find plenty of variety and outstanding hiking within these two valleys. The Little Wenatchee and White rivers are Lake Wenatchee's two main feeder rivers. One starts high in the sprawling meadows along the Cascade crest in the Henry M. Jackson Wilderness, while the other is born of melting snow and ice from the rocky and frosty southern neighbors of majestic Glacier Peak.

69 Minotaur Lake

RATING/ DIFFICULTY	ROUND-TRIP	ELEV GAIN/ HIGH POINT	SEASON
★★★/4	3.5 miles	1850 feet/ 5550 feet	July–Oct

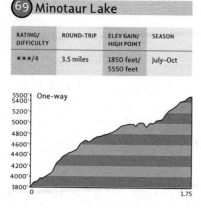

Map: Green Trails Benchmark Mtn No. 144; **Contact:** Okanogan-Wenatchee National Forest, Wenatchee River Ranger District, Leavenworth, (509) 548-6977, www.fs.fed.us/r6 /wenatchee; **GPS:** N 47 49.665 W 121 01.779

⚙ *Housed beneath the shiny granite cliffs of Labyrinth Mountain is sparkling Minotaur Lake. Fearsome like its mythological namesake? No. But the hike can be a* bit daunting and may indeed require the strength of a man-bull. Although recently rebuilt in parts, the way is more route than trail. It's short, but quite steep.

GETTING THERE

From Everett head east on US 2 for 65 miles to Stevens Pass. Continue east for another 4 miles. Just after the highway divides, turn left (exercising caution crossing the westbound lanes) onto Smith Brook Road (Forest Road 67). (From Leavenworth reach the turnoff in 30 miles.) Follow FR 67 for 6.8 miles, turning left onto FR 6704. Proceed for 0.9 mile to the road's end and trailhead (elev. 3800 ft).

ON THE TRAIL

Start beside Minotaur Creek and immediately begin the relentless climb up a steep rib—1000 feet worth in less than a mile. Upon entering the Henry M. Jackson Wilderness, the climb eases a bit as the way leaves the rib and heads to the right toward Minotaur Creek. After dropping about 100 feet, the trail swings back upward. Huckleberry patches and heather meadows begin to interrupt the hemlock.

At 1.75 miles, which you'll swear is longer, reach the outlet of beautiful Minotaur Lake. You probably won't be greeted by seven Athenian lads and seven Athenian maidens, but scores of your fellow hikers will probably be at the lake. Despite the toughness of the hike, this is a popular place. The lake's shores have been badly trampled in spots, so take care when exploring the scenic shoreline.

EXTENDING YOUR TRIP

Experienced scramblers can follow a fairly well-defined path up toward the summit of 6376-foot Labyrinth Mountain. Views of

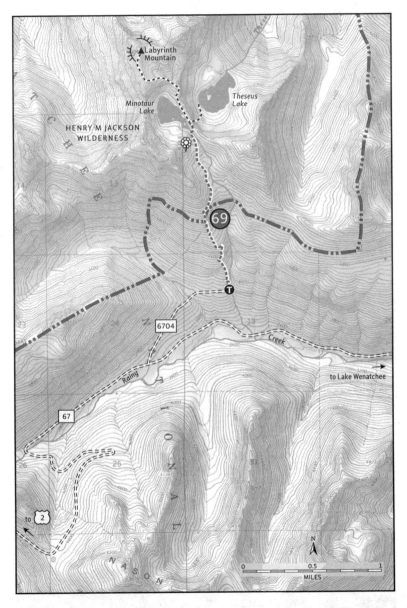

TCHEE

Labyrinth
Mountain

Minotaur
Lake

Theseus
Lake

HENRY M JACKSON
WILDERNESS

69

T

6704

19

Creek

to Lake Wenatchee

Rainy

67

25

26

31

to 2

NASON

N

0   0.5   1
MILES

the Cascade crest, Nason and Poet ridges, and beyond are awesome from this post. Much larger Theseus Lake, named for the mythological man responsible for slaying the Minotaur, lies 500 feet below Minotaur. Cross Minotaur's outlet and follow a path that heads right, to an opening on a ridge where you can stare down at the island-dotted lake.

A steep path continues to Theseus, but you won't have the lovely daughter of King Minos helping you make the climb out. And in case you're wondering, it was none other than A. H. Sylvester, first district supervisor of the Wenatchee National Forest, who placed these Greek mythology names on the map (see "Sly Sylvester" in this section).

Theseus Lake from a viewpoint near Minotaur Lake

SLY SYLVESTER

If one person can be attributed with leaving the biggest mark on the Central Cascades, it's A. H. Sylvester. A former civil engineer and surveyor, Sylvester was appointed chief forest supervisor of the Wenatchee National Forest upon its establishment in 1908. He served as overseer of the sprawling Central Cascades National Forest until 1931 and was responsible for naming well over one thousand geographic features in the region. Often naming peaks and lakes after friends, acquaintances, occurrences, and physical characteristics, Sylvester also bestowed whimsical monikers.

By Jove, he named features after Roman gods, Minoan mythology, and poets. Lake Janus, Jove Peak, Labyrinth Mountain, Minotaur Lake, Theseus Lake, and the peaks Poe, Irving, Longfellow, Whittier, and Bryant are all appellations attributed to Sylvester. He found a certain valley near Leavenworth "enchanting," and a peak hovering over Lake Wenatchee to have a "dirty face." Dish Pan Gap, Kodak Peak, Mount Mastiff, Dumbell Mountain, Mounts Maud and Saul, and Saska Peak were also named by the forest supervisor. And while Sylvester certainly left his mark on many a Central Cascades feature, one high spot along the Chiwawa Ridge honors him specifically. Hovering above Schaeffer Lake (Hike 88) is a 6913-foot peak named Mount Sylvester.

70 Rock Mountain via Snowy Creek

RATING/ DIFFICULTY	ROUND-TRIP	ELEV GAIN/ HIGH POINT	SEASON
★★★★★/4	9.8 miles	3250 feet/ 6852 feet	July–Oct

One-way
6852'
6800'
6400'
6000'
5600'
5200'
4800'
4400'
4000'
3600'
0   4.9

Map: Green Trails Wenatchee Lake No. 145; **Contact:** Okanogan-Wenatchee National Forest, Wenatchee River Ranger District, Leavenworth, (509) 548-6977, www.fs.fed.us/r6/wenatchee; **GPS:** N 47 48.456 W 120 59.773

The views from this Nason Ridge summit simply rock! Nearly every peak in the Central Cascades (and a quite a few others too, north and south) is visible from this former fire lookout site. Come in July and add a rockin' wildflower show to this visual fest. A delightful mountain stream, handsome mature forest, and a handful of resident mountain goats help make this hike a Cascades classic.

GETTING THERE

From Everett head east on US 2 for 65 miles to Stevens Pass. Continue east for another 4 miles. Just after the highway divides, turn left (exercising caution crossing the westbound lanes) onto Smith Brook Road (Forest Road 67). (From Leavenworth reach the turnoff in 30 miles.) Follow FR 67 for 6 miles, turning right onto FR 6705. Proceed for 3.6 rough and brushy miles to the trailhead (elev. 3600 ft).

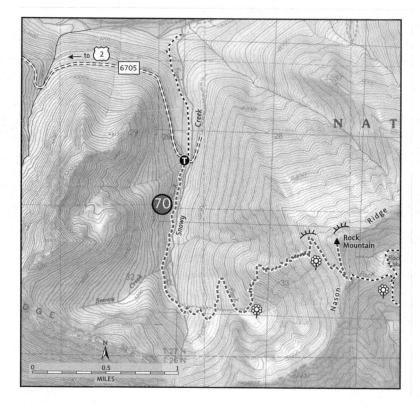

ON THE TRAIL

The trail begins gently in cool mature forest beside Snowy Creek. A far contrast from the south-side approach to Rock Mountain (Hike 44), this route stays out of the sun for most of the way, offers more varied terrain, and requires far less elevation gain. Its only major drawback is a large brushy section encountered about 0.5 mile in. In morning dew and inclement weather, expect to get soaked.

On nice grade head up the narrow valley, occasionally hopping over cascading side creeks. At 1.2 miles come to a signed junction. The faint trail right eventually gets better. Adventurous souls may want to consider a return trip to hike this lightly traveled 4.3 mile section of the Nason Ridge Trail to Rainy Pass.

For Rock Mountain, continue left. Soon cross a tributary in a draw kept open by frequent avalanche activity. Now climbing more briskly, twice cross Snowy Creek and emerge in a gorgeous lush basin (elev. 4600

Opposite: Mount Howard from Rock Mountain

ft) beneath cliffs and talus. By midsummer it reigns purple in blossoming elephant's head, spirea, aster, and monkey flower.

Turning east to cross the meadow, the trail reenters forest, and in more typical Nason fashion the way turns steep. Switchbacks are tight, and so may be your calves after negotiating this stretch of trail. At about 5700 feet begin to reach the sky, breaking out into luxuriant alpine meadows. The grade eases and the views expand as the trail approaches a 6600-foot gap on the shoulder of Rock Mountain.

At 4.2 miles reach said gap and a junction. Right drops down to Rock Lake (Hike 44). Head left instead, climbing 250 feet in 0.3 mile to Rock's 6852-foot summit. Catch your breath and then lose it taking in the stunning views. Look east along Nason Ridge to 7063-foot Mount Howard, south to the Chiwaukums and Mount Stuart, west to Hinman and

Daniel and Rainier just behind, and north to Glacier, the Monte Cristo massif, Sloan, and countless others. Directly below, Rock Lake twinkles in the sun. And marmots, mountain goats, and grouse frolic and lounge on the surrounding ridges and ledges.

EXTENDING YOUR TRIP
The lower Snowy Creek Trail can still be followed to FR 67. Brushy and unmaintained, it'll probably be put back in use when FR 6705 washes out and becomes abandoned—a fate all too common for access roads these days in Washington's national forests.

71 Heather Lake

RATING/ DIFFICULTY	ROUND-TRIP	ELEV GAIN/ HIGH POINT	SEASON
★★★/3	6.6 miles	1250 feet/ 3950 feet	July–Oct

Avalanche slopes above Heather Lake

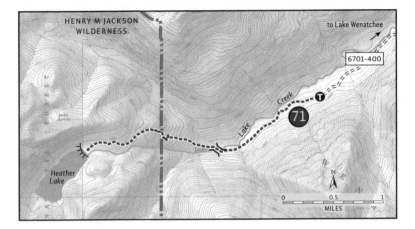

Map: Green Trails Benchmark Mtn No. 144;
Contact: Okanogan-Wenatchee National Forest, Lake Wenatchee Ranger Station (summer), (509) 763-3103, or Wenatchee River Ranger District, Leavenworth, (509) 548-6977, www.fs.fed.us/r6/wenatchee; **GPS:** N 47 51.982, W 121 04.518

👤🐾 *Hemlock or Huckleberry would be a more suitable name for this lake, as you'll be hard-pressed finding heather growing along the shores of this backcountry beauty. A misnomer yes, but a lake you'll not want to miss. Cradled beneath knolls of meadows along the Cascade crest and set in a deep forest of primeval proportions, Heather Lake is a pure gem. And the trail is a near delight! But you won't be alone here, as plenty of your fellow hikers are well aware of all of this.*

GETTING THERE

From Everett head east on US 2 for 85 miles to Coles Corner. (From Leavenworth travel west on US 2 for 15 miles.) Turn left (north) onto State Route 207 (signed for Lake Wenatchee) and proceed 4.2 miles to a Y intersection after crossing the Wenatchee River. Bear left onto North Shore Road. At 7.6 miles, after passing the ranger station and crossing the White River, the road becomes Forest Road 65. Continue west on FR 65 for 4.7 miles, turning left onto FR 67. After 0.4 mile turn right onto FR 6701. Continue for 4.7 miles, turning left onto FR 6701-400 (signed "Heather Lake T.H."). Drive for 2.4 miles to the road's end and trailhead (elev. 2700 ft). In 2014 part of spur 400 will be decommissioned and hike will begin from a new trailhead, adding distance.

ON THE TRAIL

Starting at the edge of an old clear-cut, the very well-constructed and well-maintained trail immediately enters a forest of big, beautiful ancient giants. You may end up agreeing with me that as worthy a hiking objective as Heather Lake is, this old-growth forest rivals it in beauty and majesty.

The first mile or so of this trail is pure pedestrian delight, gaining nary a foot in elevation. Cross side creeks and weave beneath towering hemlocks. At about 1.5 miles reach a heavy-duty bridge spanning Lake Creek as it cascades through a small gorge. The bridge was constructed in 2003, relegating the old log-jam crossing of the creek to the annals of hiking history.

Soon afterward, enter the Henry M. Jackson Wilderness and finally begin gaining elevation. The way turns steeper, but a cornucopia of ripe huckleberries may slow you down more than the grade. Pass a small ledge that provides a good glimpse out to Labyrinth Mountain, and then continue the upward momentum.

Eventually the way levels out once more and Lake Creek returns to your side. At 3.3

miles reach 3950-foot Heather Lake near its outlet. Stake out your spot on one of its polished, sun-kissed shoreline ledges and savor the surroundings. Grizzly Peak bears down from above. Ripples brush up against giant cedar logs. Alaska yellow cedars drape the shore. Not a heather in sight, but what a sight!

EXTENDING YOUR TRIP

Experienced and tenacious travelers undaunted by brush and windfall may want to follow a 0.5-mile way trail to 4600-foot Glasses Lake. Reach the rough route by crossing a log jam at Heather's outlet. Or just enjoy looking down at Glasses Lake from Grizzly Peak (Hike 42).

72 Pear Lake

RATING/ DIFFICULTY	ROUND-TRIP	ELEV GAIN/ HIGH POINT	SEASON
★★★★/4	12 miles	2600 feet/ 5200 feet	July–Oct

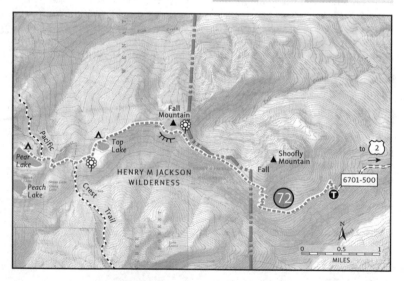

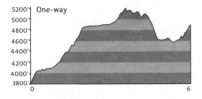

Map: Green Trails Benchmark Mtn No. 144;
Contact: Okanogan-Wenatchee National Forest, Lake Wenatchee Ranger Station (summer), (509) 763-3103, or Wenatchee River Ranger District, Leavenworth, (509) 548-6977, www.fs.fed.us/r6/wenatchee; **Notes:** NW Forest Pass required; **GPS:** N 47 52.448, W 121 05.091

■◆● *A beautiful lake perched on the Cascade crest in the heart of the Henry M. Jackson Wilderness, Pear is a succulently scenic delight. Served with a fine accompaniment of old-growth forests, wildflower meadows, and alpine views, Pear is indeed a sweet destination. Via the Top Lake Trail, however, some steep climbing is involved. But this shorter approach than Meadow Creek (Hike 27) has its advantages in the form of Top Lake, Fall Mountain, and few fellow hikers.*

GETTING THERE

From Everett head east on US 2 for 85 miles to Coles Corner. (From Leavenworth travel west on US 2 for 15 miles.) Turn left (north) onto State Route 207 (signed for Lake Wenatchee) and proceed 4.2 miles to a Y intersection after crossing the Wenatchee River. Bear left onto North Shore Road. At 7.6 miles, after passing the ranger station and crossing the White River, the road becomes Forest Road 65. Continue west on FR 65 for 4.7 miles, turning left onto FR 67. After 0.4 mile turn right onto FR 6701.

Continue for 5.6 miles, turning left onto FR 6701-500 (signed "Top Lake"). Avoid all side roads and reach the trailhead in 4 miles (elev. 3800 ft).

ON THE TRAIL

Starting in mature timber high on Shoofly Mountain, the trail quickly climbs a couple hundred feet before kicking back to a gentle slope traverse. After about 1 mile of easy ambling, short steep switchbacks alter the pace. But the drudgery is short-lived as the trail once again eases into a gentle traverse.

Fall Mountain's steep, flower-filled slopes

After entering the Henry M. Jackson Wilderness the way gradually gains elevation, cresting a 5000-foot ridge between Shoofly and Fall mountains.

Thinning forest grants views south and north along the meadow-carpeted Cascade crest. Prominent and obscure peaks compliment the emerald divide. At about 3.25 miles the way skirts beneath Fall's 5594-foot summit. Peak baggers may want to nab the pinnacle, but wildflower admirers will be perfectly content staying on the trail as it hovers at 5200-feet, brushing meadows and traveling through old groves of mountain hemlock.

Continue on—a knee-jarring descent awaits. The trail drops 700 feet, bottoming out at Top Lake (elev. 4500 ft). The forest-lined and grassy-shored body of water is a peaceful spot, but in early summer hordes of voracious mosquitoes will keep you moving. Beyond the lake the way winds through splendid albeit buggy meadows, terminating at the Pacific Crest Trail (PCT) (elev. 4600 ft) 5.3 miles from the trailhead.

Pear Lake lies less than a mile away. Turn right onto the PCT, heading north toward Canada on the long-distance thoroughfare. After approaching a rushing creek, the trail makes a short, steep climb of about 300 feet and then a quick drop of 100 feet, coming to the east end of the pear-shaped lake at a trail junction. The eastern shore is often busy with backpackers, so head a little way down the Meadow Creek Trail for quieter coves and shoreline meadows ripe for napping.

EXTENDING YOUR TRIP

The Fortune Ponds can be accessed by continuing on the Meadow Creek Trail for 1.5 miles. There's a good little climb involved, but you'll be granted an excellent view of Pear Lake. Experienced off-trail travelers may want to scramble Fortune Mountain or return to where the Top Lake Trail intersects the PCT and follow a faint path west 1 mile to equally sweet Peach Lake. And there are all of those miles of meadows south along the PCT to roam too!

73 Cady Ridge

RATING/ DIFFICULTY	ROUND-TRIP	ELEV GAIN/ HIGH POINT	SEASON
★★★★★/4	13 miles	2700 feet/ 5550 feet	July–Oct

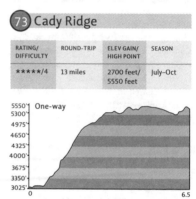

Map: Green Trails Benchmark Mtn No. 144; **Contact:** Okanogan-Wenatchee National Forest, Lake Wenatchee Ranger Station (summer), (509) 763-3103, or Wenatchee River Ranger District, Leavenworth, (509) 548-6977, www.fs.fed.us/r6/wenatchee; **Note:** NW Forest Pass required; **GPS:** N 47 55.095, W 121 05.243

When it comes to resplendent alpine meadows, the Henry M. Jackson Wilderness can't be beat. And when it comes to the finest flower romps within that wild area named for the longtime Washington senator and champion of conservation, Cady Ridge ranks supreme. A multitude of blossoms proliferate along this mile-high ridge. But it's the lupines that dominate, transforming Cady into a purple mountain majesty. And views! From the inspiring Poet Peaks, to the emerald-cloaked summits along the Cascade crest, to cloud-piercing, snow-catching, ice-harboring, horizon-dominating Glacier Peak!

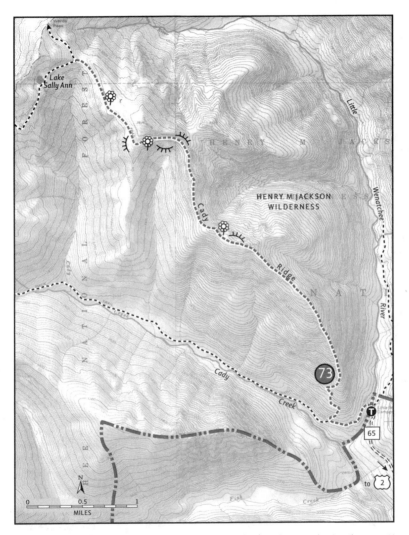

GETTING THERE

From Everett head east on US 2 for 85 miles to Coles Corner. (From Leavenworth travel west on US 2 for 15 miles.) Turn left (north) onto State Route 207 (signed for Lake Wenatchee) and proceed 4.2 miles to a Y intersection after crossing the Wenatchee River. Bear left onto North Shore Road. At 7.6 miles, after passing the ranger station and crossing the White River, the road becomes for 4.7 easy miles to 4300-foot Cady Pass, traversing magnificent old-growth forests en route. Head right instead onto the Cady Ridge Trail, which travels steep forested slopes en route to magnificent meadows.

Immediately gaining elevation, the trail gets progressively steeper as it marches up Cady Ridge. Pass a small creek in a thick hemlock grove. Depending on the snowmelt above, this may be the last source of reliable water along the trail. After a series of tight switchbacks, the way gets even steeper—and dustier and rockier too. After about 2 monotonous miles of climbing, openings in the forest begin to provide teaser views.

Thankfully, the grade begins to ease, and after about another mile of slogging the way crests a 5300-foot knoll. Look up! Glacier Peak looms above a meadow of lupine. Now the hike gets fun. Continue down the trail, being aware of marmots that have taken up residence right in the tread. Undulating between forest and meadow, the way carries on, skirting around a knoll and charging up another one.

From this 5525-foot bump on the ridge, catch your breath and enjoy the amazing view of Glacier Peak hovering over the emerald lawns of Kodak Peak. The trail then steeply drops about 100 feet and turns directly west, traversing an open side slope with spectacular views south to Nason Ridge, Mount Daniel, and the Chiwaukums. The tread here is slumping, so watch your ankles.

Cresting a 5550-foot shoulder of Cady Ridge, the trail continues for another mile through some of the finest alpine meadows this side of the Colorado Rockies. Aside from the myriad blossoms vying for your attention, hundreds of peaks demand recognition as well. Scan the Cascade crest south to Grizzly, Fortune, Benchmark, and

Lupine-filled meadows and views of Glacier Peak from along Cady Ridge

Forest Road 65. Continue west on FR 65 for 14 miles (the last 2.8 miles are rough gravel) to the road's end at the trailhead (elev. 3025 ft). Privy available.

ON THE TRAIL

Three wonderful trails begin from this spot. Take the one that veers left (west), signed "Cady Creek." The way quickly drops into a gorge, crossing the Little Wenatchee River on a solid bridge. Enter wilderness, and after 0.5 mile of easy wandering come to a junction. The Cady Creek Trail continues west

Skykomish. Look east to the lofty Poets and north to the 10,568-foot glacial giant known to the area's first peoples as Dahkobed, "the white mountain."

The trail drops to a small saddle with a sometimes-flowing spring and then makes a short, quick climb before terminating at the Pacific Crest Trail (PCT) (elev. 5350 ft), 6.5 miles from where you began. Lounge or linger long!

EXTENDING YOUR TRIP

For a great side trip, continue south on the PCT for 0.3 mile to little Lake Sally Ann (elev. 5450 ft), tucked in a snow-harboring cirque on Skykomish Peak. Explore with care, for this fragile alpine lake has endured heavy visitation. Strong day hikers or those contemplating a night out can continue south on the PCT to Cady Pass and return to the trailhead via the Cady Creek Trail for a 16-mile loop. Or head north on the PCT to Sauk Pass and return via the Little Wenatchee River Trail (Hike 74) for another glorious 16-mile loop.

74 Meander Meadow

RATING/ DIFFICULTY	ROUND-TRIP	ELEV GAIN/ HIGH POINT	SEASON
★★★★/3	12.5 miles	2475 feet/ 5000 feet	July–Oct

One-way

Looking down the Little Wenatchee River valley from Meander Meadow

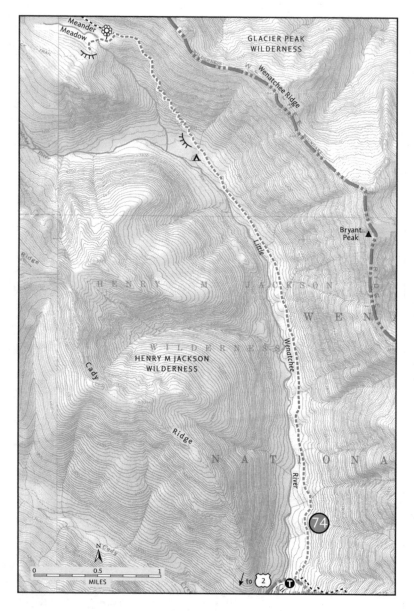

Meander
Meadow

GLACIER PEAK
WILDERNESS

W Wenatchee Ridge

Bryant
Peak

H E N R Y   M   J A C K S O N

W E N

WILDERNESS

HENRY M JACKSON
WILDERNESS

Cady

Ridge

Little

Wenatchee

N A T I O N A

River

Cady

74

N Cady

0   0.5   1
MILES

to 2   T

Map: Green Trails Benchmark Mtn No. 144;
Contact: Okanogan-Wenatchee National Forest, Lake Wenatchee Ranger Station (summer), (509) 763-3103, or Wenatchee River Ranger District, Leavenworth, (509) 548-6977, www.fs.fed.us/r6/wenatchee; **Note:** NW Forest Pass required; **GPS:** N 47 55.095, W 121 05.243

Follow the Little Wenatchee River all the way to its headwaters high on the Cascade crest. From mile-high, miles-long alpine meadows, the river meanders. And so will you upon reaching these heavenly flower gardens. The hike in is a long approach and is warm at times across brushy avalanche slopes, but it is worth every ounce of sweat expended and every annoying fly swatted.

GETTING THERE

From Everett head east on US 2 for 85 miles to Coles Corner. (From Leavenworth travel west on US 2 for 15 miles.) Turn left (north) onto State Route 207 (signed for Lake Wenatchee) and proceed 4.2 miles to a Y intersection after crossing the Wenatchee River. Bear left onto North Shore Road. At 7.6 miles, after passing the ranger station and crossing the White River, the road becomes Forest Road 65. Continue west on FR 65 for 14 miles (the last 2.8 miles are rough gravel) to the road's end at the trailhead (elev. 3025 ft). Privy available.

ON THE TRAIL

Head north on the Little Wenatchee River Trail, and within minutes come to a junction with the Poe Mountain Trail (Hike 75) and enter the Henry M. Jackson Wilderness. For the next several miles the trail gently marches up a deep valley, undulating between cool groves of old growth and herbaceous avalanche swaths. The going is easy, the trail gaining just over 500 feet of elevation in 4 miles.

The river is always nearby and plenty of feeder creeks spill into it. Views of the surrounding vernal fortress of peaks and ridges are excellent from the forest openings. However, in hot weather and when flowers are in bloom, there's no shortage of ravenous biting flies. And if the maintenance brigades haven't walked this way in some time, expect a brushy bash before breaking out into the high country.

At 4.25 miles, after crossing no less than one dozen avalanche slopes, come to a campsite at the edge of an expansive meadow (elev. 3650 ft)—a wonderful spot for wildlife watching and calling it quits if the upcoming climb doesn't sound appealing.

Continuing, cross a creek and begin with a little help from a lot of switchbacks that steeply climb out of the valley. Pause for inspiring views of Poet Ridge and the verdant valley below. At 6.25 miles, after brushing along another series of avalanche slopes, the climb eases as the trail enters a gorgeous hanging valley (elev. 5000 ft). Here a little tributary to the Little Wenatchee River meanders among blissful blossoms in summer and bountiful berries in fall. The meadows are as beautiful as they are fragile. Please be careful exploring them.

EXTENDING YOUR TRIP

From Meander Meadow the trail used to cross the creek and trudge across wetlands and heather slopes on its way to the Pacific Crest Trail (PCT). In 2007 a brand new section of trail avoiding those delicate slopes was constructed, offering a drier, more ecologically sound and direct approach to the PCT. For expanding views and excellent roaming, consider checking it out—mosey along the trail for another 0.75 mile, climbing

500 feet to intersect the PCT at Sauk Pass. Views are excellent here of Johnson Mountain, Red Mountain, and Glacier Peak. Green pyramidal 6121-foot Kodak Peak just to the north is an excellent objective. Follow the PCT north for 1 mile to a ridge crest, where a short and steep side path takes off 0.5 mile west to reach it. Strong hikers can follow the PCT south for 2.3 miles, combining the Meander Meadow hike with the Cady Ridge Trail (Hike 73) for a 16-mile loop. This section of the PCT through Dishpan Gap is among the most scenic and meadowed stretches of trail to be found anywhere.

75 Poe Mountain

RATING/ DIFFICULTY	ROUND-TRIP	ELEV GAIN/ HIGH POINT	SEASON
★★★★/4	6 miles	3000 feet/ 6015 feet	Mid-June– Oct

Map: Green Trails Benchmark Mtn No. 144; **Contact:** Okanogan-Wenatchee National Forest, Lake Wenatchee Ranger Station (summer), (509) 763-3103, or Wenatchee River Ranger District, Leavenworth, (509) 548-6977, www .fs.fed.us/r6/wenatchee; **Note:** NW Forest Pass required; **GPS:** N 47 55.095, W 121 05.243

There's nothing macabre about this peak. Au contraire, Poe's open summit ushers joyous tell-tale views of ridges, valleys, and sprawling peaks. One of the Poet Peaks, a name bestowed upon the prominent points of the Wenatchee Ridge by none other than A. H. Sylvester, Poe is not the highest, but it's the easiest to ascend. Still, this former lookout site is no easy climb. The way is steep and exposed to the eastern-slope sun—hot. But the extensive alpine views from Poe will leave you raven for some time!

GETTING THERE

From Everett head east on US 2 for 85 miles to Coles Corner. (From Leavenworth travel west on US 2 for 15 miles.) Turn left (north) onto State Route 207 (signed for Lake Wenatchee) and proceed 4.2 miles to a Y intersection after crossing the Wenatchee River. Bear left onto North Shore Road. At 7.6 miles, after passing the ranger station and crossing the White River, the road becomes Forest Road 65. Continue west on FR 65 for 14 miles (the last 2.8 miles are rough gravel) to the road's end at the trailhead (elev. 3025 ft). Privy available.

ON THE TRAIL

This is the direct way to Poe Mountain, the trail that once acted as the supply and communication line to the lookout that sat on its summit from 1933 until 1970. It's short and steep, gaining nearly 3000 vertical feet in just shy of 3 miles. A gentler route to Poe can be followed from Irving Pass (Hike 78), but even that route requires a lot of elevation gain due to its up and down ridgeline course. They're both great hikes. Do this one when the sun's not too intense or in September when the slopes are bursting with ripe blueberries and huckleberries.

Head north on the Little Wenatchee River Trail and within minutes come to a junction. Turn right on the less obvious tread and

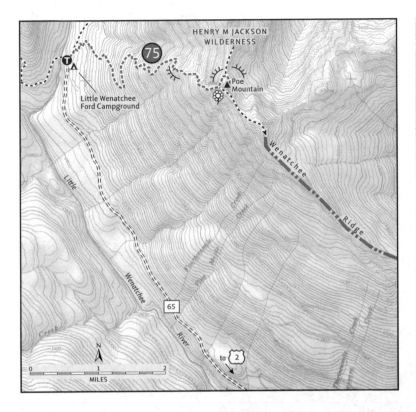

HENRY M JACKSON
WILDERNESS

75

Poe
Mountain

Little Wenatchee
Ford Campground

Wenatchee

Ridge

Little

Wenatchee

65

River

Creek

to 2

N

0   1   2

MILES

immediately start climbing. Forming the boundary of the Henry M. Jackson Wilderness, the way attacks Poe's steep western face through a dry forest of Doug-fir, silver fir, and western white pine. Views begin to open up after 1.5 miles of relentless climbing.

Switchbacks grow tighter, but the views keep expanding at every turn. So do the berry patches. At 2.6 miles come to an unmarked junction (elev. 5600 ft). The primitive path right is the Little Wenatchee Ridge Trail that heads to Irving Pass (Hike 78).

Continue left, swinging north around Poe's

summit block. Tread disappears in a small meadow—pick it up again just to the south. Pass an unmarked junction with the Poet Ridge High Route, and soon after that reach an unmarked junction with a spur that connects to the Little Wenatchee Ridge Trail.

Turn left, and after a final short push reach Poe's 6015-foot summit. Now wax poetic as you bask in scenic glory. To the south it's Nason Ridge, Labyrinth Mountain, and Lichtenberg by Jove! To the west it's Grizzly, Fortune, Cady, Johnson, and the peaks of Monte Cristo—count them! To the east it's

David and his kingdom of peaks. And to the north a dignified line-up of emerald poets: Longfellow, Whittier, and Bryant stand against the glistening backdrop of snowy white Glacier Peak.

EXTENDING YOUR TRIP
Experienced off-trail travelers can follow the Poet Ridge High Route toward Longfellow Mountain. Tread is nonexistent in places, and the route can be rough and challenging. Proceed only as far as skill and comfort levels allow.

Glacier Peak rises above the Poet Ridge.

76 Little Wenatchee Gorge

RATING/ DIFFICULTY	ROUND-TRIP	ELEV GAIN/ HIGH POINT	SEASON
★★★/2	3 miles	250 feet/ 2500 feet	May–Nov

One-way
2500'
2400'
2300'
0   1.5

Map: Green Trails Benchmark Mtn No. 144; **Contact:** Okanogan-Wenatchee National Forest, Lake Wenatchee Ranger Station (summer), (509) 763-3103, or Wenatchee River Ranger District, Leavenworth, (509) 548-6977, www.fs.fed.us/r6/wenatchee; **GPS:** N 47 52.495, W 121 00.887

Perhaps the "best kept secret" among the scores of trails within the Lake Wenatchee region, this one follows along the Little Wenatchee River at a dramatic gorge. A wonderful destination for hikers of all ages and abilities, the river puts on quite a show as it tumbles and froths over rapids and beneath ledges. Amble or while away the afternoon, or combine this hike with one of the other nearby short but sweet trails.

GETTING THERE
From Everett head east on US 2 for 85 miles to Coles Corner. (From Leavenworth travel west on US 2 for 15 miles.) Turn left (north) onto State Route 207 (signed for Lake Wenatchee) and proceed 4.2 miles to a Y intersection after crossing the Wenatchee River. Bear left onto North Shore Road. At 7.6 miles, after passing the ranger station and crossing the White River, the

road becomes Forest Road 65. Continue west on FR 65 for 8.8 miles to Lake Creek Campground. The trail begins at the far south end of the campground (elev. 2300 ft). Privy available.

ON THE TRAIL

The trail takes off south from the quiet campground and then immediately swings west. The spur that continues south follows Elevenmile Creek for a short distance to the Little Wenatchee River. It's not a bad diversion if you miss the turn. The main trail, however, continues across a bench of hemlock and huckleberry, shortly meeting up with the river at an inviting spot that encourages napping and picnicking. Directly across from the pristine waterway, Theseus Creek tumbles into it by a small campsite.

Heading upstream, the trail hugs the riverbank. Majestic Doug-firs and a few western white pines shade the way. After passing beneath a small scree slope, the trail makes a short steep climb. Notice the tread work. Is this perhaps a portion of the original trail to Cady Pass before logging roads shortened and obliterated much of the route?

Notice too that you are now at the head of the gorge. Avoid a spur that heads right, back to the road, and continue left to steeply drop back to river level. Now walk languidly along the crashing river, gazing into rapids and swirls and admiring tight chasms that thunder when the water level is high. Keep children and pooches close by at some of the gorge overlooks. Catch glimpses of Labyrinth Mountain rising above in the distance. After you pass a small punchbowl waterfall, the gorge broadens. And after passing its confluence with Lake Creek, the river once again makes a tight squeeze. A

The narrow Little Wenatchee River Gorge

spectacular rapids-fed bowl will hold your attention.

Beyond, the river resumes a more mellow flow, while the trail ends at an old road 1.5 miles from the trailhead. Return via the same route or turn right and follow FR 65 back to your vehicle.

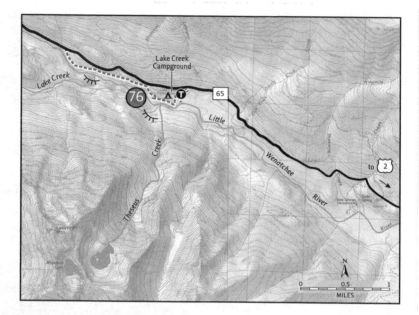

77 Soda Springs Big Trees

RATING/ DIFFICULTY	LOOP	ELEV GAIN/ HIGH POINT	SEASON
★/1	0.5 mile	50 feet/ 2250 feet	May–Nov

Map: Green Trails Wenatchee Lake No. 145; **Contact:** Okanogan-Wenatchee National Forest, Lake Wenatchee Ranger Station (summer), (509) 763-3103, or Wenatchee River Ranger District, Leavenworth, (509) 548-6977, www .fs.fed.us/r6/wenatchee; **GPS:** N 47 51.484, W 120 58.206

❌ 🚶 🐾 *Wander through a grove of big, beautiful ancient cedars on a hidden flat along the Little Wenatchee River. Then head over to a bubbling, gurgling soda spring. Children may* be disappointed that they can't have a taste of the fizzy water, but deer and other furry critters drink liberally from the mineral-laden spring.

GETTING THERE

From Everett head east on US 2 for 85 miles to Coles Corner. (From Leavenworth travel west on US 2 for 15 miles.) Turn left (north) onto State Route 207 (signed for Lake Wenatchee) and proceed 4.2 miles to a Y intersection after crossing the Wenatchee River. Bear left onto North Shore Road. At 7.6 miles, after passing the ranger station and crossing the White River, the road becomes Forest Road 65. Continue west on FR 65 for 6.2 miles to Soda Springs Campground. Follow the narrow, steep campground road to the trailhead at the far end of the campground (elev. 2250 ft). Privy available.

ON THE TRAIL

From the thickly wooded bluff housing the small primitive campground, locate the Big Tree Trail marked with a sign that simply says "Hiker Trail." With the roar of the Little Wenatchee River in the background (or its lull later in the season), drop down about 50 feet to a lush flat. Cross Soda Creek on a precarious log and enter a most impressive grove of old and towering Doug-firs, grand firs, and western red cedars. Then cross Ninemile Creek on a good log and come to a short path that leads left to a gravel bar on the Little Wenatchee.

The main trail heads to the right through a jungle of devil's club and under a canopy of trees that has been shading the ground in front of you for centuries. Turning away from the river, the trail loops around and recrosses first Ninemile (no bridge) and then Soda (on a good bridge), returning to the campground just to the north of where you began. While this trail makes for a nice family outing, it has long been neglected. Brushy areas and large blowdowns may hinder some hikers, especially the little ones.

Be sure you check out the Soda Springs before departing. Note the numerous and various animal tracks within their muddy and rusty flows.

Massive old-growth fir, hemlock, cedar, and white pine can be found along the Soda Springs Big Trees loop.

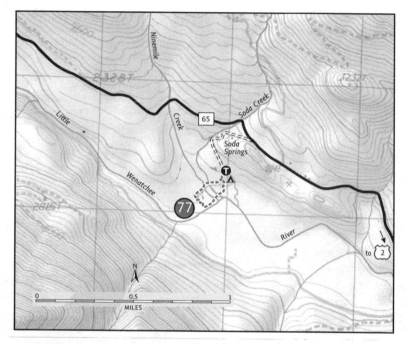

78 Poe Mountain via Irving Pass

RATING/ DIFFICULTY	ROUND-TRIP	ELEV GAIN/ HIGH POINT	SEASON
★★★★/3	6 miles	2250 feet/ 6015 feet	Mid-June– Oct

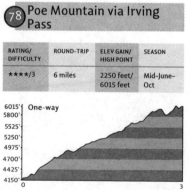

Map: Green Trails Benchmark Mtn No. 144;
Contact: Okanogan-Wenatchee National For-

est, Lake Wenatchee Ranger Station (summer), (509) 763-3103, or Wenatchee River Ranger District, Leavenworth, (509) 548-6977, www .fs.fed.us/r6/wenatchee; **Note:** NW Forest Pass required; **GPS:** N 47 53.717, W 121 02.159

Take this rolling alpine jaunt to Poe Mountain along Wenatchee Ridge and extensive views, prolific berry patches, and sublime meadows will serve as poetic justice for choosing this route. A slightly easier approach to Poe than the straight up the face of the mountain route described in Hike 75, this trail also offers a fine ridgeline ramble that allows prolonged viewing of the stunning surrounding countryside.

GETTING THERE

From Everett head east on US 2 for 85 miles to Coles Corner. (From Leavenworth travel west on US 2 for 15 miles.) Turn left (north) onto State Route 207 (signed for Lake Wenatchee) and proceed 4.2 miles to a Y intersection after crossing the Wenatchee River. Bear left onto North Shore Road. At 7.6 miles, after passing the ranger station and crossing the White River, the road becomes Forest Road 65. Continue west on FR 65 for 7.7 miles, bearing right onto graveled FR 6504 (1 mile past Soda Springs Campground). Continue for 6.3 miles (the last mile or so extremely rough and brushy) to the trailhead (elev. 4150 ft).

ON THE TRAIL

There's no time to stretch out on this route. The way commences with a steep climb, gaining 700 feet in 0.7 mile to Irving Pass, a sleepy little hollow on Wenatchee Ridge, otherwise known as Poet Ridge. From the pass, a long-abandoned, fading trail heads downward into the wild and lonely Panther Creek valley. You'll want to follow the more defined trail that heads left along the ridgeline.

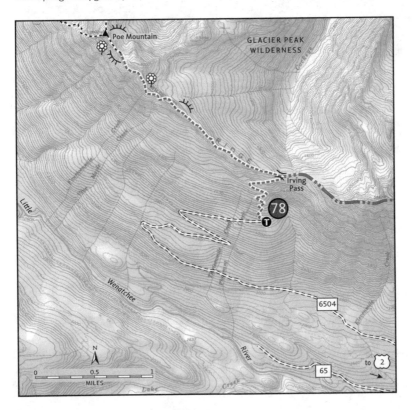

Cougar Creek valley as seen from the trail between Irving Pass and Poe Mountain

Climbing steeply again, the way pushes higher up the ridge. At about 1.2 miles, meadows and views begin. The trail continues westward across the rugged ridge, rounding bumps and knobs and steadily gaining elevation. At about 2.5 miles, the way skirts just beneath a 6000-foot knoll, passing a marshy depression before beginning a short descent.

After dropping a couple of hundred feet to a saddle beneath Poe Mountain, you'll come to a junction. The official trail continues left, meeting up with the Poe Mountain Trail at 5600 feet about 0.4 mile from the summit. The trail to the right is a boot-beaten shortcut that connects with the Poe Mountain Trail just beneath the summit. Chances are you'll choose the path that heads right, and after a short climb you'll begin to recite the prolific peaks from Poe's perspective. Glacier to the north. Rainier and an emerald swath of peaks along the Cascade crest to the west. Stuart to the south. The White Mountains to the east. And in the immediate vicinity along Poet Ridge, Bryant, Longfellow, Whittier, and Washington's Irving.

79 Hidden Lake

RATING/ DIFFICULTY	ROUND-TRIP	ELEV GAIN/ HIGH POINT	SEASON
★★/2	1.2 miles	200 feet/ 2275 feet	Apr– mid-Nov

One-way

2275'
2175'
2075'
0   0.6

Map: Green Trails Wenatchee Lake No. 145;
Contact: Okanogan-Wenatchee National Forest, Lake Wenatchee Ranger Station (summer), (509) 763-3103, or Wenatchee River Ranger District, Leavenworth, (509) 548-6977, www.fs.fed.us/r6/wenatchee; **Note:** NW Forest Pass required; **GPS:** N 47 49.298, W 120 48.383

A little lake surrounded by big pines in a hidden nook above Lake Wenatchee. This is a nice place for an afternoon stroll with kids in tow, or an evening jaunt while camping down below—just don't expect to be alone.

GETTING THERE

From Everett head east on US 2 for 85 miles to Coles Corner. (From Leavenworth travel west on US 2 for 15 miles.) Turn left (north) onto State Route 207 (signed for Lake Wenatchee) and proceed 3.5 miles, turning left onto Cedar Brae Road (signed for the south entrance of Lake Wenatchee State Park). In 0.4 mile bear left at the state park entrance, following Cedar Brae Road for another 3.4 miles to the pavement's end, where the road becomes Forest Road 6750. Bear left again in another 0.4 mile, and turn left at 0.9 mile to reach the trailhead (elev. 2075 ft). Privy available.

ON THE TRAIL

Responding to limited parking, the Forest Service constructed this new trailhead and trail to Hidden Lake in the early 2000s. The old trail from Glacier View Campground is still in place and maintained, and when combined with a short road walk it makes for a nice loop. If you're familiar with the old trail, the first thing you'll notice about the new one is that it's not nearly as steep. In fact, it's quite pleasurable and makes an ideal trail for coaxing someone into hiking for the first time.

Follow the wide, well-groomed trail through a flat of gorgeous old-growth cedars. After 0.25 mile the forest thins, and you might be able to make out Dirtyface Peak and Lake Wenatchee through the trees.

Gradually gaining elevation, greet Hidden Lake at its outlet stream near a patch of big ponderosa pines. Cross the stream on a log bridge to boulders, more big pines, and nice lakeshore lounging spots. In early season a series of cascading creeks feed into the

Hidden Lake tucked beneath Nason Ridge

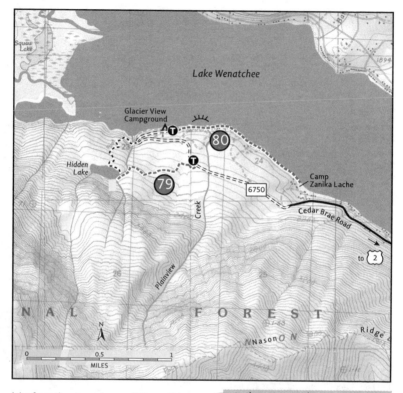

lake from the steep slopes of Nason Ridge. Enjoy the music they make as well as the symphonies conducted by the various avian residents.

EXTENDING YOUR TRIP
The old trail leaves from the big-pine and boulder grove on the west side of the outlet creek. Dropping rapidly 350 feet, the steep trail reaches the Glacier View Campground in 0.5 mile. Make a loop by following FR 6750 for 0.7 mile back to the new trailhead. Glacier View is an excellent place to set up a base for exploring other area hikes.

80 Lake Wenatchee South Shore Trail

RATING/ DIFFICULTY	ROUND-TRIP	ELEV GAIN/ HIGH POINT	SEASON
★★/1	2.4 miles	None/ 1900 feet	Apr– late Nov

Map: Green Trails Wenatchee Lake No. 145; **Contact:** Okanogan-Wenatchee National Forest, Lake Wenatchee Ranger Station (summer), (509) 763-3103, or Wenatchee River Ranger District, Leavenworth, (509) 548-6977, www .fs.fed.us/r6/wenatchee; **Note:** NW Forest Pass required; **GPS:** N 47 49.429, W 120 48.577

👪 *This lightly used trail allows you to enjoy glacier-made and glacier-fed big, beautiful Lake Wenatchee up close and personal. Saunter past quaint cottages, big trees, and shoreline ledges that grant good views up and down the 5-mile-long lake. Catch reflections of surrounding peaks twinkling on placid waters, or watch wind-whipped waves whack shoreline rocks.*

GETTING THERE

From Everett head east on US 2 for 85 miles to Coles Corner. (From Leavenworth travel west on US 2 for 15 miles.) Turn left (north) onto State Route 207 (signed for Lake Wenatchee) and proceed 3.5 miles, turning left onto Cedar Brae Road (signed for the south entrance of Lake Wenatchee State Park). In 0.4 mile bear left at the state park entrance, following Cedar Brae Road for another 3.4 miles to the pavement's end, where the road becomes Forest Road 6750. Bear left again in another 0.4 mile, and reach the trailhead at Glacier View Campground in 1.5 miles (elev. 1900 ft). Privy available.

ON THE TRAIL

Lake Wenatchee can be a busy place, its shorelines quite boisterous from Memorial Day to Labor Day. While this trail traverses public land, it passes by numerous private cabins and cottages. Most are unobtrusive and many are quite charming, harkening back to simpler and less ostentatious times. The owners of these structures lease the land from the Forest Service. Respect the owners' privacy and private property while sauntering by.

That said, you may want to avoid this trail in summer so as not to feel like you're traipsing in someone's backyard. Spring is quiet, but the trail often floods then. Fall is ideal. The

A border collie plays in Lake Wenatchee as Dirtyface Peak stands guard.

trail officially begins by the boat launch, but you may want to avoid traveling through someone's shoreline campsite. Walk the campground loop road east 0.25 mile to campsite number 20 and pick up the trail there.

Traveling along the lake's wooded shoreline, pass several large firs and cedars. At about 0.5 mile cross Plainview Creek on a log bridge, and soon come to a rocky point harboring an old bench and a big ponderosa pine. Enjoy excellent views of Dirtyface Peak rising above the lake and Mount David, too, hovering above the White River valley.

Come to another rocky point and then to excellent views down the lake to the Entiat Mountains. At about 0.9 mile leave cabins behind and enter old-growth forest. Notice the western white pines, an increasing rarity in the Cascades. At 1.2 miles the trail ends at a little bridge at Camp Fire USA's Camp Zanika Lache. Do not enter the camp. Turn around and resume pleasant lakeside rambling.

81 Lake Wenatchee State Park

RATING/ DIFFICULTY	LOOP	ELEV GAIN/ HIGH POINT	SEASON
**/1	2.5 miles	75 feet/ 1950 feet	Apr– late Nov

Map: Green Trails Plain No. 146; **Contact:** Lake Wenatchee State Park, (509) 763-3101, www.parks.wa.gov; **Notes:** Dogs permitted on-leash; Discover Pass required; **GPS:** N 47 49.429, W 120 48.577

Splendid undeveloped lakeshore and riverfront, spectacular views of towering peaks near and far, all from a pleasant loop that originates from one of Washington's busiest and best-loved state park campgrounds. But surprisingly, many campers never wander far from their fire pits and RVs, leaving these trails relatively quiet. The mosquitoes, however, are another thing. They're legendary here in May and June.

GETTING THERE

From Everett head east on US 2 for 85 miles to Coles Corner. (From Leavenworth travel west on US 2 for 15 miles.) Turn left (north) onto State Route 207 (signed for Lake Wenatchee) and proceed 4.2 miles to a Y intersection just after crossing the Wenatchee River. Bear left, and after 0.3 mile turn left into the north entrance of Lake Wenatchee State Park. In

A windy day brings crashing waves along the shores of Lake Wenatchee.

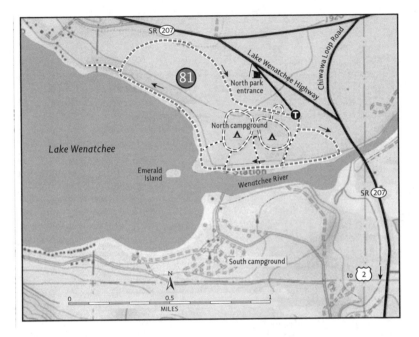

0.25 mile, just after passing the campground registration booth, come to the trailhead and parking (elev. 1950 ft). Privy available.

ON THE TRAIL

From behind a gate, pick up the trail and make a choice. Beeline straight for the river or take the longer, more scenic route? I thought you'd choose the latter. Turn left and amble through open forest of pine and fir, gently descending 50 feet or so to the Wenatchee River. Now turn right and head upriver. Nason Creek drains into the Wenatchee along this stretch. In spring the flow is quite intense. Rafters and floaters take to these waters later in the season when they're not as hazardous.

At 0.5 mile intersect the shortcut route. Continue straight along the river, passing

two spur trails leading to campground loops. At 1 mile arrive at a beautiful beach at the lake's outlet. A small wooded island guards the outflow. Huge cedar driftwood logs litter the beach. The view uplake to Dirtyface Peak, Nason Ridge, and Labyrinth Mountain is a classic. It's partially captured on Washington's special state parks license plate. Winds often whip here, funneling down from the glacially carved valley that houses the 2500-acre lake. The lake is fed by glaciers too—wade if you dare.

Continue past the beach and another campground spur, meandering through pleasant forest along the lakeshore. At 1.5 miles come to a junction. The trail left continues for 0.1 mile to the park border. Turn right and make a short steep climb of about 75 feet in open forest. Park personnel have recently cleared understory brush here, lessening chances of a serious fire sweeping through the popular park.

Now on a pleasant woods road, bear right at a junction and follow it to its terminus near the campground's loop 2. Walk the paved park road 0.25 mile back to your vehicle.

EXTENDING YOUR TRIP

There are several miles of pleasant trails in the 490-acre state park's southern unit too. In winter the park's trails are tracked and groomed for cross-country skiing. The state park makes an excellent base camp for hiking nearby national forest trails. Reservations are necessary in summer.

82 Dirtyface Lookout Site

RATING/ DIFFICULTY	ROUND-TRIP	ELEV GAIN/ HIGH POINT	SEASON
★★★★/4	9 miles	3950 feet/ 5989 feet	June–Nov

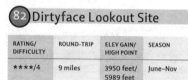

Map: Green Trails Wenatchee Lake No. 145;
Contact: Okanogan-Wenatchee National Forest, Lake Wenatchee Ranger Station (summer), (509) 763-3103, or Wenatchee River Ranger District, Leavenworth, (509) 548-6977, www.fs.fed.us/r6/wenatchee; **Note:** NW Forest Pass required; **GPS:** N 47 50.275, W 120 47.858

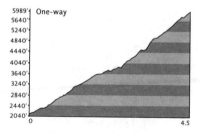 *Take this stiff climb to an old lookout site that looks out directly over Lake Wenatchee—and beyond. Hot and dry in summer, but a good choice in early season because it's often 90 percent snow-free by Memorial Day, Dirtyface provides a great heart conditioner and a lot of visual treats for the eyes. The views are stunning and expansive, from sun-baked Mission Ridge to snowcapped Glacier Peak.*

GETTING THERE

From Everett head east on US 2 for 85 miles to Coles Corner. (From Leavenworth travel west on US 2 for 15 miles.) Turn left (north) onto State Route 207 (signed for Lake Wenatchee) and proceed 4.2 miles to a Y intersection just after crossing the Wenatchee River. Bear left onto North Shore Road and in 4.5 miles come to the Lake Wenatchee Ranger Station. Turn right on a service road immediately before the parking area. Follow the road for 0.2 mile to the trailhead behind the ranger station (elev. 2040 ft). Privy available.

ON THE TRAIL

Beginning in open, mature timber, the well-defined trail ascends moderately as it traverses Dirtyface's sun-kissed southern slopes. Green timber soon yields to burnt bark and charred snags from a 2005 forest fire. Much old-growth timber, including giant ponderosa pines, survived the conflagration, but whether the trail survives it is another question. It won't be long before many of the fire-scorched trees begin to topple, forming impediments along the trail. With the Forest Service abandoning trails due to lack of funding for maintenance (and lack of enough public outcry demanding that Congress address this), Dirtyface may very well become another lost piece of our public heritage.

Gaining altitude more steadily, the way passes a spring before coming to Fall Creek tumbling down an open avalanche chute (elev. 2750). Views out over Lake Wenatchee are excellent. In May and June the flower show is too. Hop across the creek and continue climbing steeply, eventually following an old skid road through cool, unburnt timber. At about 2 miles the way intersects an old logging road (elev. 3500).

Turn left, following the old road for a gentle 0.5 mile, ending at a campsite and spring. The way then resumes as true trail and truly steep. Tight switchbacks that appear to have no end climb relentlessly. At about 4700 feet the forest thins. Ground squirrels and grouse scurry about. At about 3.8 miles come to a small ledge (elev. 5000 ft) with

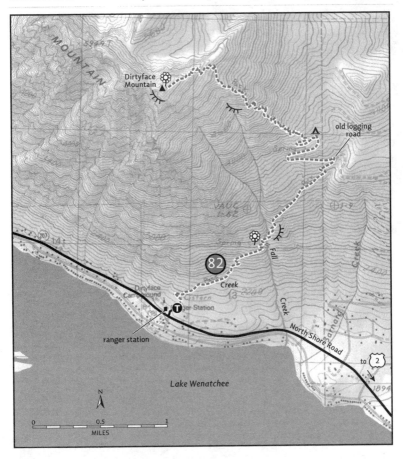

A balsamroot lines this waterfall on Dirtyface Peak.

north are especially impressive. So is the Nason Ridge to the south with its three prominent peaks, Rock, Howard, and Mastiff, lined up for your admiration. Fish Lake twinkles in the southeast. Lake Wenatchee spreads out directly below and will command most of your attention, especially its west end where the White and Little Wenatchee rivers flow into a vast marsh via spaghetti oxbows.

83 Twin Lakes

RATING/ DIFFICULTY	ROUND-TRIP	ELEV GAIN/ HIGH POINT	SEASON
★★★/3	8 miles	1000 feet/ 2850 feet	Late May– Nov

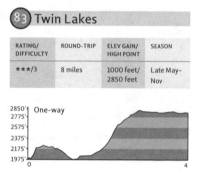

Map: Green Trails Wenatchee Lake No. 145; **Contact:** Okanogan-Wenatchee National Forest, Lake Wenatchee Ranger Station (summer), (509) 763-3103, or Wenatchee River Ranger District, Leavenworth, (509) 548-6977, www .fs.fed.us/r6/wenatchee; **Note:** NW Forest Pass required; **GPS:** N 47 55.232, W 120 53.693

Hike to a pair of pristine lakes, one quite large, both quite shallow, surrounded by big timber and wedged in a deep valley between the steep and jagged Dirtyface and Chiwawa ridges. The hike isn't overly difficult, but the terrain it traverses is rugged and remote. One of only three trails affording access into the wild Napeequa River valley, it's a brief affair here, but satisfying nevertheless, with good glimpses into this forbidding and magical corner of the Cascades.

great views to the south and east. It is often possible to reach this point in May without encountering snow.

Beyond, the trail enters the subalpine zone, passing small meadows flush with flowers and teeming with views. Reach the near-6000-foot former lookout site after a final push along a semi-open ridge crest.

Wipe sweat, apply sunscreen, pull out maps and begin swirling around to identify the myriad peaks spread out before you. Glacier, Clark, and the Chiwawa Ridge to the

GETTING THERE

From Everett head east on US 2 for 85 miles to Coles Corner. (From Leavenworth travel west on US 2 for 15 miles.) Turn left (north) onto State Route 207 (signed for Lake Wenatchee) and proceed 4.2 miles to a Y intersection just after crossing the Wenatchee River. Bear left onto North Shore Road, passing the Lake Wenatchee Ranger Station, and continue 6.2 miles to White River Road. Turn right and follow White River Road, which becomes Forest Road 64, for 6.3 miles to the trailhead at Napeequa Crossing Campground (elev. 1975 ft). Privy available.

ON THE TRAIL

A fairly well-beaten path leaves the primitive riverside campground near a row of giant cottonwoods. Immediately climbing, reach an easy-to-miss side trail at 0.4 mile that leads a short distance up a 2200-foot rocky knoll, affording a nice view down to the Tall Timber Youth Camp on the Napeequa and up to 7420-foot Mount David hovering over the White River valley.

Leveling off, the main trail traverses a couple of scree slopes before dropping 200 feet to briefly brush up against the wild Napeequa River. Continuing upvalley in a lush bottomland of cedars and cottonwoods, the trail then enters the Glacier Peak Wilderness. Soon afterward, pass a teeming-with-birds (and in early season, mosquitoes) wetland. Take in a good view of the towering serrated peaks flanking the Napeequa Valley and imagine what rugged delights lie upstream.

Delights in the form of monstrous cedar trees soon greet you on the trail as you

A hiker inspects the cabin at Twin Lakes that was built in 1949.

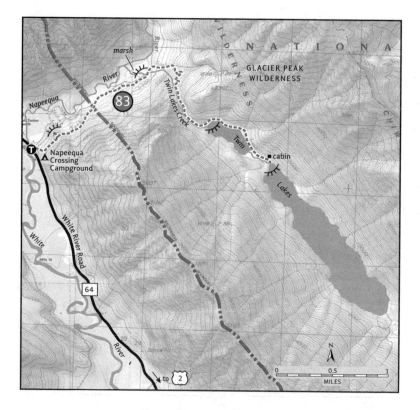

approach Twin Lakes Creek. The creek must be forded—easy to do late in the summer, but often tricky right after the snows melt. Scout upstream for a strategically fallen giant.

Once across the creek, the way climbs steeply, gaining 600 feet in about 0.5 mile and meeting back up with the creek in a tight slot canyon. The way negotiates the rocky gap via loose rock, a little ledge, and a couple times by swinging right down to creek's edge. Roaring rapids make the scene quite dramatic. At about 3.2 miles the trail and creek mellow out and the first of the

Twin Lakes, the smaller one, is encountered. The shoreline is brushy, but in about 0.25 mile is a nice lakeside ledge with a good view up to Dirtyface's forested backside.

Continue for a level 0.5 mile on brushy trail through nice forest to the bigger lake. Here you can check out a 1949 cabin used by the Washington Department of Fish and Wildlife to house personnel working at the fish-rearing station on the big twin. Walk down a small boardwalk to the lake and watch the cutthroat jump. Fishing is prohibited, unless you're a resident osprey or eagle.

84 Mount David

RATING/ DIFFICULTY	ROUND-TRIP	ELEV GAIN/ HIGH POINT	SEASON
★★★★★/5	14 miles	5200 feet/ 7420 feet	Aug–Oct

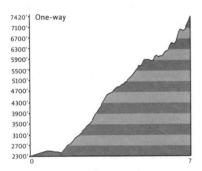

Map: Green Trails Wenatchee Lake No. 145; **Contact:** Okanogan-Wenatchee National Forest, Lake Wenatchee Ranger Station (summer), (509) 763-3103, or Wenatchee River Ranger District, Leavenworth, (509) 548-6977, www.fs.fed.us/r6/wenatchee; **Note:** NW Forest Pass required; **GPS:** N 47 57.792, W 120 56.729

Named by A. H. Sylvester (see "Sly Sylvester" in this section) for the biblical king of Judah, majestic Mount David reigns high above a heavenly kingdom of snow and ice and deep emerald valleys. With its lofty height and commanding views, it was home in the 1930s to a fire lookout. The lookout is long gone, but its legendary "throne of stone" outhouse still exists. Bountiful scenic rewards are granted to all who partake in the arduous task of summiting. The way is long (8 miles), and the climb is brutal (more than 1 vertical mile), and lingering snowfields make the route potentially dangerous (bring an ice ax). Only the most experienced and fit hikers should attempt this journey.

GETTING THERE

From Everett head east on US 2 for 85 miles to Coles Corner. (From Leavenworth travel west on US 2 for 15 miles.) Turn left (north) onto State Route 207 (signed for Lake Wenatchee) and proceed 4.2 miles to a Y intersection just after crossing the Wenatchee River. Bear left onto North Shore Road, passing the Lake Wenatchee Ranger Station, and continue 6.2 miles to White River Road. Turn right and follow White River Road, which

Mount David's "throne-of-stone" privy offers commanding views of Indian Head, Glacier Peak—and just about everything else!

becomes Forest Road 64, for 10.3 miles (the pavement ends at 6 miles) to its terminus at the trailhead (elev. 2300 ft). Privy available.

ON THE TRAIL

Cross the White River on a solid bridge, taking a moment to admire the cascade-fed gorge below. Immediately enter the Glacier Peak Wilderness and come to a junction. Right leads deep into the wilderness along Indian Creek (Hike 85). Head left on the Panther Creek Trail instead, and enjoy 1 mile of easy walking along the White River, losing about 100 feet of elevation. Take time to admire the scenic White River Falls. You'll know when they're close by the impending thunder.

Shortly past the falls you'll come to a junction (elev. 2200 ft). The Panther Creek Trail continues straight to the Panther Creek valley, where it fades into oblivion—yet another one of our treasured trails lost due to funding neglect. Fill water bottles (this is the last water source if snowfields have melted), and turn right onto the Mount David Trail and prepare to elevate your heart rate. For the next 3 miles the trail climbs steeply and relentlessly, switchbacking tightly as it gains 3000 feet!

Cresting David's high southern shoulder (elev. 5200 ft), catch your breath and prepare for your second vertical assault of the mountain. In thinning forest ripe with views, the trail now heads along the radiating ridge. Minor ups and downs keep the legs limber. At about 4.5 miles, a faint trail heads right, dropping several hundred feet into a small basin where water and backpackers may sometimes be found.

The way to David heads up and becomes increasingly difficult. The way leaves the for-

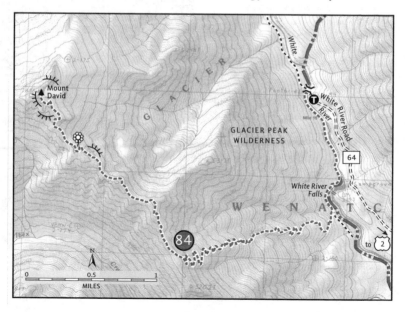

est behind to traverse open slopes of heather and scree. Use caution where the tread has slid out. Use caution, too, approaching the snowfield that usually lingers beneath the summit block. If it looks scary, turn around and be content with the wonderful views gained so far. Otherwise, proceed up ever steeper slopes, crossing loose rock and talus. The final section is a bit exposed and may be unnerving to the vertigo-inclined.

Reach the 7420-foot summit and relish in your peak-bagging achievement. Now reap your visual rewards that span the horizons. Glacier Peak dominates the northern view. The Poets—Whittier, Poe, Longfellow, Irving, and Bryant—and fellow biblical notables, Saul and Jonathan, stand proudly close-by to the south and west. Stare directly down 1 mile to the glaciated trough occupied by the White River. Follow it south to Lake Wenatchee. After you've overindulged in pure panoramic pleasures, a trip to Mount David's aerie privy is in order.

Just below the summit block try to locate the old lookout's outback outhouse. Composed entirely of rock, this throne of stone is my absolute favorite backcountry bathroom.

85 Indian Creek

RATING/ DIFFICULTY	ROUND-TRIP	ELEV GAIN/ HIGH POINT	SEASON
★★★/3	8 miles	800 feet/ 3100 feet	June–Nov

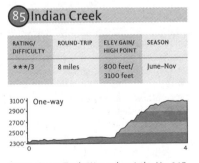

Maps: Green Trails Wenatchee Lake No. 145, Benchmark Mtn No. 144; **Contact:** Okanogan-Wenatchee National Forest, Lake Wenatchee Ranger Station (summer), (509) 763-3103, or

The White River rushes past old-growth cedars and firs along the first couple miles of the Indian Creek Trail.

Wenatchee River Ranger District, Leavenworth, (509) 548-6977, www.fs.fed.us/r6/wenatchee; **Note:** NW Forest Pass required; **GPS:** N 47 57.792, W 120 56.729

Two glacier-fed pristine rivers flow through corridors of gargantuan cedars that were old when Columbus, Cabot, and Cartier washed up on the eastern seaboard. This is a pleasant hike early or late season, crowds are nil, and chances are always good of spotting bears or other large woodland critters. Indian

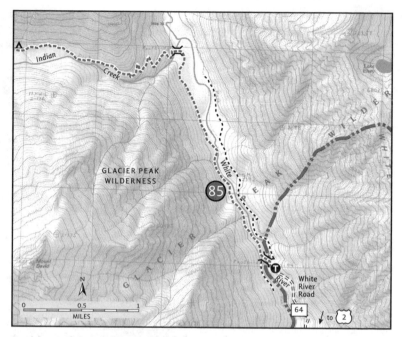

Creek is one of the best hikes in the vicinity for admiring ancient forest or when you want the wilderness all to yourself.

GETTING THERE

From Everett head east on US 2 for 85 miles to Coles Corner. (From Leavenworth travel west on US 2 for 15 miles.) Turn left (north) onto State Route 207 (signed for Lake Wenatchee) and proceed 4.2 miles to a Y intersection just after crossing the Wenatchee River. Bear left onto North Shore Road, passing the Lake Wenatchee Ranger Station, and continue 6.2 miles to White River Road. Turn right and follow White River Road, which becomes Forest Road 64, for 10.3 miles (the pavement ends at 6 miles) to its terminus at the trailhead (elev. 2300 ft). Privy available.

ON THE TRAIL

Take the trail left and cross the White River on a sturdy bridge. Admire rays of sunlight dancing on the mist that rises from the cascades crashing through the tight chasm below. Immediately enter the Glacier Peak Wilderness and come to a junction. Left leads to the dizzying heights of Mount David (Hike 84). Head right on a near-level course through towering old growth that lines the banks of the White River.

Witness some of the widest-girth western red cedar you've ever seen. Continue through cathedral groves that echo with sacred arias from the river. The forest canopy is soon broken due to the past work of heavy snows, discontent with remaining on Mount David's sheer slopes. Pass through several brushy avalanche slopes as you proceed farther upvalley. Embrace the sun and views east up the steep slopes of the White Mountains.

Cross several side creeks and a forest of stunted hemlock before the trail leaves the White River, turning westward to greet Indian Creek (elev. 2450 ft). About 2 miles from the trailhead, this is a good turnaround spot for children and hikers not interested in gaining elevation for the day. Otherwise continue, crossing the crashing creek on a good bridge and commencing to climb via a series of long, gentle switchbacks.

At about 3 miles, after passing a pretty cascade on the boulder-strewn creek, the way levels out. Indian Creek itself also mellows, and avalanche slopes soon interrupt the forest, granting views of impressive Mount David and its scarred slopes. Continue through brushy meadows best avoided in wet weather. Thickets of willow and alder and high grasses hide the creek. At about 4 miles, after crossing a small side creek, come to a campsite nestled among big cottonwoods. This is a good spot to call it a day.

EXTENDING YOUR TRIP
Strong day hikers can continue farther up the Indian Creek Trail for several more miles. Elevation gain is minimal, but several brushy spots might make travel difficult. Hikers who carry on can expect some good views of several of the Poet Peaks (along Wenatchee Ridge) and excellent wildlife-watching opportunities. The White River Trail beginning from the same trailhead, but traveling on the eastern bank of the White River, can easily be hiked for several miles before it gets tangled up in avalanche brush. The first couple of miles are pure old-growth splendor.

Chiwawa River Valley

In a Native language the Chiwawa River's name means "last canyon next to mountains," and while the river might not exactly be the last canyon in these parts, it does form one heck of a canyon, and it's next to some pretty spectacular mountains. A major tributary to the Wenatchee River, the Chiwawa is a portal into the southeastern corner of the sprawling Glacier Peak Wilderness. And some of the trails radiating out of this deep glacially carved valley are among the toughest and most visually rewarding in the region.

86 Basalt Peak

RATING/ DIFFICULTY	ROUND-TRIP	ELEV GAIN/ HIGH POINT	SEASON
★★★/4	8.4 miles	2600 feet/ 5950 feet	June–Oct

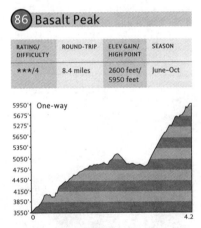

Maps: Green Trails Wenatchee Lake No. 145, Plain No. 146; **Contact:** Okanogan-Wenatchee National Forest, Lake Wenatchee Ranger Station (summer), (509) 763-3103, or Wenatchee River Ranger District, Leavenworth, (509) 548-6977, www.fs.fed.us/r6/wenatchee; **GPS:** N 47 57.358, W 120 44.151

A lonely outpost, yet easily accessible, forested Basalt Peak is oft overlooked. Four trails lead to this conical summit and all are steep. The Minnow Creek Trail is the easiest, though by no means is it easy. But hikers who brave Basalt's vertical slopes and voracious mosquitoes (they're legendary here in the Chiwawa Valley) will be rewarded with excellent views of the lofty, cloud-catching crags that flank the peak north and east.

GETTING THERE

From Everett head east on US 2 to Coles Corner. (From Leavenworth travel west on US 2 for 15 miles.) Turn left onto State Route 207 (signed for Lake Wenatchee) and proceed 4.2 miles to a Y intersection after crossing the Wenatchee River. Bear right onto the Chiwawa Loop Road and after 1.3 miles turn left onto the Chiwawa River Road (Forest Road 62), signed "Chiwawa Valley." Proceed for 9.4 miles, turning right onto FR 6210, signed "Chikamin Trailheads" (the turnoff is 1.25 miles beyond

Grouse Creek Campground). Continue on this narrow but good gravel road for 3.5 miles to the trailhead (elev. 3550 ft).

ON THE TRAIL

There's no easing into this hike—the climbing begins immediately, on soft pumice soils and under a canopy of pine and fir. Window views of peaks and ridges south and west and browsing deer should help keep your mind off of the grunt. After 0.5 mile the grade eases, the trail shifting to a gentle traverse.

Soon afterward, Minnow Creek is met in a cool, cedar-forested ravine. The trail here is muddy in spots and brushy and is in serious need of maintenance. Without adequate funding from the federal government for upkeep, this trail, like so many other Washington trails, faces the very real prospect of permanently fading from our maps and guidebooks. That would be a shame.

Views across the Chiwawa River valley from Basalt Peak's basalt cliffs

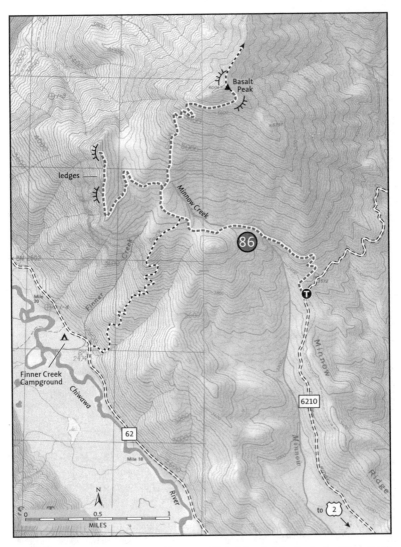

At 1 mile cross Minnow Creek and begin another steep climb, albeit short. At 1.2 miles intersect the Basalt Ridge Trail (elev. 4400 ft). Left heads 1.7 miles to the Finner Creek Campground in the Chiwawa River valley, dropping 1900 feet along the way. Head right instead, and after an easy 0.4 mile come to a junction with a spur trail signed for a viewpoint.

Not shown on maps, this trail is a mandatory side trip. Traveling for a mile and gaining only about 150 feet of elevation, this well-defined side trail leads to the upper edge of Basalt Peak's fearsome western slope ledges (elev. 4850 ft). The drop-off is grand (keep children and dogs nearby) and so are the views. Stare straight down to the oxbows of the Chiwawa River and straight out to the ice and rock of Chiwawa Ridge, capped by 8528-foot Buck Mountain. Estes Butte lies directly to the north.

After enjoying views usually reserved for raptors and accipiters, return to the Basalt Ridge Trail. Now undulating between stands of pine, hemlock, and fir, head 1.6 steep miles to Basalt's 6000-foot summit. A small meadow signals that the end of climbing is near. Just beyond and just below the summit high point is a series of ledges granting nice viewing east out to the Entiat Mountains. Find an accommodating rock for your weary body and enjoy the limited but satisfying view.

The actual summit is about 50 feet higher, 500 feet away or so, wooded and no longer sporting a lookout tower. You can follow a trail of sorts that skirts just below it to some limited views west. A better option is to continue along the Basalt Ridge Trail, dropping off of the summit cone to ledges and forest openings that afford excellent views north to Glacier Peak and its surrounding summits.

EXTENDING YOUR TRIP

For a loop, continue on the Basalt Ridge Trail for 1.2 miles to Basalt Pass. Then turn right and follow the Basalt Pass Trail for 1.7 steep downward miles to FR 6210. Walk the road to the right for 2.3 miles back to your vehicle.

87 Garland Peak

RATING/ DIFFICULTY	ROUND-TRIP	ELEV GAIN/ HIGH POINT	SEASON
★★★★★/5	10.4 miles	3550 feet/ 7400 feet	Late June– Oct

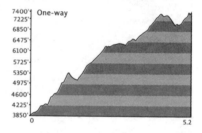

Maps: Green Trails Plain No. 146, Lucerne No. 114; **Contact:** Okanogan-Wenatchee National Forest, Lake Wenatchee Ranger Station (summer), (509) 763-3103, or Wenatchee River Ranger District, Leavenworth, (509) 548-6977, www.fs.fed.us/r6/wenatchee; **GPS:** N 47 58.718, W 120 43.598

> *The first half of this trip is a brutally steep, brushy at times, curse-inducing slog. The second half? Absolutely breathtaking! After ascending pine-dotted knolls and traversing pumice plains and rock gardens bursting with blossoms, reach a lofty shoulder on 7526-foot Garland Peak. From this vantage high in the Entiat Mountains, prepare for visual and mental overload taking in ridges and peaks for as far as the eye can see and for as long as the mind can tally.*

GETTING THERE

From Everett head east on US 2 to Coles Corner. (From Leavenworth travel west on US 2 for 15 miles.) Turn left onto State Route 207 (signed for Lake Wenatchee) and proceed

4.2 miles to a Y intersection after crossing the Wenatchee River. Bear right onto the Chiwawa Loop Road and after 1.3 miles turn left onto the Chiwawa River Road (Forest Road 62), signed "Chiwawa Valley." Proceed for 9.4 miles, turning right onto FR 6210, signed "Chikamin Trailheads" (the turnoff is 1.25 miles beyond Grouse Creek Campground). Continue on this narrow but good gravel road for 5.8 miles to the trailhead (elev. 3850 ft).

ON THE TRAIL

No sugar coating here. The first half of this hike is a real drag. And when the mosquitoes are swarming (count on it in June and July), you may wish that you never considered this hike. Be sure to pack plenty of water, for the creek at the trailhead is the last source of reliable water you'll pass.

Following the Basalt Pass Trail, immediately start climbing. The trail is brushy at times, with rough and occasionally eroded tread, and gives very little help in the form of switchbacks. After 1.7 miserable miles, reach a junction with the Basalt Ridge Trail at heavily timbered Basalt Pass (elev. 5150 ft).

Left heads to Basalt Peak (Hike 86). Go right and soon come to a junction with the Rock Creek Tie Trail, which drops 1900 feet in 1.6 miles to the Rock Creek Trail (Hike 89). Continue straight on the Basalt Ridge Trail, following rocky and eroded tread over more brushy, steep terrain. And if the sun is beating down, add hot to the list of maladies this trail inflicts.

But persevere, and soon it becomes evident why you're on this trail. Just over 0.5 mile from the pass, traverse a rock garden with good views south over the wide emerald valley of the Chiwawa River to Mission Ridge, Icicle Ridge, and the Stuart Range. Continue on, reveling in a respite from the sun when the trail reenters forest and a respite from the grind on much easier grade.

Garland Peak offers spectacular views of Glacier Peak and beyond.

At 1.5 miles from the pass (3.2 miles from the trailhead), crest a 6350-foot knoll. Hikers short on time and short on energy may want to call it a day here, content with excellent views north, south, and west. However, the best is yet to come, so consider pushing on!

Following along the crest of a ridge, the way continues. Avoiding a 6763-foot knoll,

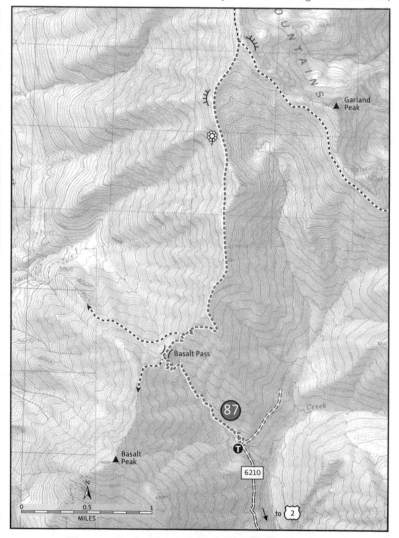

the trail drops 100 feet or so and then makes a steep climb up sun-parched meadows back to the ridgeline. From here the way turns steeper and more interesting. traversing a huge field of pumice deposited over 10,000 years ago when nearby Glacier Peak blew her top. At 5.2 miles the trail terminates (along with the climbing) at an intersection with the Garland Peak Trail on a 7400-foot knoll high in the Entiat Mountains.

Catch your breath, rehydrate, and then let your eyes go crazy scanning the sweeping views in every direction. From Mount Rainier to Glacier Peak; from the gentle Mad River country to the craggy fortress of the Chelan Mountains; and add Clark, Buck, Bonanza, and hundreds of other peaks near and far, familiar and obscure.

EXTENDING YOUR TRIP

Excellent high-country roaming can be had by following the Garland Peak Trail 0.5 mile north toward the Rampart Mountains and Devils Smokestack or south 1 mile toward Garland Peak. Scramblers revel in the good choice of nearby knolls and peaks—a few, such as Garland, are mere walk-ups.

88 Schaefer Lake

RATING/ DIFFICULTY	ROUND-TRIP	ELEV GAIN/ HIGH POINT	SEASON
★★★/4	10 miles	2700 feet/ 5130 feet	Aug– mid-Oct

One-way elevation profile: 5130', 4850', 4550', 4250', 3950', 3650', 3350', 3050', 2750', 2450' (from 0 to 5)

A hiker enjoys his lunch at Schaefer Lake.

Map: Green Trails Wenatchee Lake No. 145; **Contact:** Okanogan-Wenatchee National Forest, Lake Wenatchee Ranger Station (summer), (509) 763-3103, or Wenatchee River Ranger District, Leavenworth, (509) 548-6977, www .fs.fed.us/r6/wenatchee; **Note:** NW Forest Pass required; **GPS:** N 47 57.175, W 120 46.356

Climb to a big, beautiful sparkling lake cupped in a cirque high on the craggy Chiwawa Ridge. Silver logs line the shoreline and shine in the afternoon sun. Asters and gentians add

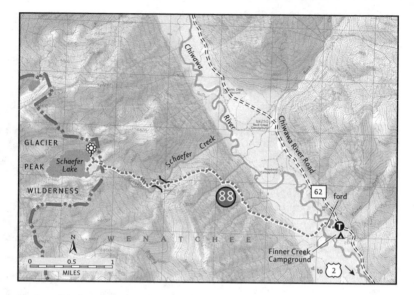

strokes of indigo and violet to the surrounding meadows. In autumn, low-lying blueberry bushes set the basin afire in crimson. While the climb can be stiff, the toughest part of this hike may be right in the beginning. If the Chiwawa River can't be safely forded, head to nearby Estes Butte or Basalt Peak instead, returning to Schaefer when river levels have subsided.

GETTING THERE

From Everett head east on US 2 for 85 miles to Coles Corner. (From Leavenworth travel west on US 2 for 15 miles.) Turn left onto State Route 207 (signed for Lake Wenatchee) and proceed 4.2 miles to a Y intersection after crossing the Wenatchee River. Bear right onto the Chiwawa Loop Road, and after 1.3 miles turn left onto the Chiwawa River Road (Forest Road 62). Proceed for 13 miles (the pavement ends at 10.8 miles) to the trail-

head, located 0.2 mile beyond Finner Creek Campground (elev. 2450 ft).

ON THE TRAIL

Begin by immediately dropping to the lush Chiwawa River flat. Pass the horse ford, soon coming to the hiker ford. For many years you could easily cross the river here by picking your way across a large log jam. But recently the jam was reduced, leaving one or two flimsy logs spanning a deep pool. Don't attempt it. Instead, ford downriver from the jam on a wide, graveled, generally shallow area. Of course this is only safe usually during late summer and early fall. If the river level is high and the water is flowing swiftly, seek an alternative trip.

Once safely across, follow the trail through about 0.5 mile of impressive cedars and cottonwoods and a "jungle flat" of dogwood thickets before leaving the flood plain. Cross a brushy avalanche slope before finally settling into good trail. Don't get too comfortable, though, for it's time to start climbing. Paralleling the Chiwawa River the way angles up steep slopes northward. A couple of creeks and window views out to Basalt Peak, Estes Butte, and up the Chiwawa Valley break the monotony of the climb.

At about 2.5 miles the trail rounds a ridge, turning westward into a deep valley high above Schaefer Creek (elev. 3600 ft). Enter a grove of big spruce trees and commence climbing steeply once more. At 3.5 miles cross Schaefer Creek on a solid bridge (elev. 4100 ft). Now through thinning forest peppered with granite boulders and ledges, the way steepens yet again. At around 4 miles (elev. 4600 ft) is a ledge just off-trail that grants sweeping views of the Chiwawa Valley and the lofty ridges and peaks flanking it. Good spot for a water break.

Climbing soon eases as the trail meets up once more with Schaefer Creek and enters the Glacier Peak Wilderness. At 4.75 miles reach placid and petite Little Schaefer Lake set amid moist meadows flourishing with flowers. Continue an easy 0.25 mile and reach big Schaefer amid more meadows and with a shimmering shoreline. Sit on a silver driftwood log, aching feet immersed in rejuvenating waters, and absorb the soothing beauty of your surroundings. Chickadees and nuthatches provide a backdrop score complementing the setting quite nicely.

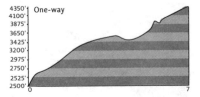

Maps: Green Trails Wenatchee Lake No. 145, Holden No. 113; **Contact:** Okanogan-Wenatchee National Forest, Lake Wenatchee Ranger Station (summer), (509) 763-3103, or Wenatchee River Ranger District, Leavenworth, (509) 548-6977, www.fs.fed.us/r6/wenatchee; **GPS:** N 47 58.196, W 120 47.343

Venture up a wide and deep valley to peaceful meadows in the heart of the Entiat Mountains. While nearby trails swarm with hikers and horseback riders, you'll more than likely only be sharing this route with ground squirrels and deer and perhaps a shy bear. While any distance along this trail makes for a nice early season wilderness probe, to reach the meadows you must ford Rock Creek twice, which is usually safe only late in the season.

GETTING THERE

From Everett head east on US 2 for 85 miles to Coles Corner. (From Leavenworth travel west on US 2 for 15 miles.) Turn left onto State Route 207 (signed for Lake Wenatchee) and proceed 4.2 miles to a Y intersection after crossing the Wenatchee River. Bear right onto the Chiwawa Loop Road, and after 1.3 miles turn left onto the Chiwawa River Road (Forest Road 62). Proceed for 14.4 miles (the pavement ends at 10.8 miles) to the trailhead, located 1.6 miles beyond Finner Creek Campground (elev. 2500 ft).

89 Rock Creek

RATING/ DIFFICULTY	ROUND-TRIP	ELEV GAIN/ HIGH POINT	SEASON
★★★/3	14 miles	1850 feet/ 4350 feet	June–Oct

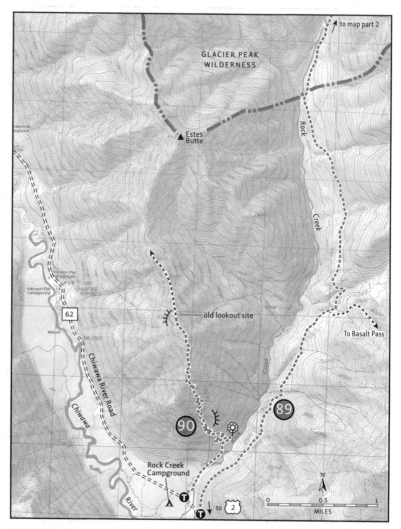

ON THE TRAIL

Begin in forest away from the creek, gradually climbing above the pristine waterway. At 2.5 miles reach a junction with the Rock Creek Tie Trail (elev. 3300 ft). The trail right climbs steeply—1900 feet in 1.6 miles—to Basalt Pass, offering an alternative approach to Basalt Peak (Hike 86).

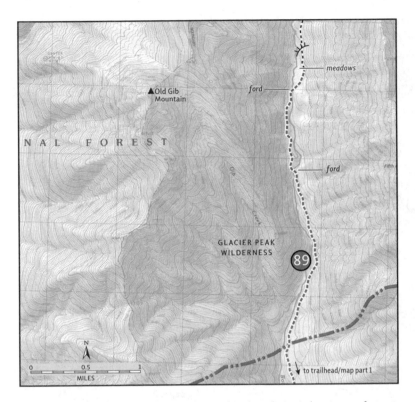

Continue straight, now well above Rock Creek. The grade eases with a few ups and downs as the trail pulls farther away from the creek. At 4 miles cross a creek coming down from the Rampart Mountains. In another 0.5 mile, enter the Glacier Peak Wilderness (elev. 3500 ft) and finally meet up with Rock Creek. Now in old growth, continue along the tumbling waterway, climbing much more steeply for the next mile.

At 6.5 miles come to the first ford of Rock Creek. If it looks deep, cold, and swift, it probably is! Call it quits, content to experience a quiet wilderness valley. If the crossing looks

safe and you don't mind getting your feet wet, proceed. Traverse a broad river flat, returning to creek's edge in another 0.5 mile. Ford the refreshing creek once more, emerging in those promised peaceful meadows.

Remove your pack, plop your fanny in the field, take a swig of water and a handful of cashews, and absorb the serenity and solitude of your surroundings. Old Gib looks down upon you from the west, while the Fifth of July Mountain and its craggy neighbors form an impressive flank to the east. A carpet of wildflowers softens the valley's harsh edges.

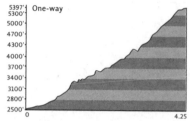

Map: Green Trails Wenatchee Lake No. 145; **Contact:** Okanogan-Wenatchee National Forest, Lake Wenatchee Ranger Station (summer), (509) 763-3103, or Wenatchee River Ranger District, Leavenworth, (509) 548-6977, www.fs.fed.us/r6/wenatchee; **GPS:** N 47 58.285, W 120 47.451

⚙ *Dry, hot, and dusty in high summer, Estes Butte makes a good choice in June or autumn. Its southern sun-baked slopes allow for early season sauntering when surrounding summits in the Entiats and on Chiwawa Ridge are shrouded in snow. Views of those jagged peaks from this old lookout site are good, and so is the one down to the broad glacier-carved valley below.*

Wild ginger carpets much of the forest floor in the lower Rock Creek valley.

EXTENDING YOUR TRIP
Strong day hikers can continue up the valley another 1.5 miles or so before the trail begins climbing to Carne Mountain. If you can arrange a car shuttle, a great one-way trip (a long day or nice overnighter) of 15.7 miles can be made by linking up with the Carne Mountain Trail (Hike 92).

GETTING THERE
From Everett head east on US 2 for 85 miles to Coles Corner. (From Leavenworth travel west on US 2 for 15 miles.) Turn left onto State Route 207 (signed for Lake Wenatchee) and proceed 4.2 miles to a Y intersection after crossing the Wenatchee River. Bear right onto the Chiwawa Loop Road, and after 1.3 miles turn left onto the Chiwawa River Road (FR 62). Proceed for 14.6 miles (the pavement ends at 10.8 miles) to the trailhead, located 1.8 miles beyond Finner Creek Campground (elev. 2500 ft).

90 Estes Butte

RATING/ DIFFICULTY	ROUND-TRIP	ELEV GAIN/ HIGH POINT	SEASON
★★★/4	8.5 miles	2900 feet/ 5397 feet	June–Oct

ON THE TRAIL

Ignore what the old guidebooks, maps, and Forest Service literature say about this hike in regard to its distance. It's not 2.6 or 3 miles long to the old lookout site on Estes Butte. It's more than 4 miles one-way—but that's good. The trail was reconstructed in the mid-1990s with an easier grade and gentler switchbacks. Despite the longer distance, this hike is now easier, and much better on your knees on the descent. It's still dry, so pack plenty of water.

The first 0.5 mile still follows an old mining road, traveling gently along Rock Creek. Then it's up, up, and away, climbing 2700 feet in 3.7 miles. Most of the way is forested—consider that a blessing, especially if eastside sun is shining. In May and June the forest floor is adorned in scads of pipsissewa (a wintergreen cousin called prince's pine back east) and wild ginger (a birthwort that tastes and smells like ginger, but beware: it's a diuretic and you'll be losing enough liquid on this hike by sweating!).

Winding up the mountain, you'll periodi-cally pass traces of the old trail. Teaser views are granted along the way, but the good show doesn't come until you reach the 5397-foot lookout knoll. Only the foundation remains of the lookout building, but there's still plenty to look out at. Take in an excellent view of the southern reaches of the Chiwawa Valley. Look west to the ridge of the same name and to Clark and Buck mountains farther out. Look east to Garland Peak and the Entiat Mountains. Enjoy the sun too—hopefully it's not too hot.

EXTENDING YOUR TRIP

The trail extends beyond the lookout knoll, climbing another 500-plus feet in 1.5 miles to the 5942-foot true summit of Estes. Feel free to continue along this mostly treed ridge if compelled to explore further. Beyond the true summit, the way continues 9.5 miles to Carne Mountain on a primitive path, hard to follow and easy to lose. It's bone dry in summer and dangerous in early season due to treacherous snow chutes.

Views across the Chiwawa River valley from the old lookout site on Estes Butte

91 Little Giant Pass

RATING/ DIFFICULTY	ROUND-TRIP	ELEV GAIN/ HIGH POINT	SEASON
★★★★★/5	10 miles	4000 feet/ 6409 feet	Aug– mid-Oct

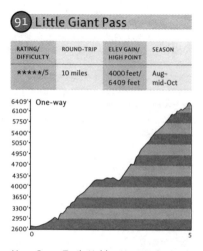

Map: Green Trails Holden No. 113; **Contact:** Okanogan-Wenatchee National Forest, Lake Wenatchee Ranger Station (summer), (509) 763-3103, or Wenatchee River Ranger District, Leavenworth, (509) 548-6977, www .fs.fed.us/r6/wenatchee; **GPS:** N 48 01.550, W 120 49.716

❌ ⚙️ *It's a little steep, a little brushy, and a little challenging getting to Little Giant Pass. But the scenic rewards? Far from little—they're gigantic! From this notch of a pass high in the Chiwawa Mountains, stand mesmerized, frozen in awe, utterly fixated on the mystifying and alluring Napeequa Valley. Gaze down at the wild Napeequa River, slithering and shining in this classic U-shaped valley, flanked by ice and rock and carpeted in vivid greenery speckled with brilliant wildflowers.*

GETTING THERE

From Everett head east on US 2 for 85 miles to Coles Corner. (From Leavenworth travel west on US 2 for 15 miles.) Turn left onto State Route 207 (signed for Lake Wenatchee) and proceed 4.2 miles to a Y intersection after crossing the Wenatchee River. Bear right onto the Chiwawa Loop Road, and after 1.3 miles turn left onto the Chiwawa River Road (Forest Road 62). Proceed for 19 miles (the pavement ends at 10.8 miles) to the trailhead, located on your left (elev. 2600 ft).

ON THE TRAIL

From beginning to end, there's nothing easy about this trail. The first challenge is met immediately at the trailhead with a ford of the Chiwawa River. A bridge once spanned the river here, but it was swept away by a furious flood back in 1972. Respect the river. It can only be safely forded in late summer when water levels run low. Even then it's still cold and the current swift, so proceed with caution. If it looks scary, head instead to one of the many other excellent hikes nearby in the Chiwawa Valley.

Picking your way across the graveled river, scan the cold waters for chinook, steelhead, and trout: cutthroat, rainbow, perhaps even bull. A car campground once existed here on the west bank of the river, but very little evidence of it remains. You'll need to snoop around a little to locate the trail. Head north a short way to a grove of mature cottonwoods, and then turn left at a rocky outwash where good, discernable tread can eventually be found.

The trail, once an old sheep drive, parallels Maple Creek for a short distance before crossing its wide gravelly wash. Now paralleling the watercourse on its north bank, the trail gently climbs under a canopy of scraggly hemlocks occasionally interspersed with white pine. Easy wanderings, however, end soon and the way turns steep and rough. Receiving little maintenance, this trail is in danger of becoming yet another casualty of Forest Service neglect (thanks largely to congressional indifference). Expect brushy sections, a lot of windfall, and areas of slumping tread.

After 2 miles of steep climbing, the way rounds a ridge (elev. 4200 ft), leaving the Maple Creek valley for the Little Giant Creek valley. Now in a cool forested grove, drop steeply 200 feet to cross a branch of Little Giant Creek (which can be tricky). The trail,

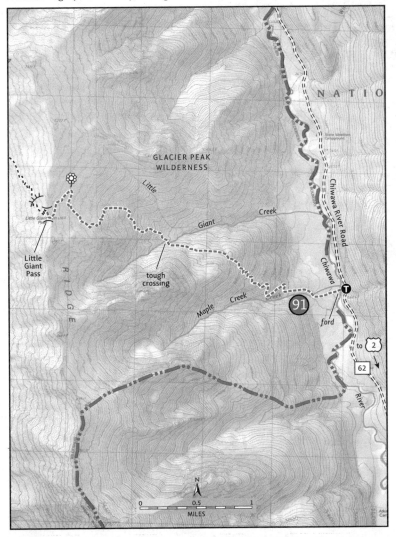

A pair of hikers stand mesmerized by the beauty of the Napeequa Valley from Little Giant Pass. (Craig Romano photo)

now downright nasty, ascends steep slopes of fire-charred forest. After crossing a minor tributary, fight through a curse-inducing patch of spirea and slide alder before emerging onto open ledges—and, thankfully, to good views out across the Chiwawa Valley to the Entiat Mountains.

Work your way up the sun-kissed ledges. Then unfortunately, it's back into the brush before reaching soothing heather and blueberry meadows blessed with a myriad of flowers and gently gurgling rivulets. Your toil now finally validated, the way continues up an open knoll (elev. 5700 ft) offering superb

viewing north to the fortress of peaks at the head of the Chiwawa Valley.

After one last steep grunt, the trail makes a long switchback through sweeping alpine meadows to the 6409-foot pass on Chiwawa Ridge. While the views so far have been excellent, they pale compared to what you are about to experience. Climb the small knoll just to the north of the pass and behold the unveiling of one of the most stunning views this side of the Continental Divide. Stare straight down to the snaking Napeequa (which means "white water"), the river slithering through fields of green beneath towering peaks topped in ice that glistens in the sun. Clark, Glacier, Buck, and scores of lesser—but just as beautiful and impressive—peaks will keep you mesmerized and captivated all afternoon long.

The trail continues into the magical valley, but the added distance, elevation change, and degree of difficulty of the path puts it squarely into the realm of the experienced backpacker.

92 Carne Mountain

RATING/ DIFFICULTY	ROUND-TRIP	ELEV GAIN/ HIGH POINT	SEASON
★★★★★/4	8 miles	3600 feet/ 7085 feet	Late June– Oct

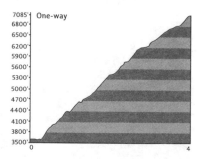

Map: Green Trails Holden No. 113; **Contact:** Okanogan-Wenatchee National Forest, Lake Wenatchee Ranger Station (summer), (509) 763-3103, or Wenatchee River Ranger District, Leavenworth, (509) 548-6977, www.fs.fed.us/r6/wenatchee; **Note:** NW Forest Pass required; **GPS:** N 48 04.975, W 120 50.098

> *One of the finest viewing outposts in the Chiwawa region, Carne Mountain will leave your head spinning as you try to identify a seemingly infinite array of peaks spread out before you: from close-ups of Maude, mighty matron of the Entiat Range, all the way to Stuart and the Enchantments. And valleys too! Peer straight down into gorgeous emerald allies housing roaring waterways. The trail is well built, albeit steep. An excellent alpine choice in early summer—come for the wildflowers. Or miss the floral show and arrive later for the larch production, which receives golden praise year after year.*

GETTING THERE

From Everett head east on US 2 for 85 miles to Coles Corner. (From Leavenworth travel west on US 2 for 15 miles.) Turn left onto State Route 207 (signed for Lake Wenatchee) and proceed 4.2 miles to a Y intersection after crossing the Wenatchee River. Bear right onto the Chiwawa Loop Road, and after 1.3 miles turn left onto the Chiwawa River Road (Forest Road 62). Proceed for 22 miles (the pavement ends at 10.8 miles) to a junction. Bear right onto FR 6211 and proceed for 2.3 very rough miles to the trailhead at the road's end (elev. 3500 ft).

ON THE TRAIL

Carne Mountain was named by A. H. Sylvester (see "Sly Sylvester" in this section) for an English clergyman and is pronounced *carn*,

A hiker works his way up the larch-laced slopes of Carne Mountain.

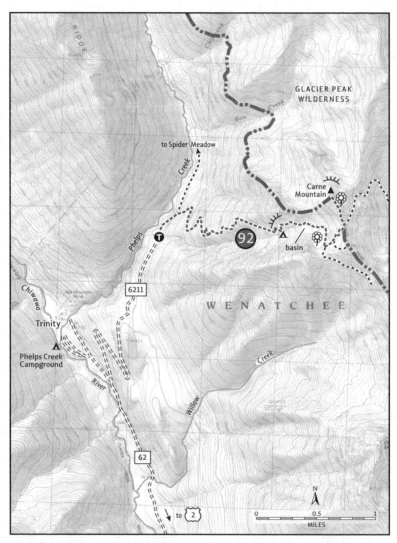

not *car-nay*, as in the Spanish word for meat—though you may feel like raw meat after attempting this steep, south-facing climb on a hot summer day. So get an early start to avoid the heat. Take a siesta on the summit and savor the scenery.

Starting from the Phelps Creek trailhead, don't despair if the parking lot is overflowing all the way down to Trinity (more on Trinity later). Ninety percent of those vehicles belong to hikers heading to Spider Meadow (Hike 93). Head down the Phelps Creek Trail a quick 0.25 mile, hopping over a refreshing creek just before coming to the junction with the Carne Mountain Trail. Time to break a sweat: the trail immediately commences to climb, switchbacking at times, shooting straight up at others.

As you wind through open forest, peek-a-boo views hint at the visual pleasures that lie ahead. After close to 2 miles of serious climbing, break out onto dry open slopes. While your eyes may be lured to scan the valley below, the myriad flowers painting the hillside may capture your attention first. Continue climbing at a good clip, passing a spur to a creekside campsite before reaching a series of tight switchbacks, views growing at each twist of the trail.

At 3 miles enter a high hanging basin (elev. 6100 ft) laced in larch and brushed with brilliant blossoms. Snow lingers late in this alpine pocket, providing a reliable water source for resident marmots and parched hikers. After a much needed respite from climbing, it's steeply up, up, and away once more. Soon reach a junction with the lightly traveled Old Gib Trail (elev. 6450 ft).

Head left, ascending through attractive groves of larches to crest a high saddle (elev. 6800 ft) between Carne's two prominent summits, coming to an unsigned junction with the Rock Creek Trail. Carne's 7085-foot summit lies left. Follow a flower-lined path 0.3 mile to reach it. Speedwell, buckwheat, gilia, gentian, lupine, paintbrush, partridgefoot, stonecrop, penstemon, buttercup, anemone, aster—what a line-up!

The panorama of pointy peaks and deep valleys is quite an arrangement as well. South it's the wild and lonely Rock Creek valley flanked by the Entiat Mountains, Old Gib, and Basalt. Look west to Buck and the Chiwawa Ridge, their glaciers and snowfields glistening in the sun. Directly below, make out remnant structures of Trinity, a former mining town, now a private ghost town. Stare north for the finale—straight up the Phelps Creek basin to its imposing watchmen: Fortress, Chiwawa, Red, Dumbell, Seven-fingered Jack, and then there's Maude! At 9082 feet, Washington's thirteenth-highest summit steals the show.

EXTENDING YOUR TRIP

If transportation can be arranged, strong hikers may want to return via the 12-mile Rock Creek Trail. This should only be attempted in late season because of two potentially challenging fords of Rock Creek. Good short explorations can be made by following the Old Gib Trail for a mile or so to the lush meadows housing the headwaters of Willow Creek. The trail can be hard to follow at times, and only experienced hikers should consider extended venturing along it. Another interesting side trip is to Carne's 6991-foot south summit, the former site of a fire lookout. The rapidly fading trail leading to it takes off from a switchback at about 6600 feet, halfway between the junction of the Old Gib and Rock Creek trails.

93 Spider Meadow and Phelps Basin

RATING/ DIFFICULTY	ROUND-TRIP	ELEV GAIN/ HIGH POINT	SEASON
★★★★/3	13 miles	1900 feet/ 5400 feet	July–Oct

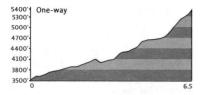

Map: Green Trails Holden No. 113; **Contact:** Okanogan-Wenatchee National Forest, Lake Wenatchee Ranger Station (summer), (509) 763-3103, or Wenatchee River Ranger District, Leavenworth, (509) 548-6977, www.fs.fed .us/r6/wenatchee; **Note:** NW Forest Pass required; **GPS:** N 48 04.975 W 120 50.098

This long but easy valley romp follows boisterous Phelps Creek to a mile-long broad flower-bursting meadow and a giant cirque beneath a formidable wall of towering peaks. But don't expect solitude, for Spider Meadow crawls with backpackers—brigades of them! The valley is large enough to disperse in, though, and Phelps Basin offers a quiet retreat from the meadow's loungers and shutterbugs and their tent cities.

GETTING THERE

From Everett head east on US 2 for 85 miles to Coles Corner. (From Leavenworth travel west on US 2 for 15 miles.) Turn left onto State Route 207 (signed for Lake Wenatchee) and proceed 4.2 miles to a Y intersection after crossing the Wenatchee River. Bear right onto the Chiwawa Loop Road, and after 1.3 miles turn left onto the Chiwawa River Road (Forest Road 62). Proceed for 22 miles (the pavement ends at 10.8 miles) to a junction. Bear right onto FR 6211 and proceed for 2.3 very rough miles to the trailhead at the road's end (elev. 3500 ft).

ON THE TRAIL

The number of vehicles at the trailhead should give you a good indication of the popularity of this hike. Spider Meadow is one of the busiest places within the Glacier Peak Wilderness.

Head down the Phelps Creek Trail, an old road reverting nicely to trail. In 0.25 mile, after hopping across a refreshing creek, come to the junction with the Carne Mountain Trail (Hike 92). Continue straight, traversing pleasant forest and crossing several side creeks, entering the Glacier Peak Wilderness at 2.5 miles.

Continuing along Phelps Creek, the delightful trail marches gently up the valley. Pass through groves of big Engelmann spruce and by tailings of old mines. The area is littered with old mines, and a few doughty prospectors still work claims in the vicinity. At 3.4 miles cross Leroy Creek, which may be tricky in periods of high runoff. On the north side of the creek you may notice a trail taking off right. This is the start of the Leroy High Route, a challenging alpine route through the Entiat Mountains.

About a mile beyond Leroy, the trail actually makes a noticeable ascent, but still quite gentle, mind you. At just over 5 miles, break out from the trees to the edge of Spider Meadow (elev. 4750 ft). Now behold the beauty of an open U-shaped valley carpeted in brilliant wildflowers. Look up to 7646-foot Red Mountain, its rusty summit contrasting nicely with its necklace of snow patches. You can call it quits here, finding a nice place to lounge by Phelps Creek, or continue farther to more dramatic scenery.

The trail carries on, blazing right up the middle of the sprawling meadows. At 5.5 miles it crosses a side creek and then climbs through a cluster of firs and enters an upper meadow. Stare up at cascading creeks coming down off of Red Mountain and Phelps Ridge. Now hop across Phelps Creek, after which the trail steepens and reenters forest. At just over 6 miles reach a signed junction. The trail left climbs to Spider Gap en route to the Lyman Lakes—it's where all of the backpackers are heading.

Hang a right on the path less taken, and in less than 0.5 mile reach the head of the wide-open cirque called Phelps Basin (elev.

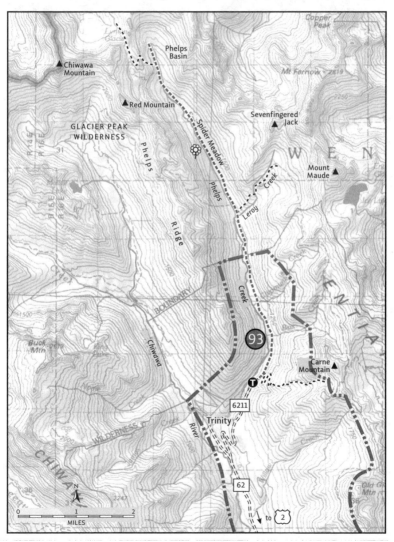

A hiker wanders through the resplendent Spider Meadows.

5400 ft). It's quite a dramatic spot, hemmed in by the vertical walls of 8421-foot Dumbell Mountain. Melting snowfields give birth to Phelps Creek here, where it tumbles through vibrant clusters of violet monkey flowers. Notice that you have the whole basin to yourself. The marmots don't count.

EXTENDING YOUR TRIP

Strong and ambitious hikers may want to make the climb to Spider Gap. Lingering snow usually warrants bringing an ice ax. Experienced off-trail travelers may want to follow the Leroy High Route for the first 1.5 miles to the headwater basin of Leroy Creek.

Opposite: Grassy meadows carpet the burned remains of forest along Miners Ridge.

entiat mountains

Mad River Valley

Mad River country is a delightful region of lofty gentle peaks and ridges, sprawling lawns bursting with wildflowers, cool subalpine forest, babbling creeks, and abundant wildlife—all traversed by an excellent and extensive trail system. The region also boasts plenty of sunshine, making this area a good choice when rain clouds cloak ridges and peaks to the west. But alas, there's trouble in paradise. The Forest Service permits motorcycles in this heavenly garden. Don't let that dissuade you from visiting, however. There are motor-free windows, and the machines are usually absent during the week.

94 Blue Creek Meadow

RATING/ DIFFICULTY	ROUND-TRIP	ELEV GAIN/ HIGH POINT	SEASON
★★★/3	11.6 miles	1100 feet/ 5450 feet	Mid-June– Oct

Map: Green Trails Plain No. 146; **Contact:** Okanogan-Wenatchee National Forest, Lake Wenatchee Ranger Station (summer), (509) 763-3103, or Wenatchee River Ranger District, Leavenworth, (509) 548-6977, www.fs.fed.us/r6/wenatchee; **Note:** Trail open to motorcycles July 15–mid-Oct; **GPS:** N 47 50.640, W 120 36.152

❌ 🔧 ⚙ 🏠 *This is an easy hike on a high plateau, alongside a delightful river to a sprawling meadow where the deer and the ground squirrels play. Unfortunately, so do dirt*

bikes, thanks to the Forest Service's misguided management. But hikers need not shun this inviting corner of the Entiat Mountains in fear of wheels and exhaust. Their presence is moderate on weekends and practically absent during the week. And there's a window of peace and quiet from snowmelt until mid-July, when only hikers and the area's wild critters are permitted to roam this enchanting high country.

GETTING THERE

From Everett head east on US 2 for 85 miles to Coles Corner. (From Leavenworth travel west on US 2 for 15 miles.) Turn left (north) onto State Route 207 (signed for Lake Wenatchee), and proceed 4.2 miles to a Y intersection after crossing the Wenatchee River. Bear right onto the Chiwawa Loop Road and continue for 5 miles, turning left onto Forest Road 61, signed "Lower Chiwawa River Road" (the turnoff is just past a river crossing and the Thousand Trails Lodge). Proceed for 1.6 miles to a T junction at Deep Creek Campground. Turn right onto FR 6101, and after 0.6 mile bear right at an unsigned junction. Continue on FR 6101 for 2.5 miles, coming to a junction at Deer Camp Campground. Make a sharp left, continuing on FR 6101 for 2.5 extremely steep and rough miles (four-wheel drive recommended) to Maverick Saddle and a junction. Park here, or continue left on a rough spur 0.3 mile to the trailhead, (elev. 4350 ft). **Note:** It's also possible to reach this trailhead by following directions for Miners Ridge (Hike 97) and continuing north on FR 52 for 3.4 miles to Maverick Saddle.

ON THE TRAIL

Like my guidebook predecessors Harvey Manning and Ira Spring, I too am appalled

The old Blue Creek Meadow Guard Station graces the upper Mad River country.

that this large roadless area teeming with wildflowers and wildlife was left out of the 1984 Washington Wilderness Act and opened up for motorized recreation (actually actively promoted by the Forest Service). Now, let me get a few things straight. I am not against motorized recreation, and the majority of dirt bikers I have encountered on the trail are among the nicest people I've met in the backcountry. It's just that motorized recreation is so ill-suited for this area. Its fragile pumice soils and meadows, abundant wildlife, and unbroken forests should be part of the adjacent Glacier Peak Wilderness. The roaded lands of the lower Mad River valley and the eastern fringes of the Chelan Mountains are ample areas for dirt biking.

Follow the wide and made-for-machines Upper Mad River Trail north through thick timber, meeting up with the Mad River within minutes. In early summer the river is truly enraged, its waters crashing and frothing, but by autumn the waterway's disposition is mellow. At 1.2 miles come to a junction with the Hi Yu Trail (elev. 4550 ft), a 3.5-mile, excessively banked for motorcycles ridgeline route to little Lost Lake (elev. 5600 ft).

The Upper Mad River Trail continues north, crossing its namesake on a large bridge and coming to the base of a large talus slope and the beginning of the Jimmy Creek Trail to Cougar Mountain (Hike 96). On good trail and easy grade, carry on to the left, through pleasant forest along the river and over a handful of feeding creeks. At 3.3 miles, at the edge of a riverside meadow, the Lost Lake Trail (elev. 5000 ft) takes off left.

After about 0.6 mile, reach a ford of the Mad River. In late summer it's a mere hop. In early summer it may require you to turn around and call it a shorter hike. Once across, continue in pleasant forest for another 0.6 mile, coming to the river once more and another ford that may be difficult in early season. Once across (again), reach a junction (elev. 5250 ft): right for Whistling Pig Meadow (Hike 95), left for Blue Creek Meadow.

Through open forest of lodgepole pine and subalpine fir, reach the edge of the sprawling pumice lawn known as Blue Creek Meadow within 0.5 mile. A half mile beyond, hop across Blue Creek and come to a junction at the old Forest Service Guard Station (elev. 5450 ft). The historic structure is in excellent condition, occasionally still used by the Forest Service. The surrounding meadows are in good shape too. Walk lightly upon them as you wander and cherish their vastness and redeeming qualities.

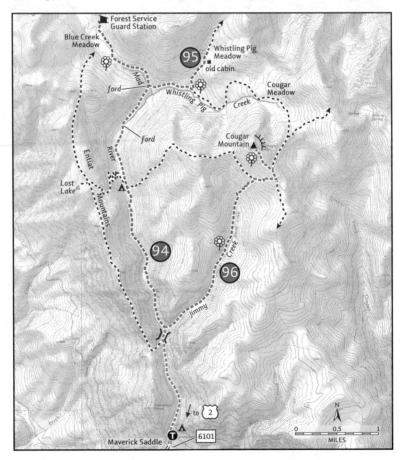

EXTENDING YOUR TRIP

Strong day hikers (or overnighters) have plenty of options for extending their stay. Two Little Lakes lie north on the Blue Creek Trail in less than 2 little miles. Meadow-ringed Mad Lake can be reached by continuing north on the Mad River Trail for 2.5 miles. Make a loop by returning via the Lost Lake Trail, or by following the Mid Tommy Creek Trail to the Hunters Trail through Whistling Pig Meadow and then back to Mad River.

95 Whistling Pig Meadow

RATING/ DIFFICULTY	ROUND-TRIP	ELEV GAIN/ HIGH POINT	SEASON
★★★/3	11.4 miles	1300 feet/ 5650 feet	Mid-June– Oct

Map: Green Trails Plain No. 146; **Contact:** Okanogan-Wenatchee National Forest, Lake Wenatchee Ranger Station (summer), (509) 763-3103, or Wenatchee River Ranger District, Leavenworth, (509) 548-6977, www .fs.fed.us/r6/wenatchee; **Note:** Trail open to motorcycles July 15–mid-Oct; **GPS:** N 47 50.640, W 120 36.152

Pigs can't fly, but can they whistle? These pigs can, because they're actually marmots, named whistling pigs by early prospectors, loggers, and trappers. And in the Whistling Pig Meadow you'll probably stumble upon one, as well as an old cabin, acres of showy blossoms, reflecting pools, and classic Mad River high-country beauty.

GETTING THERE

From Everett head east on US 2 for 85 miles to Coles Corner. (From Leavenworth travel west on US 2 for 15 miles.) Turn left (north) onto State Route 207 (signed for Lake Wenatchee), and proceed 4.2 miles to a Y intersection after crossing the Wenatchee River. Bear right onto the Chiwawa Loop Road and continue for 5 miles, turning left onto Forest Road 61, signed "Lower Chiwawa River Road" (the turnoff is just past a river crossing and the Thousand Trails Lodge). Proceed for 1.6 miles to a T junction at Deep Creek Campground. Turn right onto FR 6101, and after 0.6 mile bear right at an unsigned junction. Continue on FR 6101 for 2.5 miles, coming to a junction at Deer Camp Campground. Make a sharp left, continuing on FR 6101 for 2.5 extremely steep and rough miles (four-wheel drive recommended) to Maverick Saddle and a junction. Park here, or continue left on a rough spur 0.3 mile to the trailhead (elev. 4350 ft). **Note:** It's also possible to reach this trailhead by following directions for Miners Ridge (Hike 97) and continuing north on FR 52 for 3.4 equally rough miles to Maverick Saddle.

ON THE TRAIL

Whistling Pig Meadow, like much of the surrounding upper Mad River country, should be part of the adjacent Glacier Peak Wilderness. This unroaded high country of unbroken forest, sprawling meadows, pristine waterways, and rolling ridges is indeed de facto wilderness. But from mid-July to mid-October, motorcycles (with the blessing of the Forest Service) are allowed to disrupt the tranquility of this beautiful backcountry. Come in early summer or during the week to escape the machines. And if you do encounter one, remember that the motorists currently have

An old hunter's cabin sits in an island of trees in Whistling Pig Meadow.

a legal right to be there after July 15. By far these recreationists are nice people, so be respectful.

Following the same route used for much of the way to Blue Creek Meadow (Hike 94), head north on the Mad River Trail. At 4.6 miles, after the second ford of the Mad River (potentially difficult in high water), reach a junction (elev. 5250 ft): left to Blue Creek, right to Whistling Pig. Following the Tyee Ridge Trail, head east for 0.6 mile to another junction (elev. 5500 ft). The trail straight continues to Cougar Meadow and can be used to create a long loop to Cougar Mountain (Hike 96).

Turn left onto the Hunters Trail, passing a marshy meadow. After a short climb through thick forest, emerge at the edge of Whistling Pig Meadow (elev. 5650 ft). The trail continues straight up the flower-studded

lawn, crossing a creek to a clump of old trees hiding an old cabin. A weathered picnic table invites you to sit and linger. Sunny, grassy fields invite you to lay and lounge. Soak in the surrounding subtle beauty. Creeklets traverse the emerald field, feeding and draining small pools. Cougar Mountain's peak peeks above.

EXTENDING YOUR TRIP

For a loop that adds 3.2 miles, continue north on the Hunters Trail 0.6 mile to a junction. Turn left, hiking 2 delightful miles to the Blue Creek Trail, passing through old forest, more meadows, and to the edge of a ledge with views north to the Chelan Mountains. Then head left 0.6 mile to the Blue Creek Guard Station, and follow the Mad River Trail back to your vehicle.

96 Cougar Mountain

RATING/ DIFFICULTY	ROUND-TRIP	ELEV GAIN/ HIGH POINT	SEASON
★★★★/3	10 miles	2350 feet/ 6701 feet	Mid-June–Oct

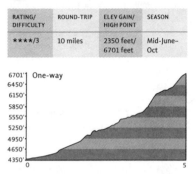

Map: Green Trails Plain No. 146; **Contact:** Okanogan-Wenatchee National Forest, Lake Wenatchee Ranger Station (summer), (509) 763-3103, or Wenatchee River Ranger District, Leavenworth, (509) 548-6977, www .fs.fed.us/r6/wenatchee; **Note:** Trail open to motorcycles July 15–mid-Oct; **GPS:** N 47 50.640, W 120 36.152

Follow a babbling brook through forests of pine and fields of dazzling wildflowers to a long-gone lookout site where the viewing still reigns supreme. Gaze out at beautiful landscapes near and far—from verdant lawns spread out directly below, to the glistening ice of Glacier Peak, to the sun-baked wheat fields of the Waterville Plateau. Heavenly? Yes. But only before the motors arrive or during the week, when chances are slim that one will come sputtering by.

GETTING THERE
From Everett head east on US 2 for 85 miles to Coles Corner. (From Leavenworth travel west on US 2 for 15 miles.) Turn left (north) onto State Route 207 (signed for Lake

Wenatchee), and proceed 4.2 miles to a Y intersection after crossing the Wenatchee River. Bear right onto the Chiwawa Loop Road and continue for 5 miles, turning left onto Forest Road 61, signed "Lower Chiwawa River Road" (the turnoff is just past a river crossing and the Thousand Trails Lodge). Proceed for 1.6 miles to a T junction at Deep Creek Campground. Turn right onto FR 6101, and after 0.6 mile bear right at an unsigned junction. Continue on FR 6101 for

A hiker looks out toward the Entiat Mountains and Cougar Meadow from the summit of Cougar Mountain.

2.5 miles, coming to a junction at Deer Camp Campground. Make a sharp left, continuing on FR 6101 for 2.5 extremely steep and rough miles (four-wheel drive recommended) to Maverick Saddle and a junction. Park here, or continue left on a rough spur 0.3 mile to the trailhead (elev. 4350 ft). **Note:** It's also possible to reach this trailhead by following directions for Miners Ridge (Hike 97) and continuing north on FR 52 for 3.4 equally rough miles to Maverick Saddle.

ON THE TRAIL

While the Jimmy Creek Trail is one of the least traveled paths in the Mad River country, it is nevertheless still legally open to motorcycles. The Forest Service has yet to "upgrade" it to a motorway. Good. However, since it is still open to dirt bikes, the few that do venture on it tear it up—and travel through fragile meadows to bypass windfall. Bad! How about demanding that the Forest Service at least close this trail to motorbikes—while we keep up the fight to get the southern Entiat Mountains into wilderness, where they rightfully belong.

Start by following the well-traveled Mad River Trail. At 1.2 miles pass a junction with the Hi Yu Trail. Continue straight another 0.1 mile, crossing the Mad River. Just before reaching an open talus area, turn right onto the unsigned and easy-to-miss Jimmy Creek Trail.

On good but lightly trampled tread, steadily climb, following Jimmy Creek through pine and fir forest that's fragrantly scented with wild blossoms by early summer. After about a mile or so, pocket meadows add to the blooming mix. Continue climbing through thinning forest and emerging lush meadows, crossing Jimmy Creek at 3.5 miles. The trail now turns steep, transforming into a deep

rocky gully thanks to motorcycle use (still any doubts about what kind of impact this form of recreation has on fragile pumice soils?).

At 3.9 miles reach a junction (elev. 6150 ft). The trail left is officially abandoned, but has been "reopened" by dirt bikes. It terminates on the Mad River Trail near the Lost Lake Trail junction. Head right, traversing fields of blooms and reaching another junction after 0.3 mile (elev. 6250 ft). Turn left to follow the Cougar Ridge Trail through more meadows and along the demarcation between burned and unburned forest from the Tyee conflagration of 1994. In no time, reach yet another junction. Head left on this spur trail to Cougar's summit.

Reconstructed for motorcycles, this path is twice as long (thanks to the banked-for-bikes switchbacks), twice as dusty, and not nearly as nice as the old summit path (which can still be followed if you snoop around for it).

At 5 miles reach the open summit of Cougar Mountain and behold the beauty of the Entiat Mountains before you. Emerald Cougar Meadow lies directly below, and Kelly and Klone mountains rise gently behind it. Amazing beauty—and a crying shame the Forest Service allows it to be disturbed by throttles. This area was one of Ira Spring's favorites in the Cascades. Mine too. An Ira Spring Wilderness would protect it and would be a fitting tribute to the late conservationist and guidebook author.

EXTENDING YOUR TRIP

For a nice loop, continue 0.5 mile north on the Cougar Ridge Trail to the Tyee Ridge Trail. Turn left, following this gentle path 2.3 miles along Whistling Pig Creek and through gorgeous Cougar Meadow. Then head back to your vehicle via the Mad River Trail, closing the loop at 13 miles.

97 Miners Ridge

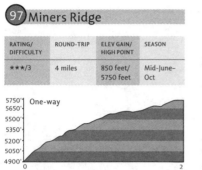

RATING/ DIFFICULTY	ROUND-TRIP	ELEV GAIN/ HIGH POINT	SEASON
★★★/3	4 miles	850 feet/ 5750 feet	Mid-June– Oct

Map: Green Trails Plain No. 146; **Contact:** Okanogan-Wenatchee National Forest, Lake Wenatchee Ranger Station (summer), (509) 763-3103, or Wenatchee River Ranger District, Leavenworth, (509) 548-6977, www .fs.fed.us/r6/wenatchee; **GPS:** N 47 48.010, W 120 34.341

After the Tyee wildfire roared over Miners Ridge in 1994 (but spared its summit), the Forest Service abandoned this easy-to-hike, flower-studded, view-filled ridgeline hike. What a shame. The tread is still intact, the views and flowers are still there, wildlife is prolific, and people are scarce. The only problem—and it's a big one—is fighting your way around hundreds of downed trees before reaching the inviting meadows that drape the ridge.

GETTING THERE

From Leavenworth head north for 2.1 miles on the Chumstick Highway (formerly known as State Route 209), turning right onto County Road 112 (also known as Eagle Creek Road). Continue for 6 miles, turning left onto Forest Road 7520. After 5.8 miles, come to a four-way junction at a saddle near the French Creek Sno-Park. Turn left onto FR 52 and proceed for 8 miles, coming to the unsigned trailhead (elev. 4900 ft), marked by a post just south of a creek crossing. Park on the west side of the road. Alternatively, you can reach the trailhead by traveling 3.4 miles south on FR 52 from Maverick Saddle (see directions for Hike 96).

ON THE TRAIL

Designation in 2008 as one of the Washington Trails Association's Top Ten Threatened Trails should help put the spotlight on this trail and hopefully "save" it, allowing hikers young and old, four-legged and two to once

Windfall presents challenges to a pair of hikers on Miners Ridge.

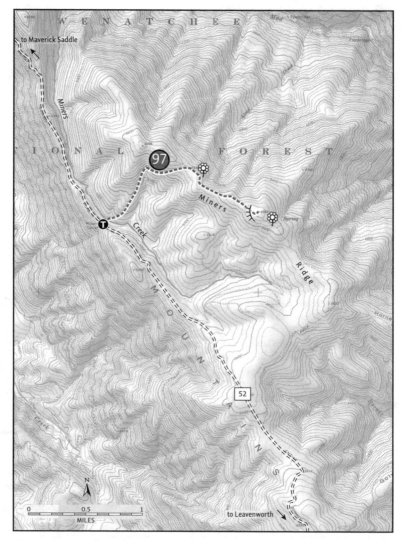

again enjoy this scenic route. Without the extensive blowdown covering the first 0.5 mile of this trail, Miners Ridge provides one of the easiest high-country rambles in the Entiat Mountains. And blowdowns or not, this is an excellent quieter alternative to the Mad

River trails, especially when the motorcycles are revving.

Starting in what appears to be impenetrable windfall, locate tread and begin an arduous approach, crossing Miners Creek and then beginning short switchbacks up a shoulder littered with fallen timber. Stay tenacious. Think like a fisher or a pine marten, finding ways to clamber over, under, and around the woody mess. It gets better.

Leaving the shoulder, the trail turns southward, rounding a drainage and entering more open woods. Blowdowns diminish. Through small meadows, silver forest, and a countryside that looks remarkably like the Kettle River Range of northeast Washington's Columbia Highlands, gently crest the ridge.

Now on excellent tread through patches of green, saunter along the ridge, coming to a wide-open meadow just below a 5750-foot high point at 2 miles. Flowers! Views

too! East to Tyee Ridge and the Waterville Plateau. South to Sugarloaf, Mission, Stuart, and Cashmere. West to the Chiwaukums and to Lake Wenatchee nestled beneath Nason Ridge. North to the snowy and craggy giants of Clark, Buck, and Glacier Peak.

EXTENDING YOUR TRIP

Consider a stop at the Sugarloaf Peak fire lookout on the way back to Leavenworth. The access road is located 3.5 miles south of the trailhead on FR 52. Park and walk the short distance to the 1949-built lookout sitting on the 5844-foot summit.

98 Lower Mad River Valley

RATING/ DIFFICULTY	ROUND-TRIP	ELEV GAIN/ HIGH POINT	SEASON
★★★/3	6.5 miles	300 feet/ 2000 feet	May– mid-Nov

Sun-kissed, flower-filled slopes along the Lower Mad River Trail

Map: Green Trails Brief No. 147; **Contact:** Okanogan-Wenatchee National Forest, Entiat Ranger District, (509) 784-1511, www.fs.fed.us/r6/wenatchee; **Note:** Rattlesnake country, be aware; **GPS:** N 47 45.533 W 120 25.628

 *Follow alongside the crashing, thrashing Mad River as it snakes through a deep canyon. Wildfire stripped most of the gorge of its green cover, but remnant big trees still grace the way. And wildflowers too, including rare and showy blooms like Tweedy's lewisia. This is a perfect destination in spring, when the high country is still buried in snow, but wildflowers are blooming like mad along this trail.*

GETTING THERE

From Wenatchee head north for 15 miles on US 97A to Entiat. (From Chelan head south for 20 miles on US 97A.) Turn left (west) onto the Entiat River Road (Forest Road 51) and proceed for 9.8 miles to the hamlet of Ardenvoir, turning left onto the Mad River Road. After 2 miles the road becomes FR 57. Continue for another 1.8 miles, turning left into the Pine Flats Campground. Find the trailhead (elev. 1700 ft) in the campground 0.3 mile farther. Privy available.

ON THE TRAIL

Good news if you've been avoiding this trail in the past due to its lack of maintenance: The Forest Service has once again begun maintaining it, and gone are the numerous large blowdowns. Of

course, regular maintenance now means that motorcycle use has increased, but this should not hinder you from hiking here. It is a great trail to build friendships with other trail users and perhaps forge a partnership to keep this wonderful low-country trail open. It would be a great way to open dialogue between all of these different trail users too.

Begin in a nice grove of big ponderosa pine. Immediately meet up with the river and follow it upstream through a narrow canyon littered with big boulders. The tread is wide and lined with horsetails. Surrounding slopes and ledges are warmed by the sun, while a constant breeze cooled by the river's tumbling waters blows along the canyon floor. At 0.5 mile enter an old burn zone. Smatterings of ancient ponderosas—their bark resilient to scorching—stand defiantly along the frothing river.

Continue through the winding canyon. Willows and other brush grow thicker along the tread. Without maintenance soon, this trail will become impassable. At 1.5 miles Hornet Creek buzzes down into the river from the west. A long-abandoned trail (extremely difficult to follow), reached by fording the river, follows the creek westward along a parallel ridge. In springtime, look along the sun-kissed slopes here for Tweedy's lewisia, a showy flower endemic only to the Wenatchee Mountains, the Methow Valley, and British Columbia's Simalkameen Valley. Look too for rubber boas, a docile constrictor snake that is common in these parts.

Continue farther, passing nice lunch spots by mesmerizing rapids and in tranquil forest groves. At 2.7 miles come to a nice series of rapids that careen over granite ledges and

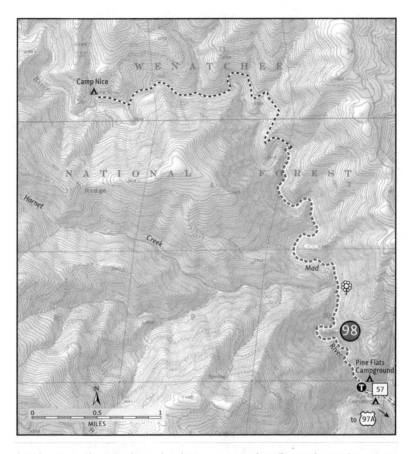

boulders. In another 0.5 mile, reach a draw that may or may not contain running water. This is a logical spot to call it a day, as the trail's conditions continue to deteriorate. Return to a noted nice riverside spot and let the resident dippers entertain you.

EXTENDING YOUR TRIP

If slumping tread, scratching brush, and blocking blowdown don't deter you, con-tinue up the valley another 3 miles to Camp Nice. En route, though, be aware that you'll be climbing several hundred feet above the river at one spot and then dropping back down to it. Solitude guaranteed.

Entiat River Valley

Like the Mad River country, the Entiat River valley enjoys plenty of sunshine throughout the hiking season. Set in a deep and long glacially carved valley surrounded by the towering Entiat and Chelan ranges, many of the hikes here travel great lengths and ascend great heights. That, coupled with the region's relative remoteness from population centers, usually assures lonesome wandering, though a few of the Entiat's more gentle trails can still attract a good crowd on a sunny weekend.

Map: Green Trails Plain No. 146; **Contact:** Okanogan-Wenatchee National Forest, Entiat Ranger District, (509) 784-1511, www.fs.fed .us/r6/wenatchee; **Note:** NW Forest Pass required. Dogs must be leashed; **GPS:** N 47 57.531, W 120 32.149

99 Silver Falls

RATING/ DIFFICULTY	LOOP	ELEV GAIN/ HIGH POINT	SEASON
★★★★/2	1.8 miles	700 feet/ 3100 feet	May– mid-Nov

A 140-foot silvery veil of refreshing mountain water draped over shiny granite slabs and lined with stately pines, this is one of the prettiest cascades in the

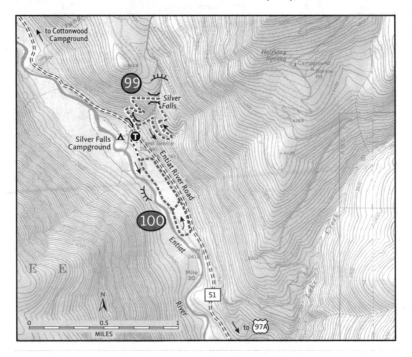

Vine maples add showy autumn colors to Silver Falls.

Cascades. And while the falls itself is a real treat, the loop trail leading to, below, and above it is sure to delight even more—especially the young set. Beautifully crafted with stone steps and bridges and adorned with attractive railings and sun-kissed benches, it's an aesthetically appealing complement to the captivating falls.

GETTING THERE

From Wenatchee head north for 15 miles on US 97A to Entiat. (From Chelan head south for 20 miles on US 97A.) Turn left (west) onto the Entiat River Road (Forest Road 51), and proceed for 29.5 miles to the trailhead, located just east of Silver Falls Campground (elev. 2400 ft). Privy available.

ON THE TRAIL

Before starting, look up at the emerald hillside across the road. Catch a glimpse of the silvery surge of cascading waters in the distance and get psyched to experience them up close and personal. Carefully cross the road and begin up a marvel-of-masonry stairway. Cool moist breezes funneling down from the falls greet you. They're especially appreciated in August, when the mercury often dances above 90 in the Entiat Valley.

Head up along Silver Creek under a canopy of cedars, and cross the creek on a delightful bridge. Then soon come to a junction. You'll be returning left, so head right. Cross the creek and enter a shaded glen. Now up you go again. Along, up, and around ledges punctuated with precariously perched ponderosa pines, kids will especially enjoy gallivanting through this grotto-like section of trail.

Savor the falls from a couple of good viewpoints, and then begin a long traverse across sunny pine groves. Continuing higher along warm south-facing slopes, take in good views of the Entiat Valley below and the Entiat Mountains above while you sip from your water bottle.

Come to the upper tier of the falls and take another break. A few more steps, a little more climbing, cross Silver Creek on a nice little bridge (elev. 3100 ft), and rejoice

that it's all downhill now. Descend on sets of stairs and make a long traverse downward. Enjoy more good valley and mountain views. Return to the lower bridge and merrily stroll back to your vehicle.

EXTENDING YOUR TRIP

The Silver Falls Interpretive Trail (Hike 100) makes a great add-on for the day, and the Silver Falls Campground makes for a nice family-friendly place to spend the night. Entiat Falls, located 2.9 miles north on FR 51, is another nice side trip.

100 Silver Falls Interpretive Trail

RATING/ DIFFICULTY	LOOP	ELEV GAIN/ HIGH POINT	SEASON
★★/1	1.2 miles	None/ 2400 feet	Late Apr– late Nov

The view down the Entiat River from the Silver Falls Interpretive Trail

Map: Green Trails Plain No. 146; **Contact:** Okanogan-Wenatchee National Forest, Entiat Ranger District, (509) 784-1511, www .fs.fed.us/r6/wenatchee; **Notes:** NW Forest Pass required. Dogs must be leashed. Trail is wheelchair accessible; **GPS:** N 47 57.329, W 120 32.054

Bring the whole family on this delight-to-hike easy trail along the free-flowing Entiat River. Derived from the Native word En-ti-at-kwa, meaning "rapid water," the Entiat that stretches along this interpretive trail is more sedate and quite soothing. Take to this trail on a warm summer evening, a crisp spring morning, or a lazy, sweltering August afternoon, when gravel beds will invite foot-soaking and casting your cares to the currents.

GETTING THERE

From Wenatchee head north for 15 miles on US 97A to Entiat. (From Chelan head south for 20 miles on US 97A.) Turn left (west) onto the Entiat River Road (Forest Road 51), and proceed for 29.5 miles to the large Silver Falls trailhead parking, located just east of Silver Falls Campground (elev. 2400 ft). Privy available. Walk into the campground to reach the start of the interpretive trail, located between campsites number 8 and 9.

ON THE TRAIL

The way starts off paved. Take the trail right and take the time to read the interpretive signs along the way. Through a rich riparian forest of mature pine, fir, and cedar, the trail soon reaches the river's edge. In late season, wide gravel bars call out to be sauntered upon. Continue downriver under big pines and on open banks that provide big views up to Tommy Ridge.

In about 0.3 mile a spur trail heads left,

offering a shortcut back. Continue right, through more cedar and spruce groves and prime riverfront property. Now on gravel tread, come to yet another shortcut spur heading left. Once again, carry on to the right, and reach a cedar grove traversed by boardwalk. Skedaddle once more along the regal river. Take time to watch flitting dippers in the rapids. Admire, too, the giant cottonwoods lining the banks. These members of the willow family are among North America's tallest deciduous trees.

The way then makes a 180-degree turn. Now through fern alleys, pine groves, and under more big cottonwoods, leisurely make your way back to the trailhead, closing this pleasant little loop.

101 Duncan Hill

RATING/ DIFFICULTY	ROUND-TRIP	ELEV GAIN/ HIGH POINT	SEASON
★★★★/4	13.6 miles	3000 feet/ 7819 feet	July–Oct

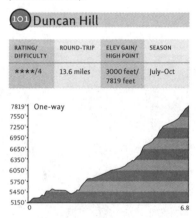

Map: Green Trails Lucerne No. 114; **Contact:** Okanogan-Wenatchee National Forest, Entiat Ranger District, (509) 784-1511, www .fs.fed.us/r6/wenatchee; **Note:** Trail open to motorcycles; **GPS:** N 48 04.477, W 120 38.605

Duncan Hill? At 7819 feet, Duncan is no hill. It's a bona fide reach-for-the-clouds mountain. And the views? No mere hill would be able to grant such a panoramic perspective of the Entiat and Chelan ranges, Glacier Peak, Mount Rainier, Mount Stuart, the Chiwaukums, the Whites, Bonanza—you get the picture. Hill indeed!

GETTING THERE

From Wenatchee head north for 15 miles on US 97A to Entiat. (From Chelan head south for 20 miles on US 97A.) Turn left (west) onto the Entiat River Road (Forest Road 51) and proceed for 34 miles, turning right onto FR 5608, signed for Duncan Ridge Trail (the turnoff is 1 mile beyond the Entiat Falls pullout). Follow FR 5608 for 5.8 winding and occasionally steep and rutted miles (be sure to bear right at a confusing junction at 5.6 miles, and left immediately afterward). The trailhead is just before the road's end (elev. 5150 ft).

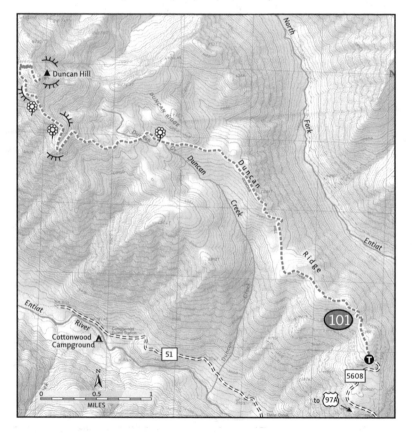

ON THE TRAIL

While this trail is open to mountain bikes and motor bikes, chances are you won't see either. You probably won't even see another hiker. Duncan Hill is off the radar screens of many recreationists. The trail, however, is in excellent shape, the tread not too rutted, the way not dusty. It's a long way across a forested ridge to Duncan's lofty summit, but the first half of the hike is fairly easy walking.

Start in a solid stand of subalpine fir and lodgepole pine, the kind of high-country forest that grouse, lynx, and snowshoe hare favor. Skirt a knoll and climb another (elev. 5580 ft). Then begin a long descent to a grassy saddle (elev. 5400 ft). Start climbing again—gently—coming to a knoll (elev. 5800 ft) with a view out over the North Fork Entiat River valley at 2.4 miles.

Continue for another easy mile, emerging from forest to a pretty little meadow with Duncan's summit peeking above. Gentle going continues, with the trail entering a cool spruce forest before crossing Duncan Creek (elev. 6200 ft), a reliable water source at 3.9 miles. The way now gets tougher as elevation gain becomes the objective. At 5 miles reach a flower-bursting, meadow-draped shoulder as Duncan's summit looms closer.

The way turns steeper—and more interesting. Crest a ridge (elev. 7200 ft) that cradles a larch-lined basin. Then skirt beneath the summit block, traversing Duncan's wide-open and steep western slopes. Enjoy breathtaking views to Garland, Fifth of July, and the Ramparts across the valley. And take a deep breath, staring 4000 feet straight down into the Entiat Valley! After another bout of steepness, albeit short, round another shoulder and come to a junction (elev. 7400 ft) at 6.3 miles.

Left leads to the Anthem Creek Trail. Turn

Devils Smoke Stack and Rampart Mountain seen from the trail up Duncan Hill

right instead, and after an exhilarating 0.5 mile across fields of granite till and pumice, through rock gardens and krummholz, reach the 7819-foot summit of Duncan Hill. There was once a fire lookout here, and now there's a solar-powered radio tower—and did I mention the unsurpassed views? To the west Glacier Peak rises above the glacier fields of Buck and Clark. Mighty Maude, Sevenfingered Jack, Fernow, and Bonanza form an impressive and impenetrable wall to the north. In the immediate vicinity, the craggy summits of the Chelan Mountains— Gopher, Pinnacle, Saska, Emerald, Cardinal, and Pyramid—form a lofty horseshoe.

EXTENDING YOUR TRIP

If transportation can be arranged, return via the knee-knocking Anthem Creek Trail to the Entiat River Trail (Hike 102). The one-way journey is nearly the same distance as the return via Duncan Ridge.

102 Myrtle Lake

RATING/ DIFFICULTY	ROUND-TRIP	ELEV GAIN/ HIGH POINT	SEASON
★★/2	8 miles	650 feet/ 3765 feet	Late May– Nov

```
3765'   One-way
3550'
3350'
3150'
      0                                    4
```

Map: Green Trails Lucerne No. 114; **Contact:** Okanogan-Wenatchee National Forest, Entiat Ranger District, (509) 784-1511, www .fs.fed.us/r6/wenatchee; **Notes:** NW Forest Pass required. Trail open to motorcycles; **GPS:** N 48 01.462, W 120 39.072

Myrtle is a quiet lake fringed with evergreens and craggy ridges. Grassy shores along its outlet encourage afternoon napping with their abundant sunshine. The destination is serene, but not so the journey. A misguided Forest Service allows motorized use on all but the last couple hundred feet of this hike. Dog- and kid-friendly during the week when use is low, this hike is nev-

Myrtle Lake in the Entiat Mountains (Craig Romano photo)

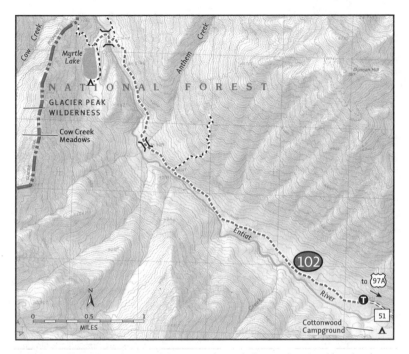

*ertheless a dusty slog. The warm lake wa-
ters, however, cleanse grubby legs along
with disheartened dispositions.*

GETTING THERE

From Wenatchee head north for 15 miles on
US 97A to Entiat. (From Chelan head south
for 20 miles on US 97A.) Turn left (west) onto
the Entiat River Road (Forest Road 51) and
proceed 38 miles to Cottonwood Campground
and the trailhead just beyond at the road's
end (elev. 3150 ft). Privy available.

ON THE TRAIL

Beginning in a mature forest of spruce and
cottonwood, the near-level dusty path takes
off up the Entiat Valley. No longer paralleled

by road, the river here is wild, its headwater
streams protected within the sprawling Glacier Peak Wilderness. Conservation-minded
citizens would do the river and its immediate
environs good by demanding that the wilderness border be moved to include all of the
remaining roadless parcels surrounding it.

Finally, after about 1.2 miles, the wild Entiat comes into view. On tread sprinkled with
soft pumice (thanks to a past eruption from
Glacier Peak), the way gently marches up the
valley, occasionally dipping slightly to break
the monotony. Openings in the pine forest
provide views westward and upward to Garland Peak and the Rampart Mountains.

At 2.2 miles reach a junction with the
Anthem Creek Trail (elev. 3450 ft), a lonely,

steep, and very demanding alternative route to 7819-foot Duncan Hill (Hike 101). About 0.25 mile beyond, cross Anthem Creek on a good bridge. Soon afterward the grade steepens to what amounts to the only real climbing on this hike. Meanwhile, the river has disappeared into a granite-walled gorge.

The way levels once again, coming to a junction at 3.6 miles. The Entiat River Trail continues straight for more than 10 miles to the meadowed basin beneath the glaciers that birth this river. Your objective, much closer, lies left via the Cow Creek Meadows Trail. Follow it, dropping slightly to cross the Entiat on a bridge, and then climb a little through a cool, forested glen to reach the lake (elev. 3765 ft). Finally, motorcycles are banned. Just before crossing Myrtle's outlet creek, a side trail takes off left 0.4 mile to busy campsites on the lake's southern shore.

A better option is to proceed forward a couple hundred feet, hopping across the outlet stream to an inviting grassy meadow on the lake's north shore. Wipe the dust off, kick back, and enjoy the serenity.

EXTENDING YOUR TRIP

Two miles and 1400 more vertical feet beyond are the Cow Creek Meadows, a sprawling, near-level lawn beneath the vertical walls of the Rampart Mountains. Snow remains in the basin year-round and wildflowers riot by midsummer. It's a remote and quiet spot and well worth any extra energy you may have upon arriving at the lake.

103 Larch Lakes

RATING/ DIFFICULTY	ROUND-TRIP	ELEV GAIN/ HIGH POINT	SEASON
★★★★/5	15.5 miles	2600 feet/ 5750 feet	July– mid-Oct

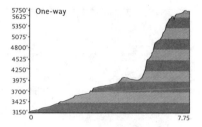

One-way

Map: Green Trails Lucerne No. 114; **Contact:** Okanogan-Wenatchee National Forest, Entiat Ranger District, (509) 784-1511, www .fs.fed.us/r6/wenatchee; **Notes:** NW Forest Pass required. First 3.8 miles of trail open to motorcycles; **GPS:** N 48 01.462, W 120 39.072

Nestled in a hanging valley high in the Entiat Mountains, the Larch Lakes and their lush environs offer quite a contrast to the sun-baked hillsides and valleys below. Ringed with blossom-bursting meadows in the summer and with clumps of the gnarly namesake trees that glow golden in autumn, it's a splendid and scenic spot. But a place this beautiful and wild is not easily reached. Steep, sun-parched slopes test your tenacity.

GETTING THERE

From Wenatchee head north for 15 miles on US 97A to Entiat. (From Chelan head south for 20 miles on US 97A.) Turn left (west) onto the Entiat River Road (Forest Road 51) and proceed 38 miles to Cottonwood Campground and the trailhead just beyond at the road's end (elev. 3150 ft). Privy available.

ON THE TRAIL

Start by following the busy Entiat River Trail (Hike 102), a dusty byway thanks to the throngs of horses, mountain bikes, and motorbikes that share it. In 2.2 miles pass the Anthem Creek Trail to Duncan Hill. Shortly afterward cross Anthem Creek on a good bridge. Then at 3.6 miles, after pleasurable walking were it not for ruts and dust, come

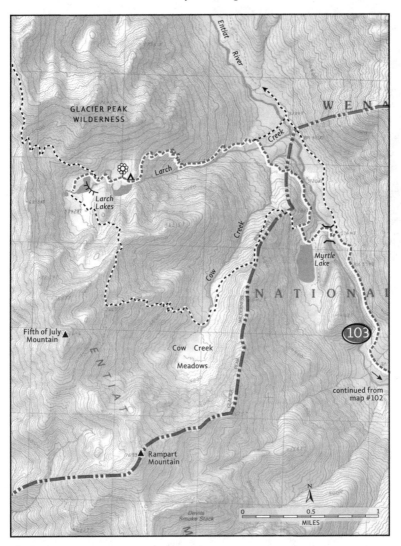

View looking down the Larch Lakes basin
(Craig Romano photo)

to a junction (elev. 3700 ft). Two choices now to the Larch Lakes. The more direct route involves continuing straight for 1.1 almost level miles to the Larch Lakes Trail. But this way requires a ford of the Entiat River—easy for horses, potentially challenging for hikers.

Head left instead on the Cow Creek Meadows Trail, crossing the Entiat on a sturdy bridge and arriving at Myrtle Lake (Hike 102) within 0.4 mile. With motorcycles no longer permitted, notice the change in the tread as you continue beyond the lake, deer track replacing tire tracks. After a short steep climb of 0.25 mile, come to a junction. Head right on the hiker-only Larch Lakes connector trail.

Side sloping along a steep timbered hill-

side above the Entiat River, the trail slightly descends, entering the Glacier Peak Wilderness in about 0.5 mile. Shortly afterward negotiate a crossing (tricky in high water) of Larch Creek, and at 1.2 miles from Myrtle Lake come to the main Larch Lakes Trail (elev. 3900 ft). Easy hiking is now over.

Turn left and parallel Larch Creek, marching upward on grueling switchbacks to the tumbling waterway's alpine source. At about 4500 feet, forest thins, allowing good views east out to Duncan Hill and to the craggy giants making up the Chelan Mountains.

A lovely waterfall soon comes into view. The Larch Lakes lie above those steep, misted granite ledges. Now on rocky tread, ascend steeply on south-facing slopes with no shade whatsoever. Best to avoid this section in midday, or be prepared to take the full brunt of the east-slope sun.

After furiously climbing the headwall into the hanging valley that cradles the Larch Lakes, rejoice—your hard labor is done. Greeting you just beyond the crest of the headwall is the first of the Larch Lakes (elev. 5650 ft). Grassy shores and sunny ledges embracing the emerald lake invite lounging. Look at all the larches too, gloriously golden in the autumn.

The grander upper lake lies 0.4 mile farther and 100 feet higher, worth any extra energy you can muster. Continue through gentian-graced and blueberry-bursting meadows. Then transition to a cool hemlock and fir grove. Head left at a junction (avoid the immediate left that goes to a set of campsites), and you're there!

Twice the size of the lower lake, the upper Larch is also twice as pretty. Occupying a flower-freckled, wide-open bowl beneath the stark north face of Fifth of July Mountain, the lake and its serene shoreline say siesta while its shallow and sandy-bottomed waters invite wading. And larches? They flank the basin and cling to the ledges and high slopes above, lighting up this little piece of alpine heaven come late September.

EXTENDING YOUR TRIP

The strongest of day hikers may want to contemplate returning via the Garland Peak and Cow Creek Meadows Trail for a lollipop loop that adds another 2 miles and more than 900 steep feet of climbing. Views are stunning along the way, especially of the Larch Lakes basin and the Cow Creek Meadows.

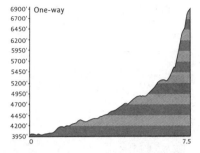

Map: Green Trails Lucerne No. 114; **Contact:** Okanogan-Wenatchee National Forest, Entiat Ranger District, (509) 784-1511, www.fs.fed .us/r6/wenatchee; **Note:** NW Forest Pass required; **GPS:** N 48 00.678 W 120 34.335

104 Fern Lake

RATING/ DIFFICULTY	ROUND-TRIP	ELEV GAIN/ HIGH POINT	SEASON
★★★★/5	15 miles	3000 feet/ 6900 feet	July–Oct

Visit a high, lonely lake in a deep wilderness valley short on visitors and long on solitude. The hike is long too, but most of it is easy, along the North Fork Entiat River. It's the final stretch

A partially frozen Fern Lake is tucked tight into the high mountains above the North Fork Entiat River valley. (Craig Romano photo)

that's a killer, a steep grunt up rock, ledges, and eroded tread. Set in a high bowl beneath granite spires and flanked with ledges, talus, and larches, Fern Lake could be right out of the Enchantment Lakes— except there will be nobody else there!

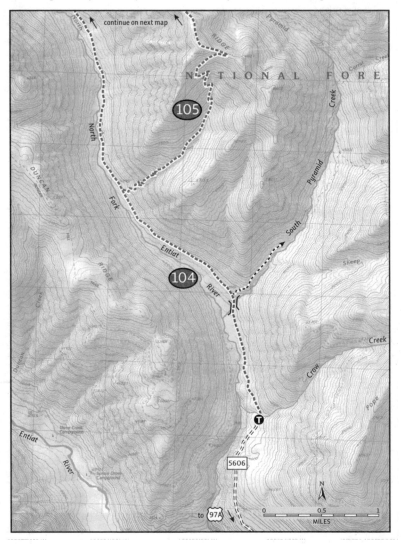

continue on next map

GETTING THERE

From Wenatchee head north for 15 miles on US 97A to Entiat. (From Chelan head south for 20 miles on US 97A.) Turn left (west) onto the Entiat River Road (Forest Road 51) and proceed 33 miles to FR 5606 (2.9 miles

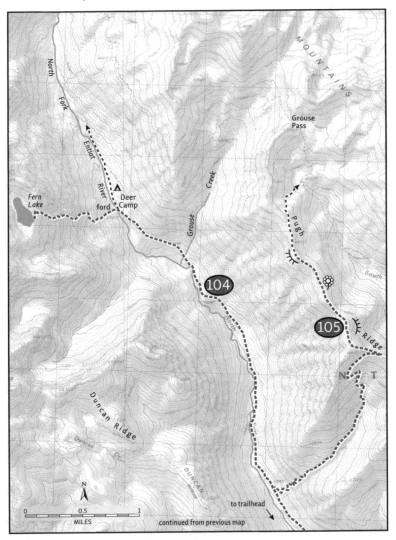

continued from previous map

beyond Silver Falls). Continue 4 miles to the road's end and trailhead (elev. 3950 ft). Privy available.

ON THE TRAIL

Coursing through a spectacular landscape of deep valley, thick forests, and sunny meadows, the North Fork Entiat River drains a crescent of rugged lofty peaks. Far quieter than the Entiat River to the south, the North Fork offers a truer wilderness experience, even though it's not in a capital W wilderness. But it wasn't always this way. The Forest Service once allowed motors to break the silence of this sprawling roadless watershed. Citizen protests led by pioneer guidebook writers Ira Spring and Harvey Manning helped rectify this misguided use of our precious natural heritage.

While this is a favorite destination among off-the-beaten path backpackers, strong day hikers will find much to their liking here too. Especially Fern Lake, one of the few alpine lakes in this corner of the Cascades and one of the prettiest this side of the Chiwawa River. Start off on the North Fork Entiat River Trail, immediately coming to Crow Creek. Hop, skip, or splash across it, and then cross South Pyramid Creek 1 mile later. This crossing is much easier, thanks to a sturdy bridge.

At 1.2 miles stay left at a junction. At 2.7 miles stay left at another junction. The trail right heads to Pugh Ridge (Hike 105). So far you've gained only 400 feet in elevation. The easy going continues. In pleasant forest continue upvalley, enjoying occasional glimpses of the river and hearing its constant bellowing. Pass through a series of meadows maintained by winter and spring avalanches.

At 5 miles come to Grouse Creek (elev. 4900 ft), which will require getting your feet wet. Climbing gently, but noticeably, (finally) reach the junction with Fern Lake Trail (elev. 5250 ft) in a cool grove of spruce and fir at 6 miles. Now it's time to pay the piper. The 1.5 miles to Fern Lake gains more elevation (1700 ft) than the previous 6 miles on the North Fork Entiat Trail (1300 ft). Yikes!

Immediately come to Deer Camp, a pleasant spot on the river. Then, ford the North Fork—easy in August, potentially difficult in early July. On light tread start climbing through thick forest. Numerous windfalls make the steep going even slower. Tread soon gets rockier and rougher as the trail breaks out of the trees onto ledges. Now working its way up a series of ledges alongside Fern's cascading outlet creek, the going gets even tougher. Pause for good views down the valley and to Pyramid Mountain peeking above Pugh Ridge.

Up shiny granite outcroppings adorned with phlox and penstemon and beneath talus piles and fractured cliffs, keep grunting upward. A stand of larches greets you at the head of the open basin housing the lake. You made it. Soak your feet or perch your weary body on a sun-warmed slab and savor the rugged scenery surrounding the secluded alpine lake. You won't find many ferns, but plenty of larch warrant a return trip in October. However, don't forget to bring your trekking poles the next time. The descent is a knee killer.

105 Pugh Ridge

RATING/ DIFFICULTY	ROUND-TRIP	ELEV GAIN/ HIGH POINT	SEASON
★★★★/5	12.4 miles	2835 feet/ 6783 feet	July– mid-Oct

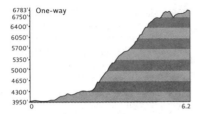

Map: Green Trails Lucerne No. 114; **Contact:** Okanogan-Wenatchee National Forest, Entiat Ranger District, (509) 784-1511, www.fs.fed.us/r6/wenatchee; **Note:** NW Forest Pass required; **GPS:** N 48 00.678, W 120 34.335

⭐ 🦴 ⚙️ *At this high and lonely outpost among the craggy giants of the Chelan Mountains, views are grand and company is rare. Pugh Ridge sits smack dab in the middle of the North Fork Entiat watershed, a de facto wilderness sans motors and quite a quiet contrast to the Entiat Valley. It's a grueling grunt to the flower gardens and breathtaking belvederes of Pugh, but worth every calorie spent.*

GETTING THERE

From Wenatchee head north for 15 miles on US 97A to Entiat. (From Chelan head south for 20 miles on US 97A.) Turn left (west) onto the Entiat River Road (Forest Road 51) and proceed 33 miles to FR 5606 (2.9 miles beyond Silver Falls). Continue 4 miles to the road's end and trailhead (elev. 3950 ft). Privy available.

ON THE TRAIL

Consider the first 2.75 miles along the North Fork Entiat River a nice warm-up. The tread is smooth, the grade slight. Only a mere 300 feet of elevation are subdued. Hit the trail and immediately confront Crow Creek. Easy to cross late in the season, in July it's a foot soaker. At 1 mile come to South Pyramid Creek, easily negotiated via a bridge. A short distance beyond, reach the junction with the Pyramid Creek Trail. Admire the vintage signpost.

Continue straight through pleasant forest, and at 2.7 miles come to the junction with the Pugh Ridge Trail (elev. 4250 ft). A side path takes off left to a campsite along the river. Take it if your water supply is low. Otherwise, head right and commence climbing. The way

A hiker takes in the view of Pyramid Mountain from the high point of Pugh Ridge.

is steep and at times rough. Animal tracks are numerous in the soft pumiceous soils. These critters also have to work hard to get to Pugh's open higher elevations.

After 1 mile and 1000 vertical feet, the grade thankfully eases and you near a creek-carrying small ravine. After passing through a soggy spring-fed meadow, the way once again steepens. At about 2 miles from the North Fork Entiat, pass a sign proclaiming "Buddy Camp" (elev. 5800 ft). No buddy of mine would want to camp there. Pocket meadows begin shortly afterward and the forest thins. At 2.7 miles from the valley, reach the meadow-carpeted ridge crest (elev. 6500 ft).

Now on faint to practically nonexistent tread, head west, climbing a couple of hundred more feet to a larch- and whitebark pine–graced knoll. Continue across open meadow along the level ridge crest for another 0.5 mile to the 6783-foot high point. Views! Golden-crowned and aptly named Pyramid Mountain dominates the show. Its Chelan Range neighbors to the west— Cardinal, Emerald, and Saska—are no less impressive. Directly to the west Duncan Hill fills the viewfinder. Beyond are the Entiat Mountains, the Chiwaukums, Nason Ridge, and Mount Stuart.

Here, from the center of the North Fork Entiat country you are afforded an unobstructed view of an unmolested drainage. The Forest Service used to allow it to be ravaged by motorcycles. Public outcry changed that. More public comment is needed to put this wild watershed into wilderness—where it belongs.

EXTENDING YOUR TRIP
Strong day hikers with good navigational skills can return via a loop that adds about 2 miles. On sketchy tread continue north

along Pugh Ridge for 1.5 more miles, reaching the Pyramid Mountain Trail. Then head east 1.4 miles to the Pyramid Creek Trail, where it's 4 miles back to the North Fork Entiat Trail.

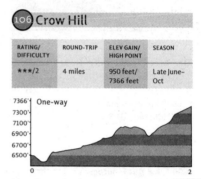

106 Crow Hill

RATING/ DIFFICULTY	ROUND-TRIP	ELEV GAIN/ HIGH POINT	SEASON
★★★/2	4 miles	950 feet/ 7366 feet	Late June– Oct

Map: Green Trails Lucerne No. 114; **Contact:** Okanogan-Wenatchee National Forest, Entiat Ranger District, (509) 784-1511, www .fs.fed.us/r6/wenatchee; **Note:** NW Forest Pass required; **GPS:** N 48 01.088, W 120 30.331

From one of the highest trailheads in the Central Cascades, set out on a delightful sky-walking, horizon-spanning, flower-lined frolic into the cloud-piercing Chelan Mountains. Rove through lonely meadows and ridges once roamed by lonely sheepherders and their flocks. And views! Colonnades of craggy peaks greet you for as far as the eye can see, and the waters of Lake Chelan sparkle more than a mile straight below.

GETTING THERE
From Wenatchee head north for 15 miles on US 97A to Entiat. (From Chelan head south for 20 miles on US 97A.) Turn left (west) onto the Entiat River Road (Forest Road 51) and

Hiking along the slopes of Crow Hill offers views of Pyramid and Cardinal mountains.

proceed 28.4 miles, turning right onto FR 59, signed for Shady Pass (the turnoff is 1 mile after Lake Creek Campground). Follow this steep, dusty, and often rutted road (high-clearance recommended) for 8.4 miles to Shady Pass and an unmarked junction. Turn left onto FR Spur 112 and continue for 1.8 miles, turning left again onto FR Spur 113 and following it for 0.5 mile to the road's end and trailhead (elev. 6500 ft).

ON THE TRAIL

The only thing difficult about this hike is the road leading to it. Starting on an old fire break, drop 50 feet or so into a small saddle and pick up real trail. Most of the immediate surroundings and the high ridge south went up in flames nearly four decades ago. Regeneration has been slow on these high thin soils on the dry eastern edge of the Cascades.

Pass through a clump or two of mature timber that survived the conflagration, and wind up open slopes of silver snags and feisty green undergrowth studded with flowers. Lupine, paintbrush, gilia, stonecrop, saxifrage, penstemon—red, yellow, purple, white!

Skirt a small knoll and at 0.9 mile intersect the fire break road. Turn left, returning to real trail soon enough. Round another knoll and break out into parkland meadows. At 1.4 miles pass an old mile sign in a clump of big larches.

Slightly descend into a meadowed saddle (elev. 6900 ft), and then make a choice. Continue on trail for another level 0.5 mile, enjoying more meadows and excellent views north of Pyramid, Cardinal, and the other Chelan Mountains. Or leave the trail and hike to the right for 0.5 mile, gaining 450 feet to the 7366-foot summit of Crow Hill.

After locating the ruins of an old cabin, probably used by shepherds long ago, start crowing about all of peaks now at your visual command. Glacier, Clark, and Buck to the west. The Stuart, Chiwaukum, and Entiat ranges to the south. Stormy and Devils Backbone to the east. The Sawtooth Range to the north. And 6000 feet directly below is Lake Chelan. Sit for a while and see if the *Lady of the Lake* makes an appearance.

EXTENDING YOUR TRIP

Continue on the trail another 0.7 mile, dropping 600 feet to a saddle and junction. Take the trail right for 2 miles, regaining 600 feet to the meadowed and lonely high slopes of 7297-foot Graham Mountain.

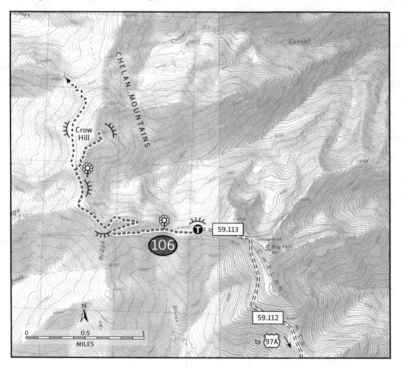

Opposite: Lake Chelan as seen from along the Rainbow Falls Trail

lake chelan

Fifty miles long, 1.5 miles at its widest, over 1400 feet deep, and flanked by craggy peaks more than 8000 feet high, fjord-like Lake Chelan forms one of the deepest canyons in North America. Fed by glaciers in the west and kissed by ample sunshine in the east, the lake has two faces. Its eastern shores bustle with vacationers and commerce, while its western shores are surrounded by wilderness. Find plenty of hiking on both ends of the lake, including a good share of family-friendly trails, especially in Stehekin.

107 Chelan Butte

RATING/ DIFFICULTY	ROUND-TRIP	ELEV GAIN/ HIGH POINT	SEASON
★★/3	4.2 miles	1350 feet/ 3825 feet	Apr–Nov

One-way

3825'
3675'
3475'
3275'
3075'
2875'
2675'
2475'
0   2.1

Map: USGS Chelan; **Contact:** Washington Department of Fish and Wildlife, (509) 686-4305, http://wdfw.wa.gov/lands/r2chelan.htm; **Notes:** Discover Pass required; or Fish and Wildlife vehicle use permit required, available statewide at retailers that sell hunting and fishing licenses; **GPS:** N 47 48.618, W 120 03.003

A favorite destination for local hang gliders and mountain bikers, Chelan Butte offers some nice recreation for those who travel by foot as well. Rising above the 50-mile-long lake and resort town of the same name, and the Columbia River too, this prominent landform affords excellent views. Visit in spring when the heat is low and the butte is streaked gold with balsamroot. And any time of year is good to visit this state wildlife area if you're intent on doing a little bird-watching. One caveat: This is a road hike, so expect a few mountain bikes and, yes, cars. Weekends can be busy and are best avoided. Your best bet is in early spring, when lingering snow patches prohibit wheels, but not feet, from exploring.

GETTING THERE

From Wenatchee follow US 97A north to Chelan. Approximately 1 mile west of downtown, turn right onto Millard Street, signed for Chelan Butte (the turnoff is just past milepost 232, directly across from the Best Western Lakeside Lodge). Follow Millard Street, which quickly becomes Chelan Butte Road. Reach the pavement's end at 1.3 miles, and 1 mile beyond enter the Chelan Butte State Wildlife Area. Continue for roughly another 0.4 mile to where the road makes a tight turn right in a forested gully. Park here, in a wide pullout area (elev. 2475 ft).

ON THE TRAIL

Though this is a road hike, it follows a pleasant and narrow dirt road through a state wildlife reserve. There are trails that climb and traverse the butte, but they're unmarked, unmaintained, and often difficult to find and follow. Save those for the locals (or befriend a few in hopes that they may guide you).

Start hoofing up the steep road, and within minutes begin looking out over slopes

Opposite: Balsamroot carpets the summit of Chelan Butte.

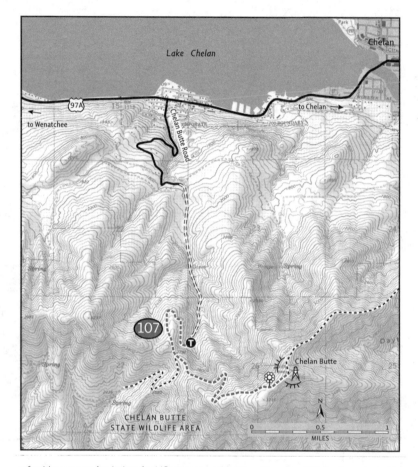

of golden grasses (and a lot of wildflowers in season) at sparkling, sprawling Lake Chelan. Watch for deer and bighorn sheep. and keep your bird book at hand, for there will be plenty of avian activity along the way. Quails are prolific.

At 0.7 mile come to a junction in a saddle; bear left. The road gets steeper and the views get better. At 1.9 miles come to another junction. The way right leads a short distance to good viewing south and should be checked out.

The way left leads 0.2 mile through a clump of pines to the tower-topped summit. Soak in the views. South, look straight down to the Columbia River and out to Mission Ridge. East, take in Badger Mountain and the wheatlands of the Columbia Plateau. To the west lie the Entiat Mountains, Stormy Peak, and Lake Chelan fading into a horizon of craggy peaks. North, it's Chelan against a backdrop of condo-sprouting hills, and those set against a better backdrop of bigger, wilder summits.

EXTENDING YOUR TRIP

From the summit you can follow an obvious trail for some distance along Chelan Butte's northeastern ridge. Eventually it will intersect a steep jeep track heading down to town near the high school. Keep an eye out for rattlesnakes and old mining relics if taking to any of the Butte's rough trails.

108 Echo Ridge

RATING/ DIFFICULTY	LOOP	ELEV GAIN/ HIGH POINT	SEASON
★★/2	2.25 miles	325 feet/ 3250 feet	Apr–Nov

Maps: USGS Cooper Ridge, or an excellent online map from the Chelan Nordic Ski Club, www.lakechelannordic.org; **Contact:** Okanogan-Wenatchee National Forest, Chelan Ranger District, (509) 682-2576, www.fs.fed .us/r6/wenatchee; **Note:** Fee required in winter for snowshoeing; **GPS:** N 47 56.228, W 120 02.549

Dig in your hiking heels on a trail called "The Shoe." Developed as a snowshoe route in the excellent Echo Ridge Winter Recreation Area, The Shoe is a sure-footed bet for good hiking too. Enjoy this easy loop as it contours along a semi-open ridge above the Chelan Valley. Sneak peeks of Washington's grand lake

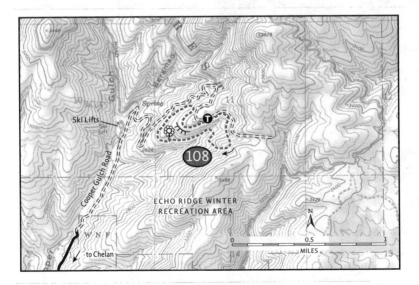

with its backdrop of lofty peaks. Come just after snowmelt for dazzling arrangements of blossoming beauties.

GETTING THERE

From Chelan head west on State Route 150 toward Manson. After driving just shy of 2 miles, turn right onto Boyd Road (signed "Echo Valley Trailhead"). Proceed for 4.5 miles, turning right onto Cooper Gulch Road. Continue for 2.9 miles to the pavement's end, just past Echo Valley Ski Tows. Then follow

Wildflowers line the Shoe Trail during spring.

gravel road 1.7 miles to the trailhead for The Shoe (elev. 3225 ft).

ON THE TRAIL

The loop begins on the south side of the road. Proceed past a small gate either left or right—it makes no difference for optimal viewing. The entire way sticks to a wide track, contouring open sunny slopes of sage and grass, punctuated with patches of pines and deer brush.

Head left to reach the loop's high point (elev. 3250 ft) after 0.25 mile. A mile beyond, after gradual downward sloping, the loop bottoms out at 2925 feet at a junction with the Switchback Alley Trail. Be sure to continue right, gradually regaining lost elevation.

The Shoe is delightful to walk in the spring, before summer's sweltering heat, or in the fall, before winter snows turn it back over to snowshoers. Wildflowers peak in May and chances of spotting wildlife are good year-round. Deer, grouse, chipmunks, and ground squirrels are abundant. Watch for ticks in spring and rattlesnakes when the snow is gone, but neither should give you much to worry about. Do pack plenty of water and don't forget your sunscreen. The Shoe is ideal for evening strolls. Watch sunlight dance on the waters of Lake Chelan and admire nearby high peaks like Stormy and Baldy and ones far away such as Cashmere and Stuart.

EXTENDING YOUR TRIP

Consider ambling along some of the other trails that make up the Echo Ridge Winter Recreation Area. Some are double-track, some are old roads, and others are all-out woods roads. Consult the Chelan Nordic Ski Club's map for orientation. Of course, a visit in winter with skis or snowshoes is in order.

STEHEKIN: "THE WAY THROUGH" REQUIRES SLOWING DOWN

In a Native language *Stehekin* means "the way through," and the Stehekin River offered First Peoples and early explorers and traders a way through the Cascade Mountains. The community of Stehekin at the mouth of the river on the northwest tip of Lake Chelan offers hikers a way back through time. Totally within the 61,958-acre Lake Chelan National Recreation Area (a unit of the National Park Service and managed as part of the North Cascades National Park Complex), the rustic and remote community of Stehekin with its fewer than 100 year-round residents feels like it's right out of the early twentieth century. And it is!

Modern amenities are few, there's only one paved road in the valley, and tourist accommodations are limited. Stehekin can only be reached by floatplane, boat, or a very long hike. But this all seems to bode well for most of the community's full- and part-time residents, as well as for folks who take the time to visit. And you'll need to make time if you want to hike here. While there are a lot of day-hiking options from Stehekin, you'll need more than a day to visit.

Most visitors arrive on the *Lady of the Lake* passenger ferry from the city of Chelan (contact the Chelan Boat Company for fares and times: (509-682-4584, www.ladyofthelake .com). There are several lodging options as well as developed albeit primitive campgrounds in the Stehekin Valley, but all frequently fill during the summer. Be sure to make your lodging arrangements before arriving.

Once you do arrive, you'll need a way to get to the trailheads. You can walk, bike (bring your own or rent), or perhaps drive if you are staying at one of the many lodges and cabins that provides a vehicle with your stay. Your other option is to take the regularly scheduled Stehekin Shuttle operated by the National Park Service. It typically makes two runs a day from Memorial Day to mid-June, and then four trips a day until early October. Be sure to contact the Park Service before visiting for current times and fares (360-854-7365, ext. 14, 360-854-7200 in winter, www.nps.gov/noca). And be sure to visit the historic Golden West Visitor Center upon arriving.

109 Chelan Lakeshore Trail

RATING/ DIFFICULTY	ROUND-TRIP	ELEV GAIN/ HIGH POINT	SEASON
★★★★/3	10 miles	1000 feet/ 1700 feet	Late Mar– Nov

One-way

1700'
1500'
1300'
1150'
0   5

Map: Green Trails Stehekin No. 82; **Contact:** Lake Chelan National Recreation Area, Golden West Visitor Center, Stehekin, (360) 854-7365, ext. 14, or North Cascades National Park, Sedro-Woolley, (360) 854-7200, www.nps .gov/noca; **Notes:** Accessible only by boat or seaplane. Passenger ferry service is available from Chelan and from Field's Point Landing via the *Lady of the Lake.* Contact Lake Chelan Boat Company for fares and times, (509) 682-4584,

Moore Point from Hunts Bluff

www.ladyofthelake.com. Dogs permitted on trail, on-leash. Rattlesnakes common, be alert; **GPS:** N 48 18.562, W 120 39.457

🚶 🌸 🏠 *Hike along Washington's dramatic fjord-like Lake Chelan, traversing sun-kissed ledges and blossom-bursting hillsides and weaving through cool forested ravines cut by cascading creeks. Stand high above the sparkling waters of America's third-deepest lake, which catches striking reflections of frosted pointy peaks. Feel rushes of wind funnel down the deep lake-cradling gorge. Listen to aspen leaves rustle, a lone loon cry, waves lap against lakeside ledges, and perhaps a rattling warning.*

GETTING THERE

Travel north from Wenatchee on US 97A for 38 miles to the Lake Chelan Boat Company in Chelan, located about 1 mile west of the city center. Or drive to Field's Point Landing, located about 17 miles northwest of Chelan via State Route 971 and the South Lakeshore Road. Take the *Lady of the Lake* to Stehekin. Disembark at Stehekin Landing and walk 0.25 mile to the Golden West Visitor Center. The trail begins just to the right of the center (elev. 1150 ft). Privy available.

ON THE TRAIL

Mile per mile, this is the most scenic hike radiating from Stehekin, and it's the only trail that embraces the dramatic shoreline of 50-mile-long Lake Chelan. Hot in summer, the Lakeshore Trail makes a wonderful destination in fall and spring—especially the latter, when a mosaic of wildflowers including chocolate lilies, balsamroot, and death camas splash the shoreline ledges and grassy slopes in an array of brilliant colors.

Starting from the Golden West Visitor Center, the trail passes park buildings, an overflow camping area, and a handful of private cabins before settling into a more natural setting. After immediately sampling high-ledge scenery, drop down closer to lake

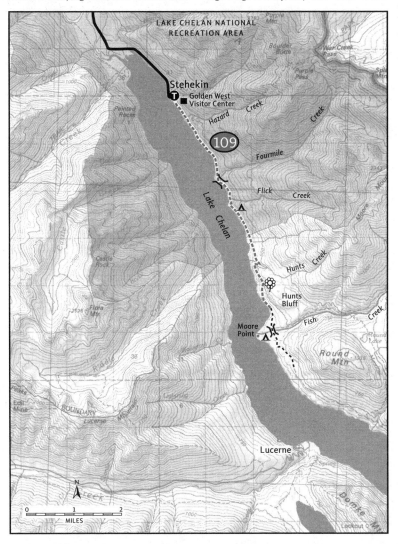

LAKE CHELAN NATIONAL RECREATION AREA

level and enter a recent burn zone. The trail undulates between patches of greenery and ghost forests created by the Rex Creek Fire of 2001 and the Flick Creek Fire of 2006. Be particularly careful while hiking in windy and rainy conditions, as the potential exists for falling snags and landslides.

At 0.75 mile cross Hazard Creek and skirt some cabins. The trail winds through and around pockets of private property. Many of the structures are simple and blend in well with the surroundings. Unfortunately, new money has found its way to these shores, with new ostentatious "cabins" sprouting up and clashing with this natural landscape and environmental sensibilities.

At just over 1 mile come to a shoreline ledge granting an excellent view down the lake to Moore Point and Domke Mountain. Continue along the scenic shoreline a short way before once again climbing above and away from it. After passing an old rock wall and compound, cross cottonwood-lined Fourmile Creek on a bridge at 2.5 miles. Drop back to lake level, passing boulders and a big "cabin," and then following cascading Flick Creek into a little chasm.

Leave the creek behind and emerge on a high bluff that grants an excellent view back to Stehekin, with 7161-foot Purple Mountain rising above it. At 3.6 miles pass the Flick Creek campground and shelter, a nice spot for a break. More fine shoreline walking follows, and then start a long ascent.

Cross Hunts Creek in a deep ravine before more climbing, emerging onto a series of ledges before topping out at 1700 feet on Hunts Bluff. Here, 5 miles from Stehekin, is a good turnaround point. Enjoy the spectacular view up the lake to Stehekin and McGregor Mountain and down the lake to Moore Point. This is quite a different Lake Chelan than 40 miles to the south, where jet skis whine in circles and condos ravenously consume the hillsides.

EXTENDING YOUR TRIP

Continue 2.2 miles beyond Hunts Bluff to Moore Point. After crossing Fish Creek on a sturdy bridge, turn right onto a short path leading to Moore Point, a historic homestead site, now a popular campground. Soak feet or take a nap on the sunny dock or inviting lawn before making the climb back up Hunts Bluff on your return. In summer it's possible to take the *Lady of the Lake* to Moore Point, allowing for a one-way hike to Stehekin.

110 Rainbow Loop

RATING/ DIFFICULTY	LOOP	ELEV GAIN/ HIGH POINT	SEASON
★★★/3	4.4 miles	1000 feet/ 2200 feet	Mid-Mar– Nov

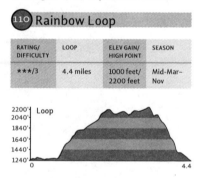

Map: Green Trails Stehekin No. 82; **Contact:** Lake Chelan National Recreation Area, Golden West Visitor Center, Stehekin, (360) 854-7365, ext. 14, or North Cascades National Park, Sedro-Woolley, (360) 854-7200, www.nps.gov/noca; **Notes:** Accessible only by boat or seaplane. Passenger ferry service is available from Chelan and from Field's Point Landing via the *Lady of the Lake.* Contact Lake Chelan Boat Company for fares and times, (509) 682-4584, www .ladyofthelake.com. Contact the Park Service for the Stehekin Shuttle from the ferry landing to trailhead. Dogs permitted on trail, on-leash. Rattlesnakes common, be alert; **GPS:** N 48 21.296 W 120 43.284

🚶 ⚙ *A Stehekin Valley classic, this popular loop takes you through mature forest, across rushing mountain creeks, and to sunny ledges that give an eagle's-eye view of Lake Chelan. Southern slopes mean that the trail usually melts out by the first day of spring. But even when snow blankets the loop, plenty of people still take to it, donning snowshoes and a happy-to-be-outside attitude.*

GETTING THERE
Travel north from Wenatchee on US 97A for 38 miles to the Lake Chelan Boat Company in Chelan, located about 1 mile west of the city center. Or drive to Field's Point Landing, located about 17 miles northwest of Chelan via State Route 971 and the South Lakeshore Road. Take the *Lady of the Lake* to Stehekin. Disembark at Stehekin Landing and take the Stehekin Shuttle to the upper Rainbow Loop trailhead, located 4.8 miles up the valley (elev. 1240 ft).

ON THE TRAIL
You can start the loop in either direction and from one of two trailheads, but the lower trailhead requires a steeper climb. It is also preferable to start at the upper trailhead so that if you miss a return shuttle, you only have a 2.5-mile walk back to Stehekin as opposed to 4.8 miles. This hike is an ideal choice if you're staying at the Harlequin Campground, in which case a 6.7-mile loop can be made by walking the road between trailheads.

Immediately begin to climb, weaving through an open mature forest with fine specimens of ponderosa pine. After skirting

A hiker looking down at Lake Chelan from Rainbow Loop Trail

a small scree slope and crossing a couple of creeks (most likely dry by midsummer), crest an open bench that provides views down to the community airstrip. Now, with the majority of climbing behind you, continue on a more leisurely way. At 1.7 miles take a break at a viewpoint (elev. 2000 ft) to look out at the Stehekin Valley, the narrow slot of a valley housing Company Creek and 8140-foot McGregor Mountain.

Traverse sunny slopes that sport pine groves and ground-hugging manzanita bushes.

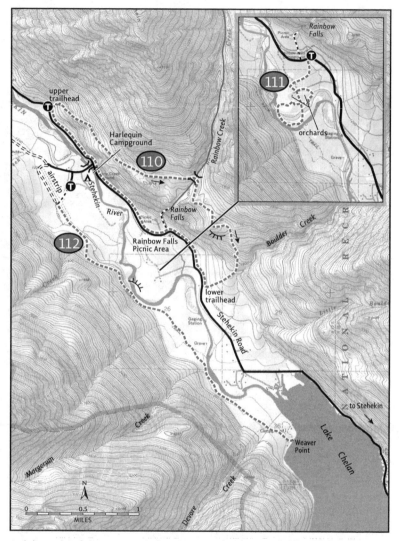

And deer. A lot of deer! At 2.4 miles reach a signed junction (elev. 2170 ft). The trail left heads deep up the Rainbow Creek valley.

Continue straight through deer brush and manzanita to a bridged crossing of boulder-bashing Rainbow Creek.

Pass big firs and cottonwoods, gently climbing the lateral moraine of a long-receded glacier. At 3 miles reach a junction with the Boulder Creek Trail (elev. 2200 ft). Continuing straight through old-growth forest, keep a lookout for a short side trail that leads left to open ledges with knockout views of Lake Chelan and the Stehekin Valley.

Beyond, the trail begins to descend, passing ledges looking out over Buckner Orchard (Hike 111). With Boulder Creek bellowing in the background switchback downward reaching the lower trailhead (elev. 1160 ft) at 4.4 miles.

EXTENDING YOUR TRIP

Walk the Stehekin River Road 0.8 mile west to Rainbow Falls and Buckner Orchard, or head up the Rainbow Creek Trail (passing some good viewing areas) for as far as time, energy, and desire allow.

111 Buckner Orchard

RATING/ DIFFICULTY	ROUND-TRIP	ELEV GAIN/ HIGH POINT	SEASON
★★/1	2.8 miles	50 feet/ 1225 feet	Mid-Mar– Nov

Map: Green Trails Stehekin No. 82; **Contact:** Lake Chelan National Recreation Area, Golden West Visitor Center, Stehekin (360) 854-7365, ext. 14, or North Cascades National Park, Sedro-Woolley, (360) 854-7200, www.nps .gov/noca; **Notes:** Accessible only by boat or seaplane. Passenger ferry service is available from Chelan and from Field's Point Landing via the *Lady of the Lake*. Contact Lake Chelan Boat Company for fares and times, (509) 682-4584, www.ladyofthelake.com. Contact the Park Service for the Stehekin Shuttle from the ferry landing to trailhead. Dogs permitted on trail, on-leash; **GPS:** N 48 20.440, W 120 41.947

An old farm truck sits idle in the Buckner Orchard.

Visit a historic orchard and homestead now maintained by the Park Service, perfect for picnics and strolls along the Stehekin River and back into time. Wander willy-nilly through the grounds, along an old irrigation ditch, and out into lovely fields along the river.

GETTING THERE

Travel north from Wenatchee on US 97A for 38 miles to the Lake Chelan Boat Company in Chelan, located about 1 mile west of the city center. Or drive to Field's Point Landing, located about 17 miles northwest of Chelan via State Route 971 and the South Lakeshore Road. Take the *Lady of the Lake* to Stehekin. Disembark at Stehekin Landing and take the Stehekin Shuttle to the Buckner Lane trailhead, located across from the access road to Rainbow Falls 3.3 miles up the valley (elev. 1225 ft).

ON THE TRAIL

Find the trailhead signed for Buckner Lane just to the west of the bridge over Rainbow Creek. Follow this delightful path as it parallels (and crosses several times on cedar-plank bridges) a century-old, hand-dug, gravity-fed irrigation ditch. In 0.4 mile the trail ends at a dirt access road at the edge of Buckner Orchard.

Before taking off to explore the rows of apple trees, old farm equipment, vehicles, buildings and assorted rusted relics, be sure to check out the privy here at Buckner Lane's terminus. Yep, it's a two seater! Talk about personal space violation!

Then locate one of several kiosks on the grounds that provide laminated interpretive trail guides—take one along with you to gain a better understanding of the delights that await you. The orchard was first homestead-

ed in the 1890s, and it continues to provide apples to residents and visitors alike. If you visit in fall you can pick a few yourself, and perhaps have the opportunity to press cider.

Be sure to follow the trail that circles the fields abutting the Stehekin River. A couple years back, the river took a big piece of the field with her to Lake Chelan. Enjoy good views of the surrounding towering peaks, wave to hikers on the trail across the river, or just lie back in the grass and watch big puffy clouds float by. Ah, the good ol' days!

EXTENDING YOUR TRIP

Do not miss Rainbow Falls, a short walk from the trailhead. The 300-foot plus waterfall is one of the prettiest and most impressive in the Cascades. Also a short walk away is a historic one-room log schoolhouse that's open for visiting.

112 Stehekin River Trail

RATING/ DIFFICULTY	ROUND-TRIP	ELEV GAIN/ HIGH POINT	SEASON
**/2	7 miles	300 feet/ 1300 feet	Late Mar– late Nov

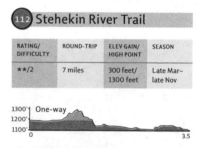

Map: Green Trails Stehekin No. 82; **Contact:** Lake Chelan National Recreation Area, Golden West Visitor Center, Stehekin, (360) 854-7365, ext. 14, or North Cascades National Park, Sedro-Woolley, (360) 854-7200, www.nps.gov/noca; **Notes:** Accessible only by boat or seaplane. Passenger ferry service is available from Chelan and from Field's Point Landing via the *Lady of the Lake*. Contact Lake Chelan Boat Company for fares and times, (509) 682-4584, www

.ladyofthelake.com. Contact the Park Service for the Stehekin Shuttle from the ferry landing to trailhead. Dogs permitted on trail, on-leash; **GPS:** N 48 20.950, W 120 42.833

McGregor Mountain rises behind the Stehekin airstrip.

Follow the glacier-fed pristine Stehekin River through dark groves of ancient cedars and along sunny banks that grant glimpses of surrounding soaring summits. Emerge on a secluded point at the head of Lake Chelan, where reflections of craggy peaks will captivate you. This is a delightful hike year-round, whether to escape summer's heat or in the dead of winter equipped with snowshoes and a sense of solitude.

GETTING THERE

Travel north from Wenatchee on US 97A for 38 miles to the Lake Chelan Boat Company in Chelan, located about 1 mile west of the city center. Or drive to Field's Point Landing, located about 17 miles northwest of Chelan via State Route 971 and the South Lakeshore Road. Take the *Lady of the Lake* to Stehekin. Disembark at Stehekin Landing and take the Stehekin Shuttle to Harlequin Bridge, located 4.2 miles up the valley. Cross the bridge and walk 0.1 mile on Company Creek Road to Harlequin Campground (elev. 1200 ft). Privy available.

ON THE TRAIL

From the Harlequin Campground (an excellent riverside base for extended exploring), follow a dirt road south (veering left off of Company Creek Road) for 0.3 mile through a Park Service maintenance yard to the Stehekin airstrip. Then turn left and follow the airstrip for 0.2 mile to the official trailhead.

Now on boardwalk, traverse a lush wetland at the head of the airstrip, taking time to admire the stunning backdrop of massive Mount McGregor. In another 0.2 mile come to a junction. The trail right heads 0.3 mile to an alternative trailhead favored by winter snowshoers.

Turn left, entering pleasant forest, and come to a log bridge crossing of Blackberry Creek. A slight descent afterward brings you to a lazy channel of the Stehekin River that's lined with big cedars. Negotiate a small stretch of ledge along the channel's edge before beginning a short climb that delivers you to an excellent viewpoint above the river, looking out to Rainbow Falls crashing into the valley.

After a short descent, finally, at 1.7 miles, come face to face with the river. Marvel at the swift-moving water. Admire the historic Buckner Orchard on the opposite bank. Then continue walking downstream, eventually parting ways with the waterway.

After another short climb and then a descent, traverse a flat of cottonwoods, poplars, and channels that may or may not be dry. Look for moose track. This largest member of the deer family, a rarity in the Cascades, can often be spotted in the Stehekin Valley. At 2.7 miles, after crossing Margerum Creek, the trail once again hugs the river. Then it's back across a forested flat, leaving the river behind. Weaver Point is reached soon enough, just after passing a junction with the Devore Creek Trail and crossing said creek.

Situated on the river's delta on Lake Chelan, Weaver Point once housed the Stehekin Valley boat landing and road before the damming of the Chelan River raised the lake's level. A few cabins still grace the point, as does a campground extremely popular with boaters. In winter and spring when the lake's level is drawn down, Weaver Point offers peace and solitude, albeit on muddy or dusty flats instead of sparkling waters.

113 Agnes Gorge

RATING/ DIFFICULTY	ROUND-TRIP	ELEV GAIN/ HIGH POINT	SEASON
★★★/2	5.5 miles	300 feet/ 2000 feet	Mid-Apr– mid-Nov

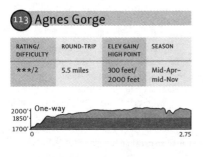

Map: Green Trails McGregor Mtn No. 81; **Contact:** Lake Chelan National Recreation Area, Golden West Visitor Center, Stehekin, (360) 854-7365, ext. 14, or North Cascades National Park, Sedro-Woolley, (360) 854-7200, www.nps.gov/noca; **Notes:** Accessible only by boat or seaplane. Passenger ferry service is available from Chelan and from Field's Point Landing via the *Lady of the Lake.* Contact Lake Chelan Boat Company for fares and times, (509) 682-4584, www .ladyofthelake.com. Contact the Park Service for the Stehekin Shuttle from the ferry landing to trailhead. Dogs permitted on trail, on-leash; **GPS:** N 48 22.844, W 120 50.417

This is an easy hike through pleasant forest to an awesome 200-foot-deep gorge carved by a rushing wild creek. Wonderful in spring when showy blossoms brighten the canyon's rim, or in autumn when stands of aspen add golden touches to the forest, Agnes will delight hikers young and old alike. But hold on to the youngsters when approaching the gorge; and the vertigo-inclined may want to skip peering down into the deep narrow chasm.

GETTING THERE

Travel north from Wenatchee on US 97A for 38 miles to the Lake Chelan Boat Company in Chelan, located about 1 mile west of the city center. Or drive to Field's Point Landing, located about 17 miles northwest of Chelan via State Route 971 and the South Lakeshore Road. Take the *Lady of the Lake* to Stehekin. Disembark at Stehekin Landing and take the Stehekin Shuttle to High Bridge, located 11 miles up the valley. From the High Bridge Guard Station, cross the bridge and walk on road for 0.25 mile (passing the Pacific Crest Trail in 0.1 mile) to

Hiking along Agnes Gorge

High Bridge Campground and the trailhead (elev. 1700 ft). Privy available.

ON THE TRAIL

Before heading out, take some time to admire the attractive High Bridge Guard Station and adjacent structures built by the Civilian Conservation Corps (CCC). Please respect the privacy of any rangers in residence. Now mosey over to High Bridge and stare straight down into the stunning narrow canyon carved by the Stehekin River. Impressive as it is, the Agnes Gorge is deeper, bigger, and longer.

Entering North Cascades National Park, walk up the Stehekin River Road and pass the Agnes Creek Trail, which is also the Pacific Crest Trail (PCT). Reach the Agnes Gorge Trail shortly thereafter, directly across from High Bridge Campground (an excellent spot to set up base camp for additional day hikes). The good trail takes off on a short and easy climb, rounding a knoll that provides excellent viewing down to the Stehekin River and the "Bullion Loop Ledges."

Now high above the out-of-sight Agnes Creek, the way continues on a near-level course through a forest of pine and fir, occasionally interspersed with cedar and giants of various species. At 1.5 miles leave the national park for the Glacier Peak Wilderness. In another 0.25 mile cross a creek, which may be tricky if it's running high. In 0.25 mile beyond that, round a bend and take in a nice view of 8115-foot Agnes Mountain guarding the valley. Now approaching the rim of the gorge, proceed with caution and take in breathtaking views of the creek churning 200 feet below.

Continue along the Agnes "catwalk," entering a cool old-growth cedar grove housing a small creek and the trail's terminus. Over a half century ago, a suspension bridge spanned the tight chasm here. It must have been exhilarating to downright nerve-wracking to cross it. Be

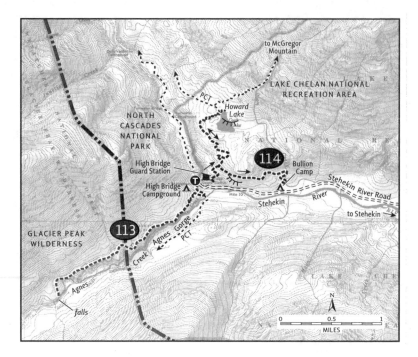

extremely careful viewing the gorge and the small cascades that plummet into it.

EXTENDING YOUR TRIP

Consider a hike on the Agnes Creek Trail (PCT), which travels along the opposite bank of the gorge. The new bridge on this trail at 0.25 mile provides a nice short option, while Fivemile Camp near the confluence of Agnes and its West Fork at 5.5 miles makes a great all-day option.

One-way

114 Howard Lake

RATING/ DIFFICULTY	ROUND-TRIP	ELEV GAIN/ HIGH POINT	SEASON
★★/2	3.3 miles	600 feet/ 2180 feet	Mid-Apr– Nov

Map: Green Trails McGregor Mtn No. 81; **Contact:** Lake Chelan National Recreation Area, Golden West Visitor Center, Stehekin, (360) 854-7365, ext. 14, or North Cascades National Park, Sedro-Woolley, (360) 854-7200, www.nps.gov/noca; **Notes:** Accessible only by boat or seaplane. Passenger ferry service is available from Chelan and from Field's Point Landing via the *Lady of the Lake*. Contact Lake Chelan Boat Company for fares and times, (509) 682-4584, www.ladyofthelake.com. Contact the Park Service for the Stehekin Shuttle from the ferry landing to trailhead. Dogs permitted on trail, on-leash; **GPS:** N 48 22.804 W 120 50.254

Hike along the Pacific Crest Trail to a shallow, wildlife-rich little lake at the base of 8122-foot McGregor Mountain, watchman of the upper Stehekin Valley. Then mosey down an old carriage road that once provided passage for prospectors at Bridge Creek. The ore is long gone, but the environs flourish with lore. And the views from this old transportation route are moving.

GETTING THERE

Travel north from Wenatchee on US 97A for 38 miles to the Lake Chelan Boat Company in Chelan, located about 1 mile west of the city center. Or drive to Field's Point Landing, located about 17 miles northwest of Chelan via State Route 971 and the South Lakeshore Road. Take the *Lady of the Lake* to Stehekin.

Disembark at Stehekin Landing and take the Stehekin Shuttle to High Bridge, located 11 miles up the valley. The hike begins on the Pacific Crest Trail at the High Bridge Guard Station (elev. 1600 ft). Privy available.

ON THE TRAIL

You won't find Howard Lake on maps just yet. State officials only recently agreed to the new name for the small body of water formerly known as Coon Lake. Why the change? Well, despite what some locals claim was a reference to raccoons (which I can't recall ever seeing in these parts), the lake's name actually came from a racial epithet for a nineteenth-century black prospector (who did work these parts). Now, I'm no big fan of political correctness (it often stifles honest discourse), and I despise revisionist history (it often deceives), but I'm all for decency and respect. Howard Lake works for me, honoring instead of disparaging a hard-working individual. The U.S. Board

Howard Lake in early spring

on Geographic Names, however, has yet to recognize the new name.

From behind the historic Civilian Conservation Corps–era High Bridge Guard Station, pick up the Pacific Crest Trail (PCT) and head north. At 0.4 mile, after negotiating a short series of steep switchbacks, reach a junction (elev. 1850 ft). Continue left on the PCT. You'll be returning to this junction later to take the trail to the right. Still gaining elevation, ignore a side trail right (it's used by equestrians to access a viewpoint), staying on the PCT through groves of big old ponderosa pine.

Emerge on a small ledge that grants viewing into the valley below. Then at 1.3 miles, arrive at Howard Lake (elev. 2180 ft). More wetland than lake, the area teems with birdlife. Mighty McGregor Mountain rises above. After enjoying the lake, head back 0.9 mile to the first junction.

Now continue east on what was once the wagon road for the mining settlement of High Bridge. Beneath cliffs, cross an open talus slope and enjoy views south into the Agnes Creek valley (Hike 113). Reenter forest and continue descending. Bear right at a junction, and in 0.3 mile (1.1 miles from the PCT junction) come to the trail's end at Bullion Camp on the Stehekin River Road. Take the shuttle back to Stehekin, or walk 1 mile on the road back to High Bridge.

EXTENDING YOUR TRIP

There are many options for hiking extensions here, especially if you set up a base camp at Bullion or High Bridge campgrounds. Beyond Howard Lake, continue on the PCT 4 miles to Bridge Creek and walk back on the closed upper Stehekin River Road; or go for shorter loops by using two connector spurs. The Bullion Loop Trail from the campground can be followed for a short distance only, since the Stehekin River took a big chunk of it away a few winters ago. Strong, determined, and masochistic hikers can shoot for McGregor's 8122-foot summit by following a 6.4-mile trail from Howard Lake. Make note—you're looking at nearly 6000 feet of elevation gain!

115 North Navarre Peak

RATING/ DIFFICULTY	ROUND-TRIP	ELEV GAIN/ HIGH POINT	SEASON
★★★★★/3	5 miles	1550 feet/ 7963 feet	July– mid-Oct

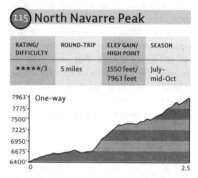

Map: Green Trails Prince Creek No. 115; **Contact:** Okanogan-Wenatchee National Forest, Chelan Ranger District, (509) 682-2576, www.fs.fed.us/r6/wenatchee; **GPS:** N 48 07.194, W 120 18.182

Ascend a cloud-snagging summit on the eastern edge of the Sawtooth Ridge, a serrated backbone of 8000-plus-foot peaks. Stare west to wind-blasted, sky-reaching rock, east to golden wheat fields crackling in the sun, and south to Lake Chelan sparkling more than 1 mile below. Come in summer for the flowers, in autumn for the larches. Come anytime for the solitude. The hike is fairly easy, but reaching the trailhead isn't. Access to North Navarre is via one of the most grueling roads this side of Bolivia.

GETTING THERE

From Chelan head west on State Route 150 for 7 miles, turning right onto Wapato Lake Road (directly across from Old Mill Park and signed "Mill Bay Casino"). Proceed for 4 miles, turning right onto Lower Joe Creek Road. In 2 miles turn left onto Grade Creek Road (signed for Antilon Lake), which becomes graveled Forest Road 82 after 1 mile. Follow this narrow, jarring, rough, agonizingly long, at times steep road for 31 miles to the Summer Blossom trailhead (elev. 6400 ft), located 2.5 miles beyond inviting but waterless South Navarre Campground. Check with the ranger station for current conditions before attempting this drive. Four-wheel drive recommended. Plan on at least 2 hours from Chelan, and watch for sunning rattlesnakes in the roadbed.

ON THE TRAIL

Composed of a string of jagged peaks exceeding 8000 feet, with glistening alpine lakes set in dramatic cirques ringed by larches, Sawtooth Ridge is one of the most strikingly beautiful regions in the entire Cascades. While the northern reaches of this ragged ridge are protected within the Lake Chelan–Sawtooth Wilderness, nearly 100,000 wild and roadless acres along its southern limits are not, leaving fragile alpine meadows and glistening alpine lakes imperiled by the motorized masses. Ask the Forest Service how they can allow such a pristine environment to be turned over to an activity better suited for speedways and racetracks.

Don't despair though, for all is not lost. The Summer Blossom Trail to North Navarre Peak has been classified motor-free. Bike- and horse-free too! Open to boots only, it's all yours to enjoy in peace. From a lofty start

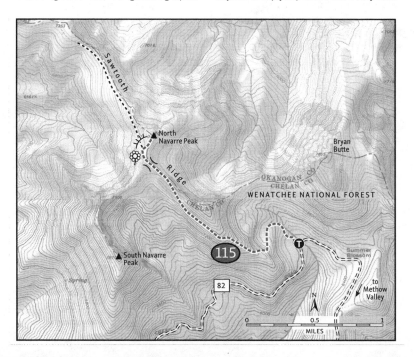

A hiker enjoys the view of Horsethief Basin from the summit of North Navarre.

at 6400 feet, head off through subalpine forest. In midsummer the lupine paints the path purple, and by September the blueberry bushes brush it red. Whitebark pines assure the presence of raucous nutcrackers and their bellowing *kraaks!*

After an easy 0.25-mile warm-up, the trail heads upward. Perhaps a small creek will be crossed, but don't count on it. Be sure to pack plenty of water for the trip up this parched pinnacle. Silver snags punctuate the greenery. In thinning forest, views of nearby peaks emerge: north to 7855-foot Bryan Butte, south to 7870-foot South Navarre Peak, all overlooking expansive meadows.

Experienced off-trail travelers can have a field day out here.

At about 1 mile, Lake Chelan comes into view. Make out the trio of little lakes just north of Manson too. Stare into South Navarre's awesome cirque. A lake should be in there. The way steepens, cresting a larch-lined saddle. Take in sweeping views north to the Tiffany Highlands. Now traversing an arête (a knife edge between two cirques), reach the wind-blasted high crest separating Navarre's two summits (elev. 7870 ft).

North Navarre's 7963-foot summit can easily be reached by heading north on faint tread for about 0.25 mile. Carpeted in alpine tundra and golden lawns and adorned with clusters of contorted pines, the mountainside environment is both harsh and fragile. Take care not to stomp delicate plants. And take care not to get swept off of your feet by the scenery. It's incredible! Especially the Sawtooth Range's procession of pyramidal peaks reaching skyward. Looking east you'll see the big-sky country across the Columbia Plateau, and south across Lake Chelan the spiraling Chelan Mountains puncture drifting clouds.

EXTENDING YOUR TRIP

Experienced strong hikers may want to continue farther along the Summer Blossom Trail. From North Navarre, the trail drops 500 feet on steep slopes and by a cliffside that may be unnerving to some. In 1.4 miles the way reaches a trail coming up from Foggy Dew Creek, and in 3.8 miles it reaches the Summit Trail at 7400-foot Deadman Pass. Nearly the entire way is in the open, teeming with alpine meadows and horizon-spanning views.

Opposite: Forested slopes of Table Mountain above Naneum Meadow

peshastin creek
and blewett pass

Situated at the extreme eastern reaches of the Central Cascades, the Peshastin Creek–Blewett Pass area is blessed with ample sunshine and an amazing diversity of plant life. Its geology is also diverse, consisting of high meadowed plateaus, deep canyons, and ancient lava flows. This is an excellent region to explore in late spring and late autumn, or when the western reaches of the Cascades are socked in with rain and clouds. There are miles and miles of trails to hike here. Unfortunately, many of those miles are open to motorcycles. But don't let that keep you away. Come late or early in the season and during the week and you'll more than likely just be sharing your trip with bluebirds and tanagers.

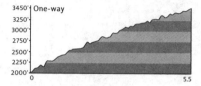

Maps: Green Trails Liberty No. 210, Mount Stuart No. 209; **Contact:** Okanogan-Wenatchee National Forest, Wenatchee River Ranger District, Leavenworth, (509) 548-6977, www.fs.fed.us/r6/wenatchee; **Notes:** NW Forest Pass required. Free day-use permit required, available at trailhead; **GPS:** N 47 27.770, W 120 40.393

Venture into a deep wilderness valley shadowed by craggy pinnacles of the Stuart Range and the Wenatchee Mountains' broad flank of summits. Located in one of the largest roadless valleys in the Central Cascades, Ingalls Creek drains a vast area of rugged

116 Ingalls Creek

RATING/ DIFFICULTY	ROUND-TRIP	ELEV GAIN/ HIGH POINT	SEASON
★★★/3	11 miles	1450 feet/ 3450 feet	May–Nov

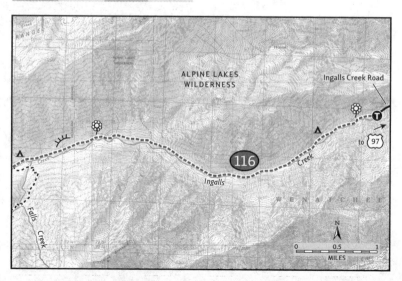

and stunning beauty. Continuously following the wilderness waterway, let rapids and ripples, crashing cascades and swirling eddies mesmerize you along the way. Come in spring and enjoy a trail lined with flowers—paintbrush, lupine, trilliums, glacier lilies, and more.

GETTING THERE

From Cle Elum follow State Route 970 east for 7 miles to US 97. Continue north on US 97 for 14 miles to Blewett Pass. Proceed another 14 miles on US 97, turning left at milepost 178 onto Ingalls Creek Road. (From Wenatchee follow US 97/2 west for 15 miles. Turn left onto US 97 and proceed for 7 miles to Ingalls Creek Road.) Cross Peshastin Creek, bear left, and continue for 1.2 miles to the trailhead at the road's end. (elev. 2000 ft). Privy available.

ON THE TRAIL

Starting from the site of a long-gone lodge and cabins (look for foundations), the well-trodden trail takes off into a forest of pine and fir that bears scars from a 1990s fire. The creek nearby is always within sight or sound of the trail—especially the latter. In late spring it can be downright deafening. Save conversation for the ride home. The roaring creek does, however, have a nice upside. It funnels a stream of cool air down the valley, providing nice air-conditioning on hot days.

At 1 mile come to a pleasant creekside campsite, which easily doubles as a stuff-your-face or cut-some-afternoon-Zs spot. There are plenty more farther upstream. Cross a small scree slope and steadily climb above the careening creek. Pass a boulder yard and big, beautiful ponderosa pines. At 2 miles the trail hugs the creek at a cavalcade of rapids before passing beneath granite cliffs. Window views

Rapids along Ingalls Creek

to the imposing surrounding summits soon open up.

After passing a lone giant pine at about 3 miles, you may see some rusty pipes and debris scattered about. An old mine perhaps? Then hop over a side creek, traverse a cool cedar grove, and cross a brushy avalanche slope before making a short, steep climb to a rocky knoll with an excellent view downstream.

Continuing, the way descends slightly to meet up once again with the raucous waterway. Approaching Ingalls' confluence with Falls Creek that tumbles down from the high slopes of Navaho Peak, the trail crosses an avalanche slope stripped down to bedrock.

It then enters a lush flat of old-growth firs and spruce, meeting up at 5.5 miles with the Falls Creek Trail (elev. 3450 ft). Head down to an inviting gravel bar and take a break. Watch for harlequin ducks and dippers while replenishing.

EXTENDING YOUR TRIP

Don't even think of checking out the falls on Falls Creek until later in the summer when Ingalls Creek can be safely forded. But do travel farther up the Ingalls Creek Trail if you desire. The next 2 miles to Cascade Creek cross open avalanche slopes and cool, old-growth groves and only climb a mere 300 feet.

117 Camas Meadows

RATING/ DIFFICULTY	ROUND-TRIP	ELEV GAIN/ HIGH POINT	SEASON
★★★/2	2 miles	350 feet/ 3200 feet	Late Apr– Nov

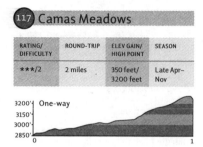

Map: Green Trails Liberty No. 210; **Contact:** Department of Natural Resources, Southeast Region, Ellensburg, (509) 925-8510, www. dnr.wa.gov; **Notes:** Discover Pass required; Respect posted private property that borders the preserve; **GPS:** N 47 28.533, W 120 35.022

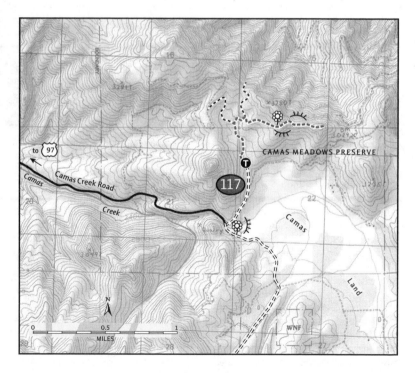

An ecological gem hidden in the Wenatchee Mountains, Camas Meadows (a.k.a. Camas Land) harbors plant species found nowhere else in the world. A sprawling, lush, near-level lawn cradled by lumpy forested ridges, Camas Meadows is a geographical anomaly in the Cascades' dry extreme eastern reaches. Too fragile to explore, the meadows are best viewed from above, as experienced on this hike. Magical in spring, brilliant in fall, and quiet in winter, it's not a bad place to be in summer either.

GETTING THERE

From Cle Elum follow State Route 970 east for 7 miles to US 97. Continue north on US 97 for 14 miles to Blewett Pass. Proceed another 16 miles on US 97, turning right (east) onto Camas Creek Road. (From Wenatchee follow US 97/2 west for 15 miles. Turn left onto US 97 and proceed for 5.3 miles to Camas Creek Road.) Follow Camas Creek Road for 3.1 miles to a Y intersection at the pavement's end. Bear left, reaching Camas Meadows Preserve in 0.1 mile. Continue another 0.25 mile to a gated road, the trailhead for this hike (elev. 2850 ft). Limited parking.

ON THE TRAIL

Administered by the Washington Department of Natural Resources (DNR), 1300-acre Camas Meadows is one of forty-nine Natural Area Preserves in the state. These areas are managed to protect high-quality examples of the state's native ecosystems and unique and rare plant and animal communities, so recreation in the preserves is extremely limited. The majority of the Camas Meadows Preserve consists of lush, fragile wetlands that sport healthy populations of its namesake as well as the Wenatchee Mountains checkermallow and the Wenatchee larkspur, which are found nowhere else in the world.

From behind the preserve sign, walk a short distance to the edge of the meadows to see this special environment. Flowering camas speckle the verdant meadows purple in May and June. Do not venture out upon the meadows, lest you risk damaging this fragile ecosystem. Field trips into the meadows, however, are periodically conducted by a DNR plant ecologist. Contact the agency about attending one of these open-to-the-public events. In the meantime, hiking to a view of the meadows from above is in order. And it's earth-friendly!

Following a series of old logging roads, this hike begins from behind a yellow gate. Walk along wetlands surrounded by aspen groves and stands of pine and fir. After 0.5 mile of

Camas Meadows

easy walking, come to a junction (elev. 2950 ft). Take the road right and immediately come to another junction. Bear right again, following the less-defined road. Walk grassy tread, gently climbing, and after 0.5 mile come to a ridge crest replete with views!

Look west to the Stuart Range and Three Brothers; north over penstemon-packed ledges to the Peshastin Pinnacles, Burch, Chumstick, and the rest of the Entiat gang. Then fix your eyes south down upon Camas Meadows, set against a backdrop of Mission Ridge, Mount Lillian, and Red Hill. Admire the meadow's aspen islands. Come October, they add brilliant golden touches to the verdant vale.

Map: Green Trails Wenatchee/Mission Ridge No. 211S; **Contact:** Okanogan-Wenatchee National Forest, Cle Elum Ranger District, (509) 852-1100, www.fs.fed.us/r6/wenatchee; **Note:** NW Forest Pass required; **GPS:** N 47 19.927, W 120 34.730

118 Swauk Forest Discovery Trail

Take to this delightful trail to learn more about Pacific Northwest tree species and silviculture (forest management), or just to enjoy abundant wildflowers and some pretty darn nice views. Appealing in late spring with its blossoms, this trail is also quite lovely in autumn when western larches splash the surrounding ridges with gold.

RATING/ DIFFICULTY	LOOP	ELEV GAIN/ HIGH POINT	SEASON
★★★/2	2.8 miles	350 feet/ 4550 feet	Late May– Nov

Balsamroot and old-growth ponderosa pines along the Swauk Forest Discovery Trail

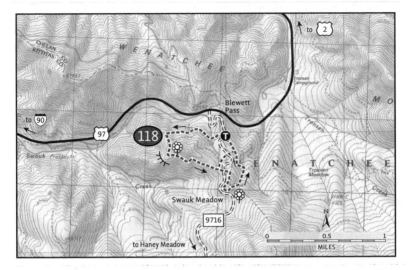

GETTING THERE

From Cle Elum follow State Route 970 east for 7 miles to US 97. Continue north on US 97 for 14 miles to Blewett Pass. (From the junction of US 2 and US 97 west of Wenatchee, follow US 97 south 21 miles to the pass.) Turn right (south) onto Forest Road 9716 and proceed 0.4 mile to the trailhead (elev. 4250 ft). Privy available.

ON THE TRAIL

Despite being located on busy Blewett Pass, this well-developed trail sees little use. Constructed by the Northwest Youth Corps in 1992, the Swauk Forest Discovery Trail is meant to enlighten visitors on forest management practices and how they are implemented by the Forest Service. Pamphlets are available at the trailhead kiosk for you to take along. And while you may not want to make twenty-five stops along the way to learn about forestry practices, definitely do stop at the tree identification plaques. I am always amazed at how many longtime hikers don't know the

difference between fir, pine, and spruce. Yeah, I know I have a degree in forestry, but this is elementary stuff. Read and learn!

The trail contours a ridge above busy US 97, meandering through patches of forest at various stages—mature, regenerating, and selectively cut. At about 0.6 mile enjoy a nice view west to Teanaway Ridge. Then traverse a sunny slope of ponderosa pines and, in June, blossoming arrowleaf balsamroot. Gradually climbing, round a ridge and head east. Watch for deer in this open forest and enjoy excellent views out to Diamond Head. In autumn, larches set this locally prominent peak aglow.

At 1.4 miles reach a junction. Turn left to shorten your trip or continue right for the best part. Cross FR 9716 and wind your way up to a 4550-foot knoll with excellent views north to Tronsen Ridge, west to Mount Stuart, and the Enchantment Range, and south all the way to Mount Rainier. Then close the loop by meandering through impressive ponderosa pine groves, returning to the trailhead in 2.8 miles. Consider a return trip in winter with your snowshoes.

EXTENDING YOUR TRIP

Just to the west is the Swauk Campground, a nice place to spend the evening after a day of hiking. Stroll the campground's little nature loop and scout the surrounding Swauk Creek meadows for elk.

119 Naneum Meadow

RATING/ DIFFICULTY	LOOP	ELEV GAIN/ HIGH POINT	SEASON
★★★/3	7 miles	1000 feet/ 5950 feet	Late May– Nov

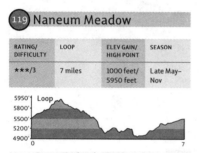

Map: Green Trails Liberty No. 210; **Contact:** Okanogan-Wenatchee National Forest, Cle Elum Ranger District, (509) 852-1100, www .fs.fed.us/r6/wenatchee; **Note:** Half the loop is open to motorcycles June 15–Oct 15. Area is popular with hunters, wear orange during hunting season; **GPS:** N 47 18.689, W 120 31.929

Spectacular fields of wildflowers. Superb views of Mission Ridge and Table Mountain and the basalt canyons that flute from them. Emerald lawns where the deer and wapiti play. The high-country meadows and forests surrounding Naneum Creek are heavenly. Almost. Most of the trails traversing them are open to dirt bikes. Sigh. But don't despair and forsake, for use is moderate—light on weekdays—and there is a good window of motorized closure. The best part of the loop is 100 percent motor-free.

GETTING THERE

From Cle Elum follow State Route 970 east for 7 miles to US 97. Continue north on US 97 for 14 miles to Blewett Pass. (From the junction of US 2 and US 97 west of Wenatchee, follow US 97 south 21 miles to pass.) Turn right (south) onto Forest Road 9716 and proceed 3.7 miles to a junction. Bear left onto FR 9712, and after 1.6 exhilarating (and to some, unnerving) miles up a steep open slope, reach a junction with FR 35. Continue left on FR 9712 for 3.1 rough miles to the trailhead at Haney Meadow, just beyond the Ken Wilcox Horse Camp. (elev. 5500 ft). Privy available.

ON THE TRAIL

Check out the old cabin before beginning. Built in 1933 by the Sinclair brothers, this well-weathered structure was used for shelter by sheepherders after its initial use as a backcountry retreat. The Sinclairs reached their cabin by horseback, and horseback riding continues to be a popular pastime in these parts. While riding is a legitimate use of these trails, the big beasties have a heavy impact on the tread. Ironically, they have torn up the trails more than the machines in many spots here. Expect a rocky and dusty hike.

From beautiful, sprawling Haney Meadow begin your journey to equally beautiful Naneum Meadow. Drop a bit to cross Naneum Creek and immediately come to a junction. The trail right will be your return. Continue straight on the closed-to-motors Grass Camp Tie Trail, climbing through a thick, cool spruce forest. At 0.8 mile, at the edge of an old cut, come to a junction with the Grass Camp Trail (elev. 5700 ft). Right goes directly to Naneum Meadow, but you'll miss the views if you take it. Go left instead for the longer scenic route.

Climbing gradually through lodgepole pine forest and basalt meadows, crest a broad ridge (elev. 5950 ft) at 1.3 miles. Window views gradually yield to all-out views, revealing peaks and canyons near and far. Lillian lies directly east, Badger and the golden Columbia Plateau are behind it. To the north Glacier Peak hovers over a serrated sea of rock and ice. Continue a little farther and enjoy views to the south: Mission Peak dominates your attention, while off in the distance Manastash Ridge begs to be recognized.

Now turning southward, the trail breaks out into the open, hugging the rim of a canyon housing Howard Creek. Look all around. Basalt cliffs. Basalt talus slopes. Basalt everywhere! You are standing on the western edge of the Columbia River basalt flows, the result of a series of massive lava flows more than 15 million years ago.

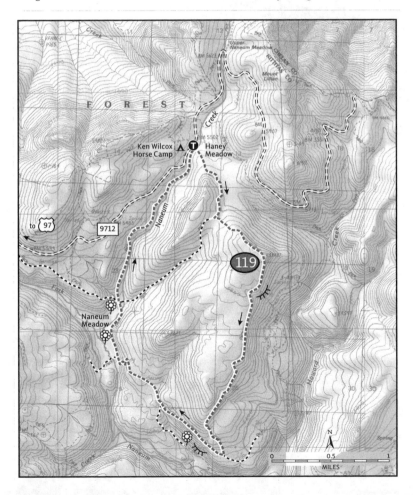

Basalt cliffs line the edge of Naneum Meadow.

Keep your eyes on the basalt-laden meadows beneath you too. Flowers! Yarrow, desert parsley, scarlet gilia, stonecrop, and lupine—lots of lupine. Continue frolicking along the dry and hot in the summer canyon rim. Upon entering cool mature forest, the trail begins to drop rapidly and steeply, coming to a junction with the Howard Creek Trail (elev. 5150 ft) at 3.7 miles.

Head right, following the heavily motorcycled trail along the smaller canyon rim of Naneum Creek. Take in good views of Table Mountain across the canyon. At 4.5 miles, just after crossing a small creek, reach the Naneum Creek Trail. Turn right, entering cool spruce forest, and then climb a little. Then on dreadfully torn-up tread, steeply drop, reaching a junction with the Naneum Meadows Trail (elev. 5050 ft) at 5 miles. Turn right, following Naneum Creek through beautiful meadows beneath an imposing wall of basalt. Look for elk and deer.

Just after crossing the shallow creek, reach a three-way junction. Right heads 1.3 miles back to the Grass Camp Tie Trail. Left goes 1.2 miles along Naneum Rim. Head straight, continuing along Naneum Creek. Gradually climbing, follow the creek 2 miles through larch groves and wet meadows back to Haney Meadow. Wash the dust off of your legs and call it a day well spent.

EXTENDING YOUR TRIP

With a good map, set out and explore the myriad side trails. The Naneum Ridge Trail is particularly attractive, passing through a landscape resembling southeastern Washington's Blue Mountains.

(120) Mount Lillian

RATING/ DIFFICULTY	LOOP	ELEV GAIN/ HIGH POINT	SEASON
★★★/3	6.5 miles	1100 feet/ 6100 feet	Late May– Nov

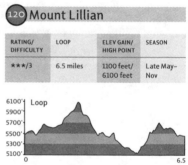

Map: Green Trails Wenatchee/Mission Ridge No. 211S; **Contact:** Okanogan-Wenatchee National Forest, Cle Elum Ranger District, (509) 852-1100, www.fs.fed.us/r6/wenatchee; **Note:** Trail open to motorcycles June 15–Oct 15. Area is popular with hunters, wear orange during hunting season; **GPS:** N 47 18.689, W 120 31.929

Spectacular sandstone spires and scenic views that extend all the way out to the sprawling Columbia Plateau are just a couple of the delights that Mount Lillian graciously offers. Brilliant wildflowers erupt in spring, and larches turn golden in fall, but do avoid this hike in the heart of summer when the sun is relentless. And avoid this area on weekends too, when it's opened to wheels, opting for quieter and much more enjoyable ambling on weekdays instead.

GETTING THERE

From Cle Elum follow State Route 970 east for 7 miles to US 97. Continue north on US 97 for 14 miles to Blewett Pass. (From the junction of US 2 and US 97 west of Wenatchee, follow US 97 south 21 miles to pass.) Turn right (south) onto Forest Road 9716 and proceed 3.7 miles to a junction. Bear left onto FR 9712, and after 1.6 exhilarating (and to some, unnerving) miles up a steep open slope, reach a junction with FR 35. Continue left on FR 9712 for 3.1 rough miles to the trailhead at Haney

Meadow, just beyond the Ken Wilcox Horse Camp. (elev. 5500 ft). Privy available.

ON THE TRAIL

While it's possible to head to Lillian's summit from a number of trailheads, by beginning from Haney Meadow you get less wear on your rig, more scenery for your enjoyment, and the opportunity to do a nice loop through this interesting landscape. Walk up the road a short distance, locating the trailheads for the Old Ellensburg Trail (that you'll be returning on), the Tronsen Meadow Trail (that you'll be ignoring), and Trail No. 1601, the Mount Lillian Trail, which you'll be taking. (If confused, continue walking up the road and pick up the trail in 0.5 mile.)

After 0.3 mile intersect a four-wheel-drive trail. Turn left on it and very shortly afterward turn right, continuing on the Mount Lillian

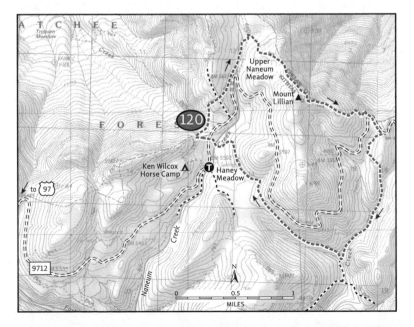

A hiker looks north from the eastern cliffs of Mount Lillian.

Trail, which here resembles an old jeep track. After another 0.2 mile intersect another four-wheel-drive road (which leads back to FR 9712, the alternative trailhead), and veer left. Locate the trailhead sign and continue, hopefully now free from confusing side trails and roads.

In spruce and pine forest and meadows, follow Naneum Creek for 0.5 mile, gently climbing to a ridge crest and trail junction (elev. 5700 ft). The way left heads to Tronsen Ridge, an excellent side trail. Go right, climbing along the ridge toward Lillian's summit. After about 0.5 mile, begin encountering outcroppings that provide excellent views. Rainier, Stuart, Glacier Peak, Mission Ridge, Badger Mountain, and the Columbia River! The drop here is precipitous, so be very careful gazing out at all of that beauty.

Continue along the ridge, cresting Lillian's 6100-foot high point. More meadows. More ledges. Then start switchbacking beneath sandstone spires and sculptures that are sure to spark your imagination. At 3 miles from your start, the trail terminates at FR 9712 (elev. 5600 ft). Walk left on the road, coming to the Howard Creek Trail in 0.1 mile. Turn right on the pleasant path and parallel the creek, gradually descending to reach a three-way junction (elev. 5200 ft) after 1.5 miles.

Take the trail to the right, the Old Ellensburg Trail, climbing along the sunny southern slopes of Lillian through meadows and larch forest. Reach an elevation of 5700 feet before descending back to Haney Meadow and FR 9712. Your vehicle waits for you just a short distance to the left.

EXTENDING YOUR TRIP

The nearby Tronsen Ridge Trail (a great hike described in *Day Hiking: Snoqualmie Region* [The Mountaineers Books, 2007]) makes for an excellent all-day adventure, particularly in autumn for the larch display.

Opposite: A hiker approaching Saddle Rock

wenatchee

The self-proclaimed "Apple Capital of the World," this Central Washington hub of industry, transportation, and agriculture sits on the banks of the Columbia River, where the cloud-piercing Central Cascades transition to the sun-baked slopes of the Columbia Plateau. Surrounded by dramatic scenery, the foothills and peaks to the west are especially appealing. In this region you'll find a growing trail system that travels to slopes bursting with spring wildflowers, lofty hills scented with pines, and craggy knobs providing knockout views of the Northwest's mightiest waterway.

121 Horan Natural Area

RATING/ DIFFICULTY	ROUND-TRIP	ELEV GAIN/ HIGH POINT	SEASON
★/1	2.5 miles	None/ 640 feet	Year-round

Map: Green Trails Wenatchee/Mission Ridge No 211S; **Contact:** Wenatchee Confluence State Park, (509) 664-6373, www.parks.wa.gov; **Notes:** Dogs must be leashed; Discover Pass required; **GPS:** N 47 27.606 W 120 19.830

Located within the 197-acre Wenatchee Confluence State Park just minutes from downtown Wenatchee, the Horan Natural Area is a wonderful place to take a quiet stroll and contemplate the beauty and importance of our state's rivers. Here the wild Wenatchee River flows into the harnessed Columbia. An oasis among parched hills, Horan is also an oasis for critters amid a rapidly developing valley.

GETTING THERE

From points west follow US 2 east toward Wenatchee. At the junction with State Route 285 (Wenatchee Avenue), which leads downtown,

Early spring color along the water at the Horan Natural Area

continue west on US 2, immediately coming to a traffic light. Following signs for Wenatchee Confluence State Park, turn right onto Easy Street, and then quickly come to another traffic light. Turn left onto Penny Road, and then make a quick right onto Chester Kimm Street, proceeding to a T intersection. Turn left onto Old Station Road, and just after crossing a set of railroad tracks turn right onto the park access road. Follow it for 0.2 mile to a parking area before entering the gated camping area (elev. 640 ft). Privy and water available.

ON THE TRAIL

Begin by taking the paved Apple Capital Trail to the right, quickly coming to a beautiful art deco–inspired bridge that spans the Wenatchee River. At the far end of the bridge, find the entrance to the Horan Natural Area. Be sure to check out the information kiosk before proceeding. Then, on a gravel surface trail, wander along oxbow ponds bursting with birds and frogs and under rows of cottonwoods. Come to a junction where you can go left or right: it doesn't matter, it's a loop.

Along the way enjoy riparian bottomlands, river views, and glimpses out to Mission Ridge and the Sage Hills. Look for muskrats among the cattails and beavers among the willows. And throughout the Natural Area, watch for birds: warblers, kingfishers, kingbirds, towhees, quails, and scores of others.

Before closing the loop, be sure to continue on the trail that ventures south for 0.4 mile to the Apple Capital Trail. Then retrace your steps and take the loop segment you didn't choose earlier, returning back to where you began, for a nice 2.5 mile saunter.

EXTENDING YOUR TRIP

The paved Apple Capital Trail makes an 11-mile loop through Wenatchee and East Wenatchee. It's a great trail to hike, bike, or run throughout most of the year. Consider spending a night at the state park's campground, set on an inviting lawn along the Columbia River.

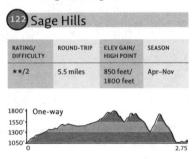

122 Sage Hills

RATING/ DIFFICULTY	ROUND-TRIP	ELEV GAIN/ HIGH POINT	SEASON
★★/2	5.5 miles	850 feet/ 1800 feet	Apr–Nov

Maps: Green Trails Wenatchee/Mission Ridge No. 211S (trails not shown), Chelan-Douglas Land Trust map, www.cdlandtrust.org /foothillsbrochure.pdf (good base map, but trails aren't accurately portrayed); **Contact:** Chelan-Douglas Land Trust, (509) 667-9708, www.cdlandtrust.org; **Notes:** Dogs must be leashed. Check for seasonal wildlife closures, typically Dec 1–Apr 1 to protect wintering mule deer; **GPS:** N 47 25.588 W 120 22.054

Hike across rolling golden hills that are wedged between the Cascade Mountains and the Columbia River. Embrace views of the mightiest river in the West, pine-topped knolls, cliff-faced buttes, and deep gulches where the deer and coyote play (and prey!). Stark most of the year, the hills are alive with brilliant colors and emanating with the sweet scent of sage in spring. Just minutes from bustling downtown Wenatchee, the Sage Hills are an important ecological buffer zone.

GETTING THERE

Follow US 2 to Wenatchee, turning south onto State Route 285 (Wenatchee Avenue). After 2 miles turn right onto Miller Street and continue for 0.8 mile. Turn right onto 5th Street, and continue west for 1.8 miles (passing Western Avenue) to where 5th angles left and becomes Number One Canyon Road. Proceed for another 0.4 mile to trail parking (signed) on right at the junction with Sage Hills Drive (elev. 1050 ft). Do not park on Sage Hills Drive.

ON THE TRAIL

Start by walking up Sage Hills Drive, bearing right and coming to the trailhead for Lester's Trail in 0.25 mile. The Sage Hills trail system has been developed and maintained because of a wide consortium of people and organizations, including the Chelan-Douglas Land Trust, the Chelan County PUD, and private citizens like the Lester family. It is imperative that you obey all rules and be a good trail user, or risk having future trail access restricted.

Skirting a housing development and powerline corridor, the trail runs along the demarcation line between urban and wild. Pressures are mounting in this rapidly growing area to consume more of this land for development. The Sage Hills are part of the larger Wenatchee Foothills Project,

Lupines and desert parsley carpet the open slopes of the Sage Hills.

spearheaded by the Chelan-Douglas Land Trust to protect these threatened lands and keep them open for recreation.

Winding through open country of golden grasses and fragrant sagebrush, the trail climbs and dips, gaining elevation in the long run. At 0.3 mile from the trailhead, reach a junction (elev. 1225 ft) with a path that heads to the Day Drive trailhead. Continue straight, soon entering land trust property, and not long afterward a wildlife preserve compliments of the local PUD.

On an easy grade, the way contours rolling hills, dips into a draw, and then begins a long ascent via gentle switchbacks to top out at 1400 feet at Five Trail Saddle, 1.5 miles from trailhead. This is a good turnaround spot if you've had enough or if the sun is a little too much to bear. You remembered to bring sunscreen and a lot of water, right?

Not done exploring? Ignore the old road left and take the trail that veers left just beyond it. Soon come to a junction. Veer right here; you'll be returning on the trail to your left. After dipping slightly into a draw, the trail heads upward to intersect a trail and old road at 2.5 miles on a ridge (elev. 1650 ft). Views are excellent here of Burch Mountain to the north, Badger Mountain to the east, and the Sage Hills and Saddle Rock to the south.

Feel free to roam the ridge to the right before beginning your return by following the trail left (don't follow the trail that goes straight, under the powerline). You'll quickly intersect another trail (elev. 1800 ft). Follow this trail left for approximately 0.8 mile back to a familiar junction just past Five Trail Saddle. You know the way back to your vehicle from here.

EXTENDING YOUR TRIP

Many connecting trails make it easy to extend your hike, but lack of signage can make it confusing. Carry a good map and have fun exploring. The new Lone Fir Spur, which connects the loop to Horselake Road, is worth checking out.

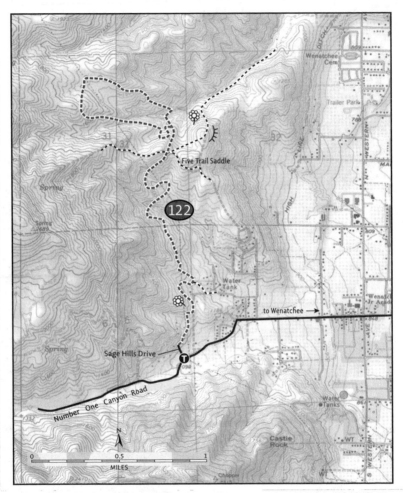

123 Saddle Rock

RATING/ DIFFICULTY	ROUND-TRIP	ELEV GAIN/ HIGH POINT	SEASON
★★/3	3 miles	930 feet/ 2000 feet	Mar–Dec

Maps: Green Trails Wenatchee/Mission Ridge No. 211S (shown on map as Old Butte), Chelan-Douglas Land Trust map, www.cdlandtrust .org/foothillsbrochure.pdf; **Contact:** Chelan-Douglas Land Trust, (509) 667-9708, www .cdlandtrust.org; **Note:** Dogs must be leashed; **GPS:** N 47 23.820, W 120 19.780

⚙ *Hike to the top of one of the rugged, rocky prominent buttes that rises above the city of Wenatchee along its western front. Then survey a dramatic landscape before you: the transition zone from lofty evergreen-covered Cascade peaks to the golden slopes of the desert steppe Columbia Plateau. Gaze out over the city that proclaims itself Apple Capital of the World and the waterway that powers the Pacific Northwest, the grand Columbia River.*

GETTING THERE

Follow US 2 to Wenatchee, turning south onto State Route 285 (Wenatchee Avenue). After 2 miles, turn right onto Miller Street and continue for 3.2 miles, coming to a junction with Circle Street. Turn right, and in 0.3 mile come to a large parking area at the road's end near the Appleatchee Equestrian Center (elev. 1070 ft).

ON THE TRAIL

From behind a gate, follow an old road turned trail. A lot of secondary paths radiate from this old roadway. Stay on the main and obvious route, unless of course you want to deviate from the beaten path. Traversing open slopes of sage, and in springtime blossoming balsamroot (a.k.a. sunflower in these parts) and other showy flowers, the way starts steep and stays steep. Except for a few scattered pines, shade is at a premium, so avoid this hike in the heat and take plenty of water.

Views of Wenatchee and the Columbia River begin almost immediately. At 0.25 mile turn left at a junction. Avoid an ugly shortcut, heading for the long switchback instead. It's steep either way, but do your part for erosion prevention and stay on the "actual" trail.

At about 0.75 mile the way eases. At 0.9 mile, come to a small pine grove at a trail junction (elev. 1800 ft). Saddle Rock's saddle becomes obvious as you get closer to this butte's eroded sandstone outcroppings. Continue left on the main trail, following

Balsamroot covers the slopes below the rocky summit of Saddle Rock.

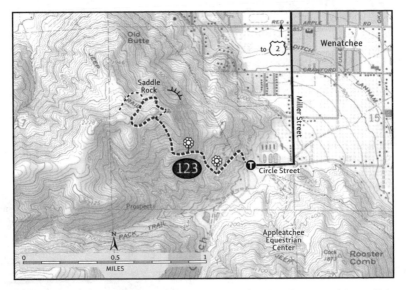

a short series of switchbacks and again avoiding ugly shortcuts (this Washington DNR property can definitely use some trail maintenance and slope rehabilitation).

At 1.4 miles come to a three-way trail junction as you crest the ridge that runs west from Saddle Rock (elev. 2000 ft). Views are good here, especially of the city and river and south to Mission Ridge and Beehive Mountain. No doubt you'll want to inspect Saddle Rock more closely, so follow the trail to the right along the ridge, coming to the rocky landmark in 500 feet. Use caution here. A trail descends from here back to the small pine grove, but it's not recommended unless you dislike your knees. Return the same way you came, saving cartilage while preventing further erosion.

EXTENDING YOUR TRIP

From the three-way junction, take the trail left 0.4 mile along the ridge to a 2200-foot knoll with excellent views west up Number Two Canyon and out to Twin Peaks. The Chelan-Douglas Land Trust has recently expanded the trail system here. Follow a new trail north to the Jacobson Trails complex off Number Two Canyon Rd.

124 Twin Peaks

RATING/ DIFFICULTY	ROUND-TRIP	ELEV GAIN/ HIGH POINT	SEASON
★★/3	7 miles	1650 feet/ 4586 feet	Apr–Nov

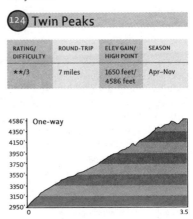

Map: Green Trails Wenatchee/Mission Ridge No. 211S; **Contact:** Okanogan-Wenatchee National Forest, Wenatchee River Ranger District, Leavenworth, (509) 548-6977, www .fs.fed.us/r6/wenatchee; **GPS:** N 47 23.632, W 120 25.833

A lone prominent peak that rises to the west above Wenatchee, Twin Peaks is virtually unknown to hikers outside of the region. Also known as Horse Lake Mountain for a tiny body of water to its northeast, Twin Peaks stands all alone, its prominence making it appear larger than its 4600 feet. Closed to motorized recreation, the old road that winds its way up pine-covered slopes to Twin's open summit is ideal for early spring and late-autumn wandering.

GETTING THERE

Follow US 2 to Wenatchee, turning south onto State Route 285 (Wenatchee Avenue). After 2 miles turn right onto Miller Street and continue for 1.8 miles, turning right onto Cherry Street. In 1 mile turn left onto Western Avenue, and after 0.1 mile turn right onto Number Two Canyon Road. Continue for 4.4 miles to the pavement's end at a turnaround. Then proceed for another 0.7 mile on rough, dirt Forest Road 7101 to a gated junction. This is the trailhead (elev. 2950 ft). The hike follows the gated road on the right, FR 7101-500. It is possible to park back at the turnaround where the pavement ends if FR 7101 is too rough.

ON THE TRAIL

Follow the old road through rows of aspen, and within 0.5 mile start edging up against a large meadow. Deer are usually present here, along with plenty of signs attesting to their presence. Ruts in the meadow also attest that illegal motorcycle riding is occurring here in this nonmotorized area. With virtually no patrolling by Forest Service personnel, don't ex-

Looking north toward the Stewart Range from Horse Lake Mountain

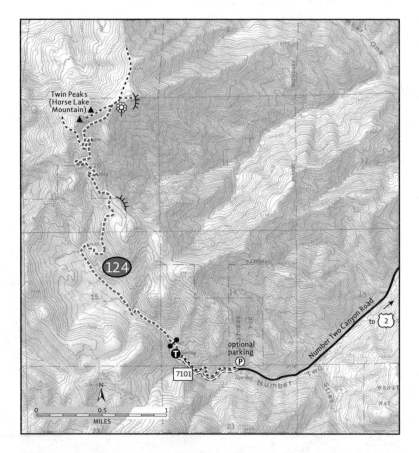

pect any enlightenment among the scofflaws.

Avoiding spurs, keep following the main track upward through pine forest, sage meadows, and groves of fir. Views out to Wenatchee and the Columbia River begin around 2 miles. They only keep getting better. At 2.8 miles come to a junction (elev. 4300 ft). Continue right, skirting Twin's eastern slopes, and come to a small saddle between its two peaks at 3.2 miles. Now follow fainter tracks to the right for 0.3 mile to the 4586-foot east summit.

There's nothing but a lone ponderosa pine to share the sweeping views with. West it's Stuart and the Enchantments, Cashmere, Three Brothers, and more. North it's Burch, Chumstick, Tyee, and the Entiats, Chelan Butte, the Chiwawa Ridge, and the little city of Cashmere below. To the south, Mission Ridge and Mount Lillian fill the horizon. And looking east you'll see the Sage Hills, Saddle Rock, and Wenatchee spread out below. Linger long, or feel free to explore more meadows to the north or Twin's slightly higher 4621-foot west summit, reached by following a steep primitive track from the saddle.

125 Clara and Marion Lakes

RATING/ DIFFICULTY	ROUND-TRIP	ELEV GAIN/ HIGH POINT	SEASON
★★/2	3.2 miles	900 feet/ 5475 feet	May–Nov

One-way

Map: Green Trails Wenatchee/Mission Ridge No. 211S; **Contact:** Okanogan-Wenatchee National Forest, Wenatchee River Ranger District, Leavenworth, (509) 548-6977, www .fs.fed.us/r6/wenatchee; **GPS:** N 47 17.652, W 120 23.923

These two little larch-fringed lakes tucked within the basaltic slopes of Mission Ridge make an ideal destination year-round. Clara and Marion offer excellent spring hiking, good heat relief in the summer, a spectacular color show in autumn, and a wonderful family-friendly snowshoeing route in winter. These are the only motor-free trails along Mission Ridge—savor this area's peace along with its beauty.

GETTING THERE
Follow US 2 to Wenatchee, turning south onto State Route 285 and driving for 4.5 miles until it turns east to cross the Columbia River into East Wenatchee. Do not cross the bridge. Instead, continue straight on Mission Street. After 0.8 mile, Mission becomes Squilchuck

Road. Continue for 11 miles to the road's end at the Mission Ridge Ski Area. The trailhead is located near the entrance to the ski area parking lot (elev. 4575 ft).

ON THE TRAIL
Follow the Squilchuck Trail (a name derived from the Chinook Jargon, meaning "muddy waters"). It leads uphill into a mature forest of Doug-fir and ponderosa pine. At 0.4 mile, after negotiating some tight switchbacks, come to a junction with the Pipeline Trail (elev. 4900 ft), a popular snowshoe route.

Continue ascending in thick, cool forest, big larches now adding to the mix. At 0.9 mile the grade eases near a crossing of Lake Creek. A

Western larch trees and basalt rock formations surround the green waters of Marion Lake.

short distance farther, reach a signed junction. The trail left leads to the little lakes. Take it.

Immediately enter a beautiful little basin flanked by giant larches and basalt spires, sculptures, and pyramids. Also find little Clara Lake. Continue on trail, now over a slight rise, reaching tiny Marion Lake within a few minutes. It is set within equally pretty surroundings, so sit back and let the sounds of nature (birds, breeze, and busy squirrels) calm your soul.

EXTENDING YOUR TRIP

The Squilchuck Trail continues beyond the Lakes Trail junction for another mile through pleasant forest, meadow, and basalt sculpture gardens to FR 9712. For a loop, continue right on the road for 1.3 miles, turning right onto the Devils Spur Trail (open to motorcycles). Follow this trail for 2.1 miles, passing an excellent viewpoint of the Columbia Valley, back to the Squilchuck Road 1 mile north of your vehicle.

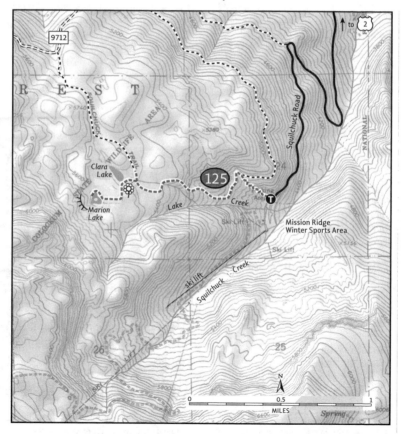

Appendix I: Recommended Reading

Knibb, David. *Backyard Wilderness: The Alpine Lakes Story*. Seattle: The Mountaineers Books, 1982.

Krist, Gary. *The White Cascade: The Great Northern Railway Disaster and America's Deadliest Avalanche*. New York: Henry Holt, 2007.

Manning, Harvey, and Bob and Ira Spring. *Mountain Flowers of the Cascades and Olympics*. 2nd ed. Seattle: The Mountaineers Books, 2002.

McConnell, Grant. *Stehekin, A Valley in Time*. Seattle: The Mountaineers Books, 1988.

Mueller, Marge, and Ted Mueller. *Exploring Washington's Wild Areas*. 2nd ed. Seattle: The Mountaineers Books, 2002.

———. *Washington State Parks: A Complete Recreation Guide*. 3rd ed. Seattle: The Mountaineers Books, 2004.

Renner, Jeff. *Lightning Strikes: Staying Safe Under Stormy Skies*. Seattle: The Mountaineers Books, 2002.

Tabor, Rowland, and Ralph Haugerud. *Geology of the North Cascades*. Seattle: The Mountaineers Books, 1999.

Wandell, Becky. *The Iron Goat Trail*. 2nd ed. Seattle: The Mountaineers Books, 1999.

Whitney, Stephen R., and Rob Sanderlin. *Field Guide to the Cascades and Olympics*. 2nd ed. Seattle: The Mountaineers Books, 2003.

Appendix II: Conservation and Trail Organizations

Alpine Lakes Protection Society (ALPS)
PO Box 27646
Seattle, WA 98125
www.alpinelakes.org

Cascade Land Conservancy
615 2nd Avenue, Suite 600
Seattle, WA 98104
(206) 292-5907
www.cascadeland.org

Chelan-Douglas Land Trust
PO Box 4461
15 Palouse
Wenatchee, WA 98807
(509) 667-9708
www.cdlandtrust.org

Conservation Northwest
1208 Bay Street, No. 201
Bellingham, WA 98225
(360) 671-9950
www.conservationnw.org

Deception Pass Park Foundation
41020 State Route 20
Oak Harbor, WA 98277
www.deceptionpassfoundation.org

The Mountaineers
7700 Sand Point Way NE
Seattle, WA 98115
(206) 521-6000
www.mountaineers.org

Pacific Crest Trail Association (PCTA)
5325 Elkhorn Blvd, PMB No. 256
Sacramento, CA 95842-2526
(916) 349-2109
www.pcta.org

Spring Trust for Trails
5015 88th Avenue SE
Mercer Island, WA 98040
http://springtrailtrust.org

Volunteers for Outdoor Washington (VOW)
8511 15th Avenue NE, Room 206
Seattle, WA 98115
(206) 517-3019
www.trailvolunteers.org

Washington Trails Association (WTA)
705 2nd Avenue, Suite 300
Seattle, WA 98104
(206) 625-1367
www.wta.org

Washington's National Park Fund
PO Box 64626
University Place, WA 98464-0626
(253) 566-4644
www.wnpf.org

Whidbey Camano Land Trust
765 Wonn Road
Barn C-201
Greenbank, WA 98253
(360) 222-3310
www.wclt.org

Wilderness Society
1615 M Street NW
Washington, DC 20036
800-843-9453
www.wilderness.org

Index

About the Author

Craig Romano grew up in rural New Hampshire, where he fell in love with the natural world. A former Boy Scout, backcountry ranger in the White Mountain National Forest, and ski bum in Vermont, Craig's true calling is the outdoors. He has traveled extensively from Alaska to Argentina, Sicily to South Korea, seeking wild and spectacular landscapes. He ranks Washington State, his home since 1989, among the most beautiful places on the planet, and he has hiked more than 13,000 miles of it, from Cape Flattery in the northwest to Puffer Butte in the southeast, Cape Disappointment in the southwest to the Salmo–Priest Wilderness in the northeast.

An avid hiker, runner, kayaker, and cyclist, Craig has written about these passions for more than a dozen publications, including *Backpacker, Adventures NW, Northwest Runner, AMC Outdoors, CityDog,* and *Outdoors NW.* Co-creator of *Hikeoftheweek.com,* he also writes recreational content for *VisitRainier.com.* Author of ten books, among them *Day Hiking Olympic Peninsula, Backpacking Washington,* and *Day Hiking North Cascades;* and co-author of five others, Craig is currently working on more Washington State guidebooks.

The author taking notes along the Agnes Gorge Trail

Craig holds several degrees: an AA in forestry from White Mountains Community College in New Hampshire and a BA in history and a masters in education from the University of Washington. He lives with his wife, Heather, son, Giovanni, and cats Giuseppe and Mazie in Skagit County, close to the North Cascades and the San Juan Islands. For more information about Craig and his writing, visit www.craigromano.com.

About the Photographer

Alan L. Bauer is a professional freelance photographer specializing in the natural history of the Pacific Northwest and its local history. He is a lifelong resident of the Pacific Northwest, having grown up on a large family farm in Oregon's Willamette Valley, and has called Washington his home for the past twenty-one years. Much of his love for the outdoors can be traced back to his life outside on the farm, working and playing—an experience he wouldn't trade for anything!

Alan's work has been published in *Backpacker*, *Odyssey*, *CityDog*, *Northwest Runner*, *Oregon Coast*, and *Northwest Travel* magazines as well as in numerous publications and books in fourteen countries. He was a featured "Master Photographer" in 2006 for his macro work in *Smart Photography*, the top-selling photography magazine in India. He regularly provides images for CD covers, textbooks, websites, presentations, and research and corporate materials. Prior to his involvement in the Day Hiking series, he was coauthor of *Best Desert Hikes: Washington* and the photographer for *Best Hikes with Dogs: Inland Northwest*.

Alan resides happily in the Cascade foot-

The photographer checking out the "throne-of-stone" on top of Mount David

hills east of Seattle with his caring family and border collie. For further information and to see samples of his work, please visit www.alanbauer.com.

1% for Trails and Washington Trails Association

Your favorite Washington hikes, such as those in this book, are made possible by the efforts of thousands of volunteers keeping our trails in great shape, and by hikers like you advocating for the protection of trails and wildlands. As budget cuts reduce funding for trail maintenance, Washington Trails Association's volunteer trail maintenance program fills this void and is ever more important for the future of Washington's hiking. Our mountains and forests can provide us with a lifetime of adventure and exploration—but we need trails to get us there. One percent of the sales of this guidebook goes to support WTA's efforts.

Spend a day on the trail with Washington Trails Association, and give back to the trails you love. WTA hosts over 750 work parties throughout Washington's Cascades and Olympics each year. Volunteers remove downed logs after spring snowmelt, cut away brush, retread worn stretches of trail, and build bridges and turnpikes. Find the volunteer schedule, check current conditions of the trails in this guidebook, and become a member of WTA at www.wta.org or (206) 625-1367.

THE MOUNTAINEERS, founded in 1906, is a nonprofit outdoor activity and conservation club, whose mission is "to explore, study, preserve, and enjoy the natural beauty of the outdoors. . . ." Based in Seattle, Washington, the club is one of the largest such organizations in the United States, with seven branches throughout Washington State.

The Mountaineers sponsors both classes and year-round outdoor activities in the Pacific Northwest, which include hiking, mountain climbing, ski-touring, snowshoeing, bicycling, camping, kayaking, nature study, sailing, and adventure travel. The club's conservation division supports environmental causes through educational activities, sponsoring legislation, and presenting informational programs.

All club activities are led by skilled, experienced instructors, who are dedicated to promoting safe and responsible enjoyment and preservation of the outdoors.

If you would like to participate in these organized outdoor activities or the club's programs, consider a membership in The Mountaineers. For information and an application, write or call The Mountaineers, Club Headquarters, 7700 Sand Point Way NE, Seattle, WA 98115; 206-521-6001. You can also visit the club's website at www.mountaineers.org or contact The Mountaineers via email at info@mountaineers.org.

The Mountaineers Books, an active, nonprofit publishing program of the club, produces guidebooks, instructional texts, historical works, natural history guides, and works on environmental conservation. All books produced by The Mountaineers Books fulfill the club's mission.

The Mountaineers Books
1001 SW Klickitat Way, Suite 201
Seattle, WA 98134
800-553-4453
mbooks@mountaineersbooks.org
www.mountaineersbooks.org

The Mountaineers Books is proud to be a corporate sponsor of The Leave No Trace Center for Outdoor Ethics, whose mission is to promote and inspire responsible outdoor recreation through education, research, and partnerships. The Leave No Trace program is focused specifically on human-powered (nonmotorized) recreation.

Leave No Trace strives to educate visitors about the nature of their recreational impacts, as well as offer techniques to prevent and minimize such impacts. Leave No Trace is best understood as an educational and ethical program, not as a set of rules and regulations.

For more information, visit www.lnt.org, or call 800-332-4100.

OTHER TITLES YOU MIGHT ENJOY FROM MOUNTAINEERS BOOKS

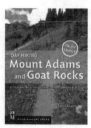

Day Hiking Mount Adams
Tami Asars
81 gorgeous hikes in the Goat Rocks, Indian Heaven,
and Mount Adams wildernesses—and more

Day Hiking the San Juans and Gulf Islands
Craig Romano
136 hikes on two dozen islands—plus Victoria,
Anacortes, Tsawwassen, and Point Roberts

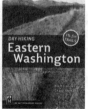

Day Hiking Eastern Washington
Craig Romano and Rich Landers
125 sunny hikes on the dry side of the
Cascades

Day Hiking Columbia River Gorge
Craig Romano
100 day hikes on both sides of the river

Day Hiking: Olympic Peninsula, 2nd edition
Craig Romano
"Romano is one of the better guidebook
writers around . . . " —*Seattle P-I*

Backpacking Washington
Craig Romano
70 spectacular weekend routes,
from the lush Hoh River and Glacier Peak
Meadows to the open ridges of the
Columbia Highlands and beyond

www.mountaineersbooks.org